Time and the Land

Four Approaches to Environmental Ethics, Climate Change, and Future Generations

by

Brendan Myers

Northwest Passage Books
Gatineau, Quebec, Canada

The original copy of this text is archived in the James Hardiman
Library, National University of Ireland, Galway.
Library index reference: TH6610 (December 2005)

This edition is published by Northwest Passage Books, 2013
Gatineau, Quebec, Canada
ISBN: 978-0-9920059-2-4

http://brendanmyers.net

Cover: the Mamturk mountain range, co. Galway, Ireland.
Photo by Brendan Myers.

Table of Contents

Acknowledgements.

My first and foremost thanks go to my supervisors, Dr. Felix O'Muirchadha and Dr. Richard Hull, as well as to department chair Dr. Markus Wörner, for their guidance and their patience. The end result is a thesis which crosses several different philosophical debates and disciplinary boundaries. Of course, any difficulties which arise because of this must be my own responsibility.

This thesis may not have been possible without a fellowship grant from NUI, Galway's Environmental Change Institute, and my gratitude is owed to this body as well. In particular, I thank its tireless administrator, Dr. Martina Prendergast. I was the lone scholar of the humanities in a research unit otherwise composed entirely of scientists, and she helped me to integrate into the unit, to solve various administrative problems as they occurred, and to find conference presentation opportunities.

I thank the other postgraduate students in the Department of Philosophy here, especially Pat O'Connor, Erynn Flynn, Allan Carr, Ed O'Toole, and the participants in two post-grad research seminars where draft chapters of this work were presented. Their research suggestions, and indeed their friendship, was enormously helpful. Similarly, I thank other friends and family members here in Ireland (they know who they are), who offered me hospitality and companionship while exploring the Irish countryside for myself. While this thesis is not the travelogue of an eco-tourist, the effect of experiencing Ireland's landscape cannot fail to have an effect on my philosophical writing. I should, indeed, thank the spirit of Ireland itself.

Time and the Land: Abstract

The central questions of this dissertation are, What is the ethical significance of the environment? What is the morally right way to interact with the environment, and what is its philosophical foundation? How should we inhabit the Earth? In general, this work aims to find an acceptable statement of environmental ethics, which satisfies two criteria, one theoretical and the other practical. On the theoretical level, the acceptable statement of environmental ethics shall be able to provide clear formal principles: it will tell us what is the ethical significance of the environment, and what is the morally right way for humankind to treat the resources and ecosystems of the planet. On the practical level, the acceptable statement of environmental ethics shall be able to give clear direction when making choices. I specify three general categories of environmental policy choice, which are Preservation, Conservation, and Depletion, and stipulate that acceptable environmental ethic must be able to tell us which one we are morally bound to prefer.

These questions are pursued through four theories of ethics which are prominent in the western philosophical tradition: In the order that I study them, they are Utilitarianism, Distributive Justice, Kantian Deontology, and Virtue Ethics. I study two varieties of Virtue Ethics: Aristotelian and Modern. I determine how each of them answers the central question of the right way to live in and with the environment and to relate to future generations, and then these answers are assessed for whether they fulfil the practical and theoretical criteria of the acceptable environmental ethic. Throughout the text, case examples of actual environmental issues and problems serve to illustrate the philosophical argument. These cases come from all over the world although special emphasis is placed on Irish and European cases.

The theme of future generations remains a constant issue throughout the work. Ways of relating to the environment are also ways of relating to the future, and some of our choices cause a future to manifest that is different from that which would manifest if we chose otherwise. It is generally accepted that pollution of the atmosphere and water, destruction of resources, and general climate change are all actions committed today which we can know with certainty will harm people who, at this time, have not yet been born, and indeed who may not be born until long after everyone presently living is dead. It follows that when calculating the harms or benefits likely to come from decisions about environmental policy, the future generations must be considered as well. Thus, my central question is not only a question about environmental ethics, but also a question of inter-generational ethics and future generations.

Furthermore, this thesis employs Derek Parfit's Non-Identity Problem as a philosophical question with which each of the four moral theories here studied is put to the test. Parfit's argument shows how certain wide ranging environmental policy decisions might harm no one in the far distant future, even if they produce situations all would agree are intrinsically repugnant. Parfit's conclusion is that we should avoid such situations but that "person affecting principles cannot explain why". Other versions of this problem also exist: for instance, the argument that as future people do not yet exist they cannot have rights. In the course of each chapter I take the Non-Identity Problem as the general philosophical challenge of future generations, and as another criterion for the acceptability of any environmental ethic. I claim that a theory which can avoid this problem is more acceptable than a theory which can not.

It is my general conclusion that no moral theory by itself can provide an environmental ethic which is acceptable on both theoretical and practical planes, and which passes the Non-Identity test. However, this thesis develops a synthesis of the best parts of each theory which can succeed where others by themselves fail. It is also one of my conclusions that in any synthesis of environmental ethics, Virtue Ethics must lead the way. I conclude that Aristotelian Virtue theory, together with its modern counterparts, is best able to provide both an acceptable answer to the question of how to relate to the environment and the future, and also avoid the Non-Identity Problem. Since the primary goal of this dissertation is the development of this synthesis of environmental thought, guided by Virtue theory, there is limited discussion of the primary sources and their associated secondary literature. The synthetic approach would be unwieldy and cumbersome if this were not so. The areas which are studied in greatest detail are those which are necessary for the development of this thesis.

The general synthesis of environmental morality which I defend consists of five general conclusions. In the first, I argue that what matters is excellence of character, not the maximisation of utility. The Non-Identity Problem, as I demonstrate, can be solved or avoided only by a moral theory in which the maximisation of utility is not what matters. Virtue Theory is one moral theory capable of sustaining that claim, and so it is able to succeed where person-affecting principles can not. In the second, I claim that the Virtuous aim for the worthwhile human life includes the aim to create and sustain the social and environmental conditions in which the worthwhile human life is possible and supported. The ecological environment in which the pursuit of a worthwhile life takes place counts as a special kind of external good, similar in some ways to the social environment which figured so importantly in Aristotle's thinking. Environmental conservation, I therefore argue, must be part of a Virtuous person's practical aims. In the second, I claim that the right amount of environmental resource development is that which obtains a parity between the aim for a flourishing life and the opportunities and abilities to succeed in that aim which are available in the environment in which one lives. In the fourth, I conclude that the future appears to the Virtuous person as a function of the present, in the form of a *telos* whose fulfilment is temporally continuous. A Virtuous person takes a care for the future through aiming at ends which are, while achievable in the present, also temporally continuous and ongoing, even beyond the agent's own lifetime. I claim that environmental conservation is such a temporally continuous end. My final conclusion is that the future which it is virtuous to aim for is the one which brings out the agent's best qualities in the course of striving for it.

Abbreviations of Primary Sources

AV   Alasdair MacIntyre, *After Virtue*

E&U   Lincoln Alison, *Ecology and Utility*

Groundwork   Immanuel Kant, *Groundwork to the Metaphysics of Morals*

JFGE   Hendrick Visser T'Hooft, *Justice to Future Generations and the Environment*

Lectures   Immanuel Kant, *Lectures on Ethics*

NE   Aristotle, *Nicomachean Ethics*

Politics   Aristotle, *Politics*

R&P   Derek Parfit, *Reasons and Persons*

RN   Paul Taylor, *Respect for Nature*

TJ   John Rawls, *A Theory of Justice*

WPM   Avner de-Shalit, *Why Posterity Matters*

General Introduction

How shall we human beings inhabit the Earth? Can the way we make use of the resources and land territory of the Earth be an issue for ethics? What way of living in and with the ecological world, using its resources for our own purposes, changing it, and dumping our waste upon it, is morally acceptable—if there such a way at all? What philosophical resources are there to provide a foundation for any answers to these questions we may propose? This work shall explore this question through the four most distinct and well known traditions of ethical enquiry in the Western philosophical tradition. They are the traditions of the 'good', the 'just', the 'right', and the 'excellent'.

The 'good', first of all, is the range of ethical thought which places the location of moral concern primarily on the greatest overall benefit and happiness conferred upon people, including oneself. Utilitarianism and Consequentialism falls under this general heading. The 'just' is of course that which is in accord with justice, and while there are many kinds of justice they are all concerned with some conception of fairness in a society's structure. Justice is fairness in a society's economics and politics, its system of entitlements owed to the society's members, its system of investigating and punishing those who infringe that system, and so on. John Rawls' Difference Principle falls in this category. The 'right' concerns the intrinsic ethical correctness of actions in themselves. A right action is an action that is in accord with one's moral duty, as defined by some conception of reason, nature, divine command, or other similar philosophical foundation. Kant's Categorical Imperative is a theory of moral right. Finally, the 'excellent' is the ethics of human moral character and identity. An action is excellent if, broadly speaking, it makes him and others concerned flourish as human beings, for this is the mark of someone possessing virtuous character. The first philosophical expression of this kind of ethics is in the writings of Aristotle, and in the last quarter of the 20th century it was revived by

Alasdair MacIntyre, Rosalind Hursthouse, Phillipa Foot, and others. The purpose of this work is to use each of these four kinds of moral enquiry to explore the problems and principles of environmental philosophy.

Environmental philosophy is the sustained intellectual inquiry into the meaning, significance, realities, and truths concerning the physical and ecological world in which we live, and the place of humankind in and with it. Philosophers have used the term 'the world' in a variety of different ways, but to environmental philosophers the term generally signifies the planet Earth with its ecological systems of global life support and interaction which underlie the social, economic, political, and linguistic contexts that are often taken to be 'worlds' in their own right. To such a philosopher, 'the environment' means the habitats and dwelling places of living beings. It also includes all the elements and processes of the world, such as precipitation cycles, seasonal changes, geological landforms, and so on, which surround life and support it. There are many types of environment: the skies and seas, the forests and deserts and mountains, temperate zones and tropical zones, and so on. But to many environmentalists, 'the environment' is anywhere that life can be found. Similarly, 'nature', a word with a long history in philosophy, takes on its more 'environmental' guise, and usually means the part of the world that is mostly untouched and unmodified by human hands, where animals and plants and other organisms live without human interference. This is the environmental philosopher's general field of enquiry. But human life is not excluded, and environmental philosophers are equally interested in the 'built' environment of towns, cities, urban areas, and the territory that we share with non-human life forms including farms and parks. There are many different types and kinds of environment, and the environmental philosopher is ultimately concerned with all of them; but most of the time he is concerned with the non-human world, and the place where it meets the human world. Environmental philosophy wants to know the philosophical significance, if there is any, of what happens there.

Environmental ethics is the inquiry into questions concerning the moral significance of the world we live in, and how human beings should act in reference to it, whether individually, collectively, or politically. It is concerned with the extraction and exploitation of the planet's material and energy resources, the production of pollution and waste, and the effects this has on human and non-human life. With this concern at the centre of attention environmental ethics aims to pronounce a judgement about our way of life. Hence it would be too simplistic to say that environmental philosophy is just a variety of applied ethics. It would be more accurate to say that environmental ethics attempts to clarify human morality within the widest and most comprehensive of all contexts: the whole of the physical world.

It is now a generally accepted scientific fact that human economic activity is causing the climate of the earth to change. Through education, news coverage, cultural events, and political communication from grass roots activism to government public service announcements, we have been aware of environmental issues and problems for about fifty years. Most of us now have a moral intuition that the kind of destructive impact human industrial and economic activity has had on the environment is morally questionable, if not altogether bad. Most of us would agree that despite the great advances in technological power and quality of life that these activities have produced, still the present-day modes of interaction with the environment have had numerous negative consequences, not only for ourselves but for the landscape as well. When we find that the world is changing and degrading into a condition which is inimical to the furtherance of life as we know it, including but not limited to human life, and when we find that our own industrial and economic activity is responsible for this change, we cannot avoid the conclusion that something we are doing is wrong. But what is the rational explanation of that conclusion, if there is one? What exactly is it that we are doing wrong? To understand this, we need to know what constitutes morally right conduct in reference to the environment. This is the central question of this thesis. What is the right mode of interaction with the environment, and what is its philosophical foundation?

These questions belong among the most serious and important questions of our time. For global warming is a real phenomenon. Here is a short survey of what we are dealing with, and some of its most dramatic possible implications.

Global warming and climate change. Since the Industrial revolution, global atmospheric levels of carbon dioxide have increased 30 percent, methane by 145 percent and nitrous oxide by 15 percent. Ice core samples have not shown such high levels of these gases in the last 400,000 years, which clearly links them to human industrial activity.[1] Ireland is not isolated from climate change effects of this kind. Several studies are now showing that the Gulf Stream, the Atlantic current which keeps most of Western Europe warm, is slowing down because Arctic ice is melting quicker than ever before, which is changing the salinity and thermodynamic properties of ocean currents. A survey by a Cambridge University professor of ocean physics recently found clear evidence of this phenomenon using a research submarine travelling beneath the Arctic ice cap. He concluded that Europe will become much colder on average in the next few decades.[2] If, as another example, the West Antarctic ice sheet fell into the sea and melted (not only because of global warming, but also under-ice volcanic eruptions), the ocean level would rise by six meters, and two billion people would die from flooding, exposure, thirst and starvation. In 1999 it was reported that the glaciers of Antarctica are indeed melting at the rate of 12 cubic miles per year, according to NASA scientists.[3] On the 19th of May 2002, an ice shelf of unusually large size —5,000 square kilometres—did break off from the

4

Larsen-B Ice Shelf of Antarctica. America's *CNN* reported that it was "about 53 miles long and about 40 miles wide", and refused to speculate about global warming.[4] By contrast, England's left-leaning newspaper *The Guardian* reported that it was "just under the size of Cambridgeshire",[5] and happily blamed it on global warming. Environmental upheavals like these pose threats to human communities around the world. By destroying crops, infrastructure, or people's homes, they can and often do kill thousands of people and ruin the lives of millions more. For example, the number of "environmental refugees" (people compelled to cross an international border due to an environmental disaster) was at the time of writing estimated to be about 25 million people world wide. That figure is 3 million more than the estimated number of political refugees. It was also estimated that there will be as many as 150 million environmental refugees by the year 2050.[6] In the year 2001, the number of people world wide who lost their homes in floods, droughts, and storms reached 170 million. At least five Pacific island states are at risk of disappearing completely, because global warming is causing the sea level to rise and submerge their territories. One of them, the Republic of Tuvalu, has recently announced that their nine islands, which are home to 11,000 people, are disappearing, and they have entered negotiations with the government of New Zealand where they hope to resettle.[7]

Environmental disasters linked to global warming and climate change are more destructive to human life than terrorist attacks. If human industrial processes are carried on in a "business as usual" manner, with its huge volumes of pollution and resource consumption, there is a very high probability that in the future there will be many more global environmental catastrophes like these here described.

It is fairly safe to say that the necessity for environmental ethics has arisen together with the discovery of how the expansion of human settlement and industrialisation has had those kinds of direct and indirect destructive effects on the world's natural ecosystems and human communities. The natural world is enormously important to us for a variety of reasons: for instance its beauty, its supply of material and energy resources, the relation between landscape and culture. Most of us, therefore, have an intuition that the environment should not be destroyed by what we do. But what is the philosophical basis for that intuition, if there is one? Is there a moral principle for living in and with the world which is suggested by the various ways the world is important to us, and the evidence of the destructive effect of so many of our actions?

§ 1. The Rise of Environmental Thought.

For centuries, philosophers referred to the landscapes, seas, and skies of the Earth as 'the wilderness', or 'the countryside', or as 'Creation', meaning the handiwork of God. The first philosopher to use this latter term in print this way seems to be Boethius, the 5th century Roman philosopher and politician who fell from the good graces of his king, and in his prison cell he composed a book called The Consolation of Philosophy. "Creation is indeed very beautiful," he wrote, "and the countryside a beautiful part of creation. In the same way we are sometimes delighted by the appearance of the sea when it's very calm and look up with wonder at the sky, the stars, the moon and the sun." But we are not to take the beauty of Creation as an object of moral concern, or as a source of virtue or moral goodness, because "not one of these has anything to do with you, and you daren't take credit for the splendour of any of them… You are, in fact, enraptured with empty joys, embracing blessings that are alien to you as if they were your own."[8] Moreover, excessive interest in the beauty of the world could be interpreted as a form of blasphemy: "the heavens are less wonderful for their foundation and speed than for the order that rules them."[9] This attitude toward the Earth prevailed among philosophers well into the early modern era.

Jean Jacques Rousseau should be credited as the first philosopher in the western tradition to refer to the landscapes of the world as 'nature', and to describe its importance to philosophical speculation. His discussion appears in his <u>Confessions</u> (1782), where he described walking alone across the Swiss Alps. With characteristic romanticism, he said: "Never does a plain, however beautiful it may be, seem so in my eyes. I need torrents, rocks, firs, dark woods, mountains, deep roads to climb or descend, abysses beside me to make me afraid."[10] Rousseau is the first major thinker of modernity to conceive of nature as a 'place', the world that is 'out there' beyond the wards of towns and cities, instead of as a principle of order or necessity which exists within living beings and the cosmos. The present debate in environmental philosophy has its roots in Rousseau's conception of nature, especially as expressed by a small number of American naturalists and theologians. Thoreau, Muir, Emerson, and Leopold published books in the late 19th and early 20th centuries describing the sublime beauty of the natural world and the threat posed to it by expanding industrialisation. These writers were influenced by, among other things, the legends and folklore of Native American and Canadian First Nations people which were then becoming more and more available in print. The letters, speeches, and biographies of 19th century Native leaders like Chief Seattle, Chief Luther Standing Bear, and Chief Joseph expressed a respect for the Earth which non-Natives were beginning to admire. Of course this may have been because Native cultures no longer posed much of a military threat, and so it was 'safe' to think of them positively. The image of the 'noble savage', just then taking hold in the popular imagination, was just as false and patronising as the image of the 'wild west'. But the words and thoughts of Native people were now being recorded for posterity, and were garnering respect among those who felt that the destruction of Native culture was a terrible tragedy, however few those people may have been at the time.

In the United Kingdom similar ideas were expressed in poetry and literature published during the period between the first and second world wars. Industrialisation and urban growth inspired a literature that condemned English society for being culturally impoverished, and alienation from nature was blamed for this impoverishment. A kind of rustic country simplicity and innocence was seen as the solution: consequently, much of this literature was written for children. Henry Williamson, C.S. Lewis, A.A. Milne, Arthur Ransome, and Rudyard Kipling are the most well known English authors in whose works these ideas are expressed. In his novel That Hideous Strength (1945), C.S. Lewis articulated his fear that industrialisation would 'cleanse' the world of everything organic, and leave it as sterile and lifeless as the moon. The most widely read and influential of these authors, surprisingly, was J.R.R. Tolkien. A chapter called 'The Last March of the Ents', in The Two Towers (1954), depicts an army of walking, talking trees which attack and destroy a factory for mass producing weapons of war. This scene is plainly an indictment of industrialisation and a glorification of the power of nature.

Much Irish literature at the time, especially the collections of folk and faerie tales published by Ella Young, Augusta Gregory, and W.B. Yeats, shares the anti-industrial, pro-nature nostalgia. The Irish artist and mystic George Russell, writing in The Candle of Vision (1931), declared with regret, "I was an exile from living nature".[11] In a lecture that Yeats delivered in New York in 1904, he said: "Whenever men have tried to imagine a perfect life they have imagined a place where men plough and sow and reap, not a place where there are great wheels turning and great chimneys vomiting smoke."[12] Certain nationalist ideas were also being articulated. In Gregory's Gods and Fighting Men (1904) there is a retelling of a mythological war between the race of the Irish gods and a race of monsters called the Fomorians, and of another one between Fionn MacCumhal's Fianna against the army of the 'King of the World', represented a victory of 'nature' over 'civilisation', as well as the hope for a politically independent Ireland.[13]

Most of this literature can be characterised as 'sentimental' or as 'reactionary', depending on how charitable one wants to be. The excellence of its artistic merit is beyond doubt. Yet its impact on political will, at the time, was minimal. Philosophers, for their part, totally ignored them. During the post-war period philosophers did not normally teach or publish on major specific social, political, or cultural issues. This was largely changed in the 1960s and1970s, when the civil rights movement and various other related movements presented important thematic problems which philosophers could not ignore. Rachel Carson's Silent Spring (1962) is widely regarded as the first major publication describing an environmental issue as a moral tragedy. In her case the issue was the widespread use of DDT as an agricultural pest-killer, which was also killing native song birds by weakening their eggshells. The title, 'silent spring', referred to the possibility that in the future, a spring season might come without any songbirds remaining alive to herald it since pesticides will have killed them. Thus she urged her readers to no longer take for granted the relation between the ecological realm and the human realm. Edward Abbey's novel, The Monkey Wrench Gang (1975), strongly influenced by Thoreau, inspired the radical environmentalist movement. This novel told the story of four friends as they destroy a dam in order to protect the animals and habitats which the altered water course would have destroyed. Because of the title of this novel, the word 'monkeywrenching' has entered the regular vocabulary of environmental activists. It refers to acts of industrial sabotage in the service of environmental protection. Finally, by the end of the 1960's an animal rights movement was well underway, initiated by books like Ruth Harrison's Animal Machines (1964) which described 'factory farming' as a morally outrageous exploitation of animals. These publications may be taken as the literary inaugurations of environmentalism in its present form.

The very first professional philosophy paper on the topic was entitled "Is there a need for a new, an environmental, ethic?", and was delivered in 1973 at the 15th World Congress of Philosophy by Australian philosopher Richard Sylvan (then Routley). He was the first philosopher to consider seriously the idea that actions which affect the environment and yet harm no one directly, nor directly infringe anyone's rights, may yet be morally wrong. He was also the first to suggest that moral indifference towards nature might be a form of human chauvinism.[14] At that time, the idea that any non-human entities could possess moral standing, be they animals, plants, species, or ecosystems, was still unthinkable—the record states that his colleagues laughed at him. The first few philosophers to discuss environmental problems thought that the restriction of moral considerability to humanity, which was treated at the time as an unquestionable moral truth, was an untenable dogma that needed to be abolished. For J. Baird Callicott, as an example, it was not the case that a justification needed to be found for extending moral standing beyond humanity. Rather, it was the case that a justification could *not* be found for continuing to restrict moral standing exclusively to humanity.[15] This was also the position of the Utilitarian philosopher Peter Singer, who almost single-handedly inaugurated the animal rights movement with two works of his own, one a book called Animal Liberation, the other an essay called "All Animals are Equal" (1974). He pointed out that the various qualities and properties of humankind to which we point as the ground of moral considerability exist also in various other species, albeit often to lesser degrees of development. Pure logical consistency, he argued, demanded that if human beings are held in moral standing for possession of language, intentionality, capacity for suffering, etc., then so are animals insofar as they too possess those same qualities. The Deontologist Paul Taylor claimed that the denial of human superiority is a necessary part of any acceptable statement of environmental ethics.[16] The first book-length treatment of environmental ethics (not just animal rights) came out the same year: John Passmore's Man's Responsibility for Nature (1974). And finally, an interest in the aforementioned theologians and naturalists was revived. The study and interpretation of one of them, Aldo Leopold, author of "The Land Ethic",[17] has become a semi-independent tradition of its own within the family of environmental ethics debates.

Environmental philosophy itself is the debate concerning ethical conduct in reference to animals, plants, the entire range of non-human life, and indeed the whole of the ecological world in which we all dwell. The debate is characterised by philosophical commitment to the view that non-human entities possess moral standing, largely due to the kind of cultural soil from which the debate grew. It is contested, of course, whether that standing is justifiable on grounds supplied by one or other of the classic Western ethical systems, or whether a philosophical principle can be discerned in the "pre-philosophical" work (I mean that non-disparagingly) of naturalists, artists, theologians, and ecologists, especially Thoreau, Muir, Leopold, Kipling, and Tolkien. It is also contested whether moral considerability lies chiefly with individual organisms (this is sometimes called biocentrism, or bio-centric individualism) or with 'holistic entities' or 'organic unities' like species and ecosystems (ecocentrism or bio-centric holism). It is also contested whether 'holistic entities' or 'organic unities' are coherent concepts or even whether they exist at all. Environmental philosophy, then, can be seen as a sustained calling-into-question of the place humanity assigns to itself in the world, and the sustained philosophical exploration of all possible alternatives to the traditional anthropocentric views. Contemporary environmentalists who have described and defended biocentrism or ecocentrism include Nicholas Agar, E.O. Wilson, Paul Taylor, Arne Naess, George Sessions, and Holmes Rolston III.

There is a major stream of thought in environmental philosophy which is not explicitly related to Utilitarianism, Deontology, or Virtue theory. It is the idea, advanced as a general working hypothesis or as a first premise in a larger argument, that what has gone wrong is our failure to recognise the environment as intrinsically, inherently valuable. Holmes Rolston III and Arne Naess are the most well-known philosophical advocates of this view. Although argument has several varieties, its general form goes like this: Because we emerged from nature, and because we find ourselves to be intrinsically valuable beings, we therefore also find that nature is also intrinsically valuable.[18] This is called 'ecocentrism', as contrasted with 'anthropocentrism', and might be seen as a variant of the 'value theory' debates which also occur in other areas of ethics. This critique of anthropocentrism is one of the original themes of environmental philosophy. Naess' "Deep Ecology" goes further than Rolston by claiming that a fully informed, rational person should consider the environment as not only intrinsically valuable but also as an extension of his sense of selfhood. It has turned out to be very difficult to provide a rational basis for ecocentrism, and much of the debate has been about whether or not it is philosophically defensible. Although much progress has been made this way, no argument in support of this position has yet been formulated that is entirely immune from logical difficulty or deep-structural criticism. Any attempts to attribute or recognise intrinsic value in non-human species, or in ecosystems, might inevitably be tainted with human interests and anthropomorphic projections. Sylvan has recently pronounced that it is a philosophically dead end.[19]

Happily, this debate need not concern me here. A rational defence for a strong ecocentrism is not the goal of this thesis. Nor am I seeking a rational defence for a blanket condemnation of all forms of interference in the natural world. What I am seeking, what environmental ethics in general is seeking, is a statement of how we are to live in and with the environment. I shall take the term 'environmentalism' to mean nothing more than the philosophical study of the environment. This basic question, 'how shall we live?' constitutes the study of ethics itself. Environmentalism is a distinct study within ethics through its exploration of how, if, and why the physical and natural landscape, in and with which we live, is ethically significant, and how, if, and why it figures into the great question of ethics.

§ 2. Theoretical Principles: Goodness, Justice, Rightness, Excellence.

Here I shall describe the methodology of this thesis and the breakdown of its five chapters. Although a defence of ecocentrism is not the goal of this thesis, the pursuit of a *an acceptable statement of environmental ethics* certainly is. This is indeed one of the goals of environmental philosophy itself. I am in search of a moral principle that can clearly tell us how to live in and with the natural world. This is the standard meaning of the term 'an environmental ethic' in the tradition of environmental philosophy. In order for an environmental ethic to be acceptable, it shall satisfy two specific criteria, one theoretical and the other practical.

First of all, the acceptable statement of environmental ethics shall satisfy a *formal* or *theoretical* criterion: it will be able to explain in what way, if at all, the ecological world in which human life takes place is ethically significant. It will be able to explain the morally correct way for us to treat the landscape of the earth. 'Landscape' here refers to the land, sea, and sky of the planet; any environment where life is possible. Some of the landscape is inhabited by humanity, and some of it is 'wilderness', where no humans dwell because it is too hostile, too remote, or too thick with other life forms to easily colonise. I shall assume that the moral significance of the landscape implies some robust moral responsibilities to (or 'for', or 'concerning') the local and global environment, however those responsibilities are explained. It is the task of environmental philosophy to explain them. The theoretical questions of environmental ethics are such questions as have already been articulated: How are we to live and to dwell in and with the environment? What moral significance, if any, is attached to the various ways we are related to the world? Are there ethical limits to what resources we can take from the environment, and to the ways we take them? An environmental ethic would be plainly unacceptable if it was unable to provide definitive answers to these questions.

The central questions of this thesis, thus stated on theoretical plane, are explored through a methodology which may strike some readers as unusual. This work does not undertake an analytic study of one author nor of one school of thought. Rather, it undertakes an examination of several schools of thought and of many authors, and seeks a synthesis of their best parts to supply answers. I shall explore not one but four traditions of ethics: the tradition of the Good, as in Utilitarianism, the Just as in Distributive Justice, the Right as in Deontology, and the Excellent, as in Virtue theory. It is the aim of this work to determine what environmental principles each of them can offer, and to compare them to each other to see which is the most acceptable. Each of the five chapters of this work undertakes to study one of these approaches. Utilitarianism is studied first, followed by Distributive Justice, Kantian Deontology, Ancient Virtue, and finally Modern Virtue.

The most prominent writer to approach environmental ethics from the Utilitarian direction is Peter Singer, whose early essays, as mentioned, inaugurated the animal rights movement. In Chapter One I examine the statements on environmental goodness which appeared in Practical Ethics (1993) and One World (2002). The most comprehensive treatment of "green" thought from the perspective of Utilitarianism in recent years is Lincoln Alison's Ecology and Utility (1991). It is important that this work should begin with Utilitarianism. This is in part because philosophy in the English-speaking world is almost completely dominated by the Utilitarian tradition, and so it is the most familiar theory for most English-speakers today. Also, the "standard" argument for why future generations matter (described below), is usually stated in Utilitarian terms.

In Chapter Two I study John Rawls' A Theory of Justice (1971; revised 1999), and alongside it two recent philosophers whose work on justice theory with special application to the problems of future generations have become noteworthy: Avner de-Shalit's Why Posterity Matters (1995) and Hendrick Visser T'Hooft's Justice to Future Generations and the Environment (1999). The study of Distributive Justice follows after Utilitarianism here, as a system of ethical thought falling between Utilitarianism and Deontology. Environmental resources, while not exactly "social goods" since they do not emerge from social relations, are appropriated from the landscape and distributed within society in a manner that can be subject to principles of just distribution.

Deontology has been a part of environmental thought from the beginning, for instance in the 'animal rights' theory of Tom Regan and the 'ecosystem rights' theory of Kenneth Goodpaster. The most important deontologist for the purpose of this thesis is Paul Taylor, whose first essay on the topic, "The Ethics of Respect for Nature" appeared in the journal *Environmental Ethics* in 1981. The general strategy of environmental deontology has been to re-write Kant's Practical Imperative, "Always treat humanity…as an end itself", such that some other, more environmentally inclusive duty-generating quality can defensibly be placed in the logical space for 'humanity'. The reason for this, as we have seen, is that early environmental ethicists claimed there was no reason for continuing to restrict moral standing to humanity. In Chapter Three I study Kant's theory directly, as expressed in his Groundwork to the Metaphysics of Morals (1785). Alongside it I study Taylor's flagship book-length work, Respect for Nature (1986).

On the subject of Virtue, there are two distinct but related debates. One is the debate concerning Virtue ethics itself, initiated in 1958 by Elisabeth Anscombe, initiated again 23 years later by Alasdair MacIntyre in After Virtue (1981; revised 1985) and then carried forth by Rosalind Hursthouse, Phillipa Foot, and others. There were other studies of the virtues before MacIntyre's text, for instance James Wallace's Virtues and Vices (1978), but MacIntyre seems to have overshadowed everyone in the field who came before him. This portion of the debate concerns the nature of the virtues themselves, their role in our decision-making, and whether Virtue-thinking can rival alternative ways of moral thinking. The other debate is on the use of Virtue theory for environmental purposes, which at this time is mostly confined to articles published in just one journal: *Environmental Ethics*. There is only one book-length treatment of environmental virtue theory published at this time: Louke Van Wensveen's Dirty Virtues (2000). However, as Wensveen demonstrates, a kind of literary proto-Virtue theory has been a part of environmental ethics from the beginning, although never explicitly presented as such. Some of the first papers to approach environmental ethics took the philosophical route of describing certain outstanding individuals whose styles of life were upheld as models of good environmentally-conscious living. Each of these figures led exemplary lives which may be taken as paradigmatic examples of virtuous existence in "balance" and "harmony" with nature. Leopold, the American forestry professor who wrote "The Land Ethic" after his retirement in the 1940's, is frequently singled out as a forerunner of environmental virtue.[20] Philip Cafaro argued that proto-Virtue theory is to be found in Thoreau's autobiographical description of isolated rural life on Lake Walden, and in Aldo Leopold's principles of forestry management. He also argued persuasively that Rachel Carson's tradition-inaugurating Silent Spring is strongly based on unarticulated Virtue theory premises.[21] Wensveen devoted two chapters of her work on environmental virtue to the "social ecology" of Murray Bookchin, a political analyst and anarchy theorist, and the "story of the universe" cosmology of historian and Catholic priest Thomas Berry, both of which she claims are saturated with proto-Virtue language.[22] In Chapter Four, I shall study an Aristotelian conception of Virtue ethics, focusing on the discourse of The Nicomachean Ethics but with reference to The Politics as well. The study of Aristotle shall constitute the pursuit of a statement of environmental Virtue on the theoretical plane. In Chapter Five I turn to modern Virtue in search of a statement of practical environmental Virtue, focusing on Alasdair MacIntyre's After Virtue and also Rosalind Hursthouse's On Virtue Ethics (1999).

This constitutes the theoretical, or one could say philosophical, aspect of this thesis. The thesis as a whole, then, is not contributing to one and only one philosophical debate. The purpose and methodology of this work is not to analyse any single moral tradition in exhaustive detail. Rather, it is to achieve a wider and more encompassing scope of vision than is possible for a thesis confined to a single debate or tradition. This is a synthetic thesis, which is to say a thesis which studies moral theory in a comparative way, with a view to what they have in common and how they may be brought together. A complete and comprehensive examination of each tradition of moral thought, including its inaugural writers and all the different variations advanced by its critics and defenders, would render the synthesising approach unwieldy, and indeed each examination would be a thesis in itself. Each chapter, then, begins with only a schematic presentation of the structure and logic of each theory. From there each chapter moves directly into the critique of the theory for the purposes of finding an acceptable statement of environmental ethics.

§ 3. Practical Choices: Preservation, Conservation, and Depletion

In addition to a theoretical criterion, the acceptable environmental ethic shall satisfy a *practical* criterion: it will be able to offer specific advice to guide our choices. If we have an array of environmental policy choices in front of us, it will be able to tell us how to choose. Given a choice between an environmental policy of protection or of exploitation, or some third policy lying between these positions, the practical criterion will be able to tell us which option we are morally obliged to prefer. The methodology of the practical aspect of this thesis concerns the way each theory guides us to choose between different competing environmental policy choices. There are three general kinds of environment-affecting choices which will be examined here. Each of them encompasses a range of possibilities, and a range of criteria for what is included and excluded from its sphere of concern.

The first is the category of *Preservation*, also sometimes called *Protection*, which can be described simply as a "complete hands-off" approach to an area which otherwise holds things which humanity needs and values for various reasons. To preserve an area of wilderness is to refrain from human development in that area. Environmental preservation can be likened to the preservation of heritage monuments or important works of art. Efforts are made to ensure the present state of the protected object remains unchanged. Of course environments, unlike paintings, are changing all the time of their own accord. It is part of the normal activity of wild animals, plants, and organisms to move, to grow, to reproduce, and to die, for

17

instance. A landscape can even destroy itself, so to speak, by some natural disaster: an earthquake or a hurricane, for instance. This is part of the meaning of Heraclitus' famous statement that one cannot step into the same river twice. The choice of Preservation is the choice to refrain from intervening in these activities. Whatever happens in a protected area, it happens without human interference. (Note that this absence of human interference is, for many environmental activists, one of the regular meanings of the word 'natural'.) In Preserved areas, little or no economic development takes place. There may be some scientific, historical, archaeological, or aesthetic interest in the area. Some people may feel pleased with the thought that certain areas of the world are preserved, even though they may never visit them. The wild vegetation contributes to normalising and regulating the climate, purifying water, and replenishing atmospheric oxygen. It is also often the case that we can protect ourselves from unforeseen diseases, poisons, and natural disasters by keeping away from certain areas. While these benefits are important, they are usually the only benefits we receive from Preserved areas, and there may be other benefits which we forgo, such as the use of raw materials, energy, or farmable land.

The second major category of environment-affecting choice is *Conservation*, which we can characterise as the choice to make use of an area's resources in a sensitive, careful, and limited way. The principle of "sustainable development", which requires that the economic productivity of an area must not exceed the area's regenerative capacities, can fall under this major category. If any industrial activity is permitted in a conserved area, the most low-impact activities possible are preferred, and may also be coupled with a restoration effort. Waste dumping in the area is also kept as low-impact as possible, preferably within the ecosystem's renewable assimilation capacity, and coupled with some kind of treatment process before the waste substances are released. The Conserved area can benefit humanity in some of the same ways that Preserved areas can, for instance by regulating climate. It also benefits humanity through the material and energy resources which we take from it.

The third and final major category is *Depletion*, which is the choice to take as much as possible, as quickly as possible. Little or no regard is given to the resource's capacity for renewal. If we choose Depletion, we receive the greatest benefit from the area's material and energy resources that it is possible to gain, at least in the short and intermediate time spans. However, most of the time, this strategy exhausts an area's resources completely, and then the area is abandoned. Sometimes restoration projects are possible afterwards, but they are generally very expensive and labour-intensive, and it is normally easier and more cost-effective to simply move to another area and continue depleting the sought-after resource there. Depletion is often chosen because the people who use the space and its resources regard their purposes as being of higher value than the conservation or preservation of the space. Depletion tends to maximise the wealth of the society that chooses it at that time, and raises the society's material standard of living to a higher level, although it may not be able to sustain this benefit for more than a few generations.

An important distinguishing quality of each of these choices is the rate of resource consumption and the volume of waste deposit over time. Preservation takes little or nothing from the world and also deposits as little waste as possible. Conservation takes up resources at an intermediary rate, and deposits waste in careful, controlled ways. Depletion takes resources as fast as possible and deposits waste wherever and however it is easiest to do so. In general, most human relations with the environment are interventions in natural processes of this kind. They are relations of material or energy appropriation, modification, and production that alters or transforms the ecological systems in which they are involved. The morally correct way to relate to the environment cannot be a "hands-off" approach to nature *tout court*. It must in some way be an intervention. Note that I am using the term 'intervention' in a way that need not carry the pejorative connotation that it usually does. To make use of environmental resources is to intervene in ecological processes, even if we do so in sustainable, non-destructive ways. These three categories of relation can be seen as three different levels or intensities of intervention.

These are categories of not only choice but also *relation*. Each of them describes a way of relating to the other animals and plants with which we share the world, as well as to the landscape which all life on Earth inhabits. The science of ecology has shown us that the world is host to many tightly intertwined systems of organic relation, called ecosystems, in which every life form contributes to the survival of other life forms which share the same landscape through exchanges of chemical and thermodynamic energy. An ecosystem can be called a system of organic mutual dependence and reliance between and among many living things, obtained through exchanges of various organic and inorganic elements and energies. We too participate in these relations. The three categories of environmental choice represent degrees of involvement and intervention in these systems of relations. Preservation intervenes as little as possible, and preferably not at all. Depletion is near-total intervention. And Conservation intervenes with them in a limited or controlled way. We must choose some form of relation to the environment to survive: we are totally reliant on the material and energy resources of the Earth for our existence. This basic fact is recognised by all environmental philosophers of every major school of thought within the tradition. We have no choice but to take resources from the world in order to eat, to shelter and clothe ourselves, and also to obtain goals of a higher order than basic survival. It is, to a large extent, the meaning and moral significance of this fact which environmental philosophers debate. Because of our total reliance on the Earth for our existence, we find that much of the time we cannot choose Preservation. We might choose it for some areas, but if we do then we must choose some variety of Conservation or Depletion elsewhere. Frequently, we Preserve some area only because we have scheduled it for use later on, after other areas have been exhausted, and so Preservation is sometimes a disguised form of Conservation. The practical enquiry of this thesis poses the question of the right way to inhabit the Earth and relate to its ecosystems and other living inhabitants in this way:

Which of these major categories are we morally bound to prefer? Which should be enshrined in public policy? Each chapter, while pursuing a theoretical statement of environmental ethics, shall also pursue a practical statement, to see which category of environmental relation is endorsed as the morally correct one. A statement which cannot provide this practical guidance shall be deemed unacceptable.

The examination of these major categories of environmental relation constitutes the practical thesis of this work, which complements the theoretical thesis concerning the synthesis of moral theories. It is important for the understanding of this work that formal and practical questions are being studied together. Unless we do this, any conclusion we might reach would be incomplete. For theoretical principles and practical choices always exist in a tight relation to each other, and so must be studied together. As MacIntyre says, "Abstract changes in moral concepts are always embodied in real, particular events… Every action is the bearer and expression of more or less theory-laden beliefs and concepts; every piece of theorizing and every expression of belief is a political and moral action." (*AV* pg. 61)

§ 4. Future Generations.

The 19th century Irish politician Sir Boyle Roche asked a rhetorical question which became famous: "Why should we put ourselves out of our way to do anything for posterity? For, what has posterity ever done for us?" The answer he was implying is of course "nothing". Posterity might benefit someone's posthumous reputation, however it can do nothing for him in the here and now. We therefore have no reason, so he implied, to do anything for future generations. Was he right? Environmental ethics is also a debate concerning the ethics of future human generations and the continuation of human civilisation.[23] The three major categories of environmental relation are also distinguished as choices concerning how much of the Earth's resources should be saved for the future. Preservation aims to save as much as possible; Conservation aims to save a generous amount but not everything; and Depletion saves little or nothing. In choosing one of these three categories we are also choosing a relation to the future. The notions of Conservation and Preservation already contain within their meanings a connection to time and the future: we 'conserve' and 'preserve' things which we want to continue to exist in the future, and to be given to posterity as they are. The environment is only one of many things we often wish to conserve: we also conserve historic buildings, artefacts, works of art, books and documents, archaeological relics, and the like. The "future generations" argument for why we ought to conserve such things, especially the environment, is quite common in the position statements of environmental activist groups, and frequently appears in environmental policy statements. For example, the Bruntland Report's well-known definition of Sustainable Development, "development that meets the needs of the present without compromising the ability of future generations to meet their own needs",[24] veritably presupposes moral obligations to not-yet-existing people. This definition was the second sentence in the Irish government's "Sustainability Strategy" of 1997, and it was further elaborated by the Minister of the Environment in his preliminary remarks to the report, in which he said: "Sustainable development is also about solidarity: solidarity between the present and future generations, between various participants in our society and between different countries."[25]

There is a standard argument for why future generations deserve to be included in our moral reasoning, which runs like this. Future people are remote to us, in a way that is similar to how people who are distant across space are remote to us. Future people are distant to us across time. The time difference between deliberately committing an act that leads to the suffering or death of another person, and the birth date of the victim of the action, so the argument goes, makes no moral difference whatsoever. If there is a time delay between an action performed today and the moment when the action harms someone, for example the time between planting a landmine and the moment it detonates, I cannot use that time delay to excuse myself from responsibility for the harm that occurred as a result. Likewise it is not relevant if the victim was not born when the mine was planted. Pollution of the atmosphere and water, destruction of resources, and general climate change leading to drastic and destructive weather disasters, are all actions committed today which we can know with certainty will harm people who, at this time, have not yet been born, and indeed who may not be born until long after everyone presently living is dead. It follows that when calculating the harms or benefits likely to come from decisions about environmental policy, the future generations must be considered as well. Thus, my central question is not only a question about environmental ethics, but also a question of inter-generational ethics and future generations.

Furthermore, I shall put each moral theory studied to the following special test. The English analytic philosopher Derek Parfit published a work on Utilitarianism entitled Reasons and Persons (1984), which contained an intriguing philosophical puzzle that complicated the problem of future generations. Parfit named his puzzle "The Non-Identity Problem". The logic of this problem describes how someone committed to Utilitarian and/or person-affecting moral principles must conclude that a policy of environmental Depletion would harm no one. Parfit claimed that exploiting the world's resources, leaving little or nothing for future people, would create an intrinsically bad state of affairs. Great suffering and depravation would result from the loss of valuable resources and the intensified levels of pollution, to the point where most people's lives are only barely worth living, if they are worth living at all. But the logic of the Non-Identity Problem renders person-affecting principles unable to explain why it is wrong to choose it. I shall explain the logic of the problem in detail in Chapter One, but here is a quick summary. Policy planning decisions like environmental policies tend to have consequences, however unintended, on how people travel and settle, how they meet, and eventually with whom they have sex and produce children. A policy choice like Depletion or Conservation, therefore, will also result in different people being born than who would have been born otherwise. It follows that the people who in the future would be affected by a Conservation policy would be different people than

23

those affected by a Depletion policy. They would owe their very existence to the choice which also created their terrible living conditions. Parfit therefore claims that the choice of Depletion is *not worse* for them, and therefore the choice *does not harm them*. We should still have an objection to such choices, but as Parfit says, "person-affecting principles cannot explain why."

This arresting philosophical puzzle has so far never been solved. The first chapter of the thesis shall describe the problem in more detail and also explore some of the Utilitarian solutions offered by various scholars. But it is not my intention here to try and solve it on its own terms. In fact my final statement on the problem itself is essentially the same as Parfit's: Person-affecting principles like Utilitarianism cannot explain what is morally wrong with choosing Depletion. But instead of attempting to refine or modify our person-affecting moral principles, I shall claim, however contentiously, that the solution to the problem *must be found outside of person-affecting ethics*. An ethical theory that places the weight of concern on what we do, in reference to a theory of moral duty or a theory of virtuous character, shall be able to succeed where Utilitarianism failed. One of my ongoing questions, among those already described, is thus whether an act can be wrong even if no one is harmed. If there is a way of answering that question in the affirmative, we will have a path to the solution to the Non-Identity Problem.

Although it is not my purpose to solve the Non-Identity Problem on its own terms, it is my purpose to find an acceptable statement of environmental ethics which incorporates our moral responsibilities to future generations. Most environmental philosophers assume that an acceptable statement environmental ethics will condemn any unnecessary destruction of the Earth's resources, habitats, and ecosystems. Similarly, Parfit presumes that by choosing Depletion we can create an intrinsically repugnant future situation which we should avoid. In the course of this work, then, I shall assume that the practical aspect of the acceptable environmental ethic includes a strong preference against causing environmental disasters, both now and in the future. We should not accept a statement of environmental ethics which justified or supported the choices that lead to, for instance, the sinking of Tuvalu and other island nations. Some environmental philosophers prefer a stronger statement, which provides proactive moral requirements for actions and choices which are environmentally sensitive and sustainable. For this thesis, I shall assume only that a statement of environmental ethics which can avoid the Repugnant Conclusion is more acceptable than one which can not avoid it. The practical aspect of this thesis is therefore not only about which practical environmental choice each moral theory would compel us to make, but it is also about the search for a defensible way of saying that causing environmental disasters is wrong, even if the logic of the Non-Identity Problem enables one to claim that no one is harmed by such disasters.

Is this a form of question-begging? If the practical criterion was nothing more than the search for a blanket condemnation of environmentally destructive actions, it might appear so. Without the theoretical criterion, the practical criterion may seem as if it is an attempt at a rational defence for an unexamined intuition systematically presupposed from the beginning. But I believe this presumption against causing environmental disasters is not unreasonable. It is, first of all, one of Parfit's own presumptions, and its appearance in his text is reflected in this one. Depletion, he claims, can create a future situation that everyone would find "*intrinsically* repugnant". The *problem* of the Non-Identity Problem is precisely that person-affecting principles can find no objection to it. Furthermore, most environmental philosophers accept that what makes an environmental ethic genuinely *environmental* is commitment to the view that animals, plants, habitats, ecosystems, and so on, possess moral standing, and must figure into our moral reasoning somehow. One need not claim that the environment is intrinsically valuable to be an environmental philosopher. But to fail to see the wrongness of causing environmental disasters, even if the reason for why it is wrong is elusive, is to fail to understand what environmental philosophy is all about. Similarly, no one argues that Utilitarians beg the question by claiming that causing harm is morally wrong. When a Utilitarian asks, 'why is it wrong to (unnecessarily) harm people?', no one objects that the speaker has already presupposed that it is wrong to unnecessarily harm people. We would be unable to do Utilitarian philosophy without that presupposition. No one objects that feminism begs the question when it claims that discriminating against women, for no other reason than because they are women, is wrong. These practical claims are not treated as instances of question-begging because their corresponding higher-order theoretical dimensions are already well known. It is systematically inconsistent, then, to claim that when environmental ethics asks 'why is it wrong to cause environmental destruction?', it is already presupposed that to do so is wrong, when the same objection is not also levied against other disciplines of ethics. Hursthouse has shown how the question-begging criticism was similarly directed at Virtue theory during its early revival, and how the criticism is similarly misplaced. It is, she said, inconsistent to argue that the notion of 'the virtuous person' is indeterminate while at the same time not saying the same of 'harm' or 'duty', the central categories of Utilitarianism and Deontology.[26]

In accord with the good philosophical practice of having as few presuppositions as possible, it *would* be an unexamined assumption if we believed that the reason to prevent environmental disasters necessarily had to be some form of ecocentrism. Environmental ethics must be open to the possibility that the answers to its questions could be found anywhere. Sometimes the view that the environment has moral standing has been interpreted to mean that our main moral duty toward it is to leave it alone. This was Leopold's view when he wrote *The Land Ethic*.[27] But most of the time, Preservation is impossible for us. In areas where Preservation is an option, it is often the case that another area must be Conserved or Depleted to create the resources required for the Preservation effort. It would be question-begging if the acceptable environmental ethic had to be a defence of one of the three major categories of relation as the most morally correct environmental choice we can make, to the exclusion of the other two. Even if we grant the obvious fact that when we interfere in ecosystems we usually ruin them, we must be suspicious of ethical statements that assert a blanket condemnation of all forms of interference. Calicott has called this "the popular wilderness fallacy".[28] There might be ways to interfere with the environment that are not destructive, which positively benefit the environment, and which are not morally wrong. We must also be open to the possibility that an acceptable ethic cannot be found at all using the philosophical resources we presently possess. If some variety of ecocentrism could be found and successfully defended, then it would be an acceptable environmental ethic. But if ecocentrism cannot be defended, and yet some variety of anthropocentrism can be, then that would have to count as acceptable.

Having said that, it does not beg the question to assume that causing environmental disasters is morally wrong. I take my cue from Parfit that a future in which people experience intense suffering, such that their lives are very nearly not worth living, is intrinsically repugnant and should be avoided. Parfit himself could not find a solution to the Non-Identity Problem, but he believed that a solution could be found by others. He said:

> When he was asked about his book, Sidgwick said that its first word was *Ethics*, and its last *failure*. This could have been the last word of Part Four [of *Reasons and Persons*.] As I argued, we need a new theory about beneficence. This must solve the non-Identity Problem, avoid the Repugnant and Absurd Conclusions, and solve the Mere Addition Paradox. I failed to find a theory that can meet these four requirements. Though I failed to find such a theory, I believe that, if they tried, others could succeed.[29]

This thesis takes up Parfit's challenge. A minimally acceptable environmental ethic shall fulfil both the theoretical and the practical criterion, but I shall assume that if it includes a reason to avoid causing environmental disasters and avoid the Repugnant Conclusion, then it is more acceptable.

§ 5. A Synthesis of Ethics, with Virtue Leading the Way

In general, this thesis seeks to make a contribution to the wide and diverse debate on environmental ethics. My primary and central questions are the same ones which concern environmental philosophers everywhere. Apart from environmental thought, the thesis makes a contribution to the debate concerning the Non-Identity Problem by suggesting a solution. And there is also a substantial contribution to the newly emerging field of modern Virtue ethics. The general themes of Conservation and Depletion, the (minimally) acceptable environmental ethic, the Non-Identity Problem as the theoretical test case, and the necessity of turning to Virtue theory, are all consistent themes in this work, providing cohesion and unity throughout.

I shall now describe my conclusions, as well as the path by which I arrive at them. The theoretical thesis, concerning moral theory, is the claim that no moral theory by itself can articulate an acceptable environmental ethic. Environmental issues reveal unusual problems of logic in each theory; it will be shown that alternative ways of thinking are called for to solve them. It shall also be shown that each theory also possesses resources which contribute to a general synthesis that is capable of stating the moral significance of the landscape, and is capable of choosing between different environmental policy options, and finally is capable of overcoming the Non-Identity Problem. Although this is not an analytic thesis, it still follows a systematic methodology. The discourse starts with Utilitarianism, since the aforementioned standard argument for our ethical responsibility to future generations is normally stated in Utilitarian terms, and because the Non-Identity Problem began as a problem for Utilitarianism. I argue that the utility of a healthy, bountiful, and beautiful environment may be very much greater than we normally estimate, and the dis-utility of a polluted and exploited environment can also be greater than is usually calculated. However, I find that environmental issues and problems, and the unique matter of future generations, lead Utilitarianism in the direction of the Non-Identity Problem and its Repugnant Conclusion.

This leaves the Utilitarian in the position of either being forced to choose Depletion, even though it can produce the intrinsically repugnant future situation, or alternatively, being left unable to explain what is wrong with choosing it. The only escape from this conclusion, I shall argue, is to call for another system of thinking in which the maximisation of utility is not what matters.

Justice is capable of articulating just such a claim, and so it is studied next in the sequence. The action is right if, according to Justice theory, it distributes to everyone his or her fair share of the world's resources. Justice theory provides strong reasons for participating in a practice of just savings of resources and social goods from one generation to the next. However, justice theory cannot by itself offer a reason for initiating such a practice. It would have to be shown that initiating such a practice is a moral duty. I therefore turn to Kantian Deontology in search of that reason. According to this tradition, the action is right if can be willed as a universal law, and it respects the humanity of others. Immanuel Kant's Categorical Imperative provides that environmental destruction is self-defeating as a law for everyone, but I conclude that this provision is sound only on a theoretical level—on a practical level, there are ways in which any particular environmentally destructive act can actually pass the test of universalisation, and thus not count as a morally wrong action. If everyone followed a universal law authorising him or her to litter, for instance, that would not make it impossible to litter. Moreover, the same problems which challenged Utilitarianism also challenge both forms of Deontology studied here, and indeed a Deontological version of the Non-Identity Problem is discovered. An action which deprives future people of their right to clean water and air, and their share of the world's other resources, might also create the people whose rights are infringed. This, Parfit would say, leaves them unable to object to the infringements of their rights. An alternative act would create different people whose rights cannot be infringed, not even in principle, which undermines the very conception of rights. A moral theory is called for in which it is possible to claim that an act can be wrong even if no one is affected, that is, no one's rights are infringed, no one deprived of his or her fair share, or no one's humanity is disrespected.

The only moral theory capable of judging an action wrong even if there is no one who can complain of being harmed, being deprived, or disrespected, is Virtue theory. For the theory is not 'person-affecting' in the usual sense of the term. The weight of moral concern, for this theory, lies not with the complaint of the moral patient. Rather, the weight of moral concern is the moral agent's own character and her pursuit of a worthwhile, flourishing life. More than any other moral theory, the moral agent's attention is drawn inward, to his own life and the purposes he creates for himself, especially the aim for happiness.

It shall be one of my final conclusions that none of the major moral theories of Western philosophy is able to make a definitive and complete statement of our moral duties and responsibilities in reference to future generations on its own. No single theory, by itself, tells the whole story of environmental ethics. A synthesis or moral theories, in which our reasoning is guided by no single principle but by the best aspects of several principles, is best able to succeed where each theory by itself fails. However, I also conclude that Virtue theory must be the leading theory in any synthesis. I wish to refute the idea that Virtue theory can be nothing more than a mere crutch to shore up other theories. I also wish to refute the widespread belief that Virtue theory can have nothing to say about environmental ethics and future generations. Indeed I wish to assert a contrary position. Virtue theory can indeed say interesting and substantial things about environmental ethics and future generations. I shall show that whenever other theories attempt to speak to environmental issues they often borrow concepts and terms from Virtue theory to overcome various conceptual aporias. Indeed one of the things that almost all the moral theories here studied have in common with each other is their use of Virtue theory's philosophical vocabulary (deliberately or accidentally). Virtue theory must lead the synthesis of ethics because only Virtue theory is able to claim that an act can be wrong even if no one is harmed, no one's humanity disrespected, and no one's rights infringed. This ability, as I shall argue, enables Virtue theory to provide a coherent and defensible statement of environmental ethics which both incorporates responsibility for future generations and avoids the Non-Identity Problem.

I shall conclude that the moral significance of the environment is that it is our home and place, the ground of human life, the field and stage of all human action. It follows from this that we should have a moral wish for an environment in which flourishing is possible and supported, both now and in the future. We should do that which will aim at creating that environment, or at least do nothing which will degrade the environment into a condition less suitable, or altogether unsuitable, for human flourishing. This position is articulated in a five-point schematic, with parts drawn from all four moral theories but with Virtue theory providing the bridge that holds them together. Aristotle and MacIntyre present a theory of the virtues which is strongly rooted in the social and political environments in which people find themselves. I argue that something similar obtains in reference to the ecological environment as well. One's catalogue of the virtues must include those which are required for the creation, maintenance, and protection of the physical or ecological environment in which the aim for the flourishing life is possible and supported.

The future appears to the Virtuous person not as the consequence of her actions but as a potential or possible future which her present actions aim at. I shall conclude that the value of continued human existence into the future is rooted in the interests and intentions of presently existing people, particularly in the aim for a worthwhile life, which is the central guiding principle of Virtue theory. I find that little can be gained by appealing to the rights, interests, or benefits which as-yet-nonexisting future people possess, or are deprived of. Paradoxes like Parfit's Non-Identity problem are bound to arise when the location of one's concern is on the complaint of others (but this is not to say that other people do not matter). The three categories of environmental choice, Preservation, Depletion, and Conservation, when viewed as a Virtuous person would view them, become potential futures which can be brought into being by present-day choices. They are potential futures in which people have, or do not have, things which exist today. A Virtuous person must decide which one of these possible futures it is morally right to strive for with her present actions and decisions, whether that future is likely to transpire or not, and whether that future transpires in that person's own lifetime or not. I shall claim that the solution to the Non-Identity Problem is the Virtuous person's discovery that a Non-Identity choices creates a different future than that which would be created otherwise, and that the morally correct one to choose is the one which will bring out the best in her character in the course of aiming for it. The morally wrong choice is the one which tends to bring out of the agent a propensity for several vices that we have strong reasons to avoid.

Virtue theory is both the youngest and also the oldest of moral theories in the Western philosophical tradition. It is coherent and robust enough to stand on its own and make genuinely unique and fruitful contributions to environmental thought. The combination of environmental ethics with Aristotelian ethics is one of the youngest hybrid trees in philosophy's garden, and it deserves a chance to grow. That growth will be difficult if certain disciplinary boundaries remain rigidly in place. It is my hope that this small contribution to its development is philosophically fruitful and beautiful, and that it will encourage further growth in the field.

---

[1] Henry Hengeveld, "The Science", pg. 15.

[2] J. Leake, "Britain faces big chill as ocean current slows" *The Times* (UK) 8 May 2005.

[3] Bruce Torrie, "Sea-Level Rise Alert", pg. 11.

[4] "New giant iceberg adrift near Antarctica" www.cnn.com, 19 March 2002

[5] "Massive Antarctic Ice Shelf Collapses" *The Guardian* 19 March 2002

[6] "Unnatural Disasters" *The Guardian* 15 October 2003.

[7] Bruce Torrie, "Sea-Level Rise Alert", pg. 11; "Pacific Islands: Climate Change, Radiation Concern Leaders" *Environmental News Service* 19 August 2002; and Patrick Barkham, "Going Down" *The Guardian* 16 February 2002.

[8] Boethius, The Consolation of Philosophy, book II, pg. 66.

[9] Boethius, *ibid*, book III, pg. 92.

[10] J.J. Rousseau, The Confessions, pg. 167.

[11] George Russell "A.E", The Candle of Vision pp. 11.

[12] R. Ellmann, Yeats: The Man and the Masks pg. 116.

[13] Both of these stories can be found in Augusta Gregory's Gods and Fighting Men, pp. 60-68, 171-200.

[14] Routley, "Is there a need for a new, an environmental ethic?" pg. 206.

[15] See, for instance, J. Baird Callicott, "Animal Liberation: A Triangular Affair"; and also his book-length work, In Defense of the Land Ethic, pp. 75-99.

[16] Taylor, "The Denial of Human Superiority", chap.3 part.5 of Respect for Nature, pp. 129-156. Reference to this text is hereafter abbreviated as *RN*.

[17] Aldo Leopold, A Sand County Almanac, pp. 237-264

[18] As an example of this argument, here are the words of Holmes Rolston III: "Nature does, of course, offer possibilities for human valuation, but the vitality of the system is not something that goes on [exclusively] in the human mind, nor is its value. The possibility of valuation is carried to us by evolutionary and ecological natural history, and such nature is already valuable before humans arrive to evaluate what is taking place. How do we humans come to be charged up with values, if there was and is nothing in nature charging us up so? Some value is anthropgenic, generated by humans, but some is biogenic, in the natural genesis. A comprehensive environmental ethics reallocates value across the whole continuum." Holmes Rolston III, "Challenges to Environmental Ethics" in Zimmerman, et. al., eds. Environmental Philosophy pg. 144.

[19] Lincoln Allison, Ecology and Utility pg. 48. Alison's text shall hereafter be referred to as *E&U*.

[20] See, for instance, Bill Shaw, "A Virtue Ethics Approach to Aldo Leopold's Land Ethic"

[21] Philip Cafaro, "Thoreau, Leopold, and Carson: Toward an Environmental Virtue Ethics"

[22] Wensveen, Dirty Virtues pp. 43-86.

[23] I stipulate here that by 'future people' I do *not* mean living children or infants who could be taken as the implicit presence of future generations. Their presence among us may be taken as the presence of time's arrow, or a kind of guarantee that the human race shall survive and outlast the lifetime of any presently living adult. But since they are alive among us now, they are part of the present generation, and not, in fact, a 'future' generation among us in the present.

[24] World Commission on Environment and Development, Our Common Future pg. 43.

[25] Brendan Howlin, T.D. Sustainable Development: A Strategy for Ireland pg. 5

[26] Hursthouse, On Virtue Ethics, pg. 28.

[27] "A thing is right when it tends to preserve the integrity, stability, and beauty of the biotic community. It is wrong when it tends otherwise." Leopold, "The Land Ethic" as cited in Zimmerman, et.al. Environmental Philosophy pp. 109-110.

[28] The Popular Wilderness Fallacy is the view that "any human alteration of pristine nature degrades it, and therefore biological conservation is served best by wilderness protection." Calicott, "The Wilderness Idea Revisited" pg. 236.

[29] Parfit, Reasons and Persons, pg. 443. References to this text are hereafter abbreviated to *R&P.*

Chapter One: The "Good"
Utilitarianism.

The history of contemporary Utilitarianism begins in England in the 19th century and early 20th century, with authors like Jeremy Bentham, John Stewart Mill, G.E. Moore, and Henry Sidgewick. The basic principle of the theory can be stated like this: the morally right action is the one which results in the best consequences overall. The best consequences overall are those which have the greatest net difference of benefit over harm, i.e. the greatest benefit and the least harm, for the greatest number of people. This is, of course, only one way of expressing the Utilitarian position, but it is one of the standard ways. Most Utilitarians who have worked the field of environmental ethics have sought for ways in which the consequences for the environment should figure into the calculus of benefits and harms for people, or for both people and animals. Here I shall present a schematic of the theory, followed by an exploration of environmental ethics from a Utilitarian point of view.

§ 1. Utilitarianism and the Environment

There are two important points which must be clarified here. The first is that for Utilitarianism, actions are to be judged right or wrong by virtue of their consequences. Nothing else matters. Right actions are, simply, the ones with the best overall consequences. Since Utilitarianism rejects the emphasis on acts-in-themselves, it follows that there are situations in which some action can be right, and in other situations the same action can be wrong. This is determined by the amount of harm and benefit the action causes, or can be expected to cause. It is not determined by its conformity or non-conformity to a rule of duty, a principle of human nature, human reason, or divine command. Utilitarianism is thus very accessible and flexible. Moreover, among all consequences the only thing that matters is the amount of utility that is caused. Utility was originally defined as 'happiness' but it has also come to mean 'benefit, 'pleasure', 'satisfaction of preferences', or 'well-being'. The action's 'dis-utility' also matters: this is the harm, pain, or suffering the action causes. Everything else is irrelevant.

The second important point here is that in calculating the utility or dis-utility that will be caused, no one's utility is to be counted as more important than anyone else's. We are to do that which results in the greatest benefit for the greatest number of people, whoever and wherever they are. No one's happiness or harm is more important than anyone else's happiness or harm. One's own self, one's friends and family, one's enemies and rivals, and others with whom one is totally anonymous, are all absolutely equal in the Utilitarian view. It is equally as good to benefit a friend as it is to benefit a stranger. This is what separates Utilitarianism from more narrow-minded doctrines like egoism and enlightened self-interest. As Bentham famously said, "Each to count for one and none to count for more than one." Utilitarianism's standard of rationality is thus an impersonal standard: those with whom we have personal relationships must have no privilege or special status in our moral decision-making.

Within this simple statement of the position, there are several varieties and possibilities for interpretation. As noted by J.J.C. Smart, each of the major authors in the Utilitarian tradition defended their own version of the principle. Smart wrote:

> Bentham, who thought that quantity of pleasure being
> equal, the experience of playing pushpin was as good
> as that of reading poetry, could be classified as a
> hedonistic act-Utilitarian. Moore, who believed that
> some states of mind, such as those of acquiring
> knowledge, had intrinsic value quite independent of
> their pleasantness, can be called an ideal utilitarian.
> Mill seemed to occupy an intermediate position. He
> held that there are higher and lower pleasures.[1]

Let us look at the notion of utility, which as stated can variously mean happiness, pleasure, and benefit. Smart shows how the concept of happiness is partly a descriptive and partly an evaluative concept.[2] It is a descriptive concept in that it would be absurd to call someone 'happy' when he is clearly not enjoying whatever he is doing, or is even in pain. As Smart says, "For a man to be happy he must, as a minimal condition, be fairly contented and moderately enjoying himself for much of the time."[3] After this minimal condition is met, we can evaluate different kinds of states of enjoyment, and even rank them against one another. Happiness is also evaluative in that it is "a long-term concept in a way that enjoyment is not."[4] Mill was convinced that whatever people desire, they desire it for the sake of the happiness which will result for them, or they desire it as part of their happiness.[5]

However, we may pursue many things for reasons other than the happiness that may result. In that case utility may consist not so much in happiness but in the satisfaction of preferences and desires, including but not limited to the desire for happiness. As explained by William Shaw, "...someone benefits a person, promotes her well being, or enhances her welfare if and only if it satisfies her desires (or as economists say, her 'preferences')."[6] The idea here is that utility is not a mental or psychological state like pleasure or happiness, which is open to some easy-to-imagine objections, but that utility is people's getting of what they want. People may want many more things in addition to happiness.[7] People may also want knowledge, freedom, the development of their natural talents, and so on. And it seems that the relation to people's desires is all that different and otherwise incomparable kinds of pleasure have in common. Thus Mill's claim that utility is happiness, because whatever we desire we desire it for the sake of happiness or as a part of happiness, may be too narrow. The desire-satisfaction view of utility is the most prominent view among Utilitarian philosophers today. Shaw says that this is so mainly because of:

> ...the prestige of modern economic theory, which
> defines utility maximisation as one's doing what one
> most prefers and explains market behaviour in terms
> of people's rational pursuit of their ends. If one

accepts the standard idealisations of positive
economics and the economists' view of rationality,
then it follows that what one prefers is what is good
for one.[8]

The desire-satisfaction position is of course not without its own
objections and difficulties. Shaw discusses five different kinds of
objections: people's desires can and do change, desires may be based
on false beliefs, a person's desires can be satisfied without the person
realizing it, a person might end up disliking her preferences once
they are satisfied, and the theory might imply we should have only
simple and easily-satisfied desires.[9] One could also add to this list
the objection that someone could have a desire to cause harm or do
works of evil.

 In reply to each of these objections, we can modify our
theory of desire-satisfaction, for instance to say that we should
satisfy only our rational desires, and that there is a list of things that
are objectively valuable which we should pursue. This principle,
usually called the 'objective-list' approach, is the claim that
"rational, ideally informed people will desire the things on the
objective list because they realise that those things are good for
them".[10] Friendship, knowledge, love, health, freedom, justice, and
the like are all examples of things that make life worthwhile, and so
should go on such a list. A list of objectively bad things could also
be drawn up, to include things which tend to bring suffering or make
life harder. Objective List theory is distinct from pleasure-seeking or
desire-satisfying Utilitarianism in that it asserts the things on the list
to be valuable whether people desire them or not, whether they are
pleasurable or not. The appeal of this approach is that we can agree
that certain goods reliably enhance or increase well-being, even if
there are different competing lists, and even if it is disputable
whether possession of such goods is all that is meant by well-being.

 According to both Smart and Shaw, there is no overall
consensus among Utilitarians today concerning what constitutes
Utility itself.[11] However, as Smart observes, while there may be
disagreement over specific technical points there is enough

approximate agreement to allow for rational and co-operative moral discourse.[12] I have not described all of the various competing theories of utility, for it is not the purpose of this chapter to achieve that consensus. I have described only three of the main contenders (happiness and pleasure, satisfaction of preferences, and objective goods) which is sufficient to show that the concept of Utility is complex and multi-faceted. To avoid getting caught up in the nuances and relative merits of each contender, which may take a whole thesis in itself, I shall assume that Utility means all three of them. If a person had any one of these things without the others, that would bring very much less utility than if one had all three of them. Each might be worthless or nearly worthless without the other two. This possibility for compromise and synthesis is a variation of that which was suggested in a tentative way by Derek Parfit (*R&P* pg. 502). But for the purpose of this study, I have now said all that needs to be said about the notion of Utility. I do not believe that the arguments in this study hang on one particular conception of Utility winning out over the others. So I need not delay any further to investigate the Utilitarian assessment of actions which affect the environment and future generations.

There are two obvious ways to apply the Utilitarian calculus to actions which affect the environment. It can be claimed that the utility of Conserved and/or Protected landscapes is very high, perhaps much higher than is normally calculated. It can also be claimed that the dis-utility of Depletion is likewise very high, again possibly more so than we might usually estimate. These two strategies are not mutually exclusive, and they can include the benefit and harms which occur to future people. When contemplating certain decisions that we can know in advance will have an impact on the future, not only in our own time but also the time of people who are not yet born, we believe that people of the future should not be (unnecessarily) harmed, just as we believe the same of present people. This belief commonly appears in government policy statements, and in the statement of grass-roots environmental activists. For instance, Alan Carter, director of the *Friends of the Earth* office in London, argued that:

> The date of birth of the victim is morally
> insignificant. The fact that the infant was not born
> when the bomb was planted makes no moral
> difference whatsoever. Some of our present actions
> will, as a matter of fact, harm persons who will exist
> in the future. If our present actions lead to the
> destruction of the life-support systems of this planet,
> billions of people who do not yet exist will die in
> horrific conditions.[13]

This belief is the core of the standard argument for why future generations must not be harmed, and it has widespread popularity. But what is the explanation of this belief, if there is one? One part of Carter's view is certainly undeniable: the birth-date of the victim of an act of harm is irrelevant to moral concerns. However, it is also the case that the longer we extend the time horizon of our concern then the more problematic the belief becomes. If we plan for the next 25 years, it is easy to imagine what we will want for ourselves in that time: for instance, clean beaches to swim in, cared-for city parks and national parks to walk and play in. If we plan for the next 50 years, it is easy to imagine what we will want for our children and grandchildren. Sympathy and benevolence for our offspring will make us want their lives to go well. But if we plan for, say, the next 300 years, we find ourselves planning for total strangers, and it becomes harder to translate our present wants and needs into policy decisions. The further into the future we look, the more uncertainties there are. We will still know that it is wrong to harm future people, and their birth-dates will still be morally irrelevant, but we will not necessarily know what we must positively do to benefit them, or whether we are obliged to benefit them at all. We might claim that the dis-utility of inconveniencing ourselves to prevent harm from befalling them may be greater than the disutility of the harm that befalls them, and that this increases as we look further to the future.

     Lincoln Allison argues that we should not bet on the possibility that future people will be able to solve all our environmental problems for us, by for instance creating new sources of non-polluting energy. That is really a non-answer to the question of what *we* should do about pollution, resource depletion, and climate change. The future is a realm of deep uncertainty. Since this is so, he says the best policy for planning for the far future should be "combined with an attitude to risk". He points out that economists normally think of risk-aversion as a preference rather than as a decision, and so it is not irrational for a heavy cigarette smoker to risk contracting lung cancer if he likes smoking and the risk is acceptable to him. The same idea, so he says, can apply to environmental conservation and future generations. "It is necessary, but difficult, to conceive of a level of risk-aversion which is both collective and long-term. What chances should we take on behalf of the people of 2100 AD? The question cannot be ducked; a non-answer is an answer, probably a poor one." (*E&U* pg. 123.)

What is it that we are risking, through a continued course of environmental depletion? Peter Singer suggested that we are risking the enormous dis-utility of *irretrievable loss*, which can sometimes be enough to outweigh even the greatest compensatory benefits. Irretrievable loss is the dis-utility of losing something which cannot be replaced and cannot be compensated for by the gain of something else. There may be no gains that would compensate for the loss of certain special art treasures and historic national monuments, for instance. Singer says that something similar applies to ecosystems, especially ancient untouched wildernesses. The extinction of a species is also permanent and irretrievable. The short term benefits that may be realised by cutting down a forest to feed the lumber industry, or drowning it behind a dam to produce electricity, may be outweighed by the irretrievable loss of continuity with the past, the loss of opportunities for recreation, scientific discovery, and aesthetic experience. This latter opportunity, which may be difficult to quantify, should nevertheless not be dismissed. As Singer points out, with reference to his own experiences as well as that of others, aesthetic contemplation of 'wilderness' and 'nature', here understood in a loose way to mean the landscape of the Earth which is not yet touched or influenced by man, rises "to an almost spiritual intensity" in many people.[14]

Alison constructed a Utilitarian theory of 'totemism' to account for the special 'magic' of the Earth and the enormous benefit and value it has for us. He introduced it as follows:

> A truly happy life must contain magic, wonder, and reverence. The most necessary and satisfying objects of these sentiments must be aspects of the planet itself. It is the surface of the earth, in all its diversity, that inspires our deepest feelings, our senses of identity and belonging, our strivings for artistic expression. To take the broad spirit of utilitarianism seriously—to want sincerely to maximise human well-being—is to recognise these truths. (*E&U* pg. 130-1)

Environmental totemism, as Allison explains it, appears to be a philosophical way of describing the aesthetic, cultural, and spiritual value landscape has for human life and society, which is so great as to be nearly immeasurable. As seen in the general introduction, environmental philosophy itself was in part inspired by poets and theologians who found spiritual inspiration in the landscape. But why should a Utilitarian accept it? Allison asserts that it is compatible with Utilitarianism, and that the power it holds over many people, offering them a sense of identity and meaning, must count as a positive benefit in the Utilitarian calculus. Allison also asserts that it is not Utilitarianism's purpose to subvert totemism, even if its theological roots are questionable or problematic. It is the degree to which it benefits people which matters. (And aside from that, "bad philosophy can be good propaganda" (*E&U* pg.144)). If it gives meaning to life then it is "to be welcomed into the utilitarian embrace", and moreover, "utilitarianism is a philosophy in defiance of its own purpose unless it acknowledges the spiritual needs which relate people to the land". (*E&U* pp. 144, 150.)

The loss of an untampered wilderness landscape can be a very great dis-utility. Singer says the irretrievable loss of an irreplaceable landscape will be compounded, since it will be borne by every generation to come, forever.[15] We can expect for good reasons that future generations will value the environment more or less the same way that we do,[16] and so the irretrievable loss of it would be for them an ongoing dis-utility. If they do not share our view of the value of nature, as is theoretically possible, nevertheless it would be wrong of us to deny them the opportunity and the choice.[17] Singer's view is also shared by Allison, who argues that the cultural, historical, and aesthetic value of nature untouched by human hands is very large, much more than most politicians or economists are normally willing to grant. We should therefore have a strong preference for risk-aversion, and for the preservation of options: "We should not allow anything to happen, if we can avoid it, which irreversibly closes down possibilities for human resources and human experiences. Two applications: no species should be extinguished and no type of landscape allowed to disappear entirely" (*E&U* pg. 123). We should also prefer risk-aversion because "There is much more to lose by ignoring warnings which turn out to be right than by reacting to those which turn out to be wrong" (*E&U* pg. 155). Allison cites favourably, although with reservations, a statement by J.S. Mill on the 'Stationary State'. In his words:

> A long-term utilitarianism [like Mill's 'Stationary State'] concerned with aspects of culture generates reasoning and policy which is very close to that of today's Greens. He fears for the spiritual consequences of over population and the loss of solitude. He argues that wild nature is under estimated as a contribution to our well-being. He believes the benefits of the competitive, acquisitive society to be an illusion. I find Mill's vision of the future highly attractive and far ahead of its time. (*E&U* pg. 124.)

It is worth noting that these views are also generally shared by the public at large. Certainly, people are willing to place a very high value on the environment today, as revealed by a number of opinion polls.

> *Public opinion.* A poll conducted in November of 2004
> which questioned of 1,000 people in each of the EU's
> 25 member states indicated that 88% of Europeans
> believe that environmental issues are equally as
> important as social and economic issues. 72% of
> those questioned said that environmental issues
> affected their quality of life "very much" or "quite a
> lot". Nine of the ten EU countries where this view is
> most prevalent are Eastern European states which
> joined the EU in May of 2004. Another poll
> conducted in February of 2005 revealed that only
> 20% of Europeans regard environmental protections
> as an obstacle to economic growth, 64% of people
> thought that environmental policies can serve as
> economic incentives for innovation, and 63% of
> people thought that protecting the environment is
> more important than economic competitiveness.[18]

Singer is well known for his view that the harms and benefits for animals and all sentient beings are important, and not just the harms and benefits for humans, and so it would be wrong to limit ourselves to a human-centred position while formulating a Utilitarian environmental ethic for future generations. Similarly, Bentham asserted that the capacity to suffer matters more than the capacity to think and speak, and so we are obliged to respect any being which can suffer whether it is human or not. The whole of Bentham's argument has been quoted in the literature often enough; the salient line is the last one, which reads: "The question is not, Can they reason?, nor Can they talk?, but *Can they suffer?*" Bentham's words were intended to apply to mainly to pets, farm animals, and beasts of burden, as his examples reveal. But there is no reason it cannot apply to animals in the wild as well. If he were alive today, there is no doubt he would be among those calling for an end to fox hunting. In the flooding of a river valley to provide hydro-electric power, the future well-being of all generations of animals occupying habitats in the flooded areas must matter to a Utilitarian. Their future well-being and the well-being of every generation of their offspring is also an irretrievable loss which counts as a massive dis-utility in the calculus.[19] This does not mean there can be no justification at all for destroying wildernesses and ancient ecosystems to meet our needs. It is possible that the dis-utility of ecosystem loss in one place can be reduced if there are other similarly special areas in the same region which are protected. The point is that the choice to destroy an area of untouched wilderness is much more complicated than it may appear, and that in many circumstances we have strong obligations not to destroy a wilderness, or to limit our use of it, because the dis-utility to result from its destruction is much higher than we might ordinarily suppose.

Singer's basic outline of a Utilitarian environmental ethic translates to the personal level as a requirement to recycle as much as possible and produce as little waste as possible; to engage in sports and recreations that do not create pollution (so water skiing and sports car racing is thus ruled out); to have smaller families; to produce food in ways that does not unduly harm animals, nor unduly destroys ecosystems. In general, a 'truly environmental ethic' (as Singer puts it) would require that we should all live less extravagantly and more frugally. Of course this does not mean that a life lived according to this broad Utilitarian environmentalism would have no luxuries at all. Singer says that the emphasis on 'simple' living' (his term for it) "does not mean that an environmental ethic frowns upon pleasure, but that the pleasures it values do not come from conspicuous consumption. They come, instead, from warm personal and sexual relationships, from being close to children and friends, from conversation...".[20] The emphasis is on the dis-utility of conspicuous consumption. Singer is not repeating Eamonn de Valera's call for a life of "frugal comfort". The claim is simply that conspicuous consumption should not go on the Objective List of utilitarian goods, because it can create the enormous dis-utility of irretrievable loss. It can also have other harmful effect on ourselves, our own future generations, the many animals whom we keep in our farms and households, and who live in the wilderness still, and all of their future generations. Singer claims the benefits and happiness that are available in an environmentally conscientious, simple life, should be enough to make life go well.

This Utilitarian environmental ethic so far emphasises only the environmental effects of personal decisions. In a more recent study, Singer considered what ethical responses we should make to the fact that we all live in one world. In one chapter he focused on the fact that we live in one atmosphere, and that actions which affect the chemical composition of the atmosphere can harm large numbers of people in unexpected ways.

> Our value system evolved in circumstances in which
> the atmosphere, like the oceans, seemed an unlimited
> resource, and responsibilities and harms were
> generally clear and well defined. If someone hit
> someone else, it was clear who had done what. Now
> the twin problems of the ozone hole and of climate
> change have revealed bizarre new ways of killing
> people. By spraying deodorant at your armpit in your
> New York apartment, you could, if you use an aerosol
> spray propelled by CFCs, be contributing to the skin
> cancer deaths, many years later, of people living in
> Punta Arenas, Chile. By driving your car, you could
> be releasing carbon dioxide that is part of a causal
> chain leading to lethal floods in Bangladesh. How
> can we adjust our ethics to take account of this new
> situation?[21]

Here, Singer identifies a need to articulate his environmental ethic on a global, political scale. His question is this: "Evidently, there are good utilitarian reasons for capping the emission of greenhouse gases, but what way of doing it will lead to the greatest net benefits?"[22] Since he is a Utilitarian, he would not support a Rawlsian-style principle of fair distribution, but he finds it useful to have such principles when broad questions about net happiness maximisation or net preference satisfaction are difficult to answer.[23] His final proposal is that we should all support a general principle of egalitarian fairness: every nation should have the same per capita future entitlement to the use of the atmosphere as a sink for waste gas. While it is not normally the principle Utilitarians would choose, Singer says that "where there is no other clear criterion for allocating shares, however, it can be an ideal compromise that leads to a peaceful solution, rather than to continued fighting."[24] He further suggests that this principle could be combined with a "polluter pays" principle, which would reduce pollution by creating a disincentive to pollute,[25] and a system of "emissions trade" which would enable rich nations to reduce their emissions without severely disrupting the economy, and poor nations gain something to trade to rich nations in exchange for other resources they need.[26] All of this he justifies on Utilitarian grounds: such a system, he claims, would produce the best result for the atmosphere and thus return the greatest benefit to sentient life on Earth.

With these Utilitarian environmental principles, one on the personal level and another on the global level, we can analyze particular environmental development choices, for instance land planning decisions and energy production methods, to see how much utility and dis-utility can be expected for all sentient beings concerned. The dis-utility of irretrievable loss is a trump card one should not play lightly, and we can analyze whether it is appropriate in each case to do so. For instance:

The Poulaphouca Dam. When the Poulaphouca Dam in county Wicklow was built in 1940, near the town of Blessington, a large portion of the Liffey river valley was flooded. The Blessington Lakes were created, and much farmland and animal habitat was lost. Two

towns were submerged and their people were
relocated.

Was it right or wrong to build the dam? If we wish to answer this
question using a Utilitarian comparison of outcomes, we can
compare the benefits and harms which were experienced by the
people and animals that inhabited the area before the dam was built,
to the benefits and harms experienced by people and animals after it
was built. In this example, the dis-utility of the loss of the land area,
of animal habitats, and of two communities, is very nearly
irretrievable. The lake could be drained, the dam dismantled, and
the land resettled, although the direct continuity with the past and the
previous communities might be irretrievable. But this loss could be
compensated for by the benefits of non-polluting hydro-electric
power, the creation of a reservoir which supplied water to many
thousands of households, and the recreational use of the lakes by
swimmers and by sailing and rowing clubs. Perhaps the loss of two
communities can be partially, if not completely, compensated for by
the creation of new communities in the places where the residents
were relocated. It may also be partially justified by the prospect that
there may have been worse alternatives.

But there is another reason why we might approve, or at least
not disapprove, of similar environmental planning decisions, even
when the dis-utility of irretrievable loss and conspicuous
consumption is much larger than in the case of the Poulaphouca
Dam.

§ 2. Parfit's "Non Identity Problem".

I shall turn now from this general account of Utilitarianism
and the environmental ethic it articulates, to a specific philosophical
problem concerning the environment and future generations. This
specific problem seems to show that certain choices which have
definitive effects upon the future, including choices which result in
irretrievable loss, may in fact harm no one, and thus may not count
as a dis-utility in the calculus. It is called "The Non-Identity

Problem". It was invented by Derek Parfit and published in his masterwork on Utilitarian ethics, <u>Reasons and Persons</u>, in 1984.

Parfit draws attention to a special fact concerning future people who might be affected by present-day environmental disasters or policy decisions. It is obviously the case that the time difference between committing a harmful act, and the harm actually occurring, is not morally relevant. "Remoteness in time has, in itself, no more significance than remoteness in space". (*R&P*, pg. 357.) By itself, this claim is a repetition of what I have called the "standard argument" for why we are morally responsible for actions which affect future generations. What Parfit adds is that we can affect future people, not only in terms of harming or benefiting them, but also in terms of who they are. What we do today will change the circumstances in which people will be born, largely through the choices we make concerning when and with whom we produce children. This presents us with the following troublesome problem: what happens if some choice that causes future people to suffer also affects the choices people make concerning when and with whom we produce children, and so is also the necessary condition for those people to exist at all? Is it still a morally wrong choice? This problem is called the "Non-Identity Problem".

Parfit explains the Non-Identity Problem with the following initial claims. First, if someone had not been conceived within a month of the time when they were actually conceived, then they would never have existed. ("The Time Dependence Claim 2" *R&P* pg. 352.) Second, if any person had not the parents they actually had, then they would never have existed. These two claims can be derived from this more general claim: If any particular person had not been created from the particular genetic material from which they were created, then they would never have existed. ("The Origin View" *R&P* pg. 352.) It follows that for any choice which, however unintentionally, affects the circumstances in which people meet and produce children, the people who will be born as a side effect of one choice will be different, non-identical people than those who will be born if one makes a different choice. The philosophical problem here is the problem of whether people are benefited or harmed in a morally relevant way by actions which not only benefit or harm them, but also affect the circumstances of their conception and thus also cause them to exist. It is Parfit's contention that an action which harms someone, but which also causes that person to exist, is an action to which the harmed person can have no objection. That contention is what makes the "Non-Identity Problem" so peculiar and troublesome.

Parfit uses three case studies to illustrate these Non-Identity situations. The first is the case of "the 14 Year Old Girl", in which a girl contemplates conceiving a child at a young age, or waiting until she is older. If she conceives early, her child will not get a good start in life, because she will not yet have all the skills and resources needed for motherhood. But if she conceives later, she will have a different child.[27] The second example is the case of "The Risky Policy". Imagine that a government planner must decide how to dispose of the waste from the country's nuclear energy plants. Each choice will have, among its effects, an impact on who is born, and possibly also on how many people are born, because it will affect which people meet, and when, for the purpose of bearing children. If the choice is made to bury it, an earthquake in the far future will damage the containment facility and the leaked radiation will kill thousands of people. But these people will owe their existence to the choice to bury the nuclear waste. If the choice is made to bury it elsewhere or not at all, different people will be born.[28] The third example is the case of "Depletion". The case is that of an imaginary gathering of businessmen and government leaders who have the task of choosing between two energy strategies, a Depletion policy and a Conservation policy. On the terms of the Non-Identity Problem, it follows that if they choose Conservation, the people who will be born will live in a cleaner environment, but those people will not be the same people as those who would be born if they choose Depletion. The alternative for the people born if Depletion is chosen is not that they will be born in a world of clean environments and bountiful resources: it is that they will not be born at all.[29] It follows that, so Parfit claims, the choice of Depletion, Risky Policy, and the 14 Year Old Girl is not worse for the people who would be harmed by those choices. The alternative situation for them is non-existence, and so Parfit claims they could have no objection and no ground of complaint against the choices that created the situation in which they live, however degraded, depleted, or undesirable it might be.

It is not difficult to find real-world examples of the kind of choices about which Parfit is concerned in contemporary environmental issues. One of the most prominent examples of Depletion which faces us today is:

> *The Price of Petroleum.* A recently published study claimed that "the world's supply of 'conventional' (that is, readily accessible) oil will peak around the year 2030."[30] It was predicted that if the price reaches US$50 and stays there, Ireland's GDP will drop by 1.0 to 1.5%, and consumer prices will rise by 1.4% more than they would have risen otherwise. Irish petroleum consumption per capita doubled between 1989 and 2001, the "Celtic Tiger" years, and today Ireland relies on imported oil for 55% of its energy needs.[31] In September of 2004 the price of oil passed US $50 per barrel for the first time in 30 years, following a sustained increase of 55% in just one year. The reasons given included the possibility of civil war in Nigeria, the world's 7th largest oil exporter, along with severe weather disasters in the Caribbean and the Gulf of Mexico which disrupted oil production in the area.[32] Civil war in Iraq was also cited: the fighting between various rebel factions and the American-backed provisional government is seen by the market as an impediment to continued and reliable oil production in the country.[33] In March of 2005, the price of oil was raised to US $57.50 per barrel, the highest it had ever been, as a result of unexpected reductions in American stockpile holdings.[34] A 'super spike' in oil prices of more than US $105 per barrel was predicted

by investment bank Goldman Sachs, one of the
world's largest traders in energy futures.[35]

It is possible to predict, as did one journalist who reported on this
situation, that the standard of living experienced by the Irish people
after that happens will be much lower than it is now as oil resources
become scarce (assuming that no alternative energy source becomes
readily available to replace it). The situation predicted for the future
would be much worse than that experienced by Ireland in the winter
of 1973, the year when an Arab embargo of oil to the West resulted
in fuel rationing, widespread electricity blackouts, a three-day work
week imposed on industry, and other social hardships for the
country.[36] In this way we can say that the depletion of oil supplies
will make future people's standard of living worse off than that
which we experience now, presuming that no alternative energy
source becomes available.

Examples of 'ordinary' non-nuclear waste management can
also serve as instances of the Risky Policy case.

> *Waste disposal.* An Bord Pleanála granted planning
> permission for a private landfill near Ballinasloe, in
> east county Galway, that would receive 100,000 tons
> of waste. An Bord Pleanála also approved the
> creation of a state-run landfill site at Cross/New Inn,
> about a mile away from the other site, which will
> have a capacity of 2 million tons.[37] One of the
> biggest waste dumps in the country is planned for an
> area near Swords, north county Dublin, which will
> enclose 350 acres of which 150 acres will be dumping
> space. The site will receive ten million tons of
> waste.[38] If pollutants were to leak from any of these
> sites, it would have bad effects on the people living in
> the area, and we would be responsible for them.

If it was possible to predict that in the far future, well beyond the
lifetime of any presently-existing person, the depletion of oil

supplies greatly reduced people's quality of life, or that an accident at one of the aforementioned waste facilities caused toxins or radioactive pollutants to enter the air or the drinking water supply, we can claim that the choices seriously harmed those whom it affected, and that it was morally wrong to choose the policies which led to those events (at least insofar as the events were foreseeable). But if the choices to build these facilities at their present locations also affected who is born, and if the accident occurred long enough after the facility was built, then the people who are harmed by future oil shortages or waste management accidents would not have existed otherwise. Parfit's problem leaves us with this: if the alternative for such people is non-existence, then their situation is not worse for them. If we know that harming people will not, in the final balance, be worse for them, is it still wrong to harm them? Choosing Depletion would be 'bad' for the people born in the future. But it would not be 'worse' for them because there is no alternative for them that is 'better'. The alternative for them is non-existence. Each of them would, presumably, find that their lives are worth living and that they would prefer life to the alternative of not having been born. How can it be wrong for us to choose Depletion, as our intuitions would suggest, if we can know that it will not be worse for the people born in the future? The conceptual difficulty was summarized by Edward Page when he wrote:

> ...it tempts the proponent of the person-affecting view into subscribing to three mutually inconsistent claims. These are (1) adopting the Depletion policy is wrong because it harms future persons; (2) an act harms somebody only if it makes a particular person worse off than they would have been had the act not been performed; and (3) the adoption of the Depletion Policy is a remote, but necessary, condition of the Depletion People coming into existence and leading lives that are worth living.[39]

The Non-Identity Problem arises when it is understood that the identities of future people after one choice we might make today will not be the same (that is, not identical) as the people who will exist in the future after another choice.[40] It seems to follow that we cannot locate on future people the moral concern for the choice. The Non-Identity Problem does not really suggest that it would not be wrong to exploit and destroy the environment, but does assert that 'the sake of future people' cannot be the reason to do so. Aside from a few rare places in his text (some to be noted in the discourse to follow), Parfit does not exactly claim that we are unable to appeal to the lives, rights, interests, or identities of future people, although much of the debate that followed Parfit's articulation of the problem has taken this route of interpreting it and attempting to solve it. It may be more of a logical than a moral problem, but it is powerful nonetheless. Its real difficulty and tenacity is revealed when an attempt is made to solve it, that is, to offer a reason why it is wrong to choose Depletion even if it would not be worse for anyone. What Parfit claims is that it may be right to choose Conservation and wrong to choose Depletion, but *person-affecting principles cannot explain why*. In his words: "We shall thus conclude that this part of morality, the part concerned with beneficence and human well-being, cannot be explained in person-affecting terms." (*R&P*, pg. 370-1.)

The crucial premise in the argument is Parfit's revision of what it means to harm someone. This revision is called "the no-worse-off principle". It is the claim that an action does not harm someone if it leaves that person no worse off than he otherwise would have been. Although it is not directly stated in Parfit's text, its implicit presence is certainly detectable in the argument and has been found there by most of Parfit's commentators,[41] and Parfit himself does not deny it in subsequent writings. It can be seen as properly following from the "person affecting view" in which it is claimed that an action is bad only if it is bad for someone. This is, of course, one possible way of formulating the essence of the Consequentialist or Utilitarian moral theory—that the consequences for people be where we locate the grounding explanation of why an action is right or wrong. But there are other kinds of person-affecting moral theories. Justice and Deontology are person-affecting theories in different ways. Parfit seems to endorse the person-affecting view of ethics with a principle called "Claim C6":

> An act benefits someone if its consequence is that someone is benefited more. An act harms someone if its consequence is that someone is harmed more. The act that benefits people most is the act whose consequence is that people are benefited most. (*R&P* pg.69.)[42]

This is re-affirmed later on, where he writes "If what we are doing will not be worse for some other person, or will even be better for this person, we are not, in a morally relevant sense, harming this person". (*R&P* pg. 374). Note the shift from the active to the passive tense of the verb "to harm"; note also the phrase "in the morally relevant sense". There may be actions which undeniably harm people, but if the harm leaves them "not worse" than any alternative, then they are not harmed "in the morally relevant sense". For Parfit, to say that an action is "not worse" for someone means only that it does not make him worse off than he would have been had the action not been done.

     This revision of what it means to harm someone seems to require one to abandon the belief that choosing Depletion or Risky Policy is wrong because of the harm that is caused to future people. In fact this revised view of the meaning of 'harm' and 'benefit' suggests that the Depletion people or the Nuclear people, for whom the alternative is non-existence, are not harmed at all. If we believe that causing someone to exist benefits that person, then these people are benefited by the choice of Depletion or Risky Policy. If we do not believe that causing to exist can benefit, still Depletion or Risky Policy is not worse for them. (*R&P* pg.374.)

     In summary, the argument for the Non-Identity Problem runs like this. In all cases, we assume that the people in Non-Identity situations have lives worth living. The people these choices cause to be badly off would not have existed had the choices not been made.

Therefore, the choices do not make them worse off than they would have been. A choice does not harm someone in the morally relevant sense unless it makes him worse off than he would have been had the choice not been made (the "no-worse-off principle"). Therefore, in the morally relevant sense, these choices harm no one. A variation of this argument also considered by Parfit emphasises benefit, and runs this way: a choice benefits someone, in the morally relevant sense, if its consequence is that that person receives a benefit that he would not have received had the choice not been made, therefore the people that these situations cause to be badly off are actually benefited.[43]

§ 3. The "Absurd" and "Repugnant" Conclusions.

There is a Utilitarian solution to this problem. Parfit concludes that it is morally right to select the choice which results in the greatest happiness for those who will live, regardless of who they are. In this sense it is not important that those who will live after one choice will be different people than those who would live after another. He says, "If in either of two outcomes the same number of people would ever live, it would be bad if those who live are worse off, or have a lower quality of life, than those who would have lived". ("The Same Number Quality Claim", *R&P*, pg. 360.) So long as we are dealing with two possible futures in which the same number of people will live, Utilitarianism is capable of offering reasons to prefer one policy choice over another. We should choose the policy which results in the greatest happiness for those who do live, whoever they are. In this case, we should choose Conservation.

Parfit finds that this principle is "plausible" but is not satisfied with it: aside from the fact that it is not general enough, what if our choices lead not only to different people being born, but also different numbers of people born? For we cannot assume that the same number of people will be born, whatever our choices. It is in "different number choices" where an insurmountable problem appears for any person-affecting moral theory. This question introduces two additional dimensions to the Non-Identity problem.

There is the problem of whether Utilitarians should be aiming to maximise the total happiness or the average happiness when considering choices that would affect large groups of future people, and there is the problem of same-number or different-number choices. The resolution of these two additional problems leads to what Parfit calls the 'repugnant conclusion' and the 'absurd conclusion'.

When deliberating about choices that will affect the future using the principle of utility, do we resolve our decisions by selecting the outcome with the best total happiness or the best average happiness? Consider the following example: A community of people, all of whom live lives well worth living, are joined by a child born to one of them who, due to some injury or disability, shall enjoy much less happiness than others in his community. In such a situation, the *total* happiness for the community is increased by the presence of a new person capable of experiencing happiness. However, in this situation the *average* happiness is actually *lowered*: and a case might be made that the morally appropriate thing to do is to euthanise the child immediately after birth. Or, for that matter, a case could be made that no harm is done by euthanising anyone whose unhappy life brings the average down for everyone else. This is called the Absurd Conclusion, and accepting the average-maximising view seems to lead straight to it.

If instead we accept the total-maximizing view, we are lead to another kind of difficulty which has to do with same-number versus different-number choices. Parfit's conclusion that it is best to choose the future which results in the best total happiness, whoever is born, leads to what he calls The Repugnant Conclusion. Its parameters in principle are as follows, in Parfit's words:

> For any possible population of at least ten billion people, all with a very high quality of life, there must be some much larger imaginable population whose existence, if other things are equal, would be better, even though its members have lives that are barely worth living. (*R&P* pg. 388)

The Repugnant Conclusion is typically explained as a spread of possible future populations who will be brought into being as a result of policy choices. If we must use utilitarian principles to choose among them, we are lead to the following difficulty. Under one choice, let us call it Policy A, there will be a certain population of people who lead happy, fulfilled lives. But it is possible that another choice, let us call it Policy B, will result in a population of people whose lives are somewhat less happy than the Policy A people but because there are more of them, the total happiness is greater. Therefore B is the desirable choice for a 'total' utilitarian. But there might be another choice, Policy C, which results in a still higher total happiness from a still larger population of people all of whom individually experience somewhat less happiness than those in Policy B. So the utilitarian must choose C. This goes on until one arrives at something like Policy Z, in which the total happiness is higher than any other option due to a gigantic population, yet the happiness experienced by each person individually is so little that their lives are barely worth living. The total-maximising utilitarian is thus lead to the difficult position of having to choose policy Z, which brings into being the vast population of miserable people. This is called the Repugnant Conclusion. It is, in Parfit's words, "*intrinsically* repugnant"; we don't need to appeal to other moral principles to see it that way.[44] It is Parfit's position that we should be able to explain why we should not make choices that lead to the Repugnant Conclusion, but that person-affecting principles cannot provide the necessary explanation.

Parfit's conclusion regarding the Non-Identity Problem is also an invitation to other philosophers to pick up the problem where he leaves it. He says:

> Because we can easily affect the identities of future
> people, we face the Non-Identity Problem. To solve
> this problem we need a new theory about
> beneficence. This theory must avoid the Repugnant
> and the Absurd Conclusions... Since I failed to find

the principle to which we should appeal, I cannot explain the objection to our choice of such policies. I believe that, though I have so far failed, I or others could find the principle we need. But until this happens, (8) is a disturbing conclusion. ("Conclusion 8", *R&P*, pg. 451.)[45]

I will argue that these problems follow from approaching the issue from the utilitarian perspective. They admit of no space for other issues or considerations: such as whether rights are infringed, whether justice is served, whether duties are fulfilled, whether virtues are in play. It is the same for the solution that Parfit is seeking. In his words:

> I am searching for Theory X, the new theory about beneficence that both solves the Non-Identity Problem and avoids the Repugnant Conclusion. More generally, Theory X would be the best theory of beneficence. It would have acceptable implications when applied to all of the choices that we ever make, including those that affect both the identities and the number of future people. (*R&P* pg. 405.)

The specific reason for studying the Non-Identity Problem in detail is this. If a solution cannot be found, then we will not be able to claim that Utilitarianism can provide a satisfactory environmental ethic. It will not be able to provide a satisfactory answer to the central questions of environmental ethics. The most we will be able to say is that we should avoid conspicuous consumption, pursue simple pleasures, and conserve or protect the areas of the world that have a special 'magic' for us. But this may be too vague for some purposes. If the Non-Identity Problem cannot be solved it will mean that the practical question of environmental ethics may prove impossible to answer with sufficient decisiveness, so long as we hold on to person-affecting principles. The Non-Identity Problem concludes that the future created by choosing Depletion is inherently repugnant, but there is no explanation for why it is morally wrong to choose it.

§ 4. A serious problem or a 'mere quibble'?

How important is this problem? D. Heyd raised the objection that our moral obligations are only to those people who are beyond the reach of the Non-Identity problem, and so we don't need to worry about it. Such people are, for the most part, only the present generation, and so Heyd believes we have no obligations to most future people. At the most, he says, we have obligations to our contemporaries, our nearest descendants, and to "transcend our time frame" by involving ourselves in projects that will last beyond our deaths.[46] Nick Fotion wrote that "never-never land" examples such as the vastly different populations of the possible futures that are used to test the utilitarian theory, "should not be the norm when it comes to engaging in criticism of ethical theories. After all, such theories are supposed to help us deal with practical, that is, real life problems."[47] Hendrick Visser T'Hooft wrote,

> This argument has become quite famous in the
> literature concerning future generations. But I have
> never been able to see its point. Imagine yourself to
> be a member of that victimized generation. What
> would your personal identity have to do with your
> moral standing as a complainant? You wouldn't
> complain in your capacity of being Peter or Paul, you
> would complain in your capacity of being a member
> (among many others) of a group of people placed in a
> situation which their forebears could have made so
> much better.[48]

The point which T'Hooft claims he has never been able to see is this. If you were one of the Depletion People, you would find yourself in a situation that your forebears could have made much better. However, you would find that if your forebears did choose to make a better situation, you would not have been a part of it. Your lot is to be placed in the bad situation your forebears created, or not to be placed anywhere at all. Parfit claims that this fact would outweigh any possible complaints that you may have about the situation.

James Woodward suggested that the real purpose of the activity is to test on hypothetical cases certain principles which are destined for use in real-life cases, and so the plethora of theoretical cases may be an enormous academic distraction.[49] Against this, Stuart Rachels defends the usefulness of the Repugnant Conclusion as a thought-experiment meant to test the plausibility of the principle of utility, and as such it is not meant to be practical.[50] Rachel's counter-argument is sound although it implies that the Non-Identity Problem is largely a theoretical problem, and not relevant to real-life policy choices. But Parfit would likely say that the problem is one that should be of interest to everyone, not just to theorists. "Since it would be merely technically impossible to face a choice between A and Z, this does not weaken the comparison as a test for our principles." (*R&P* pg. 390) Additionally, his reason for why the problem is important runs thus:

> Some people believe that this problem is a mere quibble. This reaction is unjustified. The problem arises because of superficial facts about our reproductive system. But, though it arises in a superficial way, it is a real problem. When we are choosing between two social or economic policies, of the kind that I described, it is *not true* that, in the further future, the same people will exist whatever we choose. It is therefore *not true* that a choice like Depletion will be against the interests of future people. We cannot dismiss this problem with the pretence that this *is* true. (*R&P* pg. 363, emphasis his.)

I believe there is some substance to the complaints articulated by Heyd, Woodward, T'Hooft, and others described here. Philosophy should address itself to the real world. But the Non-Identity Problem is not a purely theoretical problem with no practical relevance. It examines and calls into question some of our assumptions about the concepts and principles which underlie our practices. When the Non-Identity Problem is fully analyzed and examined, we will know whether it is the elaborate distraction that some scholars believe it to be. We will also see exactly how it renders any clear answer to the central question of this project impossible on Utilitarian grounds.

I will, however, restrict my discussion to the aspects of the problem which are easiest to apply to real-life environmental ethics cases. Therefore I will ignore the enormously complex Mere Addition Paradox. The only apparent real-world cases it might apply to are cases of separate populations living on distant undiscovered continents, or even on different planets in outer space, who are therefore unaware of each other's existence. [51] The Repugnant and Absurd conclusions appear to be relevant to large scale economic choices which have a significant effect upon wide territories, and on the communities or larger populations that inhabit them. Decisions about land planning, motorway development, other kinds of infrastructure development, certain kinds of taxation or price fixing, oil exploration and extraction, consumer product development, are all decisions that tend to have that kind of large-scale impact upon the land and upon future generations. These large-impact decisions are the ones that tend to produce the Non-Identity Problem. The future people of Ireland are not likely to owe their existence and identities to my choice of whether or not to take a train from Galway to Dublin today, instead of a bus, a private car, an aircraft, or to go to another city instead, or not to travel at all. The biography of my life will almost certainly change in various great or small ways as a result of that choice, but the fact that I came into existence will not change. By contrast, the future people of Ireland may well owe their existence and identities to the choice of whether to build more motorways, airports, and rail links around Ireland's cities, because that will affect people's mobility more generally, subsequently affecting which people meet each other, as well as how and when they meet, how and when they produce children together, and so on. Also, as a general rule, it is institutions, such as corporations or government agencies (or more precisely, those managers, executives, or legislators who control them) that make the decisions that have the kind of impact on the environment and future people about which the Non-Identity cases of Conservation and Depletion are concerned. For example:

> *The Western Rail Corridor*. Irish cabinet ministers Martin Brennan (Transport) and Eamonn Ó Cuív (Community, Rural and Gealtacht Affairs) publicly endorsed the construction of a commuter rail service from Tuam to Galway via Athenry. But they declined to endorse a longer "Western Rail Corridor" connecting Cork, Limerick, Galway, and Sligo.[52]

We can call this a Non-Identity choice, for it will predictably have a Non-Identity effect on future generations. People's options for travel would be increased, with the result that people meet each other in different ways, the biographies of their lives change, and different children are likely to be born. If the decision not to open a Western Rail Corridor is changed, that would also be a Non-Identity choice; indeed the timing of the choice may also be a Non-Identity Choice. If it is built this year, it will have different effects on the identities of future people than if it is built twenty years from now.

We are also witnessing many climate change disasters that could be seen as not only producing Non-Identity effects on future generations, but may also be regarded as Non-Identity effects on us, resulting from choices made by past generations. Consider:

> *Weather Disasters*. Continued pollution is changing the chemical composition of the atmosphere, resulting in an increase in the frequency and severity of weather disasters.[53] A scientific study commissioned in 2000 by the World Wildlife Federation concluded that "A further rise in the concentrations of greenhouse gases in the atmosphere will lead to further changes in

global climate. The consequences now expected
include a further rise of the mean global temperature,
an increase in extreme rainstorms, a substantial rise of
sea level, and changing ocean/atmosphere circulation
patterns with subsequent changing patterns,
frequencies, and intensities of extreme weather
events."[54] As if to confirm this hypothesis, four
tropical hurricanes struck the Caribbean and the
eastern seaboard of the United States in the fall of
2004, all within a six week period. In the United
States, the world's richest nation, 108 people were
killed, 3 million forced to evacuate, and property
damage was estimated by the insurance industry to
cost US$17.8 billion to repair. In nearby Haiti, the
world's poorest country, the death toll after the fourth
cyclone was estimated to be 1,650, with a further 800
still missing.[55]

Let us suppose that the cause of these storms may be traceable to the
climate destabilizing effect of industrial emissions from the burning
of fossil fuels over the last hundred years, as the WWF scientists
conclude. According to the Non-Identity Problem, the millions of
killed or displaced people could have no objection to the policy of
unrestrained coal and petroleum consumption of the economically
affluent decades of the previous centuries. The choices which
created the climate change effects also caused them to exist. But as
Parfit would agree, we should have a strong moral objection to the
policy choices which caused these deaths.

In the discussion to follow, I will show that Utilitarianism is
unable to express a moral objection to environmentally destructive
choices when they are Non-Identity choices similar to Parfit's
examples of Depletion and Risky Policy. In this Parfit and I are in
agreement. Parfit claims that the theory which will succeed must
necessarily be a theory of Utilitarian beneficence. In this Parfit and I
disagree. I claim that to overcome the Non-Identity Problem and to
find an acceptable environmental ethic, we must look to other moral

theories. Indeed I shall show how in various ways Utilitarianism itself calls for other ways of thinking. Each of the commentators to be studied here, in their own particular way, attempted a solution to the Non-Identity Problem by moving away from strict Utilitarianism or incorporating non-Utilitarian elements into their argument. Each failed to solve it, in part because of their remaining Utilitarian commitments.

§ 5. Revising Utilitarianism: Lexicality or "Higher Status" Pleasures

Lexicality is the idea that some kinds of pleasure and happiness are qualitatively preferable to others, above and beyond matters of duration or quantity. This variation of Utilitarianism goes back to J.S. Mill, who was answering the charge that the Utilitarianism, by aiming at the maximisation of happiness, only dignifies as philosophical the base and animalistic drives in man, the drive for animal pleasure.[56] Mill argued that a life that is good enough for an animal is not good enough for a human being. Some pleasures are better than others, and that a rational person would normally prefer the better pleasures even if lesser pleasures are easier to attain, and even if seeking these higher pleasures tends to be accompanied by more pain.[57] This leads to his famous statement that "it is better to be a human being dissatisfied than a pig satisfied; better to be Socrates dissatisfied than a fool satisfied."[58] This principle of ranking pleasures as higher and lower has come to be called the principle of *Lexicality*. The Utilitarian environmentalism as Singer and Allison present it is, like the Utilitarianism of Mill, strongly lexical: some pleasures are better than others. The benefit of the existence of untouched, untampered landscapes is of a very high order, and the dis-utility of its irretrievable loss is likewise very high, easily enough to outweigh the benefits of unrestrained consumption.

Stuart Rachels applied lexical reasoning in his attempt to solve the Non-Identity Problem. He believes that the theory of beneficence which Parfit seeks is a form of Utilitarianism that includes Lexicality in its calculations. He devised a theory of hedonic (pleasure-seeking) well-being which he calls 'the Quasi-Maximizing Theory', which incorporates four principles. For the present purpose, two of these four principles must be mentioned. The first is the Conflation principle, by which "one state of affairs is hedonically better than another if and only if one person's having all the experiences in the first would be hedonically better than one person's having all the experiences of the second"[59]. This principle invites us to translate multi-person comparisons into single person comparisons. The second is the principle of Lexicality, the important one here, by which some pleasures are more "dignified" than others and thus cannot really be compared with each other. Rachel's view is like Mill's in that some pleasures are better than others, but it is more strict than Mill's view in that small quantities of the higher pleasures are better than any quantity of lower pleasures. "Ecstacy *trumps* mild pleasure in the sense that the smallest possible duration of ecstacy is hedonically preferable to any duration of mild pleasure."[60] In other words, Rachels is claiming that no number of ordinary-happy experiences are as good as one fully blissful experience. Bliss is a more 'dignified' condition than mild pleasure. This is supported by "the strong preferences of competent judges".[61] This provides a reason for objecting to the Repugnant Conclusion on Utilitarian grounds. It can be claimed that if one person had all the experiences of the Conservation future, that would be better than if one person had all the experiences of the Depletion Future. We may also object to the Repugnant Conclusion by claiming it is a future in which people lack the 'higher status' pleasures.

After a brief defence of the contestable parts of his theory, Rachels moves into an attempted critique of Parfit's various problems. Parfit would likely reject the 'conflation' aspect of the Quasi-Maximising View because he might regard the Conflation principle as a disguised variation of "same number choices", in that it invites us to imagine that one person has all the experiences of each possible outcome, so that we may judge which is best. If we ignored the differences between people's lives, such as by 'identifying' with other people (Parfit asserts that this is John Rawls' suggestion[62]) it would no longer be possible to postulate principles of distributive justice: it would no longer be possible to distribute the 'good things' in life (material resources, happiness, etc.) among different people. Rachels' Conflation principle invites us not to identify with other people but to imagine them as though they were one person. Though something like this has been used to explain the Utilitarian view before,[63] Parfit rejects it. One who argues that "sets of lives are like single lives… would explain the Utilitarian view in ways that undermined this view. It is clearly a mistake to ignore the fact that we live different lives. And mankind is not a super-organism." (*R&P* pg. 331).

Parfit says that the Lexical View entails an unacceptable variation of the Absurd Conclusion: that the presence of people whose lives are in the lower categories of happiness (call it the Mediocre Level) would make it worse than a possible future in which no people exist at all.[64] But Rachels believes this objection to be too strong:

> …a theory of well-being cannot entail that one outcome is worse *simpliciter* than another. Here the claim is that an outcome P with persons is worse than an outcome W without persons. But this doesn't follow from P's being bad in terms of well-being, since P's population might bring with it goods outside the domain of well-being. For example, P might include love, courage, artistic creation, human cultures, scientific discovery, and so on, which might have value independently of well-being. P might be better than W because of such goods despite being worse in terms of well-being.[65]

I see this move as a step away from person-affecting Utilitarianism, for the following reason. Lexicality does *not* assert that the dignified pleasures outweigh lesser pleasures, although it may seem so at first. If that was the claim of Lexicality, then longer lasting mediocre pleasures might still out-balance shorter durations of dignified pleasures. Rather, Lexicality asserts that dignified pleasures "outclass" or "overrule" the others, and puts them beyond comparison. "Ecstacy *trumps* mild pleasure", as Rachels put it, and so no finite duration of mild pleasure could ever outweigh ecstacy. "Five seconds of ecstacy are better than any finite duration of mild pleasure".[66] This is a division that in some sense is foreign to the usual way in which Consequentialism compares outcomes, because the pleasures of the dignified class count for more than their 'share' in the utilitarian calculus. Rachels offers two explanations: one is "the strong preference of competent judges", (a possible appeal to authority, of which I will say no more) and the other is the claim that certain things (love, courage, etc.) may have value "independently of well being".[67] This claim seems to assert that these goods have inherent or intrinsic value. The plain existence of these goods is treated by Rachel's argument as an end in itself, independent of any people enjoying them or being affected by them (for that is what is implied by disconnecting them from people's well-being), and thus they are independently able to "tip the balance" in favour of the future that possesses them.

Thus, Rachels has moved away from person-affecting principles although he may not have moved completely away from Consequentialism. We are still to consider them as consequences, among the others: if our actions today bring into being a future world in which love, courage, and the like exist, then that is a consequence of our actions. Consequentialism may take one or more of these intrinsic goods as its token along with or instead of people, although that is not quite what Rachels claimed—he claimed only that the future that possesses them might fare better in the calculus, regardless of the well-being of the people in that future. But suppose we did take one of these goods as consequentialism's token, as Rachels' claim implies. Perhaps the total-utilitarian should relate her obligations not to future people but instead to future love, future courage, or 'future happiness'.[68] But how can one produce these goods without relating them to people? They can not be disconnected from human experience. For any non-person token for consequentialism, one should always ask, for whom does the token matter? Additionally, I see a way in which this may imply a new variation of the repugnant conclusion. For any future in which there is a sizeable amount of the selected token, there might be another future in which the amount is greater although it is less intense, or more thinly spread among more people. In one possible future there are 1,000 units of courage spread evenly among 100 people, giving them 10 units each, and in another possible future there are 2,000 units of courage spread among 500 people, giving them 4 units each. Thus, it seems that so long as we remain within consequentialism, something like the Repugnant Conclusion tends to arise.

Rachels' main purpose in introducing intrinsic goods into the calculus is to demonstrate that things are not as simple as Parfit's Absurd Conclusion and Repugnant Conclusion apparently paint them to be, and to meet Parfit's objections to the Lexical view. Let us look again at the Repugnant Conclusion. It states that for any population of people with a high quality of life, even as many as ten billion, "there must be some much larger imaginable population whose existence would be *better*, even though its members have lives that are barely above the Mediocre Level".[69] Rachels does not find it so repugnant. He asserts that the Lexicality principle would require us to choose the first option, the smaller population of blissful people, since their higher quality of life would 'trump' the greater number of less happy people. From Parfit's perspective this is a variation of the Average Principle, which he rejected as leading to the Absurd Conclusion. "It is always better if an extra life is lived that is worth living. But no amount of Mediocre lives could have as much value as one Blissful life". (*R&P*, pg. 414) Rachels demonstrates his case by reversing the Repugnant Conclusion's terms: "If there were ten billion people living, all with Agonizing lives, there must be some much larger imaginable population whose existence would be *worse*, even though its members have lives that are barely below the Bad Mediocre Level"[70]. In this pain-emphasizing version, in which the suffering of the people is added up instead of their happiness, the utilitarian is still forced to choose the second possible future, with more people with more total suffering, but because each person in the second future experiences less suffering individually, it isn't repugnant to choose it. If this pain-emphasizing version is not repugnant, he says, then neither is the pleasure-emphasizing version. Parfit does not accept Lexicality because "The existence of ten billion people below [the Mediocre level] would have less value than that of a single person above the Blissful Level. If the existence of these people would have less value than that of only one such person, its value would be more than outweighed by the existence of one person who suffers, and has a life that is not worth living". (*R&P* pg. 528, fn. 40.)

In Rachels' reversed version of the Repugnant Conclusion, one life of severe torture may outweigh the lesser suffering of ten billion others. This unfortunate person, the Agonizing Life, which is presumably the analogue of the Blissful Life, must be so terrible that it *does* outweigh the ten billion Mediocre Lives. Rachels finds this a welcome prospect, but I am not so sure. Rachels asserts that ten billion Mediocre lives are outweighed by the one Agonizing Life: if we reverse the terms again, back to their original position, we find ten billion Miserable lives outweighed by one Blissful life. If it is morally preferable to choose a future in which there are ten billion people living melancholy, drab lives and one person living a Blissful life, something is wrong with the principle of Lexicality. A situation like this is not hard to imagine: it is rather like a feudal monarchy in which a large population of slaves produce the material wealth that a small group of nobles enjoy. Today we would regard such a situation as terribly unjust—we might even think that a slave rebellion in that situation would be praiseworthy. By maintaining the analysis at the abstract level, and not applying it to real-world situations (and the real-world application is, as Woodward observed, the whole point of the exercise) we may become blinded to the real implications of what we are proposing.

Like Parfit at the end of his intellectual travels, Rachels must admit that he still has not found what he was looking for. "I haven't, of course, shown that the Quasi-Maximising Theory is completely adequate—that it is Theory X—but its success in dealing with Parfit's problems shows that we should explore it further."[71] Moreover, there are problems with Rachels' theory still. Lexicality could be called into question: perhaps there are situations in which mediocre pleasures that last long enough *are* better than shorter durations of higher class pleasures. Lexicality might find some kinds of unjust social orders, like feudal monarchies powered by slave labour, to be unobjectionable. I also observe that the principle of Lexicality, in which certain dignified pleasures overrule lesser pleasures in the utilitarian calculus, is in some sense a disguised step away from person-affecting principles. We cannot use a consequentialist comparison of outcomes for why some experiences belong in the dignified class and others do not, although we may find a place for the dignified pleasures in the utilitarian calculus.

This is admitted by Allison as well: "The acceptance of 'higher' pleasures or of a condition of a dissatisfied wisdom which might be preferable to satisfied stupidity is a large step on a retreat back to deontology." (*E&U* pg. 131.) The work of determining what pleasures are lexically dignified cannot be performed by Utilitarianism, although Utilitarianism may be able to measure and compare them against other pleasures once they are determined. *Utilitarianism thus calls for another way of thinking.* Rachels does not take that further step into the position of suggesting that "Theory X" might not be consequentialist in nature. He remains bound to "solve the game", as it were, within the boundaries that Parfit has set: that Theory X will be based on a principle of Beneficence. So long as we remain bound to the person-affecting principles that Parfit's problems test, we will be bound to certain presuppositions that Parfit assumes and which Rachels does not question. Most importantly, for the purpose of this project, if the Non-Identity Problem cannot be solved, then we will be forced to conclude that person-affecting principles like Utilitarianism can not provide an acceptable environmental ethic. They may be able to describe the moral significance of the landscape, for instance with principles like Alison's Totemism. But they will not be able to tell us how to choose between different environmental policy choices when Non-Identity effects on the future are involved.

§ 6. Non-Identity cases and non-being.

Few authors have treated the specific theme of the non-existence which is the alternative for future people born in Non-Identity situations. There is an unique conceptual difficulty here. As T'Hooft wrote, "One wonders also whether it really makes sense to ask people to consider the possibility that they wouldn't have existed at all". (*JFGE* pg. 50-1.)

There is an analogy to be made between Parfit's three main illustrative stories and cases of "wrongful life" which arise in bioethics debates concerning disability. Indeed one of Parfit's 'puzzling cases', which introduces the Non-Identity problem, is a similar situation: the story of "the 14 year old girl", who chooses to conceive at her young age even though it would give her child a bad start in life. The Non-Identity Problem asserts that if she waits until she is older, she would conceive a different child, not the same child, and so conceiving while young will not be worse than the alternative for that child. A particular variation that Parfit discusses is the case of a woman who knows that she will transmit a particular disease to her child if she conceives now, but not if she conceives some years later: if she conceives now, she would transmit the disease to her child but if she conceives later, she would have a different child, and this different child would not have the disease.

A 'wrongful life' is a life of such severe suffering, due to some unusual handicap or genetic disease, that the parents ought to have made use of genetic screening techniques, or not conceived a child, or possibly even aborted the child once conceived, so that the wrongful life does not come to be. It is claimed that we harm a child by burdening him with certain disabilities: but this is not the same as harming a child already born. This is explained by Buchanan, et.al., as follows:

> If a mother or anyone else knowingly and responsibly
> caused harm to an already born child so serious as to
> make its life no longer worth living, that would
> constitute extremely serious child abuse... That is a

different and arguably more serious wrong than
wrongful life, where the alternative to the life not
worth living is never having a life at all.[72]

There is a limit to what may be claimed, for not every case of a life
that is of poor quality is a case of wrongful life. Joseph Feinberg, for
example, argues that if there is a legitimate way to claim that the
child was harmed by his mother, then that might create a slippery
slope in which people launch wrongful-life lawsuits for being
illegitimate, or ugly, or of below average intelligence. He therefore
claims that if the child believes life as a handicapped person is better
than no life at all, then the child could not have a grievance against
his mother.[73] This, we have seen, is one of Parfit's premises as well:
he claims that the Depletion people can have no objection to the
choices which created the Repugnant Conclusion because the same
choices also caused them to be born in the fist place. But this leads
to an interesting incoherence in the case. Buchanan says:

> …nonexistence is not any kind of condition, so it is
> clearly not a condition that could be better for the
> infant than the existence it has. When the alternative
> is nonexistence, there is no individual who is made
> worse off by being conceived and born.
> Nonexistence is not a condition that is better for an
> individual than actual existence [except] in rare cases
> like having Lesch-Nyhan or Tay Sachs disease; it is
> no condition at all, and so it is not better or worse
> than any other condition.[74]

If being harmed "requires being made worse off than one otherwise
would have been",[75] as Parfit would say, then one is lead to the
conclusion that a person currently living a wrongful life could have
no objection to the choices that lead to his birth. However, since
non-existence is no kind of condition, it cannot be better or worse
than existence. On this basis, Matthew Hanser claims the Non-

Identity problem is not a real problem. The first of his arguments, this one considering the Risky Nuclear Policy, runs as follows:

> There is no doubt that these people suffer harms: had
> the radiation not leaked, they would have gone on
> living happy lives. And they would not have suffered
> these harms had we chosen another policy, for then
> they would not have existed and so would never have
> been harmed at all. It is thus a consequence of our
> choosing the Risky Policy that people end up being
> harmed more than they would have been had we
> chosen differently.[76]

Hanser claims that since the people born after a Risky Policy would not have existed otherwise, therefore they would not have been harmed otherwise. Therefore the choice *does* harm the Nuclear People in a morally relevant way. As Hanser puts it, "an act does not harm someone in the morally relevant sense unless its consequence is that that person is harmed more than he would have been had the act not been performed".[77] It follows that the act of choosing Risky Policy harms people in a way that *satisfies* the criterion of the no-worse-off principle: the alternative for them is to not be harmed, since that is implied by not existing, and thus the choice of Risky Policy harms them more than they would have been. "They would not have suffered these harms had we chosen another policy, for then they would not have existed and so would never have been harmed at all".[78] Since we do harm future people in a morally relevant sense, Hanser concludes that we do leave them worse than they would have been, and thus he claims that the whole Non-Identity argument is rendered unsound.

Note that Hanser's formulation of the no-worse-off principle is not precisely the same as the version found by Woodward, Buchanan, and others. This is partly because Parfit's formulation is nowhere openly stated in the text: it is merely detected in the argument by Parfit's commentators. It may be helpful to illustrate the differences in a diagram.

Parfit's implicit version	Hanser's revised version
An act does not harm someone in the morally relevant sense if its consequence is that it leaves someone no worse off than he would have been had the act not been performed.	An act does not harm someone in the morally relevant sense unless its consequence is that the person is harmed more than he would have been had the act not been performed.
The people these choices cause to be badly off would not have existed otherwise.	The people these choices cause to be badly off would not have existed otherwise.
Therefore, these choices leave them no worse off than they would have been. Therefore, these choices harm no one in the morally relevant sense.	Therefore, these choices harm them more than they would have been otherwise. Therefore, these choices do harm them in the morally relevant sense.

The formulation Hanser uses follows properly from Parfit's premises, including the crucial premise that the alternative for future people in Non-Identity situations is non-existence, and moreover the argument supports both variations equally well. And each supports opposite moral conclusions regarding whether people in Non-Identity cases are harmed. The relevant difference is the alternative formulation of the no-worse-off principle.

Note that Hanser's version of the no-worse-off principle is very similar to Parfit's own reformulation of what it means to harm someone: "An act harms someone if its consequence is that someone is harmed more". ("Principle C6" *R&P*, pg. 69.) Hanser would agree that there is no deep disjunction between the two forms of the principle. Taking it as one's first premise, one may conclude that if non-existence implies not being harmed, then one is indeed 'harmed more' by choices like Depletion or Risky Policy.[79] It follows that future people harmed by Depletion or by Risky Policy can indeed have an objection to the choices that harmed them. In this way

Parfit's own premises can lead one to a very different, diametrically opposed conclusion.

This is one of the hypothetical cases that may turn out to have a real-world counterpart. An obvious real-life instance of Parfit's Risky Policy scenario of nuclear waste burial is:

> *Sellafield.* This is a mixed oxide nuclear fuel reprocessing plant in Sellafield, England. Discharges from the plant pollute the Irish Sea with radiation. Greenpeace Ireland launched a legal challenge against the UK government on the grounds that its detrimental environmental impact outweighs its economic benefits. Ireland also took the United Kingdom to court for withholding information about the facility's capabilities and its economic viability.[80] An accident similar to what happened at the nuclear energy generating plants in Chernobyl, Ukraine, on 26 April 1986, and at Three Mile Island, Pennsylvania, USA, on 28 March 1979, could conceivably occur at Sellafield as well. The possibility prompted the Irish government in 2002 to send the entire population a small supply of iodine pills to help mitigate the effects of radiation exposure, should an accident occur.[81]

If an accident did occur at the nuclear plant in Sellafield, the Irish Sea would be irradiated, as would the atmosphere, and thousands of people would experience severe suffering or death from radiation exposure. We can call choice to build the facility an instance of Parfit's Risky Policy. Parfit's argument asserts that if an accident occurred, the people harmed could have no objection; Hanser's argument, by contrast, asserts that the people can have an objection.

Hanser goes further than that: he claims that not only are both versions of the no-worse-off principle very similar, but also that they are both false. Parfit's formulation "does not purport to say how an action must be related to the event of someone's suffering a harm in order for it to be at least prima facie objectionable…".[82] Hanser's own formulation does attempt to describe that relation, but in his view does not do so correctly: "…in order for an action to harm someone in the morally relevant sense, it must result in the person's *being harmed* more than he would have been had the act not been performed. It leaves the notion of someone's being harmed unexplained".[83]

In a second argument Hanser deals with another of Parfit's reasons for why the objection to an act that causes people to be badly off cannot be that it harms them in the morally relevant sense. In this second case, the no-worse-off principle takes the form of the necessary and sufficient criterion for an action to benefit someone in the morally relevant sense: an act qualifies as benefiting someone "…if its consequence is that that person receives a benefit that he would not have received had the choice not been made".[84] This makes it appear as if an action benefits the people that it causes to be badly off, provided that they have lives worth living and that they would not have existed otherwise. However, no agent could be *morally* responsible for the existence of particular people even if it is known that people will exist after one choice who will not exist after another. A distinction must be drawn between the *cause* of someone's life and *responsibility* for it. Hanser says:

> Most such actions affect the identities of future
> people only because they *accidentally* (even if
> predictably) affect who has sex with whom and
> when… the agents of actions only *accidentally*
> affecting the identities of future people cannot
> plausibly be taken to act in order to ensure one group
> of people's coming into existence rather than
> another's… The mere fact that I can predict that
> people will exist if I choose this policy who would
> not exist if I were to choose a different policy will not
> make me responsible for their existence. If the
> responsibility will belong to anyone, it will belong,
> presumably, to their parents.[85]

The feature of accidentally affecting the identities of future people is part of both the Risky Policy and Depletion cases by which Parfit illustrates his argument. As the effect on the identities of future people is accidental, we consequentially can not locate on them the justification for our choice in either of these situations.

To summarise Hanser's case: he began by pointing out that non-existence in some sense renders people immune from harm, whereas Parfit emphasises only that non-existence cannot be worse for them. A different form of the no-worse-off principle enabled Hanser to claim that even though the alternative for Non-Identity people is non-existence, Non-Identity choices still harm them in the morally relevant way. Also, the accidental way in which people's identities are affected by Non-Identity choices means that Non-Identity choices do not benefit the people they harm, at least not in a way that imposes on us moral responsibility for it. Hanser concludes by claiming that there is no such thing as the Non-Identity Problem as Parfit presented it, and there is no need for a special explanation for why it is wrong to choose Depletion or Risky Policy.[86] As it happens, Hanser concedes that "Depletion" is still a problematic case, but for reasons to do with intergenerational distributive justice and not to do with Non-Identity reasons.

It can be objected that in some situations, such as the case of the 14 Year Old Girl, or in cases of Wrongful Life, if not in further-future cases like Depletion and Risky Policy, we do have direct moral responsibility for who has sex with whom and when, or we do have moral responsibility arising from the failure or refusal to genetically screen for disease or handicap, or to abort the child, where the facilities exist to do so and when it can be known in advance that the child about to be born will be the subject of a wrongful life. We might, then, claim that the wrong of Wrongful Life outweighs the benefit of mere existence. But it may not be clear which version of the concept of harm we should use. It is also not clear if, how, or why causing someone to exist can benefit that person. It is also not clear that the claim 'X is not harmed' can logically follow from the premise 'X does not exist', as Hanser claims it can. For it would seem that the X must be an existing person who is or is not harmed. With the word 'is', the existential indicator, in play, the claim 'X is not harmed' already implies an existing X. Hanser's argument may be subject to the very same logical problems which he claims are also present in Parfit's argument.

Given these difficulties, it is worth digressing for a moment to consider Parfit's case for why causing someone to exist benefits that person. The case is presented as a semi-independent argument in an appendix after the end of <u>Reasons and Persons</u>. Parfit's most direct confrontation with the comparison of existence to non-existence is found in the beginning of this argument, and runs as follows.

> Some objectors claim that life cannot be judged to be either better or worse than nonexistence. But life of a certain kind may be judged to be either good or bad— either worth living, or not worth living. If a certain life is good, it is better than nothing. If it is bad, it is worse than nothing. In judging that some person's life is worth living, or better than nothing, we need *not* be implying that it would have been worse for this person if he had never existed. (*R&P* pg.487.)

All Parfit has done, here, is claim that the judgement "a life is worth living" can mean the same as "it is better than nothing", and that the judgement "a life is not worth living" can mean the same as "it is worse than nothing". He has not actually dealt with the objection that life cannot be better or worse than non-existence. He has simply decided to be less strict about it. The main body of his argument is an induction by analogy, and runs as follows. Someone can decide whether or not to continue living or to die. Someone could look back on a part of his life and think that, if he knew beforehand what was to come, he could decide whether or not he wanted to live it out. If people can make such decisions about parts of their lives, they can make such decisions about whole lives. (*R&P* pg.487) The difficulty lies in whether the condition of "ceasing to exist" can be treated the same as "having never existed", as Parfit claims they can. (*R&P* pg. 488.) I claim that they can not. Death is an actual event that happens to existing people. Non-existence is a non-event that happens to no one. Similarly, Harm is an actual condition that can affect real people. Non-existence is no kind of condition which affects no one. One can look back or forward on one's life to decide if it was, or will continue to be, worth living, but there is a deep difficulty in putting oneself in the theoretical, counter-factual position of *the moment before one's own birth* in order to judge one's whole life that way. At least when anticipating the future of one's own life, one is still in a position to be the architect of one's life (at least by the decision whether or not to commit suicide), whereas in the theoretical pre-natal position, one could not affect one's own life. No one can choose whether or not to be born. There is a related difficulty concerning whether existence can be a natural quality possessed by things. Parfit says, "Some claim that, because it lacks some of the features of other predicates, *existing* is not a predicate. Others claim that this only shows *existing* to be a *peculiar* predicate. We can similarly claim that causing someone to exist, who will have a life worth living, gives this person a peculiar benefit." (*R&P* pg. 490) It is possible that Parfit is referring to Kant's well known objection to Anslem's 'Ontological' Argument for the existence of God, which is that existence is not a predicate.[87] If Kant is right, it follows that Parfit cannot make "similar" claims about existence as a benefit. But I lay these comments aside for the time 'being'. They are, even by Parfit's admission, inconclusive.

I return now to the theme raised at the beginning of this section. In both versions of the no-worse-off principle, the alternative for the people involved is non-existence: that is what is denoted by being "not worse" or "not harmed more" *than they would have been*, according to both Parfit and Hanser. The provisio "then they would have been" in Non-Identity situations is non-existence. But a closer look at the comparison of existence to non-existence must take us back to the fact that non-existence isn't any kind of condition. Non-existence cannot be worse than existence; likewise, it cannot be better. There are no bearings of comparison. It simply does not fit the case to say that a person who does not exist is not harmed. If the alternative for Non-Identity people is non-existence, then it makes equal sense, or equal nonsense, to say that non-existence leaves them no worse off, or that it leaves them unharmed. Actually, the alternative for Non-Identity people is to not *be* anything, neither better nor worse off, neither harmed nor benefited.

Someone who is alive can prefer to exist than not to exist, and one can find the rare cases of Wrongful Life so abhorrent that most would agree they should not have come to be. It is probable that most people would choose non-existence when faced with the kind of situation imagined by Feinberg, in which God offers a person the choice between being born with Tay-Sachs disease or immediate and permanent annihilation.[88] A future characterised by pollution, disease, resource scarcity, severe weather disasters, rising oceans and rising global temperatures, might also be a future that no one would want to live in, if they had the choice. The peculiar difficulty raised by the Non-Identity Problem is that people born into such a future could not have lived in another kind of future. Yet there is a deeper difficulty. It may be claimed that non-existence is not worse for people as an alternative, and that non-existence implies not being subject to harm. These claims are half-truths: the more complete truth is that non-existence cannot be any kind of alternative for people: not worse, not better, not harmed, not benefited. There is no basis for choosing one conclusion about non-existence over another. Any utilitarian comparison of outcomes in which non-existence is involved cannot avoid the deep difficulty here described. Such comparisons apparently qualify as 'empty questions' by Parfit's own criterion.[89] And yet they are at the heart of the Non-Identity Problem as he presented it.

For the purpose of this section, it is sufficient simply to point out this difficulty. I end it with a few questions. Given that the comparison of existence to non-existence is deeply problematic, what are we to make of claims like Parfit's that if a certain life is good or bad, it is better or worse than nothing? Likewise, what are we to make of the problem of "wrongful life", in which we can claim that someone's quality of life is so bad that he or she should not have been born? There are a number of possibilities. We might be less strict about the logical demands of the comparison. Perhaps the comparison is coherent when treated as a kind of literary or metaphorical device. Someone could say his life is "better than nothing", or "worse than nothing", with the intent to express his feeling about the value or disvalue of his life. If such an expression is 'merely' literary or metaphorical in nature, it would not be empty. Nor would it imply that the value of life which it affirms is absolute, or all-or-nothing. It need not be a contradiction to claim that life is valuable and yet it is not wrong to swat flies or to clean bacteria from one's blood stream. Another way we could be less strict about the logical demands of the comparison with non-existence is by claiming that the value of life may be in some sense a property of life itself, and not dependent on a comparison with non-existence or on a consequentialist value theory. This is claimed by philosophers who defend some form of ecocentrism. Still another way might be for people to compare their lives to the approaching cessation of their own existence, that is, to their death. In this case, someone is not comparing existence to non-existence, but deciding whether their own particular existence is worth continuing. This evaluation may require a certain standpoint—the standpoint of existence. As-yet-unborn future people do not have this standpoint. It may therefore be senseless, as T'Hooft claimed, to ask people to consider the prospect that if certain conditions had been different, they would not have existed, and thus not have been harmed.

The only conclusion which can be drawn here in a definitive way is that Depletion and Conservation cannot meaningfully be compared with each other when they are treated as Non-Identity choices. They must be compared with non-existence, which is a deep impossibility. It is thus impossible for us to decide which choice we are morally bound to prefer. The ability to make such a decision was, as stated in the general introduction, a criterion for the acceptability of a statement of environmental ethics. It seems to me that the only way to resolve this impasse is with an ethical theory that can render a judgement without involving a comparison of outcomes.

§ 7. Should we make people happy or make happy people?

It may be argued that because of present economic, social, and environmental policies, humanity is already headed toward something like the Repugnant Conclusion. Consider:

> *Global Population.* The world's population is rising. The most recent predictions suggest that there will be 8.9 billion of us by the year 2050, and most of this population growth will be in the world's poorest countries.[90] A report issued by the World Wildlife Federation suggested that by 2050 the world's ecosystems will no longer be able to support this population growth.[91] Environmental scarcities are now known to create political conflict and economic turmoil. For instance, poor countries may be less able to adapt to climate change and global warming, resulting in mass deaths and mass population migrations on scales that will almost certainly be much greater than ever before.[92]

We should find this prospect disturbing. One might argue that in this situation, we are obliged to maximise the happiness of whatever number of people there are, but not necessarily obliged to increase the number of people. Avner De-Shalit considered this as a way in which the Repugnant Conclusion could be avoided without abandoning the principle of total utility. This is also the view of Narveson, who wrote that our purpose should be to do that which results in "…the greatest happiness *of* the greatest number and not… the greatest happiness *and* the greatest number… we are in favour of making people happy, but neutral about making happy people. Or rather, neutral as a public policy, regarding it as a matter for private decision".[93] On this view, we should not maximise total happiness by maximising the number of people. However, de-Shalit argues that this requires one to go outside of utilitarian principles because it would place the group of people the Utilitarian calculus must account for to a fixed group (i.e. those who are presently living), and assert that the happiness or suffering of only that group of people matters. But, the principle of utility, insofar as it claims to be a universal, impartial and impersonal principle, must include as many people as possible; ideally, it should include everyone, including future people. (Indeed, In Parfit's Mere Addition Paradox, the puzzle requires a "God's eye view" in which the happiness of "extra people" whose existence is unknown to the main group of people must still be counted.) Accepting Narveson's claim as a solution to the Non-Identity Problem thus requires the Utilitarian to abandon the universality and impartiality of his principle. In his words,

> ...her solution to these paradoxes is alien to utilitarianism, making the utilitarian principle dependent on a society of a given size, a certain community of people, and asserting that it is the happiness of this community and these people that we should consider. The solution bars the entry to non-members of the society, who, not being included in this calculation, are not equally respected. But what, then, has become of the idea of universal ethics and impartiality? (*WPM* pg. 73.)

It seems unclear what the justification for that move outside of Utilitarianism would be, if it is not simply and exclusively "to solve the Non-Identity Problem". Narveson's solution thus serves as another example of an attempt to solve the Non-Identity Problem by means of compromising the principle of Utility.

Observing the difficulty involved in calculating the utility to future people who will owe their number, identity, and existence to our choices, de-Shalit concludes thus: "...the argument is quite simple: as utilitarian person-regarding principles encounter unavoidable and insurmountable challenges, one must return to non-person-regarding principles". (*WPM* pg.76) By this point, I must agree. Parfit's presupposition that Theory X will be a Utilitarian theory of beneficence (c.f. *R&P* pg. 451) is what makes it impossible for him to find it. The problems within the theory are sufficient and serious enough to warrant looking elsewhere for a philosophical explanation for why we must avoid the Repugnant Conclusion, and for a satisfactory principle of environmental ethics. These failures are, in my view, reasons for departing from Utilitarianism.

§ 8. Summary Remarks for Chapter One.

I conclude that in the Non-Identity problem, Utilitarianism has created a puzzle which it is unable to solve within its own terms alone. The theory that Parfit thinks he is seeking to overcome the Repugnant Conclusion is a theory of Utilitarian beneficence. But every attempt to solve the problem here studied which used utilitarian principles alone, or which countered the problem using utilitarian objections, has failed. We should now be prepared to face the possibility that utilitarianism itself is at fault. As Allison (a committed Utilitarian) puts it, "As a doctrine, utilitarianism seems to collapse which ever way it turns. Interpreted broadly, it contradicts those qualities which are distinct about itself, while interpreted narrowly it defeats its own purpose." (*E&U* pg. 131.)[94] Why, then, do so many Utilitarians continue to cling to Utilitarianism? "For all its faults", says Allison, "broad utilitarianism is the least silly approach to policy available: its premises are the most defensible logically and the closest to contemporary western values." (*E&U* pg. 131.) I can find no serious disagreement with this latter statement (although I would not wish to characterise any moral theory as more or less silly than any other). Yet I also find that the various ways Utilitarianism points beyond itself cannot be ignored, and ought to be explored. As I see it, the only way to move forward is to assert that the maximisation of utility is not what matters.

The Non-Identity Problem began as a real problem. Its inferences seemed at first to follow properly from agreeable premises. I believe that what Parfit has inadvertently shown is that if one wishes to propose the reason to avoid future environmental disasters, it is necessary to do so without appealing to the effect on the people of the future. We may be able to do so in "same number" cases by appealing to something like Parfit's Same Number Quality Claim, cited earlier. But the conceptual difficulty involved in the revised concept of harm, and in the comparison with non-being, remains unsolved: and that is what gave birth to the problem in the first place. At any rate, in "different number" cases, we cannot appeal to the Same Number Quality Claim.

The utilitarian tradition as embodied in Parfit has become expert in calculating out to the last possible parameter, and to every conceivable level of elaboration and complexity, the consequences and implications for human happiness and well-being that may follow on after our choices and decisions. By that very expertise, the utilitarian calculus itself has created the problems which now puzzle us. I see it as having become something like a huge labyrinthine prison. A labyrinth captures its inmates and holds them not by its walls, locks, and gates, but by the hypnotic quality of its organisation. To escape from a labyrinth, it normally takes only a slight shift in perspective, and this is sometimes enabled by the intervention of something from outside, which does not follow the labyrinth's rules. Thus to find the reason to reject the Repugnant Conclusion, and thus to arrive at an acceptable environmental ethic, I find it necessary to depart from consequentialist, utility-maximising principles. We require a theory in which the maximisation of utility is not what matters. The acceptable statement of environmental ethics will be a theory in which it is possible to claim that an act can be wrong even if it produces the greatest utility, or can be right even if it produces the lesser utility, or can be wrong even if it harms no one.

---

[1] J.J.C. Smart, "An outline system of utilitarian ethics" in Utilitarianism: For and Against, pg. 12-13.

2 "Now to call a person 'happy' is to say more than that he is contented for most of the time, or even that he frequently enjoys himself and is rarely discontented or in pain. It is, I think, in part to express a favourable attitude to the idea of such a form of contentment and enjoyment. That is, for A to call B 'happy', A must be contented at the prospect of B being in his present state of mind and at the prospect of A himself, should the opportunity arise, enjoying that sort of state of mind. That is, 'happy' is a word which is mainly descriptive (tied to the concepts of contentment and enjoyment) but which is also partly evaluative." Smart, *ibid*, pg. 22.

3 Smart, *ibid*, pg. 22.

4 Smart, *ibid*, pg. 23. The distinction is elaborated as follows: "We can talk of a man enjoying himself at a quarter past two precisely, but hardly of a man being happy at a quarter past two precisely. Similarly we can talk of it raining at a quarter past two precisely, but hardly about it being a wet climate at a quarter past two precisely." [pg. 23.]

5 "...pleasure, and freedom from pain, are the only things desirable as ends; and that all desirable things (which are as numerous in the utilitarian as in any other scheme) are desirable either for the pleasure inherent in themselves, or as means to the promotion of pleasure and the prevention of pain." John Stuart Mill, *Utilitarianism*, in On Liberty and Utilitarianism pg. 118.

6 William H. Shaw, Taking Account of Utilitarianism pg. 53.

7 In this way the Utilitarian notion of happiness is distinct from other philosophical notions of happiness, for instance that of Aristotle who believed that nothing could be added to happiness. More will be said of the differences between Utilitarian and Aristotelian notions of happiness in chapters 4 and 5.

8 Shaw, Taking Account of Utilitarianism, pg. 53.

9 Shaw, *ibid.*, pg. 54-6.

10 Shaw, *ibid.* pg. 57.

11 Shaw, *ibid.* pg. 63-4

12 Smart, "An outline system of Utilitarian ethics" in Utilitarianism: For and Against pg. 26

13 Alan Carter, "In Defense of Radical Disobedience" pg. 38.

14 Singer, Practical Ethics, pg. 272.

[15] "There are some things which, once lost, no amount of money can buy back. Thus to justify the destruction of an ancient forest on the grounds that it will earn us substantial export income is unsound, even if we could invest that income and increase its value from year to year; for no matter how much we increased its value, it could never buy back the link with the past represented by the forest." Singer, Practical Ethics pg. 270.

[16] "Can we be sure that future generations will appreciate wilderness? Perhaps they will be happier sitting in air-conditioned shopping malls, playing computer games more sophisticated than any we can imagine? That is possible. But there are several reasons why we should not give this possibility too much weight. First, the trend has been in the opposite direction: the appreciation of wilderness has never been higher than it is today, especially among those nations that have overcome the problems of poverty and hunger and have relatively little wilderness left. Wilderness is valued as something of immense beauty, as a reservoir of scientific knowledge that it provides, and because many people just like to know that something natural is still there, relatively untouched by modern civilisation. If, as we all hope, future generations are able to provide for the basic needs of most people, we can expect that for centuries to come, they, too, will value wilderness for the same reasons that we value it." Singer, Practical Ethics pg. 271. Allison confirms this point as well, observing that the interest in nature and the wilderness is "a very modern instinct which has increased steadily and geometrically since industrialisation." (c.f. pg. 148 in *E&U*).

[17] "Finally, if we preserve intact the amount of wilderness that exists now, future generations will at least have the choice of getting up from their computer games and going to see a world that has not been created by human beings. If we destroy the wilderness, that choice is gone forever." Singer, Practical Ethics, pg. 272-3.

[18] "Europeans Rank Environment Equal to Economic, Social Issues" *Environmental News Service* 2 May 2005.

[19] Singer, Practical Ethics, pg. 275-6.

[20] Singer, Practical Ethics, pg. 288.

[21] Singer, One World, pg. 19-20.

[22] Singer, One World, pg. 41.

[23] "Perhaps it is because of the difficulty of answering such broad questions about utility that we have other principles like the [distributive justice] ones we have been discussing. They give you easier answers and are more likely to lead to an outcome that approximates the best consequences (or is at least as likely to do so as any calculation we could make without using those principles)." Singer, One World, pg. 41.

[24] Singer, One World, pg. 41.

[25] Singer, One World, pp. 43-4.

[26] Singer, <u>One World</u>, pp. 46-9.

[27] "This girl chooses to have a child. Because she is so young, she gives her child a bad start in life. Though this will have bad effects throughout the child's life, his life will, predictably, be worth living. If this girl had waited for several years, she would have had a different child, to whom she would have given a better start in life." *R&P* pg. 358.

[28] "As a community, we must choose between two energy policies. Both would be completely safe for at least three centuries, but one would have certain risks in the further future. This policy involves the burial of nuclear waste in areas where, in the next few centuries, there is no risk of an earthquake. But since this waste will remain radio-active for thousands of years, there will be risks in the distant future. If we choose this Risky Policy, the standard of living will be somewhat higher over the next century. We do choose this policy. As a result, there is a catastrophe many centuries later. Because of geological changes to the Earth's surface, an earthquake releases radiation, which kills thousands of people." *R&P* pp. 371-2.

[29] "As a community, we must choose whether to deplete or conserve certain kinds of resources. If we choose Depletion, the quality of life over the next two centuries would be slightly higher than it would have been if we had chosen Conservation. But it would later, for many centuries, be much lower than it would have been if we had chosen Conservation. This would be because, at the start of this period, people would have to find alternatives for the resources that we had depleted... Because we choose Depletion, millions of people have, for several centuries, a much lower quality of life. This quality of life is much lower, not than it is now, but than it would have been if we had chosen Conservation. These people's lives are worth living; and, if we had chosen Conservation, these particular people would never have existed." (*R&P* pg. 361-3).

[30] Paul Roberts, <u>The End of Oil</u>, pg. 5

[31] Cliff Taylor, "Oil prices should be Republic's wake-up call" *The Irish Times* 14 May 2004, pg. 5.

[32] Mark Tran, "Oil price surge 'threatens global growth'" *The Guardian* 28 September 2004.

[33] "Oil prices hit record high amid uncertainty over Iraq" *The Irish Times* 21 August 2004; Ashley Seager, "All eyes on Iraq as oil price nears $50" *The Guardian* 21 August 2004.

[34] Tavia Grant, "Oil crosses $57 a barrel" *The Globe and Mail* 17 March 2005

[35] Mark Tran, "Oil price surges after 'super spike' predicted" *The Guardian* 1 April 2005.

[36] Damian Corless, "Why the Oil Apocalypse is Closer Than You Think", *The Irish Independent* 15 May 2004, pg. 6.

[37] Lorna Siggins, "Permission Granted for Controversial Landfill in East Galway" *The Irish Times* 21 May 2004, pg. 2.

[38] Tim O'Brien, "350-acre north Dublin site proposed for super-dump" *The Irish Times* 7 September 2004.

[39] Page, "Global Warming and the Non Identity Problem", in Tae-chang (ed) <u>Self and Future Generations</u>, pg. 112. The 'person-affecting view' referred to here is the view that an action is bad if it is bad *for* someone.

[40] Parfit does not consider that the condition of the world in which the future generations will exist, be it badly polluted or respectfully cared for, will also figure into the identities of future people in that the environment affects human health, nutrition, population density, and the other cultural and environmental factors that figure into our biographies. It is sufficient for his purposes that future people will exist, or not, as a result of our actions made today.

[41] For instance, it was detected by Thomas Schwartz, who interpreted Parfit as arguing that a person can have no complaint that an act harmed her unless the act left her worse off than she would have been had it not been done. C.f. Schwartz, "Obligations to Posterity" in Barry and Sikora, (eds.) <u>Obligations to Future Generations</u> pp. 3-13.

[42] Note the shift from the active to the passive tense of the verbs 'to benefit' and 'to harm'. Explaining this further, he writes, "(C6) revises the ordinary use of the words 'benefit' and 'harm'. When I claim to have benefited someone, I am usually taken to mean that some act of mine was the chief or immediate cause of some benefit received by this person. According to (C6), I benefit someone even when my act is a remote part of the cause of the receiving of this benefit. All that needs to be true is that, if I had acted otherwise, this person would not have received this benefit. Similar claims apply to 'harm'". (*R&P* pg. 69). This will come up again in the discussion of the Non-Identity Problem and non-being.

[43] Both versions of the argument are presented once in each of the three main puzzling cases that introduce the problem (the 14-Year Old Girl, Depletion, and Risky Policy—chapter 16 of *R&P*). The second, benefit-emphasising variation assumes that the benefit of existence (if it is a benefit) is greater than the harm caused to these people by the choices that also brought them into existence.

[44] Parfit's full text here reads: "This conclusion is *intrinsically* repugnant. And this conclusion is implied by the Impersonal Total Principle, which is a particular version of the Principle of Beneficience. To avoid the Repugnant Conclusion, we must try to show that we should reject this version. We must try to find a better version: Theory X." *R&P* pg. 390.

[45] Parfit also adds, hopefully, that "in the meanwhile, we should conceal this problem from those who will decide whether we increase our use of nuclear energy. These people know that the Risky Policy might cause catastrophes in the further future. It will be better if these people believe, falsely, that the choice of the Risky Policy would be against the interests of the people killed by such a catastrophe. If they have this false belief, they will be more likely to reach the right decision." *Ibid*, pg. 451-2.

[46] D. Heyd, Genethics: Moral Issues in the Creation of People cited in E. Page, "Global Warming and the Non-Identity Problem" in Self and Future Generations pg. 112.

[47] Nick Fotion and Jan C. Heller, eds. Contingent Future Persons (Dordrecht: Kluwer Academic Publishers, 1997) pg. 96.

[48] Hendrick Visser't Hooft, Justice to Future Generations and the Environment pg. 50. (this text is hereafter referred to as *JFGE*.) T'Hooft seems to misunderstand the argument with the last sentence that I quoted: for while it is true that a Depletion Person is in a situation that could have been better, it could not have been better for him: and that is what Parfit claims is so important and troublesome. He would not have been Peter or Paul: he would have been Peter or there would be no Peter.

[49] "...what is ultimately of interest—the point of the whole exercise, if it is not to be purely academic—is the evaluation of possible actions, policies, and institutional arrangements. But Parfit's discussion strongly suggests that such real life cases will often have (potentially) morally relevant features that are excluded from most of the hypothetical cases that motivate his discussions ... When we consider also that Parfit is unsuccessful in finding a version of principle X which deals in a fully adequate way even with his hypothetical cases, the case for a theory which includes both consequentialist and nonconsequentialist elements from the start and which focuses on actual choice situations becomes even stronger." James Woodward, "The Non-Identity Problem" pg. 831.

[50] Stuart Rachels, "Contingent Future Persons", pg. 165.

[51] Mere Addition is what happens when "in one of two outcomes, there exists extra people (1) who have lives worth living, (2) who affect no one else, and (3) whose existence does not involve social injustice". (*R&P*, pg. 420.) Imagine two scenarios that are identical in terms of the number of people and the total happiness they possess, except that one of the two scenarios includes 'extra' people who are unknown to the 'main' population. These extra people change the total and the average utility of the scenario in which they exist. This, plus the fact that the extra people and the main population do not affect each other and do not know of each other's existence, renders it very difficult to choose which scenario is better. To make matters more complicated, the Mere Addition Paradox comes in three different varieties. The second version is described by Stuart Rachels as "one of the great achievements of twentieth-century ethics". In it a long series of possible future histories are laid out, each of which is asserted to be better than the one before it but the last one is worse than the first.

[52] Lorna Siggins, "O Cuiv calls for realistic approach to rail corridor" *The Irish Times* 24 May 2004.

[53] "Report: Climate Change causing jump in natural disasters" *Reuters* 29 September 2000

[54] P. Vellinga and W. J. van Verseveld, Climate Change and Extreme Weather Events, pg. 35.

[55] "1650 dead as hurricane pounds Haiti coast" *Reuters / The Irish Times* 27 September 2004.

[56] "To suppose that life has…no higher end than pleasure—no better and nobler object of desire and pursuit—they designate as utterly mean and grovelling; as a doctrine worthy only of swine, to whom the followers of Epicurus were, at a very early period, contemptuously likened…" John Stewart Mill, "Utilitarianism", in On Liberty and Utilitarianism pg. 118-9.

[57] "Now it is an unquestionable fact that those who are equally acquainted with, and equally capable of appreciating and enjoying, both, do give a marked preference to the manner of existence which employs their highest faculties. Few human creatures would consent to be changed into any of the lower animals, for a promise of the fullest allowance of a beast's pleasures; no intelligent human being would consent to be a fool, no instructed person would be an ignoramus, no person of feeling and conscience would be selfish and base, even though they should be persuaded that the fool, the dunce, or the rascal is better satisfied with his lot than they are with theirs… A being of higher faculties requires more to make him happy, is capable probably of more acute suffering, and certainly accessible to it at more points, than one of an inferior type; but in spite of these liabilities he can never really wish to sink into what he feels to be a lower grade of existence." Mill, *Utilitarianism*, pg. 120.

[58] Mill, *Utilitarianism*, pg. 121.

[59] Stuart Rachels, "A Set of Solutions to Parfit's Problems" pg. 215.

[60] Rachels, *ibid*, pg. 219.

[61] Rachels, *ibid*, pg. 216.

[62] Parfit describes Rawls' position on Utilitarianism this way: "Many Utilitarians answer moral questions with the method called that of an *impartial observer*. When such an utilitarian asks himself, as an observer, what would be right, or what he would impartially prefer, he may *identify* with all of the affected people. He may imagine that he himself would *be all* of these different people. This will lead him to ignore the fact that *different* people are affected, and so to ignore the claims of just distribution as between these people... While an identifying observer imagines himself as being *all* of the affected people, and a Rawlsian imagines himself as being *one* of the affected people, without knowing whom, a detached observer imagines himself as being *none* of the affected people." (*R&P*, pg. 331.) It is possible, however, that Parfit is here misrepresenting Rawls' view. Rawls does not exactly assert that we should identify with all people: he asserts that we must impartially decide the best way to distribute resources as if we were "behind a veil of ignorance" concerning what he himself would get.

[63] Gauthier, Practical Reasoning, pg. 126.

[64] Variant (A) of the Absurd Conclusion, which Parfit claims is a consequence of the Lexical View, reads: "Suppose that, in some history of the future, there would always be an enormous number of people, and for each one person who suffers, and has a life that is not worth living, there would be ten billion people whose lives *are* worth living, though their quality of life is not quite as high as the Valueless Level. This would be *worse* than if there were no future people." (*R&P* pg. 415.)

[65] Rachels, *ibid*, pg. 223.

[66] Rachels, *ibid*, pg. 220.

[67] In this second case, it is possible that Rachels conflates Lexical pleasures with the "goods outside the domain of well-being". But I will not dwell on this problem. These "goods outside the domain of well-being" might be consistent with Sidgwick's "ideal goods": the arts, sciences, and the highest achievements of culture, which matter more than general utility.

[68] As suggested by J. B. Stearns, "Ecology and the Indefinite Unborn" pp. 439-61.

[69] Rachels, *ibid*, pg. 224. Compare this to Parfit's own weakened version of the Repugnant Conclusion, offered in his own consideration of Lexicality: "If there were ten billion people living, all with a very high quality of life, there must be some much larger imaginable population whose existence would be *better*, even though its members have lives that are barely above the Valueless Level". Parfit, *ibid*, pg. 415.

[70] Rachels, *ibid*, pg. 224.

[71] Rachels, *ibid*, pg. 232.

[72] Buchanan, Brock, Daniels and Wilker, <u>From Chance to Choice</u> pg. 240.

[73] "If we insist that there is some relevant sense in which the infant... has been harmed by his mother, that could have the unfortunate consequence of legitimizing wrongful life suits for harmful states such as illegitimacy, ugliness, below average intelligence, and the like... I do not think that the child can establish a grievance against [his mother] so long as he concedes that his handicapped existence is far preferable to no existence at all..." J. Feinberg, "Wrongful Life and the Counterfactual Element in Harming" in <u>Freedom and Fulfillment</u> pg. 27, 31.

[74] Buchanan, et.al., *ibid*, pg. 234

[75] Buchanan, et.al., *ibid*, pg. 234. This is the formulation of the no-worse-off principle that appears implicitly in Parfit's text, also discovered by Woodward and others.

[76] Matthew Hanser, "Harming Future People", pg. 56.

[77] Hanser, *ibid*, pg. 55.

[78] Hanser, *ibid*, pg. 56.

[79] "One might have thought that the real moral of Parfit's first example was precisely that sometimes it is best *not* to maximise the number of people that you personally benefit. If there are several in need of aid and several capable of giving it, and if I have no special obligation to any of those in need, the thing for me to do s to coordinate my actions with the actions of others so as to ensure that as many as possible are benefited. It is only the idea that the correct action to perform must be the one that has me personally benefiting the greatest number that puts pressure on us to revise the use of the word 'benefit' to fit this case." Hanser, *ibid*, pg. 57 (note 15.)

[80] "Ireland takes UK to court over Sellafield Plant" Press release by Greenpeace (UK), 21 October 2002.

[81] Dick Ahlstrom, "Households to be posted iodine tablets from today" *The Irish Times* 18 June 2002

[82] Hanser, *ibid*, pg. 57. This is, presumably, on the basis of Parfit's switch from the active to the passive tense of "to harm" in his discussion of Principle (C6), quoted earlier. Hanser interprets (C6) as follows: "…I think that it is meant to explain the new, morally relevant senses of the active constructions 'X benefits Y', and 'X harms Y' *in terms of* the ordinary, unexplained senses of the passive constructions 'Y is benefited' and 'Y is harmed'… [Parfit's no-worse-off principle] is best seen as a cross between what it is for an act to harm someone in the morally relevant sense and an account of what it is for someone to suffer a harm as a result of something that happens to him." Hanser, *ibid*, pp. 54, 58.

[83] Hanser, *ibid*, pg. 55-6.

[84] As paraphrased by Hanser, *ibid*, pg. 59. Hanser argues that this is not precisely the same as his own reformulation of the no-worse-off principle for his first argument. It is similar to what Parfit called the Two-State Requirement: "We benefit someone only if we cause him to be better off than he would otherwise at that time have been". *R&P* pg. 487.

[85] Hanser, *ibid*, pg. 61-2. Emphasis added. Hanser may be here accusing Parfit of making "too big a deal" of the "superficial facts about our reproductive system" that Parfit says give rise to the problem. See Parfit's comments on page 363 of *R&P* on why the problem is not "a mere quibble", and section 4 of chapter 1 of this thesis.

[86] Paraphrasing Hanser's conclusion, *ibid*, pg. 62-3.

[87] In the Critique of Pure Reason, Kant says, "Being is obviously not a predicate, i.e. a concept of something that could be added to the concept of a thing. It is merely the positing of a thing or of certain determinations in themselves. In the logical use it is merely the copula of a judgement. The proposition 'God is omnipotent' contains two concepts that have their objects: God and omnipotence; the little word 'is' is not a predicate in it, but only that which posits the predicate in relation to the subject." Kant, Critique of Pure Reason A598/B626, pg. 567.

[88] Cited in Buchanan, et.al., *ibid*, pg. 235. Here the theoretical pre-natal position, which I criticised earlier, appears as a useful thought-experiment.

[89] Parfit's criterion for emptiness comes from his discussion of personhood and identity, and runs as follows: "When we ask an empty question, there is only one fact or outcome that we are considering. Different answers to our question are merely different descriptions of this fact or outcome. This is why, without answering this empty question, we can know everything that there is to know… When an empty question has no answer, we can decide to *give* it an answer… This is not a decision between different views about what really happened. Before making our decision, we already knew what happened. We are merely choosing one of two different descriptions of the very same course of events." *R&P* pg. 213-4.

[90] "40% rise in world population by 2050" *Associated Press* 25 February 2005.

[91] Mark Townsend and Jason Burke, "Earth will expire by 2050" *The Observer* 7 July 2002.

[92] Robert McLeman and Barry Smit, "Climate Change, Migration, and Security", pg. 5

[93] Jan Narveson, "Utilitarianism and New Generations", as cited in Avner de-Shalit, <u>Why Posterity Matters</u>, pg. 72-3. This text shall hereafter be referred to as *WPM*.

[94] To be clear, by 'broad' Utilitarianism Alison means the Utilitarianism of Mill, which accepts lexical pleasures. The 'narrow' Utilitarianism is that of Bentham, in which all pleasures are equal.

Chapter Two: The "Just"
Rawlsian Distribution

As was seen in the preceding study, Parfit claimed that the people born in the future after environmentally disastrous choices like Depletion and Nuclear Policy, insofar as they are Non-Identical to those who would have been born otherwise, cannot have an objection to those choices. He also claimed that we should avoid making those choices even if person-affecting principles are unable to provide a reason why. The various consequentialist solutions to the problem that were studied were shown to be unsuccessful. We must look to other moral theories for our solutions.

It might be objected that if we ignore consequentialist considerations, the future generations might disappear: it seems only in terms of the consequences for them that they appear in moral problems at all. But there are other ways in which the future generations appear to us. We can claim, for instance, that they have rights, or that it is unjust to leave them with little or nothing and to burden them with excessive pollution and waste. These are not utility-maximising principles, although they are still person-affecting principles. They may be able to succeed where Utilitarianism failed.

This project asks the question, what is the morally correct way to treat the environment? This chapter shall use the framework of distributive justice as presented by John Rawls in his well known work, A Theory of Justice, to approach this question. Might the wrongness of choosing Depletion be a problem of improper or unjust distribution? Can we affirm that, even if the Depletion people are 'not harmed', and that the Depletion future has the greatest total utility, nevertheless it is unjust to choose it? My working hypothesis for this chapter is that the Non-Identity choice of Depletion would not be chosen by parties in the original position, for the reason that it distributes social goods across generations unjustly. Depletion, I shall argue, is a failure of the Just Savings principle. What matters for this purpose is not that the Depletion people have more utility among them, but that a moral agent in the present who chooses

Depletion leaves the people of the future, whoever they are, with so little. A moral agent in the original position of not knowing what generation he would belong to would find it unjust for one generation to receive a great quantity of environmental resources from its predecessors only to consume most of them and leave little or nothing for its successors. I shall explore this hypothesis in the discourse to follow to see how well it is supported by Rawls' own principles, and whether it can stand as an acceptable environmental ethic.

§ 1. John Rawls and Distributive Justice.

The opening statement of A Theory of Justice reads, "Justice is the first virtue of social institutions, as truth is of systems of thought.",[1] and then a few pages later, he says, "the primary subject of justice is the basic structure of society, or more exactly, the way in which the major social institutions distribute fundamental rights and duties and determine the division of advantages from social co-operation." (TJ pg.7) The characterisation of justice as a social principle is an ancient theme: in antiquity, Plato regarded justice as a social structure in which three functional specialisations of society, as corresponded with three parts of a person's soul, are in proper order. Rawls' own contemporary, H.L.A. Hart, in a work that appeared ten years before the publication of A Theory of Justice, claimed, "Justice constitutes one segment of morality primarily concerned not with individual conduct but with the ways in which classes of individuals are treated. It is this which gives justice its special relevance in the criticism of law and of other public or social institutions."[2] Thus Rawls participates in a tradition of sorts by claiming that justice is a virtue of social institutions.

Rawls' theory develops a conception of a person as a citizen, a member of a society which also includes other individuals who are leading different lives. This conception is expressed in the thought-experiment of the "original position" and the "veil of ignorance", a position which contains within it the idea that society should be regarded as a system of co-operation between free and equal citizens. To summarise it: Rawls claims that the just basic structure of society is the one which individuals in an original position behind a veil of ignorance would want to live in. The original position is a theoretical position, a thought-experiment, (not a metaphysical condition of actual as-yet-unborn persons)[3] in which everyone bargains with each other about what the most just and equitable distribution of social goods should be. In the original position, everyone is a free and equal citizen, and possesses perfect knowledge of the structure of the society, but stands toward it as if he or she has not yet joined it. The 'veil of ignorance' prevents everyone from knowing who they will be, or what place they will occupy, in the society observed from the original position. As Rawls says, "Among the essential features of this situation is that no one knows his place in society, his class position or social status, nor does any one know his fortune in the distribution of natural assets and abilities, his intelligence, strength, and the like." (*TJ* pg.11.) The veil of ignorance here symbolises the objectivity and the impartiality with which the process of settling upon a just system of distribution should proceed. Rawls claims that someone in such a position would want a basic structure of society that adhered to two particular principles. The first is that "each person is to have an equal right to the most extensive scheme of equal basic liberties compatible with a similar scheme of liberties for others", and the second is that "social and economic inequalities are to be arranged so that they are both (a) reasonably expected to be to everyone's advantage, and (b) attached to positions and offices open to all." (*TJ* pg.53)

These two principles are, as Rawls claims, meant to be applied not to individuals but to society as a whole. "These principles primarily apply, as I have said, to the basic structure of society and govern the assignments of rights and duties and regulate the distribution of social and economic advantages." (*TJ* pg. 53.) Society is here understood as *a system of distribution*: society is a system by which social goods and values (liberties and opportunities, rights and legal protections, wealth and income, etc.) are distributed among individual people. It is reasonable to include environmental goods such as clean air and water among these social values, although Rawls refers to them only incidentally. (I shall soon show how environmental goods can be factored into the distribution.) Distributive justice itself may be seen, then, as the justice of the distribution arrangement. Justice is obtained if social values are distributed in a way that is advantageous to everyone. This leads to what Rawls calls 'the difference principle': any inequalities in the distribution must be acceptable to those who receive less. "The social order is not to establish and secure the more attractive prospects of those better off unless doing so is to the advantage of those less fortunate." (*TJ* pg.65) Thus, Rawls claims that some forms of inequalities may still be just: they are just if they are to the benefit of the least well off. Under such a principle, injustice is not simply equated with inequality, but with inequalities that are not to the benefit of all, or which are unacceptable to the representative man who gets the smallest share. Rawls uses the example of comparing the initial life prospects of an entrepreneurial man in a property-owning democracy with that of an unskilled labourer. He says, "What, then, can possibly justify this kind of initial inequality in life prospects? According to the difference principle, it is justifiable only if the difference in expectation is to the advantage of the representative man who is worse of, in this case the representative unskilled worker." (*TJ* pg.68) For Rawls, then, justice does not have to involve absolute equality. But it must involve *consensus*. Only if it is agreeable to all can it be considered fair. The Original Position is the thought-experiment with which Rawls believes people would achieve consensus. The Difference Principle provides the incentive which, he claims, would make people willing to accept certain inequalities, and which would motivate them to maximise the overall wealth of the society in which they will live.

Unique problems arise when future generations are factored in. Rawls says that the question of justice between generations "subjects any ethical theory to severe if not impossible tests." (*TJ* pg. 251) But that does not mean that normative expressions of moral principle cannot be formulated at all. The most common expression of intergenerational justice is the claim of intergenerational impartiality: no single generation, including one's own, has more right than any other to claim access to the world's resources. The distribution principle, which claims that the just basic structure of society is one which favours the least advantaged, applies to future generations in that the difference principle must account for the long-term prospects of the least favoured group in the distribution. To distribute social values not only among individuals within a single generation, but also between different generations, each generation must save some social values (resources, technology, knowledge, achievements of culture, etc.) for the next generation. This requires a 'just savings principle'. Rawls says,

> Each generation must not only preserve the gains of culture and civilisation, and maintain intact those just institutions that have been established, but it must also put aside in each period of time a suitable amount of real capital accumulation. This saving may take various forms from net investment in machinery and other means of production to investment in learning and education. (*TJ* pg.252)

Rawls claims that the problem of determining how much to save for future generations can be solved by referring back to the original position. Individuals in the original position have complete information about the type of society they will be a part of, but no information about what position in it they will occupy; Rawls adds that the veil of ignorance also prevents knowledge of what place in history they will have. They will not know how far their society has developed technologically, economically, socially, artistically, or politically, nor will they know what resources will be available. One's place in history is considered among the contingent or accidental characteristics and circumstances which we are to overcome in order to produce a principle of justice more objectively. As one's place in history is such a contingent circumstance, it follows that the living, present generation cannot give preference to its own interests and needs over the interests and needs of other generations. The preference for one's own time must be rejected from the start, or else no principle of just savings can be formulated. Justice among generations must be "governed by the same conception of justice that regulates the co-operation of contemporaries". (*TJ* pg.257) A just savings principle can be thought of as the requirement for each generation to take on its fair share of the responsibility to preserve a just society.

Rawls rejects the idea that the original position contains within it representatives or members of every generation who will ever live. In the original position, one bargains only with one's contemporaries. Rawls says that the original position "is not to be thought of as a general assembly which includes at one moment everyone who will live at some time; or, much less, as an assembly of everyone who could live at some time"; this would "stretch fantasy too far".[4] A just savings principle "cannot literally be adopted democratically", presumably because the members of preceding and subsequent generations are not bargaining with one's own generation in the original position. But Rawls claims that it is not necessary to bargain with members of other generations because:

> ...the conception of the original position achieves the same result. Since no one knows to which generation he belongs, the question is viewed from the standpoint of each [generation] and a fair accommodation is expressed by the principle adopted. All generations are virtually represented in the original position, since the same principle would always be chosen. (*TJ* pg.256)

The idea is that anyone should be able to adopt the original position at any time. Any generation could adopt Rawlsian principles of justice. Members of other generations need not be present in the original position since, in the original position, behind a veil of ignorance concerning which generation one will belong to, one will arrive at a just savings principle which is advantageous for all generations.

The just savings principle is the claim that justice must somehow involve saving certain "primary social goods" for subsequent generations. The just savings principle must include a rate or a schedule of savings, defining how much is to be saved for the future. Rawls states at the outset that "it is not possible, at present anyway, to define precise limits on what the rate of savings should be. How the burden of capital accumulation and of raising the standard of civilisation and culture is to be shared between generations seems to admit of no definite answer." (*TJ* pg.252-3)[5] But as noted, this does not mean that no moral principle of justice across generations can be produced at all. A further difficulty in formulating a just savings principle is the disparity of power between present and future generations: as noted early in chapter one, there can be no real exchange or reciprocity between ourselves in the present time and the people of the future. Our activities today will have an impact on their living conditions, and we will receive from them neither their thanks nor their protest. Rawls says the parties bargaining with each other in the original position:

> ...try to piece together a just savings schedule by
> balancing how much they would be willing to save
> for their more immediate descendants against what
> they would feel entitled to claim of their more
> immediate predecessors. Thus imagining themselves
> to be fathers, say, they are to ascertain how much they
> should set aside for their sons and grandsons by
> noting what they would believe themselves entitled to
> claim of their fathers and grandfathers. (*TJ* pg.255-6)

This outlines the basics of Rawls' position on justice towards future generations. Because of Rawls' well-known opposition to Utilitarianism (to be examined in the discourse to follow), he is often taken to be a kind of Deontologist. However, there is reason to believe he is not. David Miller claims that the two parts of Rawls' second principle of justice "are not distributive principles in the same strong sense as ordinary principles of justice. They do not specify some property of the individual which will determine what his share of society's goods shall be… in this respect the contractual theory of justice resembles utilitarianism." Furthermore, "although Rawls' theory is not strictly aggregative, because it does not allow the few to be deprived to obtain a greater balance of happiness for the many, it is not distributive either since it contains no principles directly prescribing an allocation of benefits and burdens to persons.".[6] Miller's implication is that Rawls' position is a disguised form of Utilitarianism. However, the non-aggregative nature of Rawls' position places it in opposition to Utilitarianism, and this cannot be swept under the rug. It is what makes the theory distinct. It would be closer to the truth to say that Rawls's theory of Justice is neither Deontological nor Utilitarian, but rather a theory which bears some features of both theories and in many ways stands between them.

§ 2. Environmental Circumstances of Justice

I emphasised from the beginning that for Rawls, as for other philosophers in his tradition, justice is a social principle. How animals, plants, landscapes and ecosystems are treated is not necessarily irrelevant to justice, but they are is not the central concern. The central concern of justice is the structure of society and how people treat people. The thought-experiment of the original position clearly stipulates that the people bargaining with each other for a fair distribution of social goods behind the veil of ignorance are all members of a social or political community. Rawls claims that his theory of justice is not a complete theory covering the whole of ethics: one of the missing pieces is right conduct towards "animals and the rest of nature" for which "no account is given". Rawls further explains:

> Certainly, it is wrong to be cruel to animals and the destruction of a whole species can be a great evil. The capacity for feelings of pleasure and pain and for the forms of life of which animals are capable clearly

imposes duties of compassion and humanity in their case. I shall not attempt to explain these considered beliefs. They are outside the scope of the theory of justice, and it does not seem possible to extend the contract doctrine so as to include them in a natural way. (*TJ* pg.448)

It is fairly clear from this statement that justice is an exclusively anthropocentric principle. Still it should be possible to formulate a theory of environmental justice without retrofitting ecocentric principles on to the general framework. I shall assume, then, that the people in the original situation, although they do not know who they will be, do know that they will be people. They know that they will not be animals or plants. They know that they will inhabit a human political and social world characterised by the various facts of human society that Rawls allows them to know. They know this because the Original Position is a theoretical position which a *person* (and not an animal or plant) adopts in order to consider problems of just distribution.

It need not follow from this that no provisions at all are to be made for the landscape. It follows only that any provisions for landscapes made on the basis of justice will be made for the sake of the human community. The principle of distribution is a good point of reference for environmental ethics, for the kind of wrong that is often said to be involved in environmental problems is the injustice of being deprived of certain environmental resources, such as clean air and water, arable land, certain non-renewable energy supplies like petroleum, and so on. Human life and culture, and even a basic standard of dignity, depend in large measure upon the availability of these and other environmental goods. Most of the primary goods which Rawls mentions are goods which emerge from social relations: opportunities, legal protections, material wealth, and so on. Clearly, environmental goods like raw materials, land territory, and so on, do not emerge from social relations. They emerge from the landscape. How, then, can they be subject to principles of justice? There are three obvious ways. (1) Rights of access, ownership, use, and disposal of environmental resources clearly do emerge from social relations. We can assume that the distribution of these rights can be subject to principles of justice, although that is not the same thing as saying that a natural resource should count as a social good. But it is a plausible, if indirect, way of subjecting the distribution of environmental resources to principles of justice. (2) Environmental resources, once appropriated from the landscape, become part of the society's total wealth and so part of the social goods which are subject to principles of just distribution. This too is plausible, although again it is not the same as saying that environmental goods are social goods. It says that environmental goods are first transformed into social goods by the input of human labour, and then become subject to principles of justice once they are so transformed. (3) We could regard the resources of the earth as primary 'natural' goods, rather than as 'social' goods. It seems obvious that society benefits from the availability of natural goods. Although they do not emerge from our social relations, their existence and our use of them is what makes all social relations possible. We can therefore claim that natural goods can and should be distributed much the same way social goods can be. These three ways of subjecting the use and distribution of environmental resources are all plausible in their own way, and it should be noted that they are not exclusive of each other. On the basis of any one of them, we can claim that the distribution of environmental resources can be subject to principles of justice.

As environmental policy choices, Depletion and Conservation are also distribution choices. A society that chooses Depletion appropriates for itself the greatest share of the world's environmental resources, typically at the expense of other societies, both in the present and in the future. Conservation appropriates fewer resources, and Preservation appropriates almost none at all. Could we object to the Repugnant Conclusion by claiming that the generation which chooses Depletion takes more resources from the landscape than it has a right to take? Rawls claims, as we have seen, that an unequal distribution of social goods is justified if it maximises the size of the smallest share, and thus makes the lot of the worse-off better than it would have been. We find this principle in John Locke's justification for unequal distribution of wealth, as well as in the modern economic principle which has come to be known as "trickle-down theory". Could it be the case that a society may justifiably enrich itself by choosing Depletion if the choice makes life better off for its poorest members, and helps enrich poor nations as well?

To put the case in context: Ireland, while not one of the world's wealthiest nations, has become much more affluent and the standard of living enjoyed by most of its citizens compares favourably to the standard of living enjoyed by citizens of the world's leading industrial and commercial nations. This rapid economic growth has come to be called "the Celtic Tiger", a name reminiscent of the economic growth of the "Five Asian Tigers" which experienced double-digit economic growth for most of the 1980's. However these years of economic growth also saw considerable increases in the amount of pollution produced, for both the Asian Tigers and for Ireland. Consider:

> *Ireland's Kyoto Target.* In 1992 Ireland signed the United Nations Framework Convention on Climate Change, also known as the Kyoto Protocol, and ratified it in 1994. By ratifying this agreement, Ireland committed itself to an allowable increase in carbon dioxide emissions of no more than 13%. That limit is already well exceeded. The Organisation for Economic Co-operation and Development predicted that Ireland's CO_2 output will increase 63% between 1990 and 2010 (roughly 484% above the Kyoto target).[7]

Ireland has thus appropriated more shares of the world's waste assimilation capacity than the agreed-upon allotment. A Rawlsian might argue that, while this failure to meet the Kyoto Protocol target is a breach of agreed-upon contractual obligations, it is justified if it makes the condition of the least well-off party better than it would otherwise be.

At present, there can be no doubt that environmental goods are distributed with radical inequality. Wealthy nations have more food, more minerals and metals, more oil and gas, and so on, and they produce more than their fair share of waste. That is to say, they appropriate more shares of the Earth's waste-assimilation capacity than poor nations do. Expressed as purely economic figures, the gap between the rich and the poor is staggeringly wide:

> *World wealth distribution.* It was estimated in 1990 that
> the top 20% of the world's population possessed
> 82.7% of the world's Gross National Product, 81.9%
> of world trade, 94.6% of all commercial lending,
> 80.6% of all domestic savings, and 94.0% of all
> research and development.[8] By the year 1997 there
> were 447 billionaires who owned more wealth than
> the total annual income of half of the rest of the
> world.[9] A journalist described this disparity in a
> particularly dramatic way. The difference between
> the Republic of Tanzania, and Goldman Sachs, is that
> one is an African country that makes US $2.2 billion
> per annum and distributes it among its 25 million
> citizens. The other is an investment bank that made a
> profit of US $2.6 billion in 1992 and distributed it
> among its 161 shareholders.[10]

A good case can be made, on the basis of evidence like this, that Rawlsian principles have failed us. Their application to economic practice has not in fact improved the condition of the worse-off person. Singer, taking a global view, holds this position. He points out that the guiding justification for unequal use of the atmosphere as a sink for waste gas has never been fulfilled in practice. The example he gives is the use of the atmosphere by rich nations as a global sink for their waste gases, where he says:

> ...the [Rawlsian] argument does not work, because
> many of the world's poorest people, whose shares of

the atmosphere's capacity have been appropriated by the industrialised nations, are not able to partake in the benefits of this increased productivity in the industrialised nations—they cannot afford to buy its products—and if rising sea levels inundate their farm lands, or cyclones destroy their homes, they will be much worse off than they would otherwise have been.[11]

Singer is a Utilitarian, and part of his reason for discussing the Difference Principle is to describe its weakness. The Difference Principle, and similar justifications for inequality, has been the argument cited by rich nations to justify their appropriation of the lion's share of the world's environmental wealth.[12] Since the facts are that the unequal distribution of resources has not improved the well-being of the worse-off, but has actually worsened their lot, Singer claims that the principle itself must be abandoned. Certainly, we should not pretend that the facts are other than what they are. A Rawlsian, on being confronted with the evidence, could claim that our practical applications of the principle have failed us, but not the principle itself. If Depletion does not in fact maximise the minimum share, therefore people in the original position would not choose it. They would choose one of the two alternatives, which are Conservation and Preservation.

We have, here, a first tentative confirmation of my working hypothesis. We have as well the prospect that the Difference Principle may be an acceptable environmental ethic, despite its deliberate exclusion of plants, non human animals, and ecosystems. It explains what is morally wrong with causing environmental disasters. But would this confirmation also obtain across future generations? As an extension of the hypothesis, we can claim the following. One generation's excessive use of the atmosphere as a sink for waste gases, to the point of excluding future generations from being able to use the atmosphere the same way themselves, would worsen the lot of future generations, not improve it in some other, compensatory way. Pollution and pollution-induced climate disasters would render future generations less able, or even unable, to benefit from the wealth created by the previous generation(s). We could also claim, as part of the hypothesis, that it is unjust for one generation to receive so much from its predecessors only to leave little (or nothing) to its successors.

Some forms of resources are renewable, and so one generation's use of them would not deprive future generations of their entitlement to use the same resource. But each generation must restrain its use of the resource so as not to undermine its capacity for renewal; not to do so would be an injustice to the people of the future. Consider:

> *The North Atlantic Cod Fisheries.* The World Wildlife Federation has warned that the world's stock of cod fish may disappear completely by the year 2020. Global catch declined from 3.1 million tonnes in 1970 to 950,000 tonnes in 2000. North America's cod catch declined 90% since the 1980's, and Europe's catch declined 25% in the same period.[13] Ireland's fishing industry was recently accused of fraudulently under-reporting catch records, falsifying log books, and ignoring EU quotas, in order to catch more fish and return greater profits.[14]

An investigation is underway. If it concludes that the allegations are true, the implication for justice is that the Irish fishermen were appropriating more than their share of the cod fishery, thus depriving other nations and future generations of their entitlement. Consider also:

> *The Canadian Cod Fishery.* In 1993, Canada voluntarily shut down its entire Atlantic cod fishing industry to prevent over-fishing. Nearly 70% of the population of Newfoundland, Canada's poorest province, lost their jobs due to the closure of the industry. Then in 1994, the Canadian Navy arrested and impounded a

Portugese fishing boat that was trawling for cod in international waters. Canada had effectively imposed on to Portugal its voluntary abdication of its share of the North Atlantic cod fishery.

I was living in Newfoundland at the time. I went to the harbour to see the Portugese boat being towed in by the Coast Guard. A large and angry crowd had assembled there, and the Portugese crew was kept below deck by the Navy sailors to protect them from the stones and eggs the crowd was throwing. This event caused a minor international scandal: the Canadians had effectively taken the role of an international police force to protect the cod stocks. In the light of the predicted world-wide collapse of the cod fishery, this highly controversial action may turn out to be exactly the sort of thing which must be done to protect the capacity of renewable resources to replenish themselves, and so ensure that future generations receive their share of those resources. The injustice to the Portugese fisherman, the temporary denial of their entitlement to fish cod in international waters, may turn out to be much less than the injustice to the people of the future who would be permanently deprived of their share of the cod fishery if nothing had been done about over-fishing.

If this hypothesis is to stand as an acceptable environmental ethic, the situation of pollution and depravation must be the kind of situation in which the virtue of justice is called for. Is Parfit's "Depletion" case an example of what Rawls would call "a circumstance of justice"? I shall take some time to discuss this question since, as shall be shown, in the doctrine of the circumstances of justice there are grounds for holding that distributive justice cannot be applied to the problem of future generations. This doctrine is the claim that the need for justice arises in conditions of social conflict between equals or near-equals. On the one hand, these conditions of conflict give rise to the need for justice to provide a solution, and on the other hand they are within the ability of justice to solve. In Rawls' words:

> [The] circumstances of justice obtain whenever
> persons put forward conflicting claims to the division
> of social advantages under conditions of moderate
> scarcity. Unless these circumstances existed there
> would be no occasion for the virtue of justice, just as
> in the absence of threats of injury to life and limb
> there would be no occasion for physical courage. (*TJ*
> pg. 110)

In principle, a situation is a circumstance of justice if it is a situation of conflicting claims put forward by parties bargaining with each other from positions of near or approximate social symmetry. One such situation is the circumstance of 'moderate scarcity', the condition of resources which "are not so abundant that schemes of co-operation become superfluous, nor are conditions so harsh that fruitful ventures must inevitably break down." (*TJ* pg. 110) The possibility and necessity of justice arises to solve conflicting claims of ownership or access to scarce resources. Climate change, global warming, and resource depletion appear to be useful examples of moderate scarcity: as certain important non-renewable resources like petroleum become harder to reach, social conflicts are produced among competing claims to access and to use them. The recent war in Iraq is an example of this. Obviously most of these conflicts are among people contemporaneous with each other. But some of these conflicts are also between temporally separated generations, and in one place in the discussion of the conditions of justice this is what Rawls focuses upon. He takes the claims of future generations to be a special case of duties to third parties (people who are absent from the original position):

> The question arises, however, whether the persons in
> the original position have obligations and duties to
> third parties, for example, to their immediate
> descendants. To say that they do would be one way
> of handling questions of justice between
> generations... we can require the parties to agree to

principles subject to the constraint that they wish all
preceding generations to have followed the very same
principles. By an appropriate combination of such
stipulations, I believe that the whole chain of
generations can be tied together and principles agreed
to that suitably take into account the interests of each.
(*TJ* pg. 111)

Besides moderate scarcity, the other circumstances of justice are
moderate selfishness and relative equality. The circumstance of
moderate selfishness we find in Rawls' principle of rationality, in
which he assumes that the parties in the circumstances of justice are
seeking to maximise their own share (I shall have more to say about
this later). And the circumstance of relative equality is that the
parties are all more or less equals in terms of wealth and power, for
instance they are more or less equally able to retaliate against each
other for alleged wrongdoing. As Rawls says, "their capacities are
similar in that no one among them can dominate the rest". (*TJ* pg.
110) The final thing to note here is that Rawls claims to have
inherited the doctrine from David Hume,[15] for whom justice is a
matter of property and reciprocity.

This doctrine has been criticised from several directions.
One direction, spearheaded by Brian Barry, is that (at least) two of
these three conditions of justice might not necessarily obtain for all
possible generations. At some time in the future, the condition of
moderate scarcity might disappear: some new energy source might
be discovered or invented which makes abundant energy freely
available to all (cold fusion comes to mind as a plausible example),
or alternately some resource might dry up almost completely, leaving
future generations in a condition of acute scarcity, of the kind that
Rawls said would cause 'fruitful ventures' to 'break down'. If that is
true, then intergenerational justice is not possible because the
circumstances of justice do not necessarily obtain for all
generations.[16] Rawls assumes that the parties in the original position
know about the conditions of justice, and aside from various facts
about what human society is generally like, that is all that they know

when behind the veil of ignorance.[17] It follows from this, as Barry explains, that "Rawls is committing himself to the proposition that the circumstances of justice hold in all generations (past, present and future) since the people in the original position do not know what generation they belong to."[18] If moderate scarcity, moderate selfishness and relative equality are the conditions from which the need for justice arises, then intergenerational justice is only possible so long as those conditions obtain. Barry holds that it is always possible that a situation will arise in which one of these conditions does not obtain.[19]

More troublesome than the condition of moderate scarcity is the condition of relative equality. Among contemporaries, if there are two or more parties with conflicting claims to some resource or social good, and one of them was much more socially powerful than the other, let us say a party of able-bodied people and a party of people with disabilities, then so long as the less powerful party can be oppressed then the matter is not an occasion for justice. This clearly runs counter to our moral intuitions. As an illustration of this, Barry asks us to imagine "someone who, asked whether or not South African policies are unjust, replied that the answer would depend on an estimate of the white's ability to hold down the rest of the population indefinitely."[20] Hume also noticed this implication but was not disturbed by it. He claimed that we might be bound to treat the less powerful party with humanity, but never with justice.[21] We have seen this already with Rawls' exclusion of animals, plants, and ecosystems from the Original Position.

Barry's criticism could be countered by claiming that the point of view we should be using is the original position, where obvious inequalities like slavery or poverty do not exist. In the original position, everyone is a free and equal moral person. Rawls' case against racism and discrimination may be taken as the precedent for this: behind the veil of ignorance, no one would know whether he will be black or white, rich or poor, male or female, and so on. Membership in a certain race, class, gender, or culture would be an accidental characteristic which, behind the veil of ignorance, no one could use to secure a special advantage. But if the circumstances of justice only hold in the original position, then they become theoretical rather than practical, and there would appear to be no point in saying that they are the occasions of conflict in the real world which warrant a just solution.

The condition of relative equality, according to Rawls, also underwrites the Just Savings principle. For behind the veil of ignorance we are compelled to reject a preference for one's own time, just as we must reject a preference for one's own race, class, gender, or culture. But in this case, the condition of relative equality cannot possibly obtain, not even in theory. Rawls requires that the parties in the original position are equal in that "no one among them can dominate the rest", among the other ways that they are equal, and yet the forward passage of time ensures that earlier generations are totally invulnerable to, and in many ways able to dominate, later generations. A present generation can do things which affect future generations, supplying them or depriving them of some needed resource, but the future generation reciprocates nothing in return, and neither can it retaliate if it feels it has been cheated. While the circumstance of moderate scarcity might obtain, or not, from time to time (and that is problematic enough), and while wide disparities among contemporaries might be imagined away by the thought-experiment of the original position, there is certainly no equality between members of one generation and a following generation. As Barry says, there is no equality between one generation and its successors.[22] The implication of this claim is that since there is no equality between present and future people, because "time's arrow" points in only one direction, then there is no justice between them either. It is not that there is injustice instead: the claim here is that the principle of justice does not apply. Hendrick Visser T'Hooft, a strong supporter of Barry's position, argued that the case is not only that the conflicting claims for scarce resources are unequal between generations, but that the condition of conflict itself, between relative equals or otherwise, cannot arise:

> Let us admit as a general proposition that a conflict of interests is the necessary occasion for an intervention

of distributive justice. Now a competition for scarce resources does not *exist* between generations unless the presently living generation is willing to grant a claim to future people in the first place. As this willingness derives from its sense of justice, it follows that justice precedes (so to speak) the "circumstances" that are said to be antecedent to it! (*JFGE*, pg. 93)

The claim here is that the power of present people over future people is sufficiently comprehensive that future people cannot have a claim on scarce resources unless present people decide that they do. Again, the circumstances of justice do not obtain, and therefore, so the argument goes, neither does justice itself. If this criticism stands, it will be the case that Rawlsian principles of justice do not offer a satisfactory or acceptable environmental ethic. It will be unable to explain the moral significance of the environment, nor whether it is better to choose Conservation or Depletion, and will be unable to overcome the Non-Identity Problem.

This catalogue of criticisms need not (yet) force the conclusion that my provisional hypothesis is wrong, or that Depletion does not pass the test of the Difference Principle. It is, rather, a reason why actions affecting future generations might have nothing to do with justice, which for my hypothesis is troublesome enough. There might still be other grounds for claiming that the failure to save for future generations is unjust, even if conditions of moderate scarcity or relative equality do not apply.[23] What we can conclude from the foregoing discussion is that such grounds, whatever they are, can not be a straightforward matter of mutual reciprocity. With future generations, no reciprocity is possible. The relation between a predecessor generation and a successor generation is a relation of giving and receiving, but not a relation of direct reciprocation, that is, no direct trades occur. The giving and receiving flows in only one direction; there is no mutuality involved. But there are other conceptions of justice besides that of reciprocity.

What alternatives are there to the Humean conception of justice as reciprocity which can give a strong theory of intergenerational justice? We might, for instance, claim that the parties in the original position know that they will have natural attachments to the members of the generation that follows theirs. Rawls states that there is limited altruism in the original position— the parties' conception of the good is "not presumed to be egoistic or selfish". They may assume that once the veil of ignorance is lifted, they find that they have natural ties to others, for instance ties of affection and sentiment for family members and close friends, or various social and legal responsibilities to others. As a general rule, they are mutually disinterested: "they are not willing to have their interests sacrificed to the others." (*TJ* pg. 111) Ties of altruism and natural affection are suspended in the original position because Rawls wishes to ensure that the principles of justice do not depend on "strong assumptions". The parties in the original position "try to advance their conception of the good as best they can, and that in attempting to do this they are not bound by prior moral ties to each other." (*TJ* pg. 111). But Rawls stipulates that there is a "motivational assumption" with which the parties are presumed to be interested in the welfare of their immediate descendants. The parties know that most of them will find, once the veil of ignorance is lifted, that they are mothers and fathers, and that they love their children. Certainly, they will all find that they are themselves children for part of their lives. A present generation and its descendants thus form "a continuing line of claims. For example, we can assume that they are heads of families and therefore have a desire to further the well-being of at least their more immediate descendants". (*TJ* pg. 111) We might also claim that in seeking for the good of their own children (if not for any other children) they will be seeking for their children not to be killed, harmed, or made to suffer unnecessarily, and so on. They will also be seeking some essentially social goods: litter-free playgrounds and well-appointed schools, for instance. The provision of these social goods tends to require general community co-operation: so, someone behind a veil of ignorance who knows that he will be a father would find it rational to pay his fair share to ensure the provision of social goods for his children, and to compel others to pay their fair share as well.[24] In this way, justice to future generations is taken care of without relying some (impossible) principle of mutual reciprocity, so long as each generation looks after its own successors, and trusts that every other generation will do the same. This "motivational assumption" was developed by John Passmore into what he called "the chain of love", in which the concern and care each generation has for its own children and grandchildren repeats itself with each generation and thus forms an ongoing continuity, like links in a chain.[25] But in the situation Passmore describes, justice is heavily reliant upon emotional sentiment, which a principle of justice should not presuppose.[26] Barry claims that if Passmore is right and intergenerational justice is dependent on ties of caring and sentiment, then it will follow that we do not care about them, it will not be unjust to leave them with nothing.[27] A claim of justice should be binding even on those who have no offspring, or who have no "natural sentiments" for children or for the next generation.

It can thus be seen that Rawls' theory of justice to future generations pulls in opposite directions: on one hand he must assume that the parties in the original position possess natural sentiments in order to make possible an intergenerational justice, but on the other hand he wishes to maintain the detached objectivity of the veil of ignorance. On the one side he has the Humean theory of justice as co-operation for mutual advantage, or reciprocity, and on the other side, Kantian impartiality. The problems with the circumstances of justice arise because of the tension between these two ideas.[28] As Barry says,

> One way of accounting for the complexity and
> difficulty of Rawls' theory of justice is to recognise
> that it is an attempt to incorporate both Hume and
> Kant in a single theoretical structure. Since Hume
> and Kant are commonly, and reasonably, regarded as
> occupying polar positions in moral philosophy it is

hardly surprising if the result of Rawls's endeavours suffers from a certain lack of unity.[29]

This tension, as we will see, always remains close to any attempt to articulate a conception of intergenerational justice. The summary point here is that while Rawls makes it clear that justice is tied to society as a historical entity, as the very notion of a Just Savings schedule and the suspension of preference for one's own time implies, the occasion for justice between generations cannot be accounted for in terms of direct reciprocity among equals.

§ 3. Justice and Temporal Continuity.

T'Hooft suggested a non-reciprocal form of intergenerational justice which he called "Virtual Reciprocity". I take the appearance of the word 'virtual' here to denote something similar to what computer programmers mean when they say 'virtual reality': without invoking any metaphysical concepts, it refers to something which approximates or substitutes for something else that is 'original' or 'real'. Also, I do not take it to refer to an Aristotelian principle of character ethics. Virtual Reciprocity is a special refinement of Rawls' Just Savings schedule. He introduces it with a "camping ground" analogy, as follows:

> ...it is an intuitively convincing idea that hikers
> arriving at a campsite must be able to find it clean and
> with firewood cut and neatly stacked, and that they
> must leave it in the same conditions. The whole
> practice of hiking would be undermined if such rules
> were not observed. This camping ground intuition
> finds a more general form in the idea of responsible
> stewardship, which inspires legal regimes like trust or
> usufruct. One is supposed to maintain a resource at
> such a level that it remains capable of future use by
> others. (*JFGE* pg. 60)

The justice of the camping ground analogy is this: it is just for campers to clean up after themselves, for if all, or most, hikers left their campsites spoiled and useless for other hikers, the activity of hiking would become impossible for everyone. Similarly, the general idea of Virtual Reciprocity is that one generation, receiving a benefit from its predecessor, becomes duty bound to pass on that benefit to the successor generation. "Generation B 'pays' generation A by passing on comparable benefits to generation C." (*JFGE* pg. 60-1) A right to claim something from one person or generation is matched by an obligation to provide something similar to another.

This system has a Kantian flavour: the duty is based on the claim that failure to uphold the duty involved in the practice would "undermine" the practice, and so something like the Kantian test of universalisation is at work here. It can therefore seem unclear what this has to do with reciprocity, even 'virtual' reciprocity. As Barry claims, simply receiving a benefit does not by itself create an obligation to pass on a similar benefit.[30] Barry's more general contention that Rawlsian Just Savings principle unsuccessfully marries Humean and Kantian principles also obtains here. But T'Hooft asserts that there is more going on in a robust principle of intergenerational virtual reciprocity. In his words:

> There must have been something more: the intention
> to start an intergenerational practice that is to the
> good of all subsequent generations, since it
> establishes a pattern of passing on benefits in the
> absence of which no generation would be able to
> *expect* those benefits from its predecessor generation.
> So generation B doesn't "just" receive benefits from
> generation A: it receives them in its capacity of first
> beneficiary of a practice... (*JFGE* pg. 61)

Here, 'virtual reciprocity' is the claim that when one generation passes on social goods like environmental resources to future generations, the transfer happens in the context of a practice, or something equivalent, in which goods are transferred together with

120

the understanding that they are to be transferred again; the transfer is contingent upon the recipient party understanding that this practice is in place. The 'virtual' element of Virtual Reciprocity is the duty to reciprocate a benefit received although not necessarily to the same party from whom the benefit was received; and the 'reciprocity' element is the claim that the practice is initiated with the presumption that it would be mutually advantageous to everyone. The crucial premise is this: without the practice in place, a recipient generation would have no reason to expect or demand anything from its predecessors. An incentive thus exists for a generation to continue the practice. This would be an acceptable form of Just Savings principle, and a confirmation of my working hypothesis. Depletion is wrong because the generation that chooses Depletion obtains a special benefit for its members by participating in a practice without doing its own fair share to perpetuate that practice. The example of the camping ground is one instance of this. The whole range of things that we do which can loosely be called 'development' and 'progress', of which scientific research is the paradigm, also exemplifies this principle. We receive and benefit from a body of developed knowledge from our predecessors, and we contribute to it while passing it on to future generations. We would not receive anything from previous generations if they did not do the same.

But what incentive would the first generation in the sequence have for starting it? Initiating such a practice apparently carries no benefit or advantage in itself. There might be a strong duty to start the practice if it has not already been started, but what would be its rationale? One possibility is the Kantian test of universalisation; a natural first place to look since T'Hooft expresses the practice of Virtual Reciprocity in loosely Kantian terms. If no generation initiated the practice, then no generation would be able to expect or demand anything from its predecessors. Therefore, in the original position of not knowing which generation one belongs to, and thus faced with the possibility that one's own generation is the first generation, one would have to initiate the practice.

This rationale is not completely satisfactory. It brings to the foreground the tension between the Humean conception of justice as reciprocity and the Kantian conception of justice as universal hypothetical assent.[31] It is beyond the scope of this chapter to resolve this tension. But I shall say that, leaving this tension aside, the Kantian solution ignores the possibility that the parties bargaining behind the veil of ignorance may already know that they are not the first generation: they know this precisely because they are bargaining about how to distribute resources and social goods already received from their predecessors. The rationale of a practice provides an incentive for *continuing* the practice, but not for *initiating* it, so long as it is connected with the Humean conception of reciprocity.

Furthermore, this principle will not be very helpful if we find that we are the recipients of a practice of environmental destruction. A previous generation may have reasoned that its own interests matter more than any other generation's interests, and, assuming that every generation would reason similarly, made something like Depletion into its Just Savings schedule. A present generation, receiving very little from its predecessors and seeing the precedent for resource hoarding and conspicuous consumption, may believe that future people have no entitlement to claim anything more from them. Therefore, they too make Depletion into their Just Savings schedule, as do their successors, and so on. It seems clear that even if each generation understood it was receiving goods from predecessors in terms of a practice of Virtual Reciprocity, it might find itself partaking in a practice which in the long run did not maximise the smallest share, and which in the future inadvertently creates the world of the Repugnant Conclusion. Clearly, then, the rationale for continuing a practice for Virtual Reciprocity, while strong, is not by itself an acceptable statement of environmental ethics. We must be concerned not only for what reasons may exist for initiating a practice of Virtual Reciprocity, but also what kind of Virtual Reciprocity practice we have cause to initiate.

Another possible rationale for initiating Virtual Reciprocity could be the proviso of John Locke to leave "as much and as good" for others when taking resources from nature. [32] For Locke this proviso is grounded in a theological claim: God gave nature to all of humankind, and so when one exercises his God-given right to make use of the resources of nature, one must respect that others possess the same right to do likewise.[33] God initiated the practice, so we need not worry about initiating it ourselves. This duty would be sufficiently rooted in the present. Also, we can assume that Locke would not approve of causing environmental disasters, for he says "Nothing was made by God for man to spoil or destroy".[34] But I would prefer, if possible, not to rely on the complex and controversial metaphysics of a variety of religion. To introduce the idea of God into the picture also introduces too many other complex questions, not the least of which is the question of whether God exists, and whether he (!) is what we think he is. And the final conclusion of this study of justice should be acceptable to those committed to other religions, or committed to no religion. It is generally good philosophical practice to have as few background assumptions as possible. We cannot, therefore, rely on Lockean principles for a rationale to initiate a practice of virtual reciprocity across generations.

The rationale preferred by T'Hooft for both partaking in, and if necessary initiating, a practice of virtual reciprocity, is in the claim that the future generations "figure into the present meaning of things". We will be able to find the rationale for intergenerational justice, he asserts, not by trying to overcome the one-sided imbalance of power the present generation holds over the future, which both T'Hooft and Barry claim is insurmountable, but instead by finding the way(s) in which one's present picture of the future is worthwhile to one's present life. In T'Hooft's words:

> …what we are concerned with when we want to
> secure equal opportunities for future generations is to
> make room for our own experience of the good, by
> giving it a future it cannot do without.
> Intergenerational justice takes on the character of an
> instrument for keeping open a sufficient spectrum of

life options across time. This instrumental role makes it serve a wider aim than it has by itself. (*JFGE* pg. 100)

To establish this principle, T'Hooft first of all presents the case for why the parties behind the veil of ignorance know that they are members of a present-time generation. He claims that it is impossible for the parties in the original position to suspend the knowledge that they are living beings inhabiting a present time. "If we consider the original position as a thought experiment which one must actually be capable of making in order to test the social arrangements of real life, it is impossible to let the veil of ignorance fall over that very primal piece of knowledge which consists in being alive, i.e. of belonging to the living generation." (*JFGE* pg. 101). While the parties in the original position may not know *which* generation in their society's history they belong to, as required by Rawls' suspension of a preference for one's own time, they can know that the generation they belong to will be a *present* generation. [35] For we live "within time", and the very expression "future generation" does not have any meaning for us unless it is in reference to the present time of the speaker. The terms "past" and "future" cannot have meaning unless the "present" is fully presupposed.[36] But as a present generation, they seek temporal continuity and permanence for the things that are of value to them, especially including the society in which they live. T'Hooft says,

> ...there is a natural understanding of society as an ongoing reality; the search for continuity is woven in a self-evident way into most of our social practices and institutions, or even characterises their meaning. Let me mention (inter alia) the family, education, saving (investment), legal regulation, the pursuit of political stability, or the conservation of monuments and other artistic products. Because of the pervasive presence of time, its very being is for society

equivalent to surviving, caring for things going on.
(*JFGE* pg. 114)

Justice, which has as its object the articulation of what is fair and right in the social co-existence of individuals,[37] is for T'Hooft already bound together with conceptions of time and continuity, and this provides the social context in which relations between present and future generations are to be properly understood. In order to *be* a generation, although one does not know which one, one must already know that there are predecessors and successors. A present generation is motivated to initiate and/or sustain a practice of inter-generation Just Savings (or "Virtual Reciprocity") because that is already part of what it means for individuals to socially co-exist with each other through time.

For this idea to work, T'Hooft depends heavily on the principle of "trans-generational communitarian justice" articulated by Avner de-Shalit in Why Posterity Matters. De-Shalit's principle is a reflection, on the institutional plane, of the personal and psychological aspiration to transcend one's limitations. Since we are temporal and historical beings, it will follow that any particular human society is a temporal and historical reality as well. De-Shalit argues that the notion of 'community' extends across several generations and into the future.[38] We may be able to transcend our present time by participating in institutions that will continue to exist beyond our deaths. The bonds of connectivity which, according to de-Shalit, obtain between the members of a trans-generational community are not those of 'a chain of love'; like Rawls, de-Shalit does not want to found justice on ties of sentiment.[39] Rather, the bonds of the trans-generational community are, according to him, connecting ties of "moral similarity". We expect, or assume, that the values of the future generations will be similar to our own.

How can we know that a future generation's moral opinions will be similar to one's own? De-Shalit claims that present people project their intentions into the future. A present person 'constitutes' himself by continuities of intentions.[40] This continuity of intentions connects a present self with his past and future selves, and need not be "doomed" when one dies:

> There is no reason to think of death as the point
> where our future selves cease to exist: if the notion of
> continuity is based on the fact that our future selves
> respond to our present selves, intentions, and desires,
> then posthumous situations, which respond to our
> intentions and desires, can be considered as some
> kind of continuity as well. In short, I find it very
> difficult to see a precise reason why the fulfilment of
> one's desires and intentions should stop when one
> dies. (*WPM* pg. 39)

Note that de-Shalit clarifies that this posthumous extension of the continuity of one's intentions "is a psychological rather than a metaphysical argument." (*WPM* pg. 39). The argument here is that the continuity of intentions which for de-Shalit forms the basis of the unity of one's selfhood over time can be enriched and strengthened by an investment in future good. A part of one's identity in the present is what one expects will come of one's actions, ideas, and choices in the future, even after one's death. To this, T'Hooft adds only that part of what it means to value something is to want the things that one values to have a future. A present generation's intention to project its values into the future is, for T'Hooft and de-Shalit, sufficient incentive for a present generation to initiate a Just Savings schedule and/or a practice of Virtual Reciprocity.

I observe the following about this particular rationale for obligations of justice to future generations. It is not an argument for why they are entitled to receive a savings of primary social goods from us. It says nothing about what rights, qualities, or endowments they possess which enable them to claim a just share of our resources. Nor is it an argument that we owe duties to them. It is an argument for why it may be part of a present person's good to project his values and intentions into the future. This is, in my view, an intuitively appealing idea. But I am not sure what it has to do with *justice*. For no theory of justice can tell us why we ought to have sentiments for our children and grandchildren. Similarly, justice cannot tell us why children should have sentiments for their parents and grandparents. If it is 'natural' that we have these sentiments, then there is no need for justice to provide a reason for us to have them. And a theory of justice would not be able to tell us whether these sentiments are indeed natural. We would have to go outside the bounds of justice theory to find that answer. And that is precisely what both T'Hooft and de-Shalit did. They found the conceptual resources they needed in the hermeneutics of selfhood provided by Alasdair MacIntyre's Virtue theory, whose concepts of practices, traditions, and "Narrative Selfhood" were cited favourably by both scholars. While this is not an unwarranted or illegitimate move in my view, it is not a means of overcoming the one-sidedness of the power inequality between temporally separated generations which both T'Hooft and de-Shalit apparently take it to be.

De-Shalit says that through the projection of one's continuity of intentions into the future, one "interacts" with the intergenerational community. (*WPM* pp. 40-50).[41] This may very well be a kind of communication, like a letter sealed in a box that is not opened for many years, or even for centuries. But it is not in any way an *interaction*: the future generations do not communicate back to us. T'Hooft considers the possibility that the project of making a future for one's values "is not just a question of posthumous reputation… the real issue is whether or not a work is an achievement, that is, whether it deserves recognition, and that, indeed, may be something which only future generations will be in a position to decide. So future generations can benefit us or harm us". (*JFGE* pg. 123-4) This can be interpreted as saying that future generations benefit or harm our projects, intentions, values, and other things transmitted to them, and insofar as they continue to be "ours" after our death, they benefit or harm "us". As an attempt to overcome the one-sidedness of power inequality between temporally separated generations, it is like a new form of the ancient principle that has come to be known as Wisdom of Solon, which is that no one is to be counted as happy until he is dead, for it is not until then that the whole of his life can be assessed. Aristotle's own counter-argument against Solon is applicable here also: we should not wait for the judgement of future people to know whether we have done right by them, just as we do not wait for their judgement to know whether our lives were happy. We should be able to discern this on our own, during our lifetimes.

At the close of this line of enquiry, what is the state of my working hypothesis, that Depletion is a failure of the Just Savings principle? So far, it is holding up rather well, but there is one troublesome place in its groundwork. The groundwork runs as follows. Rawls' Just Savings Schedule is the practice of Virtual Reciprocity. Any generation benefits enormously from participating in the practice; foremost among the benefits is a rationale for expecting or demanding social goods from predecessors. We may also speculate that a generation might suffer if its predecessors saved the wrong things. This practice can be formulated in a deontological cast: paraphrasing Rawls, each generation gives to the future what it believes it would be entitled to receive from its past. The troublesome place is in the incentive to initiate the practice. Any generation may have a wish to put its values and intentions in a framework that extends beyond the lifetime of its members. This wish is interesting and compelling, but appears to have little or nothing to do with justice, and so justice is unable to provide a rationale for initiating the Just Savings schedule using its own principles. This difficulty might be mitigated or eliminated if there was a "Right Intention" principle, able to separate what values and intentions would be right to project into the future from those which would be wrong. Neither Rawls, de-Shalit nor T'Hooft attempted to do this. Now, it appears that the Kantian principle does not require a defeat or a revision of the one-sidedness of power inequality between temporally separated generations, as a principle of Humean reciprocity does. In that respect it is the stronger of the two, and so I will explore it in Chapter 3. I also believe the "teleological" hermeneutic of selfhood introduced here deserves to be revisited on its own terms, and this shall be done in Chapters 4 and 5. A "Right

Intention" principle of the kind demanded here shall be suggested in Chapter 5, where it shall be called "The Gift of the Future".

I believe my working hypothesis is not rendered impossible or groundless by the mere act of importing something from another branch of philosophy into its foundation. The import warrants only the claim that justice doesn't tell the whole story of ethics by itself, which at any rate none of the authors here studied would deny. I therefore need not delay any further before putting it to the test of the Non-Identity Problem. In so doing, one central presupposition comes to the surface. Rawls, de-Shalit, and T'Hooft all took it for granted that future generations will eventually and inevitably exist.[42] The Non-Identity Problem puts that presupposition into doubt by the way it examines the choices and circumstances that bring a future generation into being. It is probably a safe assumption that no generation will ever collectively agree to stop reproducing. But that is not what the Non-Identity Problem renders questionable. What the Non-Identity Problem questions is our ability to know the identities of the people of the future. For any deontological theory of ethics, duties are owed to persons. We must therefore be able to identify who they are.

§ 4. Justice *contra* Utilitarianism.

As is well known, Rawls' Theory of Justice was originally written with the explicit purpose of providing a strong and challenging alternative to Utilitarianism. The famous passage where the critique of Utilitarianism is expressed with the greatest force appears early on:

> This [Utilitarian] view of social co-operation is the consequence of extending to society the principle of choice for one man, and then, to make this extension work, conflating all persons into one through the imaginative acts of the impartial sympathetic spectator. Utilitarianism does not take seriously the distinction between persons. (*TJ* pg. 24)

The claim made here is that when a Utilitarian distributes happiness, he does so in a way that does not account for the separateness and uniqueness of persons. The Utilitarian, as Rawls explains, considers how placing a cost or a burden on himself at one time can be justified by a benefit to be received at another time, and then applies this to society as a whole. While Rawls affirms "it is right for a society to maximise the net balance of satisfaction taken over all of its members" (*TJ* pg. 23), it remains unjust to benefit one person at the expense of another. This contrast between Rawlsian Justice and Utilitarianism also appears in the matter of intergenerational justice. A Rawlsian goods-distributor rejects a preference for his own time, since in the original position he would not know what his own time is, and so he would want a fair distribution of social goods for all generations. But Rawls contends that is not enough: it is still necessary in Rawls' view to overcome the Utilitarian claim that one generation can receive greater benefits if it compensates for another generation's sacrifices. Rawls rejects this for the following reason:

> The utilitarian doctrine may direct us to demand
> heavy sacrifices of the poorer generations for the sake
> of greater advantages for later ones that are far better
> off. But this calculus of advantages, which balances
> the losses of some against the benefits to others,
> appear even less justified in the case of generations
> than among contemporaries. Even if we cannot
> define a precise just savings principle, we should be
> able to avoid this sort of extreme. (*TJ* pg. 253)

Parfit, replying to Rawls in <u>Reasons and Persons</u>, found himself compelled to agree in principle to the doctrine of the separateness of persons: "It is clearly a mistake to ignore the fact that we live different lives. And mankind is not a super-organism". (*R&P* pg. 331.) Parfit claims in response that the Reductionist view of personal identity can justify one's overlooking the separateness of persons.[43] When a Rawlsian considers some system of distribution, he imagines that he will be one of the people affected without knowing whom; a Parfitian Reductionist, on the other hand, takes a detached view, imagining not that the affected people are to be treated as though they are one person, but rather imagining that he will not be one of the affected people (*R&P* pg. 331). Harms and benefits matter, according to this view, but the persons experiencing them (strangely enough!) do not. As an example, if some burden is to be imposed on a child, it can be justified if a benefit will be conferred on someone to compensate; and on Parfit's view, it does not matter whether the person who receives the compensating benefit is the same person in adult life, or someone else.[44] Indeed Parfit argues that if the same person receives the compensating benefit later in life, the effect may be no different than the effect of conferring the benefit on someone else. For one implication of the Reductionist view is that the various parts of a person's life can be treated like separate lives. As he says, "We may regard some events within a person's life as, in certain ways, like birth or death. Not in all ways, for beyond these events the person has earlier or later selves. But it may be only one out of the series of selves which is the object of some of our emotions, and to which we apply some of our principles." (*R&P* pg. 328).[45]

While it is not the purpose of this study to assess and to judge Parfit's Reductionist view of personal identity, it remains important to draw out the background accounts of personhood behind each respective moral theory. For any Deontologist, duties are owed *to persons*, and not to impersonal experiences like harm and benefit, for which reason the separateness between persons is important. This explains why, when T'Hooft and de-Shalit found it necessary to articulate a theory of selfhood, they did not articulate a Reductionist theory. Because Parfit holds the Reductionist view, he does not quite confront the force of Rawls' basic objection to Utilitarianism. On one level, it is a straw man: Rawls does not anywhere claim that Utilitarians treat humanity as though it is a super-organism (although another scholar whom Parfit considers certainly does).[46] Rawls does claim that Utilitarians maximise goods and benefits in a way that treats the differences between persons as unimportant. Parfit does not deny this; in fact he champions it. Reductionism, Parfit claims, is a theory of personal identity in which the differences between people are 'less deep', or less morally relevant.[47] This serves to bring people together, he says, and to give them more incentive to care about one another.[48] But there is one place where, ironically, Parfit also insists that something very like the separateness of persons is vital. It is in the claim that the people born after one Non-Identity choice are separate from the people born after another such choice. The separateness of the Depletion people from the Conservation people is not a matter of degree. It is a total non-identity (hence why the problem is so named). The non-identity between them is the very reason why he claims that Non-Identity problems arise. The Depletion people are not identical with the Conservation people; the alternative for them is non-existence, and not existence as Conservation people. Here, if not elsewhere in Parfit's theory, an appeal to the Reductionist view of personal identity will not lessen or reduce the separateness of persons—or to be more specific, it will not lessen or reduce the separateness of those who will be created as a result of Non-Identity choices.

As stated, deontology requires that duties are owed to persons, and so we must be able to identify who they are. When future generations are taken into account, this becomes a problem. If we say we have a duty to leave a just savings of social goods for future people, then we have a duty to future persons themselves. But as observed by Narveson, who considered whether there is a duty to procreate and to ensure the continuation of the human race, an unusual logical problem appears here. She says,

> If we do not carry out this 'duty', we suddenly find
> that there is nobody we can claim to have let down, to
> have defaulted or failed in discharging our duties to
> them. The existence of the supposed subjects of this
> obligation is contingent on our fulfilling it. But if
> there is no subject of obligation, then, given the
> person-regarding view, there is no obligation. Which
> means that there can be no such thing as an

'obligation to perpetuate the human race', for an obligation that only exists if it is fulfilled, i.e., which logically cannot be violated, is clearly mistaken.[49]

Narveson is considering only whether we have a duty to procreate, and thus to perpetuate the human race; he is not considering a duty like the Rawlsian Just Savings principle. The claim here is that if we have a duty to future generations to cause them to be born, that duty is owed to no one if we fail to fulfil it. "For it makes no sense to say that one has done some kind of damage to a possible person by refusing to make that possibility actual."[50] It follows, Narveson claims, that there is no rational ground for a supposed duty to perpetuate the human race.

Narveson's argument here against duties to create future generations is in the background of the Just Savings principle. If future people have a right to claim their share of the world's environmental resources, and if we do not in fact save anything for them, it follows that no one's rights are trampled and no duties are unfulfilled. For the selection of a Just Savings principle is like the Non-Identity choice of Conservation, and the choice to save nothing for the future is like Depletion, for this reason. The work of procuring goods for the future can have an accidental effect on how people move, settle, meet each other and produce children, with the result that a group of future people is created who would be non-identical to the people who would be born if we chose not to save anything for the future. Thus our choice to implement some Just Savings Schedule not only saves social goods for future generations, but also creates the same future generations for whom those social goods are saved. If we have a duty to save for future people, then, that duty becomes either impossible to violate or impossible to uphold. For if we choose Conservation, we create people by whom we cannot fail. If we choose Depletion, we find that the choice of *not* saving for the future creates Depletion people, and we automatically fail to fulfil our duty to save for them. And by choosing Depletion, the Conservation people will never exist and therefore it cannot be claimed that they are entitled to anything, or that we failed to fulfil a duty to save anything for them. If we choose Depletion, there will be no Conservation people to whom we owe anything, and so there will be no strong reason to choose Conservation instead. And if we choose Conservation, there will be no Depletion people to whom we owe anything, so it cannot be claimed that by choosing Conservation we do right or wrong by the Depletion people. If what matters is how one does "by what people there are" (Narveson's terms) then it follows that by choosing Depletion we create people to whom we owe duties we cannot fulfil. This may be a reason to refrain from choosing Depletion. But no reason exists to prefer the alternative of Conservation: for if we choose Conservation, then we create people to whom we owe duties we cannot fail to fulfil, which Narveson claims is absurd.

The difficult logic here creates a Justice-based version of the Non-Identity Problem: principles of justice are unable to defend the claim that future people are owed anything by us. It is therefore unable to explain why it would be wrong to chose Depletion. It follows that my working hypothesis for this chapter cannot be a solution to the Non-Identity Problem. I am not convinced that Rawls' original position can change this conclusion. Let us say that a moral agent in the original position of not knowing which generation he would belong to would not want to be one of the Depletion people. He would want to be one of the Conservation people. It follows that he would not make the choice that brings the Depletion people into being. We may find this in the very standard of rationality which the Rawlsian distributor holds. For Rawls, reason is not total or average maximisation, but self-maximisation. As he explains, the parties in the original position:

> ...assume that they normally prefer more primary
> goods rather than less. Of course, it may turn out,
> once the veil of ignorance is lifted, that some of them
> for religious or other reasons may not, in fact, want
> more of these goods. But from the standpoint of the
> original position, it is reasonable for the parties to
> suppose that they do want a larger share, since in any

case they are not compelled to accept more if they do
not wish to... The concept of rationality invoked
here, with the exception of one essential feature, is
the standard one familiar in social theory. Thus in the
usual way, a rational person is thought to have a
coherent set of preferences between the options open
to him. He ranks these options according to how well
they further his purposes; he follows the plan which
will satisfy more of his desires rather than less, and
which has the greater chance of being successfully
executed. (*TJ* pg. 123-4)

The one feature that constitutes the exception to this general concept
of self-maximisation is that persons in the original position do not
experience envy. As Rawls sees it, envy "tends to make everyone
worse off" and is "collectively disadvantageous". (*TJ* pg. 124)
Parties in the original position "do not try to gain relative to each
other", but rather, likening it to a game, they try "to get as many
points as possible judged by their own system of ends". (*TJ* pg. 125)
The parties in the original position also know they can count on one
another to respect whatever final principles of distribution and of just
savings they collectively agree to. "They are rational in that they
will not enter into agreements they know they cannot keep, or can do
so only with great difficulty." (*TJ* pg. 126) They can trust that they
will not be cheated by others, as they have no incentive to cheat
others. Other than these caveats, the standard of rationality upheld in
Rawls' theory is that of 'intelligent self-maximisation'.[51] Thus,
someone in the original position of not knowing what generation he
will belong to, would want a distribution of resources across
generations that maximises the minimum share, just in case he ends
up as the minimum share-holder.

What matters here, then, is not the total utility to come about
as a result of one Non-Identity choice or another, but the way in
which a person makes choices; and it is Rawls' assumption that a
person makes choices on the basis of rational self-maximisation,
without envy or mistrust. The notion of *shares* may be important

here. It does not easily correspond with either total utility or average utility. Actually it is not a measure of utility at all—it is a measure of how many social goods (material wealth, social opportunity, and so on) a person possesses. But let us assume for the sake of the argument that the utility experienced by future people can roughly correspond with the shares of social goods distributed to them, at least insofar as distributing social goods to someone benefits that person. Since Rawls is preoccupied with social goods, and not with the properties of people which entitle them to claim a share of them, i.e. it is not a theory of what is someone's "due", this seems to me a legitimate interpretation.

The just distribution is the one which maximises the minimum share, as Rawls would say, and not the one that produces the highest total or highest average overall. So let us consider the choices of Depletion and Conservation as though they are distribution choices for a present generation. In this way, the interests, rights, or responsibilities to future people disappear, and so we do not find ourselves carrying out inviolable and/or impossible duties to the people of the future. Which choice maximises the minimum share? In the Depletion future, everyone's share of social goods is so little that their lives are only barely worth living. The perspective of distributive justice, resting upon the deep truth that people live separate lives, finds that the meagre share apportioned to each of the Depletion people is not justified or balanced out if the total shares available to distribute are greater than the total shares available to the Conservation people. The choice of Depletion spreads the available social goods too thinly. The choice of Conservation, while there are less total shares to distribute, maximises the minimum share, and so in that there may be a rational ground for choosing it.

But is that how the choice would appear to the parties in the original position? I think not. Someone in the original position knows that whatever generation he is a member of, it is a *present* generation. He knows he is one of the living; he knows that he is not a future person. Therefore he has no fear of finding that he is one of the Depletion people once the veil of ignorance is lifted. So a fear of finding that he is one of the Depletion people would not exist to motivate him to choose Conservation. He might decide that choosing Depletion maximises the minimum share for his own generation, and so his self-maximising standard of reasoning would compel him to choose it. Although this may appear as an unjust preference for one's own time, it is not. The parties behind the veil of ignorance still do not know which generation they belong to. But they necessarily know they belong to a living present generation, and with this knowledge they can also know that they will not be members of the Depletion and/or Conservation generations to come. I agree with T'Hooft: It is too hyperbolic to claim that the veil of ignorance suspends a person's knowledge of being a living member of a present generation. I am not sure what, if anything, it can mean to say that someone will find that he is a "future person" or a "potential person" once the veil of ignorance is lifted. This "stretches the fantasy too far" as surely as bargaining with every generation in the history of one's society, or everyone who will ever live, would stretch it. Whatever generation he finds himself to be a part of, he will find that it is "the present generation", his own generation. The original position is a thought experiment that a living person can adopt at any time, to obtain an objective and impartial perspective on problems that require a just solution. It is not a metaphysical position that as-yet-unborn people adopt before entering the real world, without knowing when, or even if, they will enter it. Since the parties in the original position all know that they are contemporaries, they can collectively agree to save nothing for future generations.

Suppose instead that the people in the original position considered Conservation or Depletion not as a distribution strategy for their own generation, but as a Just Savings schedule for every generation. If every generation made Depletion their Just Savings schedule, the parties would find themselves members of an enormously large population, receiving from their predecessors a large volume of social goods which can only be spread out thinly. If they chose Conservation, they would inherit a lesser total of social goods but, being a smaller population, would be able to increase the size of the minimum share. But I do not want to claim that the Original Position enables one to "get around" the Non-Identity problem, and usefully compare the Conservation and Depletion people to each other instead of to non-being. I think that would undermine the Deontological perspective. For the Deontologist, what matters is not whether it is better to be one of the Depletion People or Conservation people; what matters is which choice it is a moral duty to prefer, or to reject. And, more to the point, everything here depends on the rationale for initiating a Just Savings or Virtual Reciprocity practice in the first place, the rationale for each subsequent generation to sustain it, and whatever logical means might obtain to avoid the problem of bearing inviolable and/or impossible duties to future people. We have seen how the principles of Justice cannot supply that rationale on its own. Within the bounds of objectivity and impartiality symbolised by the veil of ignorance, the choice to save nothing for the future is neither unjust nor irrational.

§ 4. Summary Remarks for Chapter Two

At the beginning of this chapter it was hypothesised that every generation should have a fair entitlement to a share of the world's environmental resources, and that it is wrong for one generation to deplete the environment because to do so is to take more than its fair share. The construction of two new electricity stations to burn turf, at Lanesborough and at Shannonbridge, which will require 1,500 hectares of raised bog land each year, could be treated as an unjust appropriation of our generation's entitlement to the use of the turf from raised bogs as fuel.[52] However, the closer examination of the principles of distributive justice failed to uphold this hypothesis. It was found that the 'circumstances of justice' do not obtain across generations. Certain unavoidable absurdities were found in the claim that future people are 'owed' anything when their existence and their identities depend on our choices. And it was also found that when the choice to save or not to save for the future was treated as a Non-Identity choice, Depletion maximised the size of the minimum share. Rawlsian Distributive Justice was unable to provide a solution to the Non-Identity Problem.

Nevertheless, the search for an acceptable environmental ethic through Distributive Justice has not been futile. It was found that the reason to conserve the environment for the sake of future generations can lie in the present generation's own interests and values. De-Shalit and T'Hooft both argued that the future 'figures into the present meaning of things'. I found this idea compelling; my only substantial criticism was that I could not see what it had to do with Justice. As mentioned, it appears more like a step in the direction of Virtue theory. Since this insight cannot be followed up without departing from Justice theory, it is here that the discourse on Justice must end. Before turning to Virtue theory, I shall explore the deontology of Immanuel Kant, which may also be able to shed light on reasons to conserve the environment for the future. I am aware that from a historical point of view, it is odd to study Kant *after* studying Rawls. However, as was seen, there was a strong possibility that Virtual Reciprocity, or something like it, can be grounded in the Kantian principle of universal assent. I am engaged in a project of philosophical 'reverse engineering' here, in search of the primary ideas which moral theories have in common and which underlie the things which otherwise make them distinct. I therefore depart from Rawls, and step back a few generations to Kant's time, to see if his Deontology can provide an environmental conservation ethic and a future generations ethic that can pass the Non-Identity test.

---

[1] Rawls, A Theory of Justice pg. 3. This text is hereafter cited as *TJ*.

[2] H.L.A. Hart, The Concept of Law, pg. 153.

[3] In the revised (1999) edition of his text, Rawls clarifies that he also takes this position to be purely theoretical: He says, "This original position is not, of course, thought of as an actual historical state of affairs, much less as a primitive condition of culture. It is understood as a purely hypothetical situation characterised so as to lead to a certain conception of justice." (*TJ* pg. 11)

[4] Rawls, Political Liberalism, pg. 139.

[5] Rawls also says, "it is impossible to be very specific about the schedule of rates (or the range of rates) that would be acknowledged; the most that we can hope from these intuitive considerations is that certain extremes will be avoided." (*TJ* pg. 255.)

[6] Miller, Social Justice, pp. 42-3, 50.

[7] Earth Summit Ireland, Telling it like it is, pg. 14.

[8] United Nations Development Program, Human Development Report 1992 pg. 34-6.

[9] McMurtry, Unequal Freedoms, pg. 145.

[10] As cited in McDonagh, Passion for the Earth, pg. 9.

[11] Singer, One World, pg. 29-30.

[12] "The putatively historical grounds for justifying private property put forward by its most philosophically significant defenders—writing at a time when capitalism was only beginning its rise to dominance over the world's economy—cannot apply to the current use of the atmosphere. Neither Locke nor Smith provides any justification for the rich having more than their fair share of the finite capacity of the global atmospheric sink. In fact, just the contrary is true. Their arguments imply that this appropriation of a resource once common to all humankind is not justifiable. And since the wealth of the developed nations is inextricably tied to their prodigious use of carbon fuels (a use that began more than 200 years ago and continues unchecked today), it is a small step from here to the conclusion that the present global distribution of wealth is the result of the wrongful expropriation by a small fraction of the world's population of a resource that belongs to all human beings in common." Peter Singer, One World pg. 31.

[13] "Cod may be wiped out in just 15 years" *Irish News* 13 May 2004

[14] "Gardai to investigate claims of fraud in Donegal fisheries" *The Irish Times* 13 October 2004.

[15] "Hume's account of [the circumstances of justice] is especially perspicuous and the preceding summary adds nothing essential to his much fuller discussion." (*TJ* pg. 110). Hume expresses the conditions of justice as follows: "the rules of equity or justice depend entirely on the particular state and condition in which men are placed, and owe their origin and existence to that utility which results to the public from their strict and regular observance. Reverse, in any considerable circumstance, the condition of men; produce extreme abundance or extreme necessity; implant in the human breast perfect moderation and humanity, or perfect rapaciousness and malice—by rendering justice totally useless, you thereby totally destroy its essence and suspend its obligation upon mankind." David Hume, "An Enquiry Concerning the Principles of Morals", in Aiken (ed.) Hume's Moral and Political Philosophy pg. 188-9.

16 Barry's own words are: "We may be confident that moderate selfishness is here to stay but we cannot be sure of moderate scarcity (maybe at some time in the future the whole human race will be destitute) and the lack of equality between us and our successors is guaranteed by "time's arrow", which enables us to affect our successors while depriving them of the ability to affect us. A lot therefore hangs on the question of whether the doctrine of the circumstances of justice is true or not…" Brian Barry, "Circumstances of Justice and Future Generations" in Sikora & Barry, Obligations to Future Generations, pg. 209.

17 "As far as possible, then, the only particular facts which the parties know is that their society is subject to the circumstances of justice and whatever this implies." (*TJ* pg. 119)

18 Barry, "Circumstances of Justice", pg. 214.

19 More generally, Barry holds that the doctrine of the circumstances of justice is false. "Circumstances of Justice", pg. 207.

20 Barry, "Circumstances of Justice", pg. 222. Barry was writing here before the abolition of Apartheid.

21 "Were there a species of creatures intermingled with men, which, though rational, were possessed of such inferior strength, both of body and mind, that they were incapable of all resistance, and could never, upon the highest provocation, make us feel the effects of their resentment, the necessary consequence, I think, is that we should be bound by the laws of humanity to give gentle usage to these creatures, but should not, properly speaking, lie under any restraint of justice with regard to them, nor could they possess any right or property, exclusive of such arbitrary lords. Our intercourse with them could not be called society—which supposes a degree of equality—but absolute command on the one side, and servile obedience on the other. Whatever we covet, they must instantly resign." Hume, Enquiry, pg. 190-191.

22 "If the doctrine of the circumstances of justice is true, it must follow that there can be no place for justice between the generation of those alive at any given time and their successors. For it is clear that… there can be no getting around the total absence of equality." Barry, "Circumstances of Justice", pg. 223.

[23] Barry says, "We could concede that the presence of the circumstances of justice constitutes a *sufficient* condition for a society to have uniform rules of justice without allowing that the circumstances of justice are *necessary* conditions for the application of the concept of justice." Barry, "Circumstances of Justice", pg. 224-5. But one implication of this is that the Humean position which Rawls relies on, that justice has no external and independent criteria, collapses. "For they depended upon the notion that justice is a device for reaching agreement among approximate equals and that justice has no place where agreement does not have to be reached. But, at the same time, the view that the circumstances of justice are sufficient conditions for the application of the concept of justice is quite consistent with the truth of the view that there are no independent and external criteria of justice". [pg. 225].

[24] "The argument often made (e.g. by Nozick) that individuals should be content to give charitably themselves and not to seek to coerce everyone into doing so overlooks the public good aspect. If someone's good is a litter-free environment (rather than a tiny bit less litter) it makes sense for him to support coercion [e.g. taxation, etc.] to stop everyone littering..." Barry, "Circumstances of Justice", pg. 227.

[25] Passmore says, "Now, in fact, men quite often do make heroic sacrifices. They make them out of love. It is as lovers that they make sacrifices for the future more extensively than any Benthamite calculus would admit to be rational... There is, then, no novelty in a concern for posterity, when posterity is thought of not abstractly—as the 'future of mankind'—but as a world inhabited by individuals we love or feel a special interest in." J. Passmore, Man's Responsibility for Nature pg. 88-89.

[26] Rawls says, "(a) conception of justice should not presuppose, then, extensive ties of natural sentiment. At the basis of the theory, one tries to assume as little as possible." (*TJ* pg. 111-2)

[27] "If people care for their children's welfare, and if the welfare of the next generation is a public good, it is unfair not to contribute to it. But it would not be unjust for people not to care about the interests of their children. The limits of caring are the limits of justice." Barry, "Circumstances of Justice", pg. 227-8.

[28] This tension was first commented upon by Peter Danielson, "Theories, Intuitions and the Problem of World-Wide Distributive Justice", and further developed by Barry in "Circumstances of Justice" (*ibid.*), "Justice as Reciprocity" in Kamenka (ed.) Justice: Ideas and Ideologies pp. 50-78.

[29] Barry, "Circumstances of Justice", pg. 228.

[30] Barry says that it is not possible "to sustain a completely general principle to the effect that the receipt of a benefit creates a *prima facia* obligation to pass on a similar benefit to others... if someone offers me a toffee apple, out of the blue, and I accept it, does my enjoyment of the toffee apple create even the tiniest... obligation to distribute toffee apples to others?" Barry, "Justice as Reciprocity", as cited in *JFG* pg. 61.

[31] "Justice as rational co-operation and justice as hypothetical universal assent diverge as we leave the self-contained society of contemporaries to which Rawls confines the application of his theory of justice. The strains become manifest when we look at the problem of justice between contemporaries in different societies, justice between different generations of members in the same society, and (compounding the two) justice between different generations on a world wide basis." Barry, "Circumstances of Justice", pg. 237.

[32] "For this labour being the unquestionable property of the labourer, no man but he can have a right to what that is once joined to, at least where there is enough and as good left in common for others." John Locke, Second Treatise of Government, V, 27, pg. 17

[33] "God, who has given the world to men in common, has also given them reason to make use of it to the best advantage of life and convenience. The earth and all that is therein is given to men for the support and comfort of their being. And though all the fruits it naturally produces and beasts it feeds belong to mankind in common, as they are produced by the spontaneous hand of nature; and nobody has originally a private dominion exclusive of the rest of mankind in any of them, as they are thus in their natural state..." Locke, Second Treatise of Government, V, 26, pg. 17.

[34] Locke, Second Treatise of Government, V, 31, pg. 19.

[35] The basis for this claim is best exemplified by this passage: "Man is a being that lives in time, whose life indeed is temporal through and through, and for whom the future consequently is a constitutive dimension of his existence, as much as his remembrance of the past. Every time that we position ourselves in time by saying "now", we already find ourselves on the way towards the next minute, the next day, the next year. It is no exaggeration to say we *are* in time, that our being is a being-in-time, positioned between past and future." *JFGE* pg. 113.

[36] *JFGE*, pg. 102. An important implication of this which T'Hooft emphasises is this: "So I have the greatest difficulty with authors who declare it not be counter-intuitive to imagine, as concerns the parties to the original position, that they don't know whether they belong to the current generation, and so must consider the risk of turning out to be (!) a future generation—or who even endow those parties with the faculty of considering themselves as 'possibly existing' individuals who realise that they have (!) an interest in being actually existent." *JFGE* pg. 102-3.

[37] "it is an ancient wisdom that justice has the vocation of organising the existence between individuals." *JFGE* pg. 106.

[38] "if one accepts the idea of a community in one generation, including the principle that this entails certain obligations to other members, then one should accept the idea of a transgenerational community extending into the future, hence recognising obligations to future generations. I am claiming here that the constitutive community extends over several generations and into the future, and that just as many people think of the past as part of what constitutes their 'selves', they do and should regard the *future* as part of their 'selves'. These are the relations that form the transgenerational community, which is the source of our obligations to future generations." *WPM* pg. 15-16.

[39] C.f. *WPM*, pp. 32-4. His summary comment runs as follows: "...sentiments and emotions are inadequate to explain the transgenerational constitutive community, and in fact may even be suspect, especially if they are not controlled by reason or provoke negative reactions, such as a rejection of the stranger or the non-conformist. On the other hand, sentiments, even when positive in their results, may be too weak to serve as the moral grounds for our obligations to future generations. We know that we do have some obligations to future generations; nevertheless, the sentimental view of the community does not guarantee even basic obligations to future people. People, for example, may have had sentiments of sympathy for the struggle led by "Solidarity" in Poland, yet they did nothing actively." [pg. 33-4.]

[40] "Actions, then, are inseparably related to motives, wills, intentions, concerns. In recognising this, we can now see our lives as a long continuity, as a network of intentions and actions which are correlated and which reflect our wish to continue the self beyond temporal—as well as physical—boundaries." *WPM* pg. 37.

[41] De-Shalit cites MacIntyre's definitions of "tradition" in favour of his argument; and it occurs to me (as it did to T'Hooft) that 'tradition' may be a better word for what he has in mind than 'interaction'.

[42] "...the uninterrupted habitation of the planet is taken for granted. The moral point of view (as instanced by the search for justice) doesn't, by itself, require the *existence* of its constituency; so it is not capable of resisting a call for the collective suicide of humanity. This may be considered a quite fantastic eventuality. Now this is precisely what I want to suggest: that the difficulty in taking that extreme hypothesis seriously reveals an elemental (and therefore poorly articulated) assumption of the perpetuity of human life on the planet, which forms the horizon of our experience of the good across time." (*JFGE* pg. 100-1). Also, "The search for continuity builds upon an implicit confidence in constant generational renewal." (pg. 116)

[43] "Utilitarians reject distributive principles because they believe in the Reductionist View." (*R&P*, pg. 331). The Reductionist view of personal identity is the view that personal identity is a 'less deep, less involved' matter than non-reductionism, consisting only in 'Relation R', which is "psychological connectedness and/or continuity, with the right kind of cause. Since it is more controversial, I add, as a separate claim: In an account of what matters, the right kind of cause could be any cause." (*R&P* pg. 215).

[44] This argument appears in the case of 'the child's burden'. Parfit says, "If we are reductionists, we may compare the weakening of the connections between the child and his adult self to the absence of connections between different people. We shall give more weight to the fact that, in this example, this child does not care what will happen to his adult self. That it will be *he* who receives the benefit may thus seem to us less important. We might say, 'It will not be *he* who benefits. It will only be his adult self." (*R&P* pg. 333).

[45] Also: "If we are Reductionists, we regard the rough subdivisions within lives as, in certain ways, like the divisions between lives. We may therefore come to treat alike two kinds of distribution: within lives, and between lives." (*R&P* pg. 333-4).

[46] That other philosopher is Gauthier, in <u>Practical Reasoning</u>. He argues that to maximise utility for humanity means "to suppose that mankind is a super-person" (*R&P* pg.334).

[47] "On the Reductionist view, we are less impressed by this truth [the separateness of persons]. We regard the unity of each life as, in its nature, less deep, and as a matter of degree. We may therefore think the boundaries between lives to be less like those between, say, the squares on a chess-board—dividing what is all pure white from what is all jet black—and more like the boundaries between different countries. They may then seem less morally important." (*R&P* pg. 339).

[48] "I now live in the open air. There is still a difference between my life and the lives of other people. But the difference is less. Other people are closer. I am less concerned about the rest of my own life, and more concerned about the lives of others." (*R&P* pg. 281).

[49] Narveson, "Future People and Us" in Sikora & Barry, <u>Obligations to Future Generations</u> pg. 43-4.

[50] Narveson, "Future People and Us", *ibid* pg. 44.

[51] As Rawls puts it, "his dominant interests are in himself, not merely, as they must always be, interests of a self." (*TJ* pg. 111)

[52] Earth Summit Ireland, <u>Telling It Like It Is</u>, pp. 14-15.

Chapter Three: The "Right"
Kantian Deontology

The preceding two studies looked at the case for environmental conservation from two very different moral perspectives, but in one respect they were similar: both of them embody (other)-person-affecting principles. Both of them place the 'burden of proof' that a moral wrong had been done, so to speak, on other people. We know that we have done wrong when we receive the other person's complaint. In the case of Utilitarianism, it is the harm suffered by the other person, or in Parfit's terms, the 'fact of being made worse off', which makes an action wrong. In Rawlsian Justice theory, it is the unjust distribution among persons that makes an action wrong. However, the complaint of the deprived party is still the location of moral concern. Since both principles were in their own way person-affecting, they were unable to overcome the Non-Identity Problem.

In this chapter, I shall explore Kantian Deontology, to see if it can sustain an acceptable environmental ethic and overcome Parfit's Repugnant Conclusion. What is the morally correct way to treat the environment? Can an acceptable environmental ethic be stated in Kantian terms? Since in the Kantian system it is moral duty which matters, it is possible to claim that an act which produces the greatest utility may still be contrary to duty. Kantian ethics is still person-affecting, but in a way that is distinct from the previously studied forms of person-affecting ethics. As we shall see, it is the irrationality or inhumanity of the act itself which makes an act contrary to duty. It is *prima facia* possible, therefore, that Kantian thought can avoid the Non-Identity Problem. In the manner of an 'expanding circle', to borrow Aldo Leopold's phrase, I shall seek a satisfactory Deontological environmental ethic in a sequence that starts from the individual human moral agent, moving to the other animals, then to the land and elements of the Earth, and finally through the dimension of time to the rights of future generations.

§ 1. The *Groundwork* Applied to Environmental Problems.

Immanuel Kant's project as articulated in his <u>Groundwork of the Metaphysics of Morals</u> is to discover and explain the laws of the moral sphere of our lives, and indeed to show how the laws of morality do not constrain our freedom, but rather that they arise from our freedom. Unlike laws of nature, which cannot be ignored, laws of morality take the form of imperatives that prescribe the sort of action we should or ought to do. In particular his project is, as he put it, "to seek out and establish the supreme principle of morality".[1] As his starting place, he begins with three propositions.

The well-known first proposition of his text runs as follows: "It is impossible to conceive anything at all in the world, or even out of it, which can be taken as good without qualification, except a *good will*." (*Groundwork* pg. 61, emphasis his.) This introductory claim asserts that the will, the autonomous capacity to pursue an end, is the only intrinsic good, the only thing that is good in itself. To say that it is good for something else would be to place a qualification upon it. This is not to say that every will is a good will; it is to say that the only thing that could potentially be an intrinsic good is the will.

The will is the capacity of a free moral agent for creating a project, a purpose, or an end, for himself to pursue. Yet the value of a good will does not lie in the projects or ends which it pursues, but in the fact that it acts from duty. Kant defines the will as follows:

> Everything in nature works in accordance with laws.
> Only a rational being has the power to act in
> accordance with his idea of laws—that is, in
> accordance with principles—and only so has he a
> will. Since reason is required in order to derive
> actions from laws, the will is nothing but practical
> reason. If reason infallibly determines the will, then
> in a being of this kind the actions which are
> recognised to be objectively necessary are also
> subjectively necessary—that is to say, the will is then

147

a power to choose only that which reason
independently of inclination recognises to be
practically necessary, that is, to be good.
(*Groundwork* pg. 80)

The will, as Kant describes it, is the autonomous faculty of
recognising laws prescribed by reason, and conforming one's actions
to them. The connection between reason, a good will, and an action
done from duty is very close: for the purpose of reason, as Kant
argues, is to produce a good will.[2]   The moral worth of an action is
in its conformity with duty as recognised by the will, and not in the
results expected to be attained by the action. Indeed, an interest in
results or consequences Kant would say stems from subjective
personal inclination, and not from reason.[3] Someone could do
something which he is duty-bound to do, but the action would not be
praiseworthy as a moral action unless it is motivated by duty. Kant
says,

> ...to preserve one's life is a duty, and besides this
> every one has also an immediate inclination to do so.
> But on account of this the often anxious precautions
> taken by the greater part of mankind for this purpose
> have no inner worth, and the maxim of their action is
> without moral content. They do protect their lives *in
> conformity with duty*, but not *from the motive of duty*.
> (*Groundwork*, pg. 65-6; emphasis his.) [4]

A consequentialist principle of action Kant would call an
"imperative of prudence", an "imperative of skill", or a
"hypothetical" imperative, capable of recommending certain courses
of action but not capable of commanding the will, and not capable of
demonstrating that the recommended course of action is a duty.[5]
This follows from his initial premises, in which it was claimed that
only the will can be considered morally good. Since only the will
can be morally good, actions can be judged as morally right or
wrong only in reference to the will. An action is good if the will

which initiated the action is a good will.[6] And as noted, a will is a good will if it acts from duty, as opposed to inclination or personal desire. These two propositions in Kant's view lead to the third, in which duty is defined. Kant says, *"Duty is the necessity to act out of reverence for the law*. For an object as the effect of my proposed action I can have an inclination, but never reverence, precisely because it is merely the effect, and not the activity, of a will."* (*Groundwork* pg. 68)[7] Thus, before any formal articulation of principles, laws, or imperatives, Kant sets the stage by asserting three points: that only the will can be intrinsically good; that the good will is the one which acts from duty and not from a personal inclination, and that duty is "respect for the law". Having articulated these three important points, the question of what law does the good will respect now arises.

The kind of imperative which can command the will with the force of a moral law is a categorical imperative. Kant distinguishes the categorical imperative from the hypothetical imperative (likened to the "imperative of prudence"):

> Hypothetical imperatives declare a possible action to
> be practically necessary as a means to the attainment
> of something else that one wills (or that one may
> will). A categorical imperative would be one which
> represented an action as objectively necessary in itself
> apart from its relation to a further end... [The
> categorical imperative] is concerned, not with the
> matter of the action and its presumed results, but with
> its form and with the principle from which it follows;
> and what is essentially good in the action consists in
> the mental disposition, let the consequences be what
> they may. This imperative may be called the
> imperative of *morality*. (*Groundwork*, pg. 82, 83-4.)

Any action or project that the will can initiate can be made into an imperative, which is a verbally articulated principle of action: "I ought to do such and such". To root out the hypothetical imperatives from the imperatives of morality, Kant claims that the imperatives of morality are ones which are universal, which means that they are binding upon all rational beings; whereas by contrast hypothetical imperatives are merely useful for some particular purpose under certain conditions. There can be only one universal imperative, according to Kant, and he calls it the categorical imperative. There can be only one because the categorical imperative has no condition behind it to limit it, as do hypothetical imperatives. It is, rather, the imperative which limits all other imperatives; the categorical imperative is, to put it somewhat paradoxically, 'limited by its universality'; it conforms to no higher-order principle than its own necessity. Kant declares it as follows: "act only on that maxim through which you can at the same time will that it should become a universal law." (*Groundwork* pg. 88) Kant uses several examples to illustrate his point: the contemplation of suicide, the incurring of debts that cannot be repaid; the development of skills and talents; the offering of help to others in need. The explanation which appears in these examples is that an action is wrong if, rendered as a law for everyone, it would be logically contrary to human freedom to do it, or it would undermine one's own interests, or it would even become empirically impossible to do.

Having achieved the categorical imperative, described its content and with illustrations shown its plausibility, Kant observes that "we are still not so far advanced as to prove *a priori* that there actually is an imperative of this kind—that there is a practical law which by itself commands absolutely and without any further motives, and that the following of this law is a duty." (*Groundwork* pg. 92.) This is what necessitates the move from the categorical imperative to the practical imperative. And before embarking on his *a priori* proof that the categorical imperative exists and has the force of duty, he reminds us again that he is not searching to base the moral law in a "special characteristic of human nature", by which he means feelings, inclinations, and propensities; these are values he calls instrumental or 'contingent'.[8] The proof of the categorical imperative will be found, he insists, in something that has value in itself.[9] Very quickly, he declares that "man, and in general every rational being, *exists* as an end in himself, *not merely as a means* for arbitrary use by this or that will; he must in all his actions, whether they are directed to himself or to other rational beings, always be viewed *at the same time as an end.*" (*Groundwork* pg. 95.) The articulation of the practical imperative, therefore, contains within it the affirmation of the value of humanity as an end in itself. It is worth quoting the entire paragraph in which the practical imperative appears.

> If then there is to be a supreme practical principle and —so far as the human will is concerned—a categorical imperative, it must be such that from the idea of something which is necessarily an end for every one because it is an *end in itself,* it forms an *objective* principle of the will and consequently can serve as a practical law. The ground of this principle is: *Rational nature exists as an end in itself.* This is the way in which a man necessarily conceives his own existence: it is therefore so far a subjective principle of human actions. (*Groundwork* pg. 96)

The point to note about Kant's moral theory here is the relationship between reason and freedom: Kant claims they imply one another. This move was anticipated in the earlier argument in which hypothetical imperatives were rejected as candidates for moral duties. This good will may be subject to the limitations of duty, but its duty arises from the exercise of the agent's own faculty of reason. Thus the laws of duty arise from a process of self-legislation, and in this process the will is *autonomous*; it generates its own law, it does not receive its law from some contingent quality of human nature. For Kant, only a being that is self-legislating by means of reason is truly free, and only a free being is a moral agent. This autonomy is what makes rational nature an end in itself. The articulation of the practical imperative continues as follows:

But it is also the way in which every other rational being conceives his existence on the same rational ground which is valid also for me; hence it is at the same time an *objective* principle, from which, as a supreme practical ground, it must be possible to derive all laws from the will. The practical imperative will therefore be as follows: *Act in such a way that you always treat humanity, whether in your own person or in the person of any other, never simply as a means, but always at the same time as an end.* (*Groundwork* pg. 96)

The move from subjectivity to objectivity, from knowing one's own rational nature to be an end in itself to knowing that other beings are also ends in themselves, is enabled by the claim that "every other rational being conceives his existence on the same rational ground that is also valid for me." This move is an argument by analogy: intuitively or internally knowing that my own capacity for autonomous reason is an end in itself, I must also know that the capacity for autonomous reason possessed by other beings is also an end in itself. If I treat my own existence as an end in itself on account of my capacity for autonomous reason, then logical consistency demands that I must treat others who possess autonomous reason the same way. I might use others as a means to a certain end, as in the case of "using" a shop keeper to purchase a load of turf bricks with which to heat my house, but if I use someone else's *freedom* as a means to a separate end of my own, for example by exploiting someone's generosity to obtain the load of turf without paying for it, then I am acting morally wrongly. Kant demonstrates how to use both the categorical and practical imperatives with examples. The test of universalisation, to determine whether some act is a moral duty, is the test of whether the maxim of the action would contradict itself if it was a maxim for all rational beings. Such a maxim would be self-contradictory if, were it made a law for all rational beings, it would become impossible to do the action which the maxim commands.

Can the Categorical Imperative address environmental problems, especially the sort of problems which have irreversible impacts upon the future? Could there be a Kantian 'Land Ethic'? Could Parfit's Repugnant Conclusion be morally wrong because choosing it would be contrary to duty? It may seem, at first, that environmental destruction cannot pass the test of universalisation, and so in Kant we can find an acceptable environmental ethic. On this theme, Onora O'Neill wrote:

> The principle of destroying natural and man-made environments, in the sense of destroying their reproductive and regenerative powers, is not universalisable. Nobody can coherently view the irreversible destruction of the means of life as an inclusive principle that is available for all: rather they rely on the fact that at least some others preserve rather than destroy (parts of) the natural world, and its productive capacities, so preserve some means of life, on which they and their destructive activities depend.[10]

A similar case applies to the ethics of future generations. It is not universalisable for one generation to do nothing to clean up the pollution and waste it causes, or is caused by its predecessors, assuming for instance that it can count on future ingenuity and progress to solve its environmental problems. For if every generation reasoned that way, then no generation would take up the responsibility to solve the environmental problems which affect it and which affect every subsequent generation. We cannot rationally defer responsibility for present environmental problems on to future people. This we can take as a reason for some generation to initiate and continue a practice of intergenerational just savings, as was discussed in the previous study. "Free riding" on the benefits received from the past and the hoped-for progress and ingenuity of future generations cannot logically be a law for everyone. If each generation relied on its successor generations to clean up its pollution and waste, and to create or discover new resources to compensate for the loss of those which are depleted, then no generation would conserve its resources, no generation would create or discover new resources, and no generation would clean up its pollution and waste.

To apply this principle to practice, one might consider case examples like the ones which Kant does.

> *Littering in public parks.* Suppose that I am enjoying an afternoon lunch sitting on a park bench in the Claddagh, watching the sea birds and the sunlight on the hills of county Clare across the bay. I might find it easier and more convenient to leave my rubbish behind when I am finished, instead of spending the extra effort to take it to a public rubbish bin, or to take it home with me. I might note that my own rubbish on this occasion, being so little, would not by itself noticeably diminish the quality of the park. A real-life example of this kind of thinking is the casual thoughtlessness of smokers who drop their cigarette butts wherever they are. The well-publicised smoking ban in Irish workplaces resulted in a sharp rise in the number of cigarette butt litter on urban streets. One study carried out in the north county Dublin town of Swords found that since the smoking ban was enacted, the volume of cigarette butts on the streets increased by 20%, although bins were used where they were provided.[11]

A similar situation applies on a social scale as well. We could also consider:

> *Illegal dumping.* This is a serious environmental and criminal problem in Ireland. It proliferates because legal dumping is expensive, and because it is a high-profit, low-risk kind of crime. Two illegal dump

discovered in adjacent fields in county Meath
contained a total of 20,000 tonnes of waste.[12] Illegal
dumpers often travel far: one illegal dump discovered
in Fermanagh, Northern Ireland, was found to contain
rubbish from Waterford and Cork.[13] Punishments for
illegal dumpers who are caught tend to be light: for
instance, one waste company operator was handed a
nine-month suspended sentence.[14]

Kant's categorical imperative instructs us to consider not the
immediate consequences of one's own action, but to consider one's
actions in terms of the universalisation of the maxim of the action: or
to put it another way, when I choose to do something, I choose for all
humanity. The case against littering can run like this: there cannot
be a law for all rational beings whose purpose is to enhance the
enjoyment of public parks by means of freely spoiling the qualities
that make it enjoyable. Therefore I cannot consider it right to drop
the rubbish under the bench, but instead I must dispose of it
appropriately. (As an aside, while finishing this thesis I walked to
the park next to the Claddagh and found that there were no rubbish
bins in sight.) For similar reasons, I cannot participate in an illegal
dumping operation. To do so would be contrary to the enjoyment of
the whole landscape.

The next example which we can put to a Kantian test
is:

Public transport. Suppose that after I finish my lunch I
need to travel from Galway to Dublin quickly, and I
may choose to take a private car or a public train or
bus. I might find the choice of the private car
attractive since I will be able to plan my own arrival
time, stop where I choose, and get there faster as well.
Cargo transport by road in Europe increased by 54%
since 1980, passenger transport by road by 46% in the
past ten years, and passenger transport by air has
increased by 67% in the past ten years.[15] This says

nothing of the problems of increased air pollution which the engines of private cars produce. An activist group called Sustainable Transport Ireland claimed that because of rising oil prices and increasing gridlock on Ireland's roads, public investment should go into improving existing roads and railways, and into public transport, not into new roads. One of its researchers said, "Motorways open up land for development in the most inappropriate way. We have to get away from long distance commuting, which is destroying people's lives."[16]

However, if it were a law for all rational beings to prefer private transportation when public transport is available, it would contradict itself. Rather like the situation in which people in a crowded lecture hall stand up in order to get a better view of the speaker, which results with everyone standing and thus no one having a better view, the consequence of everyone preferring the private car over the bus or train is an increase in traffic congestion, as well as traffic accidents and fatalities, which reduces and potentially eliminates the advantages that private transport has over public transport. Thus in general, a universal law to facilitate freedom and efficiency of movement contradicts itself if it reduces people's freedom and efficiency of movement. I am obliged in this situation to take a bus or train to Dublin instead of personal transport. But what about:

> *Air Travel.* I might choose to fly to Dublin instead of take the bus or train, which is a 'public' transportation system (although the aeroplanes are privately owned) and which would get me there in a mere half hour. Air travel in Europe was predicted to double between 1998 and 2010, with attendant increase in pollution and fuel consumption.[17] Aviation accounts for 13% of all carbon dioxide emissions from transport, and about 2% of all man-made carbon dioxide. One trans-atlantic flight from Europe to America produces

about as much air pollution as most people produce in a lifetime of driving a private car.[18]

It appears that even though aviation is still a system of mass transport, the problems of traffic congestion and pollution which obtains for private cars also obtains with regard to air travel. I must still prefer the train or the bus. The last example is:

Resource development and depletion. Suppose I am going to Dublin because I am an executive of An Bord Pleanála, and must attend a meeting to consider applications for planning permission for several resource development projects. I might be asked to adjudicate the development of an off shore gas field. Mayo County Council recently approved a request by Shell Inc. to develop a gas field off the coast of Mayo, although An Bord Pleanála denied a previous application as a result of protest by local people.[19]

Here we have the familiar categories of environmental policy already introduced: Protection, Conservation, and Depletion. In the case of resource development, such as water, energy, building materials, and so forth, it might be advantageous for the community, and profitable for the companies involved, to take as much of that resource as possible, and as quickly as possible, without consideration of the ecological capacity of replenishment, in the case of renewable resources like water, or the limited supply, in the case of non-renewable resources like natural gas. Such a development programme would quickly exploit the resource beyond its capacity of renewal, or would empty out the resource altogether. Reason can never consent to a maxim whereby a resource development project is elevated to the level of a universal law, because it is a contradiction to deplete some resource to the point where the resource can no longer be depleted. I take my hint here from Kant's first illustration of the Categorical Imperative, the example of suicide, in which it was shown that a law which has as its aim the continuation and improvement of life cannot sanction the destruction of life.[20] A law that affirms the value of something (life in Kant's example, an environmental resource in the case of depletion) contradicts itself if it allows the destruction of that thing of value.

Short illustrations like these are useful ways to approach specific problems, but not enough by themselves to answer the question of whether Kantian ethics can usefully contribute answers to the overall problem of environmentalism. They cannot by themselves answer the question, carried forward from my study of Rawls, of what reason might exist to initiate a practice of inter-generational resource savings. My three examples, moreover, might contain further theoretical problems. A straightforward universal maxim to litter, disconnected from reference to special surroundings like public parks, is not in itself contradictory because if everyone felt free to litter wherever they are, that would not make it impossible to litter. Littering does not have within it an internal logical contradiction; that is, it does not undermine human freedom, and so it is not contrary to duty. The same applies to the construction of waste dumps. If every central government and local authority built waste dumps on every available parcel of land not already scheduled for some other purpose, that by itself would not make it impossible to build waste dumps. In my second example: traffic congestion, accidents, and fatalities might be reduced by building more roads, safer cars, engines that run on hydrogen, electricity, or vegetable oil (the technology already exists), and by getting more police officers on the roads, enough to render the principle of preferring cars over buses and trains no longer self-refuting. The problems of air traffic congestion and pollution might be reducible in much the same way. The Vancouver Olympics, planned for 2010, will provide hydrogen-powered vehicles to transport the thousands of athletes, media people, and spectators to and from the city centre, the airport, and the ski resort where many of the events will take place.[21] A Norwegian corporation is developing an ocean-going cargo ship, which will be powered by solar panels, sails, and hydrogen fuel cells, and which will produce no emissions at all.[22] In my final example: while it may be wrong to exploit some resource to the point of destroying that resource, then what if there are other deposits of the resource available? What if the resource is a basic requirement of life, such as water, leaving us no choice but to exploit it? With these further considerations in mind, Depletion may actually *pass the test of universalisation*, as was seen with the example of littering. For example, Kant claims it is wrong to tell lies because to do so would undermine confidence in the correlated practice of promise-keeping and truth-telling.[23] If Depletion was a law for everyone, would it undermine the practice of its own correlate, which is survival and civilisation (understood as a temporally continuous, inter-generational human society)? There are good reasons why the answer can be "no". First of all, survival and civilisation could not be possible at all without some amount of Depletion. We need to use of the resources of the planet, especially basic requirements like water. We would not be able to eat, to build houses and communities, and so on, if we did not deplete the environment in some way. It may be true that too much depletion can undermine survival and civilisation, by creating shortages and pollution. An American report showed that air pollution is dense enough to create a 1-in-1200 chance of contracting lung cancer, which is 500 times greater than the protective standard stipulated in the U.S. Clean Air Act.[24] But here we find ourselves not condemning Depletion outright, but instead trying to find how much Depletion is acceptable. The range of acceptable Depletion may be very wide indeed: wide enough to include the situation described by Parfit as the Repugnant Conclusion.

Moreover, Conservation, as a mediating term between Depletion and Preservation, also allows for us to take the resources we need to live and thrive, although in a less intrusive way. Preservation, while potentially imposing burdens of scarcity and deprivation upon human society, might not be self-defeating if it does not entail undermining human life itself. For it appears that the Categorical Imperative disallows an environmental policy choice only if it would result in the collapse of civilisation itself. The Repugnant Conclusion, as Parfit described it, is not quite that disastrous. It entails a dramatically reduced quality of life for those who do live, but it does not entail that human life would not be possible. It appears, then, that Kantian deontology is unable to supply an explanation for why it is wrong to choose the Repugnant Conclusion. So long as the human race can move to new deposits of some resource, invent new technologies to access hitherto inaccessible resources, and so on, then Depletion is not a self-contradictory act. So long as the human race is physically dependent upon the resources of the planet for survival and civilisation, then some level of Depletion is obligatory for us. We might claim that Conservation is a low-grade, tolerable form of Depletion which achieves the same result in a sustainable way. But this does not change the conclusion that Depletion is not self-contradictory as a law for everyone. We have as yet no reason to prefer one choice over the other.

Although Depletion, as an environmental policy choice, passes the test of universalisation, the Categorical Imperative is not the whole of Kant's ethics. There is also the Practical Imperative. In the previous study, it was concluded that if a practice like Virtual Reciprocity existed, it would be morally right to do one's part to maintain it. The reason for this was partially Kantian: if non-participation in the practice was a universal moral law, no generation would have any reason to expect or demand anything from its predecessors, and the whole practice would be undermined. However, I was unable to find a reason within the logic of justice for initiating such a practice in its absence. Could the Practical Imperative supply a reason for initiating a practice of Intergenerational Savings or Virtual Reciprocity, which as we saw in the previous chapter Distributive Justice could not do? If so, then Kantian deontology may provide a reason for why it is wrong to choose Depletion. To answer this question, let us shift to the practical level and its central principle, which is humanity as an end in itself. Since Kantian deontology is concerned not with the recipient of an action but with the act itself, might it succeed where Utilitarianism falls short? To answer the question of whether there can be a Kantian environmental imperative, it is necessary to explore why humanity is the 'end in itself' of the practical imperative, and from there explore whether the principle of humanity can be extended to include non-rational beings such as animals and ecosystems.

§ 2. Humanity

Kant's moral theory places on a concept of humanity the privilege, or the burden, of being the sole and exclusive bearer of intrinsic value. From where does the idea of humanity come, and why identify it alone as the location of goodness without qualification? Kant's argument follows a kind of methodological reduction (a reduction in the sense of 'leading back'). In his discussion of different kinds of imperatives, Kant makes a remarkable claim of value theory. "Who wills the end, wills…also the means which are indispensably necessary and in his power". (*Groundwork* pg. 84-5) For example, one who wills to make bread must also will to fetch water and flour, to knead the dough, and so on. His case for the intrinsic goodness of the good will is that the will posits no purpose outside of itself. This moment of the argument is 'reductive', in that it 'leads back' to a first cause, and it is repeated in the discussion of the practical imperative. Kant's claim is that in order for me to will some end, I must also be able to will the causes of that end and ultimately I must be able to will *my own will* as foremost among the various causes. Humanity as the "supreme limiting condition of all subjective ends" is placed in the position of the original object of that which is to be willed, the principle that limits all other principles, rather a like a conceptual "unmoved mover". This is the only sequence of reasoning in the text of the Groundwork for attributing intrinsic value exclusively to humanity, other than the discussion of freedom and the will. Elsewhere, humanity as an end in itself, and the will as the only thing that can be considered good without qualification, is simply assumed without supporting argument. Indeed he says early in the work that the concept of the will as an intrinsic good needs only to be clarified, not argued, as if it is a concept that is self-evidently true and which any rational being may grasp.[25]

Thus, the importance of humanity is not so much argued for as it is systematically presupposed. Yet if Kant's argument is a methodological reduction, then why stop at humanity? The answer that Kant would give is that only the human will has no purpose outside of itself—only the human will has no purpose but that which it gives to itself through its autonomous exercise of reason. This is a troublesome position for environmentalism, for there appears to be no place for non-rational beings such as animals, or for communities of living beings like ecosystems, in his ethical thinking. Yet there need not be a contradiction between environmentalism and Kantian humanism in principle. Environmentalism is not misanthropy. Additionally, any environmental ethic is still going to address itself to human moral agents, and so a place for humanity in environmentalism is not eliminated, and perhaps cannot be eliminated. But could Kantian ethics go further?

Since Kant ascribes moral agency only to human beings, on account of the human capacity of autonomous reason, he is traditionally interpreted as specifically excluding animals from his moral theory. Kantian ethics usually presupposes a 'patient-agent parity' in which only moral agents can have moral standing. It can be wrong to torture or kill an animal only if, as the standard interpretation of Kant's position goes, doing so would develop in the agent a tendency to do the same to people. This position is attributed to Kant by Christina Hoff, John Passmore, and others.[26] It is not without precedent in Kant's work: for instance, in his <u>Lectures on Ethics</u> Kant says "Our duties toward animals are merely indirect duties toward humanity". He clarifies this as follows:

> If a man shoots his dog because the animal is no
> longer capable of service, he does not fail in his duty
> to the dog, *for the dog cannot judge*, but *his act is
> inhuman* and damages in himself that humanity which
> it is his duty to show toward mankind If he is not to
> stifle his human feelings, he must practice kindness
> towards animals, for he who is cruel to animals
> becomes hard also in his dealings with men. We can

judge the heart of a man by his treatment of animals.[27]

The philosophically interesting thing here is the question of whether it can be intrinsically wrong to do something even if no moral agent is harmed, and no moral agent's rights are infringed.

Hoff interpreted this passage from Kant's lectures to mean that, in the case of the man who shoots his dog, it is humanity and not the dog who is the victim.[28] However this is not quite right: she makes it appear as if Kant is saying that there is nothing intrinsically wrong with harming animals, or even that one cannot do harm to animals. This interpretation was criticised by Tim Hayward for equivocating on the word 'to wrong'. He says:

> for while 'to (do) wrong (to) someone' must usually mean 'to do someone an injustice', it can also be used to mean 'to do harm to'—a quite distinct idea. Hoff takes advantage of both senses: on the one hand to record—the element of truth—that Kant denies that humans can do an injustice to animals; and on the other to suggest—the element of absurdity—that Kant thinks that if one beats a horse then the horse is not the victim, as if one cannot do harm to animals.[29]

In the <u>Lectures on Ethics</u> Kant claims that gratuitous cruelty to a dog is still cruelty, and still wrong. Since a moral agent's treatment of beings who are not moral agents is not irrelevant nor outside the sphere or morality, it follows that the 'patient-agent parity' view typically ascribed to Kant does not hold—at least not in the way Kant is usually interpreted. Kant affirms that the man in his example has a duty not to shoot the dog, but Kant denies that the duty is owed *to the dog*. It seems impossible to avoid interpreting Kant as saying that it is impossible to do injustice to the animals. Kant does not claim that the dog has a right to not be shot. Insofar as rights involve the ability of the right-holder to make a claim upon another moral agent to be treated in a particular way, that is, the ability to place someone under a duty to him (a standard definition of a moral right, also used by Hayward) Kant therefore can be correctly interpreted as claiming that non-rational beings do not have rights. The dog "cannot judge" (not the way we do) and thus cannot impose a claim of rights upon another being by judging that an action did or did not fulfil a duty to him. Moreover, as Kant would not recognise that they possess human reason, therefore they are not moral agents. Nevertheless, Kant still claims that it is wrong to shoot the dog. A non-rational being, like a dog, is not in Kantian terms a moral agent, for moral agency is a capacity of reason to formulate universal principles of morality, and to choose to act on them, and thus only a rational being can be a moral agent. But since Kant claims that it is still wrong to shoot the dog, there might be a case to be made that for Kant, non-rational beings may still possess *moral standing;* that is, non-rational beings may still be deserving of our respect.

The traditional interpretation of 'moral standing', which Kant uses, is that for something to hold moral standing it must have some good of its own, which usually takes the form of an interest or an end which it pursues, in which the duty of moral respect is grounded. We could claim that insofar as animals pursue various goods, they are therefore entitled to hold moral standing, and it does not matter that they are not moral agents. If we were to grant this for the sake of the argument, Kant would deny that we can know the aims of other animals with the same subjective immediacy and certainty with which we can know our own.[30] To claim to know the interests and ends of non-rational beings requires very strong knowledge claims which Kant would find impossible to accept.[31] Furthermore, Kant would say that the goods and ends which animals pursue are not generated by the exercise of autonomous reason. The ends and interests of non-rational beings are generated by their instincts, and perhaps also by their genetically-encoded patterns of behaviour. On this basis it may be claimed that they lack true freedom, since it is the capacity of autonomous reason which, for Kant, enables a being to possess freedom and thus entitles that being to consideration as an end in itself. The traditional Kantian disjunction between freedom and nature, introduced early in the preface of the Groundwork,[32] implies that insofar as a being acts according to its nature, it is not free. A being's nature, in the Kantian definition, is its activity and behaviour as governed by universal laws that are not subject to judgement or choice but rather are given by its own constitution.[33] Human reason aims at nothing other than itself, whereas animal instinct aims at particular ends of the sort that Kant would regard as 'hypothetical' and 'prudential'; i.e. to eat, to seek shelter, and so on, and which, moreover, are not motivated by freedom. As Kant says in the Lectures, "All animals have the faculty of using their powers according to will. But this will is not free. It is necessitated through the incitement of *stimuli*, and the actions of animals involve a *bruta necessitas*." (*Lectures* pg. 121)

The Kantian answer to the question of animals is that they do not possess moral standing on their own, because they are not free beings. However there *is* a Kantian argument for why it is right to respect them, although it is not for the sake of the animals themselves, nor for their interests (and that is not a criticism of the argument). We have duties *concerning* non-rational beings, even if they are not duties directly *towards* those beings. In the example of the man who shoots his dog: if the man is under a duty not to shoot the dog, it is because the act 'damages the humanity in himself', not because the dog is a free being nor because it has interests or ends which are to be respected. There is no question of respecting the humanity of the dog in this case, for the dog is not a human being. Nor is it a matter of respecting the 'dog-ness' of the dog (the presumed correlate of the 'humanity' of a human being), for Kant would deny that animals have the capacity of autonomous reason and self-legislation by means of the will that human beings possess, and which entitles human beings to be respected as ends in themselves. The reason Kant would claim it is wrong to gratuitously harm or kill non-rational beings is because there is an 'inhumanity' in the act. But if this 'inhumanity' is not a violation of a duty *towards the animal*, then what is it? In this case it does not precisely appear as the categorical 'good-in-itself' of the interests of the moral patient, which we are duty-bound to respect, but is somewhat closer to being *a particular quality or characteristic of the moral agent who performs the act*. A shift has taken place: whereas with regard to other moral agents, our duties are *to* them (as well as to the humanity within the agent); but when the recipient of the action is not a moral agent, the duty is specifically and entirely towards the "humanity" within the moral agent who performs the action. Not to damage one's own humanity is for Kant a primary moral duty: "the prior condition of our duty to others is our duty to ourselves; we can fulfil the former only insofar as we first fulfil the latter." (*Lectures* pg. 118) As Kant explains it, each person has a duty to himself to do nothing which would undermine his dignity, and that this is a prerequisite to all other duties. This is stated repeatedly, for instance: "We must also be worthy of our manhood; whatsoever makes us unworthy of it makes us unfit for anything, and we cease to be men." (*Lectures* pg. 110) And, "Only if our worth as human beings is intact can we perform our other duties; for it is the foundation stone of all other duties. A man who has destroyed and cast away his personality, has no intrinsic worth, and can no longer perform any manner of duty." (*Lectures* pg. 121.)

This emphasis on a characteristic quality of the moral agent is a step in the direction of Virtue ethics, although a tentative one. Certainly this move is implied by Kant's remark that we can judge a man's heart by his treatment of animals, and that our duty to ourselves is the prior condition of our duty to others. It is also implied by statement that the requirement to uphold one's own dignity:

> …demands that he shall prove and examine himself to see whether his dispositions are morally pure. The springs of disposition must be examined to discover whether they are honour or illusion, superstition or pure morality. Neglect to do this is exceedingly detrimental to morality. If men were to examine the grounds of their religion and actions, they would find that honour, compassion, prudence, and habit were more conspicuous in them than morality… we ought constantly to watch ourselves, and exercise a certain

vigilance, *vigilantia moralis*, in our actions. This
watchfulness ought to be directed upon the purity of
our disposition and the strictness of our action.
(*Lectures* pg. 125)

The vocabulary of Virtue theory dominates this passage. However,
there is a very specific sense in which 'humanity' is meant in
Kantian terms, which does not allow a virtue-theory interpretation
along tracks laid in ancient times by Aristotle or in modern times by
MacIntyre and others. For Kant, the only qualities of humanity that
matter are freedom and autonomous reason. An act damages the
humanity of the agent if it is motivated by a passion that clouds
one's exercise of autonomous reason. Thus, for an act to damage the
humanity of the agent, it must be a heteronomous, or *irrational*, act.
It is an act which is not a product of the free exercise of autonomous
reason, but is in some way an abdication of freedom, a product of
instinct, emotion, or that which Kant would refer to as a being's
'nature' (which for Kant is the diametric opposite of freedom, as we
have seen). Here we have an example of an act which is not self-
defeating as a law for everyone, but is nevertheless morally wrong.
If a man kills an animal for no particular reason, he abdicates his
autonomous reason and thus transgresses his own humanity.

The same may be claimed of acts which unnecessarily
damage the environment. According to a report released by 1,360
scientists from 95 countries, "Human activity is putting such a strain
on the natural functions of Earth that the ability of the planet's
ecosystems to sustain future generations can no longer be taken for
granted."[34] World-wide pollution and resource depletion, if it should
undermine the future of humanity, can be taken as an irrational act
which transgresses our own humanity. Since it is the self-
contradictory property of the heteronomous act which makes it
wrong, we can assume that this conclusion holds even if Depletion
was a Non-Identity choice, in which the people who live will be
different than those who would live if we choose otherwise.
However, Parfit's Depletion case does not undermine the future of
humanity, but rather creates a future in which humanity continues to

live (if not thrive and prosper). Kant argues that so long as someone still possesses her dignity, it may not matter that her conditions are hard. As he says:

> Socrates lived in a state of wretchedness; his
> circumstances were worthless; but though his
> circumstances were so ill-conditioned, yet he himself
> was of the highest value. Even though we sacrifice
> all of life's amenities we can make up for their loss
> and sustain approval by maintaining the worth of our
> humanity. We may have lost everything else, yet still
> retain our inherent worth. (*Lectures* pg. 121.)

This principle of duty toward oneself, therefore, does not offer a reason to prefer or to reject either Conservation or Depletion. Neither choice entails an abdication of human freedom, and neither choice undermines humanity's future, even if it is conceded that one of them creates an repugnant future. The principle of duty to the self has not (yet) proven able to deliver an acceptable environmental ethic.

With the Deontological principles discussed so far, there appears to be only one kind of action concerning the environment which clearly and unequivocally constitutes a failure of moral duty: an act which concerns the environment but the primary and direct moral patient is another person or a group of people. Acts which aim to deceive people about the full extent of the environmental crisis of our time, or which aims to cover up information about it, can fall in this category. Oil corporations frequently donate large sums of money to advocacy groups, think-tanks, and researchers to undermine the claims and arguments of environmental campaigners, and to sow scepticism in the public mind.[35] The anti-environmental backlash, supported by industry, has been extraordinarily successful in painting the environmental movement as anti-jobs, anti-human, anti-business, anti-Christian, Communist, elitist, terrorist, closed-minded, utopian, Pagan, unscientific, and naïve. Environmentalists have had their cars bombed, their homes vandalised, burglarised, and burned, their pets killed or mutilated, been shot at, received death threats, received intimidation lawsuits, been assaulted and harassed, framed for murder or other criminal offences, and been driven out of their homes. They have even been killed.[36] The most famous example of this pattern of action is the case of:

> *The Ogoni People of Nigeria.* Ken Saro-Wiwa, a community leader from Ogoniland, Nigeria led thousands of his people in protest against the environmentally destructive drilling practices of Shell Oil in his native Ogoniland. He was framed for murder, brutally tortured while imprisoned, and on 10 November 1995 he and eight others were hung. The two main witnesses for the prosecution had already signed affidavits saying that they were bribed by the military and by Shell to testify against Saro-Wiwa, but this was dismissed by the military court as "too good to be true". The repression of the protest in Nigeria continued, leading to 1,800 Ogoni killed and 80,000 left homeless. Although this situation was well publicised, no nation in the world boycotted the flow of oil from Nigeria or from Shell in protest.[37]

It is abundantly clear that acts which deceive, scapegoat, or harm people in these various ways are morally wrong. In Kantian terms, the oppression of the Ogoni people would be contrary to one's interests and one's freedom if made into a universal law, and so it is contrary to moral duty. Even if we cannot agree on what is the right way to respect the environment, or even if we cannot agree on whether the environment is deserving of our respect, we can certainly agree that these acts fail to respect the humanity of other people, and should be morally condemned. But this position might not be completely adequate for all cases. There may be acts which damage the environment but which directly disrespects no one. We are clearly obliged to respect those who take up environmental activism as their cause, at least on the grounds of their membership in the human race, if not on the grounds of their commitment to environmental activism. But we do not yet know whether there is a duty to do as environmental activists do.

Before continuing with this direction, I shall digress from the exegesis of Kant to consider another form of Deontology, which may shed light on whether we have moral responsibilities concerning nature from a different direction. A non-anthropocentric principle may be tested as an alternative. The deontologist who has done the most to pursue this line of thought is Paul Taylor, in a respected theory of environmental ethics which he advanced in his 1986 book, Respect for Nature.

§ 3. Animals and Plants

Many environmental ethicists believe that freedom and autonomous reason are not relevant to a being's moral standing. What would that mean for our moral responsibilities toward animals, plants, and the environment in general? It can be claimed, as an alternative to the Kantian position, that freedom and autonomous reason are not what matters, but instead what matters is only that the being has a good of its own, or that it is a "teleological centre of life", as Taylor says. When Taylor speaks of the denial of human superiority, he speaks of the denial of arguments which, for whatever reason, single out the human species as the only species possessing moral standing.

Could animals and non-rational beings possess moral standing, even if we grant the Kantian claim that they do not possess freedom? There is a growing body of scientific evidence that animals do have ends which they pursue. There are many species whose members have a capacity for suffering, language, decision-making, family bonding, goal-oriented behaviour, tool use, emotional sensitivities, and so on, at least as well as human infants and toddlers. There are many instances of group co-operation such as mutual grooming and group hunting strategies. Some species such as primates, cetaceans, and canines even display what appears to be rudimentary politics, as their group behaviour patterns include hierarchies of authority, territorial sovereignty, distinctions between members and outsiders of tribal groups, and forms of punishment (usually exile). Alasdair MacIntyre devoted several chapters of a recent book to humankind's presuppositions of our natural difference from, and superiority over, the other animals (including one whole chapter on dolphin society), and how in the case of some species the grounds for our assumed separateness from animals is highly questionable.[38]

    We have seen how Kant would reject any claim that we can know the aims and ends of animals. Taylor bypasses this controversy by asserting that it is not necessary to make such claims. What matters, for Taylor, is whether a being has a good of its own. While we can doubt whether a being even has interests, it remains intelligible to speak of what is good or bad for it. This, Taylor asserts, is an objective criterion.[39] It is not necessary to make the strong knowledge claims about a being's inner subjective state which Kant would find unacceptable.[40] It matters only that we can say of a being that it can be benefited or harmed, which Taylor says is a straightforward and uncontroversial thing to claim.

> To benefit a being is to bring about or to preserve a
> condition that is favourable to it, or to avoid, get rid
> of, or prevent from occurring a condition that is
> unfavourable to it. To harm it is either to bring about
> a condition unfavourable to it or to destroy or take
> away a condition favourable to it. The terms
> "favourable" and "unfavourable" apply to something
> whose well-being can be furthered or damaged, and
> this can meaningfully be said only of an entity that
> has a good of its own. (*RN* pg. 61-2)

Since it does make sense to say that there are things which benefit or harm animals and plants, we can therefore claim that they are entities which have a good of their own. Taylor asserts that this holds good for plants and animals equally (*RN* pp. 66-7). We can make this judgement "from the perspective of the organism's life, even if the organism itself can neither make nor understand those judgements." (*RN* pg. 67) Furthermore, Taylor claims that since they are beings with a good of their own, they are beings with inherent worth. This he says entails two moral judgements: that "the entity is deserving of moral concern and consideration", and that "all moral agents have a prima facie duty to promote or preserve the entity's good as an end in itself and for the sake of the entity whose good it is." (*RN* pg. 75)

Taylor's argument, it appears, is meant to increase the range of entities to whom we owe our moral duties, to include not just persons, but all beings who have a good of their own. Moral duty has a formal criterion which requires that duty cannot defeat itself as a prescription for everyone; Taylor essentially affirms Kant's Categorical Imperative here.[41] It also has a material or practical criterion which specifies a particular duty-generating token which we are obliged to respect as an end in itself. The practical criterion generally follows a pattern like, 'Act in such a way that you always treat X as an end in itself'. The token of our moral duty, here designated as the 'X' of the general pattern, is normally an empirical or objective quality possessed by that to which we owe the moral duty of respect. For Kant, that token is humanity, or more precisely, autonomous human reason, both within ourselves and within others. For Taylor, it is any entity which possesses 'inherent worth', which includes humankind but casts the net wider to include anything which can have a good of its own. All persons are beings with a good of their own, but not all beings with a good of their own are persons. As he says, "The idea that all persons are bearers of inherent worth just in virtue of their being persons is… the ultimate ground of all duties in a moral community." (*RN* pg. 78) This he claims is also the general pattern for environmental ethics.[42] Why should we accept this change in the standard view of deontology? Because, in Taylor's view, "only this way of regarding them [animals and plants] is coherent with how we must understand them when we accept the belief-system of the biocentric outlook on nature." (*RN* pg. 80)

This biocentric outlook, as Taylor defines it, is an *attitude* which someone would adopt if he fully understands and accepts four basic facts: (1) our existence as biological creatures who are "but one species of animal life"; (2) the "significance of our ecological situation" as members of a complex and integrated whole natural world; (3) a "sharpened awareness" of the "moment-to-moment existence of each living thing"; and (4) a disposition to view ourselves and other living things impartially, such that "none is then deemed more worthy of existence than another". (*RN* pp. 156-7) As to the rational defensibility of this outlook, Taylor claims that it "satisfies certain well-established criteria for the acceptability of a philosophical world view", and that "insofar as moral agents are rational, factually enlightened, and have a developed capacity of reality-awareness, they will adopt those [biocentric] criteria as the basis for deciding what outlook on nature to accept as their own." (*RN* pg. 158.) The first three of the four basic facts are empirical facts to which Taylor is right to call special attention. The first and second concern humanity's relation to the environment, and the third to the goods of non-human beings.

The fourth part of the biocentric attitude, the disposition to view ourselves and other animals and plants impartially, appears to be a moral rather than a factual claim, and it may seem at first to presuppose Taylor's conclusion that we have a strong moral duty to respect nature. However, Taylor would argue that the doctrine of human superiority has been an unquestioned basic assumption of Western philosophical thought for thousands of years. As Taylor explains, this idea has come to us mainly from three historical sources. The first is classical Greek humanism, which asserts that only the capacity for reason enables a being to achieve a worthwhile life, and that only humans have it. (*RN* pp. 135-8). The second is Christian monotheism and the idea of the Great Chain of Being, which Taylor characterises as a projection of human values on to God and the order of the cosmos. (*RN* pp. 139-142). The third is Cartesian Dualism, which holds that animals do not have souls nor minds, and behave as mechanical automata, and may not even feel pain, which is contrary to much of what we now know of animal behaviour. (*RN* pp. 143-6) To Taylor, it is question-begging to defend the doctrine of human superiority, or even to assume an anthropocentric point of view, and that to deny this doctrine and this point of view is to be free of unquestioned and unexamined presuppositions. Taylor's comments seem to hit the mark with regard to Kantian deontology: we have seen how Kant presents no arguments for the moral value of freedom and autonomous reason, but simply presupposed its value as an obvious given.

There are various ways in which this position can be both supported and also criticised. But instead of examining various counter-arguments and replies, I wish to ask what implications there are for the Practical Imperative if we change its token, as Taylor claims we must do. Would it enable us to articulate an acceptable statement of environmental ethics? Would it point the way towards a solution to the Non-Identity Problem? Certainly, with regard to motorway building, littering, waste disposal, and pollution, and the Non-Identity choice of Depletion as an environmental policy, we can claim that the interests of animals and plants are violated by the harm such actions do to them. It thwarts their pursuit of their good. To use Taylor's terminology, such actions "harm" animals and plants because they "create conditions which are unfavourable to them". By interfering with or destroying their habitats, we damage their pursuit of their own kind of well-being. This, however, is something we may be unable to avoid. To obtain certain necessary amenities for human life and civilisation, including food, it is necessary to occupy land, to deplete certain resources, to displace the habitats of many animals and plants, to put them to work for us, or even to kill and eat them. By extending the token of the Practical Imperative, conflicts between human interests and the 'interests' of animals and plants are inevitably created. Taylor proposed five "priority principles" to help adjudicate between such conflicting claims. They are self-defence, proportionality, minimum wrong, distributive justice, and restitutive justice (*RN* pp. 263-307). However, even if we can arrive at fair principles to adjudicate between competing claims in an acceptable way, as Taylor claims we can, still we cannot escape using the animals and plants of the world as a means to an end. Taylor is forced to admit that his priority principles:

> ...do not yield a neat solution to every possible conflict situation. Each principle represents one cluster of morally relevant considerations one must take into account, and these considerations can serve as rough guides in reaching decisions about what duties outweigh others. But the principles do not function as premises in a deductive argument. We cannot deduce from them, along with the facts of the case, a true conclusion expressible in a normative statement about what ought to be done, all things considered. (*RN* pg. 263)

Unless this conflict can be resolved, it will be premature to say that the denial of human superiority offers anything new to the quest for an acceptable environmental ethic. Moreover, adding extra duties towards animals and plants seems to complicate, rather than clarify, the Non-Identity choice between Conservation and Depletion. We would fail in our duty of respect to animals and plants no matter which choice we made. Although Taylor's 'priority principles' would have us err on the side of Preservation, instead of Conservation or Depletion, in order to minimise the disrespect done to them, this does not fully resolve the situation of conflicting responsibilities.

I leave this conflict suspended in order to draw special attention to another observation. We found earlier in Kant's discussion of the duty to oneself a reason for why acts which are not self-defeating as universal laws might still be wrong. They are wrong if they damage the humanity of the agent who performs them. This, we saw, was an implicit step in the direction of Virtue theory. Taylor provides an explicit treatment of the role of virtue. He says that since the biocentric outlook is an attitude, it is *necessarily* expressed as a quality of one's character.

> The central tenet of the theory of environmental ethics that I am defending is that actions are right and character traits are morally good in virtue of their expressing or embodying a certain ultimate moral attitude, which I call respect for nature. When moral agents adopt the attitude, they thereby subscribe to a set of standards of character and rules of conduct as their own ethical principles. (*RN* pg. 80)

Rules of moral duty and of excellent moral character are for Taylor inextricably connected. The virtues are "*needed* for doing what is right and refraining from what is wrong," because they provide to the moral agent "the steady ability to do the right thing with the right aim and for the right reasons" in circumstances when "confusion of mind and weakness of will are not uncommon" (*RN* pg. 88, emphasis his). An act which damages the environment, such as an environmental policy choice like Depletion, would be in the view of both Kant and Taylor a failure of moral duty if it is an expression of poor moral character. For Taylor, who denies the doctrine of inherent human superiority, the quality of the agent's character which matters is the biocentric outlook itself as an ultimate attitude.

An emphasis on the virtues may help extricate us from the impasse between human interests and animal and plant 'interests' which emerges when human superiority is denied. The moral agent could choose to do that which manifests virtue, when he is at a loss concerning his duty toward different moral patients that are more or less equally worthy of respect. There may be relevant differences between the choices in terms of what qualities of character they call upon, or appear to manifest. In Taylor's view, virtue has two aspects. One is the deliberative aspect, in which it is "the capacity of a moral agent consistently to avoid confusion of mind and distorted thinking about duties, obligations, and responsibilities of a certain specific type". The other is the practical aspect, in which "a person of good character is the one who has the capacity to act in accordance with one's deliberative reasoning and judgement..." (*RN* pg. 87).[43] We can say that in Taylor's system of ethics, an un-virtuous act is one which is motivated by poor reasoning and clouded judgement. The virtues which Taylor names are all virtues required for perseverance in the fulfilment of moral duty. They are Conscientiousness, Integrity, Patience, Courage, Temperance or self-control, Disinteredness, Perseverence, Steadfastness-in-duty. (*RN* pp. 201-2.) Virtue for Taylor is the disposition to obey one's moral duty, consistently and regularly, and for the right reasons.[44] This, of course, is not the Aristotelian meaning of a virtue. It is more Kantian in its essence: Taylor claims that it is the attitude which fully informed and rational people would take when making choices that affect the environment. However, we should take the appearance of Virtue language in the theory as a sign that *who we are* is at least as important to ethics as what we do. "We are not fully moral beings", says Taylor, "until our inner character and our external practice are in perfect congruence." (*RN* pg. 215) We have a duty, therefore, to develop moral character. But it would seem that the duty to develop moral character must be stated, and can only be stated, in anthropocentric terms.

§ 4. The Land.

That is the Deontological situation for the moral standing of non human animals and plants. What about systems of many beings and the material elements which bind them together, such as ecosystems, landscapes, and environments? In Kant's <u>Lectures on Ethics</u>, he said that our duties toward nature and toward inanimate objects, like our duties toward animals, are indirect duties to humanity: "No man ought to mar the beauty of nature; for what he has no use for may still be of use to some one else. He need, of course, pay no heed to the thing itself, but he ought to consider his neighbour."[45] The idea here appears to be that to mar the beauty of nature is to disrespect others who might gain some use or enjoyment out of nature. But it is not explained exactly how this fits into his system of ethics as a whole. The issue regarding the quasi-Virtuous use of the term 'humanity' and its disjunction from the moral agent's surroundings appears here as it did in the case for animals. Consider the case of:

The Bog of Allen. In 2003, An Bord Pleanála approved a plan to divert water from Pollardstown Fen and the Curragh Aquifer, part of the extensive Bog of Allen in county Kildare (a Class 1 habitat, protected by the European Union by the Habitats Directive) into the county Kildare water supply. This project is being carried out illegally—the required Environmental Impact Statement was done improperly, and in violation of several EU environmental conservation directives.[46]

The most we can say about this situation, with the moral resources we have so far found in Kant's system, is that while neither Depletion nor Conservation nor Preservation is logically contrary to duty, we should err on the side of Conservation in order to avoid disrespecting others. This conclusion might be useful for most practical purposes, but is not completely satisfactory because it is not definitive enough. Certainly, to avoid the Non-Identity Problem, we need something more precise than a rule of thumb.

There is, however, a whole dimension of his thought which may indicate that one's surroundings are indeed morally relevant, contrary to what has been said until now. Kant had a personal and professional interest in the study of geography, and in fact he taught lectures in physical geography forty-eight times in his teaching career, almost as many times as he lectured on metaphysics and logic. He lectured on ethics only twenty-eight times.[47] An understanding of how Kant placed geography among the sciences may be helpful in seeking a Kantian answer to problems of environmental depletion and conservation. For this section, I will take geography to include the modern sciences of ecology and environmental studies, and related disciplines, as I take it that had those sciences existed in Kant's time, he would have included them in his framework as well.

As claimed by Robert Burch, "no philosopher before Kant had explicitly set out to determine philosophically the nature and role of geography as such, nor to establish specifically the place of the discipline with respect to the 'origin' and 'arrangement' of 'the whole of our knowledge'".[48] For Kant, a body of knowledge is a science if it organised into a system. A system is "the unity of the manifold cognitions under one idea." In the Critique of Pure Reason, Kant further explains,

> What we call science, whose schema contains the outline and the division of the whole into members in conformity with the idea, i.e. *a priori*, cannot arise technically, from the similarity of the manifold or the contingent use of cognition *in concreto* for all sorts of arbitrary external ends, but arises architectonically, for the sake of its affinity and its derivation from a single supreme and inner end, which first makes possible the whole.[49]

For geography to be a science, then, it cannot be simply a catalogue of information. It has to be unified by something. The founding idea of geography as a science, for Kant, is that it is the study of our home, the world in which we live, the total context of our lives. Geography tells us "where things are to be found", not just in terms of a collection of facts, but mainly in terms of the integral world of our experiences. In his lectures on geography, Kant said, "the world is the substratum and stage upon which the play of our skill proceeds. It is the ground upon which our knowledge is acquired and applied."[50]

I shall call this the principle of *Groundedness in the World*. This refers to the quality, property, or condition of belonging to the world, living in and with it, and being inseparable from it. It refers to the functions, potentialities, and faculties of a being which are inseparably a part of the world, lived in and with the world, operates or functions in relation to things in the world, and in various ways is connected to the world. It is the recognition that the world, however we approach it and whatever way we conceive of it, is the field and stage on which we play out our lives. We have seen something like this already in Taylor's Biocentric Attitude, as well as in Alison's principle of Totemism. Within this framework, geography is divided into natural science "proper" and a "historical doctrine of nature". Burch explains,

> Kant's thesis is that the history of nature proper is a diachronic account of nature made up of a suite of synchronic accounts of nature of the sort that a geographical description would provide. Thus, he claims that "genuine history is nothing other than a continuous geography"… Geography proper is a "description" of the whole earth as it presently is, albeit not from one experience of the earth as a single object of outer sense, but from "perceptions which taken together, would constitute the experience". By contrast, the history of nature proper is a "narrative". It not only must construct the synchronic moments that make up the history itself, as if each moment were the result of a geographic description, but also to tell the story of "what kinds of changes have been gone through in all periods".[51]

As this quotation from Burch shows, there is a certain element to Kant's view of geography that might find a comfortable home in existentialism, phenomenology or hermeneutics. Two particular Kantian positions reveal this. The first is the view that the range of genuine knowledge is limited to the range of possible experience. This is an empirical position wherein experience is the systematic unity of all perceptions in which the only possible *a priori* knowledge is the knowledge of the conditions for the possibility of experience. [52] The second is a dialectic between the subject and the object of experience. We exist as conscious beings only in relation to the world of which we are conscious. As Kant says in the <u>Critique of Pure Reason</u>:

The supreme principle of all synthetic judgements is, therefore: Every object stands under the necessary conditions of the synthetic unity of the manifold of intuition in a possible experience. In this way synthetic *a priori* judgements are possible, if we relate the formal conditions of *a priori* intuition, the synthesis of the imagination, and its necessary unity in a transcendental apperception to a possible cognition of experience in general, and say, *The conditions of the possibility of experience in general are at the same time conditions of the possibility of the objects of experience,* and on this account have objective validity in a synthetic judgement *a priori.*[53]

These two positions enable Kant to move from a purely formal definition of nature, as the existence of things in accordance with laws that configure and govern their existence, to a more phenomenological definition of nature as "the conceptual-complex of appearances", and hence the world of our lived experiences. On this phenomenological definition, things exist as 'objects of experience', and not as 'things in themselves'.[54] As a science, the geography which interested Kant so intensely, and perhaps also today's science of ecology as well, is not so far removed from the world of our experiences as are other sciences which have the same subject-matter, such as physics and chemistry. One could claim that Kant's geography was "pre-critical". Geography falls short of physics in that it is not so easily suited to mathematical formulation, but on the other hand, the geographer is not perceptually distanced from his object of study by theoretical and mathematical models, or devices that measure forces or chemicals not detectable to the sensory organs of our bodies. Geography, conceived as a study of the world in which we live and find our place and home, which is to say the study of our groundedness in the world, provides:

...the general framework within which *all* our knowledge of nature is to be ordered. It does so in the sense that it serves as the middle-term between the common knowledge of the world we have in life, whose guiding principles are not critically demonstrated [i.e. formally expressed *a priori* with mathematics or logic], and the methodical positing and precise mathematical calculation of the world of nature that is the work of physics.[55]

A complete exegesis of Kantian phenomenology is not necessary for this study. What is at stake here is whether Kant's geography attributes any moral significance to the environment. As shown by the geographer J.A. May, who made a comprehensive study of the influences of, and on, Kant's geographical thought, there were in Kant's day three ways to study the earth. One was mathematically, which involved measuring distances, depths, heights, and so on; another was politically, which involved studying human communities; and the third was geographically which appears to Kant as falling somewhere in between.[56] Kant defined geography, and the singular unifying principle which makes it a science, as follows:

Physical geography considers only the natural condition of the earth and what is contained on it: seas, continents, mountains, rivers, the atmosphere, man, animals, plants and minerals. All this, however, not with the completeness and philosophical exactitude which is the business of physics and natural history, but with the reasonable curiosity for the new of a traveller who seeks out everywhere what is noteworthy, peculiar, and beautiful, and compares his accumulated observations according to some plan.[57]

What brings geography together as a complete and whole science is that geography is to be explored "with the rational curiosity of a traveller", who does not bumble about at random, but has a plan to seek out what is interesting and beautiful. This plan, as Burch explains, consists in regarding the world "not just as an object of knowledge but the stage upon which they move, the place where they live and journey." The plan of the rationally curious traveller enables her to have a "preconception" with which she may "anticipate future experience". Thus geography teaches not what the world is, but "how to know the world".[58] What makes the world our home and place in the terms of Kantian geography is not only that it is the resource base of civilisation, but that it is the field and stage whereon the play of our life and our skills is enacted. It is the place where all of our thoughts and actions are performed. We do not simply take things from it—we live in it, respond to it and interact with it.

The ethical significance of the earth, it would seem, is that it is our home. To damage the environment, then, is to damage our home, which we can regard as an irrational act and therefore an act which damages the humanity within the agent who performs it. But what Burch believes he has revealed is not so much a new discovery in Kant's writings as a new difficulty: there is a tension between the phenomenological conception of world as the totality of lived experience, and the empirical conception of the world as simply the collected total of all existing things.[59] Kant's other philosophical commitments, such as to empirical realism and to transcendental idealism, do not allow him to follow up this phenomenological idea of the world as the home-place wherein our lives, experiences, and skills are played out. How Kant can be committed to all of these philosophical positions at the same time is one of the most difficult challenges for Kantian scholarship. On the conceptual level, our groundedness in the world is a phenomenological *a priori* concept. One of Kant's primary philosophical projects is to analyse *a priori* concepts, especially in epistemology; as he says in the first Critique: "A great part, perhaps the greatest part, of the business of our reason consists in the *analyses* of the concepts that we already have of objects."[60] His ethical theory as well as his geography is largely an extension of that project to the practical field. *A priori* concepts logically precede empirical experience and practical reason. They are not objects we think about or act upon. They are, rather, instruments for thinking, and as such, in his vocabulary, they are not practical but 'transcendental'.[61] For Kant, the idea that the world is our home-and-place is already an *a priori* concept; it is the organising idea for reason of which geography can be called a science. The idea organises not the structure of the practical world, but the structure of the "conceptual-complex of appearances"; which is to say, it organises how we experience the world. This commitment to the *a priori* pulls away from emphasis on the world as it appears to us and as we experience life in it. Kant's moral theory, derived entirely from *a priori* reasoning, rejects any contextualisation of moral principles and duties in contingent or 'accidental' situations of time, place, culture, climate, or ecological surroundings. Kant always insists that humankind is radically separated from natural surroundings. Indeed it could be said that the purpose of his whole philosophical career is to reconcile the separate worlds of nature and freedom, or of causality and morality, as he states most concisely in the Third Critique.[62] Yet these very surroundings are crucial to any philosophy of the environment, and to any study of geography. The very point of environmental philosophy is to enquire into precisely those physical, climactic and ecological contexts, often in relation to our own social and political contexts, and to ask what is the morally correct way to live within them. The disjunction between nature and freedom, Burch explains, also prevents Kant from fully understanding the dialectical relationship between ourselves and the world in which we live. "The root of the problem", according to Burch, "is that Kant does not fully appreciate the dialectic that governs the relation of human being and the natural world."[63] As a consequence of this Kant does not explore the significance of our groundedness in the world and the nature of our relation with it.

Moreover, as shown early in the first Critique, *space itself* is an *a priori* concept. Preceding (logically, not temporally) any empirical knowledge we may have of things in space, we already have in our minds a concept of what space is, and that *a priori* concept of space enables us to experience the world, and ourselves in relation to it, empirically and intelligibly. [64] We are able to find our home and place in the world because the concept of space is already within us as an *a priori* concept. But the *concept* of space, internalised within a person's mind, is not the practical home-and-place context of our lives.

May showed how Kant's thinking eventually expanded to include a kind of *moral* geography, and indeed a speculative moral anthropology. He indicates that Kant might eventually have resolved the tension Burch described in the direction of the empirical study of the world. Kant's moral geography, according to May, studied "what is moral in man, the variety of differences between his natural attributes, over the whole earth", focusing not on different kinds of government or the sequence of their rulers, but on "an understanding of more permanent features such as the position and situation of different countries, their produce, customs, trade and commerce, and population", with the aim of producing "a sort of 'moral map' of the human race".[65] According to May, this moral map would have contours following the fourfold classification of temperaments described in the ancient world by Hippocrates (melancholy, sanguine, choleric, and phlegmatic).[66] It appears that Kant thought we have certain natural dispositions given to us by our physical constitution and the condition of the world in which we live. But Kant also claims that what matters is what we decide to do with these dispositions:

> The sum of the pragmatic anthropology in respect to the destination of man and the characteristic of his development is as follows. Man, on account of his reason, is destined to be within human company and to cultivate, civilise, and moralise himself within it by means of art and science, no matter how great his animalistic tendency may be to resign himself passively to the incitements of leisure and luxury which he calls the state of happiness, but rather [he is destined on account of his reason] to make himself worthy of humanity in combat with the obstacles

which are affixed to him through the rawness of his nature.[67]

The idea here appears to be that humankind is grounded in nature (this is the "rawness" of his nature) but is 'destined' to overcome this groundedness and "make himself worthy of humanity". This is an acknowledgement of the role and the influence of the world on human life, but again, we find Kant's other philosophical commitments rendering him unable to follow up on this acknowledgement. At any rate, Kant says too little on this matter for any researcher to make a definitive statement of his meaning. No one, not even the most committed eco-centrist, would say that possession of a certain temperament derived from environmental influences determines the whole of someone's character, or makes him more or less a candidate for moral standing. It is a deep truth that we must always make choices in life, and that the choices themselves, as well as the ability to make them, shape a very large part of who we are. And in the <u>Lectures on Ethics</u> Kant declares that "anthropology observes the actual behaviour of human beings... whereas moral philosophy alone seeks to formulate rules of right conduct, that is, what ought to happen." (*Lectures* pg. 2) The most we can say with some confidence is that our groundedness in the world has moral significance because it is our home, and because it has some influence in the shaping of human character. But so long as we remain within the Kantian system, we would not be able to specify that significance very precisely because it would always be over-ruled by the importance of other concepts.

In 1755 Kant wrote three articles on the causes of earthquakes in response to one which devastated the city of Lisbon that same year. Much of it is concerned with scientific speculation which is not important here, however Kant includes several remarks to the effect that natural disasters should be taken as a sign that we do not know how God evaluates our worth in comparison to the worth of other things in nature, and so we should not think of ourselves as more important than anything else. Kant's own words on the matter are:

Man is so much taken with himself, that he considers
himself only as the sole object of the dispositions of
the Almighty, as if these had no other aim, than him
alone, in the regulation of the measures in the
government of the world. We know that the whole
complex of nature is a worthy object of the Divine
Wisdom and of its dispositions. We are a part of them
and would be the whole.[68]

The general idea here appears to be that we should not think of the
devastation of earthquakes as God's punishment for wickedness,
because such thoughts arise from an erroneous belief in the
importance and superiority of man. This is confirmed in the *Critique
of Judgement*, where he says:

...external nature is far from having made a particular
favourite of man or from having preferred him to all
other animals as the object of its beneficence. For we
see that in its destructive operations—plague, famine,
flood, cold, attacks from animals great and small, and
all such things—it has as little spared him as any
other animal.[69]

These remarks may seem surprising, and contrary to what has been
shown of his thought previously. In his ethical studies, Kant regards
humanity as the only end in itself. Here, by contrast, Kant appears to
be saying that humankind is not more important than anything else
in the eyes of God. It is possible to interpret this as an eco-centrist
position as it declares the value of humanity to be equal with that of
landscapes and natural environments. But again, Kant's text is very
sketchy here, and this apparently eco-centrist position, which owes
more to theology than to ecocentrism, can be attributed to him only
very loosely and tentatively. His ethical philosophy makes it clear
that humanity is to be treated as an end in itself. Furthermore his
critical philosophy holds humanity to be the teleological end of

nature. This position is stated most concisely in the parts of the
Critique of Judgement where the teleology of nature is discussed. In
a chapter entitled "The teleological system in the extrinsic relations
of organisms", he argues that if anyone were to ask what the purpose
of plant life is, it would be concluded that it exists to provide
sustenance to herbivorous animals. If one then asks why herbivores
exist, the answer would be to provide sustenance to carnivores. The
question could be repeated all along the food chain, until:

> At last we get down to the question: what is the end
> and purpose of these and all the preceding natural
> kingdoms? For man, we say, and the multifarious
> uses to which his intelligence teaches him to put all
> these forms of life. He is the ultimate end of creation
> here upon earth, because he is the one and only being
> upon it that is able to form a conception of ends, and
> from an aggregate of things purposively fashioned to
> construct by the aid of his reason a system of ends.[70]

Today one might answer this sequence of questions by saying that
plants and animals and life on earth exists for no purpose, and that
the benefit which living things provide to each other in the food
chain is quite accidental. But the point to pay attention to in this
passage is the claim that humankind is the only being on earth able
to form its own ends, and that nature has apparently fashioned
humankind to be capable of forming its own ends, and for that
reason 'he is the ultimate end of creation here upon earth'. The
humanism and even anthropocentrism of this passage is clear: nature
exists to promote and support humankind. This point appears again
in the next section, "The ultimate end of nature as a teleological
system":

> True, he [man] is a principle in respect of many ends
> to which nature seems to have predetermined him,
> seeing that he makes himself so; but, nevertheless, he
> is also a means towards the preservation of the

finality in the mechanism of the remaining members. As the single being upon earth that possesses understanding, and, consequently, a capacity for setting before himself ends of his deliberate choice, he is certainly titular lord of nature, and, supposing we regard nature as a teleological system, he is born to be its ultimate end.[71]

The idea here is that the teleology of nature, the purpose towards which all of its processes and activities aim, is the production of humankind, or at any rate the production of a being capable of freedom, understanding, and choice. This appears to be the window through which the reconciliation between nature and freedom which Kant envisions can be sighted.

This principle is repeated in a short essay from his later works entitled "Idea for a Universal History from A Cosmopolitan Point of View", in which he defends nine theses about what the ultimate end of human history is. Some of the principles articulated in the essay repeat his thoughts from the <u>Critique of Judgement</u>. The most interesting of which, for the present purpose, are the first, the fifth, and the eighth, which read:

[1st Thesis] All natural capacities of a creature are destined to evolve completely to their natural end.

[5th Thesis] The greatest problem for the human race, to the solution of which Nature drives man, is the achievement of a universal civic society which administers law among men.

[8th Thesis] The history of mankind can be seen, in the large, as the realisation of nature's secret plan to bring forth a perfectly constituted state as the only condition in which the capacities of mankind can be fully developed, and also bring forth that external

relation among states which is perfectly adequate to
this end.[72]

We may read from this essay that the development of a being's
capacities requires definite environments, and that the 'greatest
problem for the human race' is to create the environment in which
our specific faculty, reason, may evolve completely to its natural
end. For the purpose of articulating an environmental ethic in
Kantian terms, however, the positioning of humankind as the end of
nature makes it impossible to specify the moral significance of the
environment with much precision, even with the principle of
Groundedness in play. For Kant's emphasis is on the *social*
environment; he says nothing in these texts about the ecological
environment. His remarks about Nature as a teleological system
with Man as its end render unwieldy any attempt to re-cast Nature as
the ecological field and stage of our lives.

 Furthermore, the principle of Groundedness seems to have
limits, and we cannot always regard the world as our proper home.
In the essay on earthquakes, Kant says,

> Man was not born to build everlasting cottages upon
> this stage of vanity. Because his whole life has a far
> nobler aim. How beautifully do all the devastations,
> which the inconstancy of the world shows even in
> those things that appear to us the greatest and most
> important, contribute to put us in mind that the goods
> of the earth cannot satisfy our instinct for happiness?
> [73]

The philosophical message here appears to be that natural disasters
should be taken as evidence for 'the inconsistency of the world' for
which reason we should not look to it in order to 'satisfy our instinct
for happiness'. Again, Kant's remarks are very sketchy; there does
not seem to be enough material with which to make a definitive
statement about what Kant regarded as the appropriate attitude we
should adopt towards the fact of our groundedness in the world. At

most, we can say that the world does not exist 'for' humanity. But I would hesitate to attribute this position to Kant in a systematic way, as it is contrary to some of his statements about the teleology of nature. It is undeniable that Kant regarded humanity as the only being that must be treated as an end in itself. The tension Burch discovered between his theoretical commitments and his empirical discoveries remains unresolved, even if we can claim, however tentatively, that in his later writings Kant saw humankind as a creature whose being is realised in history and in physical embodiment, and not just in the thought and action of the (disembodied) mind and spirit.

With the conception of the moral significance of the world which we have, however sketchy it may be, we are now prepared to consider the choice between the Non-Identity environmental policies of Conservation and Depletion. For this purpose, we can think of them as plans for exploring the world and living in it, which we can put to the test of the Categorical Imperative. We can assume that while we choose our plan for living in the world freely, there may be plans which are irrational to choose because they fail to account for our groundedness in the world, and thus risk undermining our humanity and depriving us of a future. Can looking at the acts themselves, rather than their consequences, resolve any of the issues of the Non-Identity Problem? The only way to do this is if we interpret the principle of groundedness not as an epistemological concept, but as the embodied world of our life and action. This is the alternative which, as Burch claimed, Kant was unable to follow up due to his other philosophical commitments, although as shown by May, Kant's thoughts were indeed turning in this direction. On this level, it makes sense to say that Conservation and Depletion represent ways for using our Groundedness, and living in the world. At first it may seem that to ask the categorical imperative to judge our overall use of the world as our home and our place, instead of to judge individual actions, is a straightforward expansion of Kant's principle. The answer it would give may appear straightforward as well: it is irrational to live in the world in a way which, if everyone lived that way, would render the world unliveable, unfit for life, impossible to know, to move in, and to explore. If everyone used the world's resources greedily and gratuitously, and/or took them in a manner that does not take into account the ecological capacities of resource renewal or waste assimilation, then survival and civilisation would collapse as they disappeared. To undermine the resource base of survival is a self-defeating, irrational act when formulated as a law for everyone. Some way of living in and with the world sustainably must be found. At minimum, this Kantian environmentalism would not support unlimited and unfettered Depletion. This, if it is sound, would count as an acceptable environmental ethic.

However, I find that environmentally destructive acts fail the test of universalisation only at this abstract, world-encompassing level. Unless some means can be found to state the principle of groundedness in practical terms, rather than in theoretical terms, it will follow that acts which damage or degrade the world in which we are grounded can be criticised only on the theoretical level, and not at the practical level. We will be able to claim that it is morally wrong to do something which makes the world less easy, or even impossible, to live in. However we would never be able to pin-point any specific, particular action which fails the test of universalisation and thus is outlawed by duty. We will be able to say that it is wrong to make the world less healthy, less beautiful, less fertile, less clean, and so on. But we will be unable to claim that such actions are contrary to duty. Thus we would not be able to say why it is wrong to toss rubbish around in public places, use highly polluting fuels for transport and energy, and withdraw resources from the earth in exploitative, unsustainable ways. There is no *particular* environmentally destructive act which, if it were a law for everyone, undermines human freedom. We could say that such acts, as laws for everyone, render the world less suited to serve as the field and stage of our lives, in much the same way Kant said that natural disasters represent limits to the extent we can call the Earth our home. But that is not the same as saying that that such acts, as laws for everyone, become impossible to do. It could be claimed that to perform an act which causes a serious environmental disaster, rendering it less fit to serve as the field and stage of human life, is to disrespect one's humanity, and the humanity of everyone else who is grounded in the world. But as shown, the Kantian notion of 'humanity' is too narrow to support this claim very easily. We have no grounds to prefer either Conservation or Depletion; neither one of them fails the ethical test of universalisation. Deontology has thus far proven unable to provide an acceptable statement of environmental ethics.

This conclusion holds in part because of a weakness of the Categorical Imperative in general, which is that many non-moral maxims and even many silly maxims can pass the test of universalisation quite handily. As MacIntyre says, maxims like "'Keep all your promises throughout your entire life except one', 'Persecute all those who hold false religious beliefs' and 'Always eat mussels on Mondays in March' will all pass Kant's test, for all can be consistently universalised." (AV pg. 46.) Similarly, a maxim like 'Let everyone put their rubbish in the public bins except for me' can pass the test, as can similar maxims relating to pollution and mass transport. Life would be annoyingly inconvenient if everyone lived by such a principle. But it would not be impossible. And as MacIntyre argues, "to invoke considerations of convenience would in any case be to introduce just that prudential reference to happiness which Kant aspires to eliminate from all considerations of morality." (AV pg. 46.)

A possible exception to this conclusion, already alluded to, may be an act of 'omnicide', an act which destroys the whole world in a single moment. Kant's remarks on suicide in the Groundwork and the Lectures on Ethics may be illuminating here: he says in the Lectures that a moral agent "may not use his freedom against himself." (*Lectures* pg. 120) It is consistent with this view that an act freely chosen which destroys the material basis of life is contrary to freedom and thus contrary to moral duty. But it does not seem possible to formulate such an action as a universal law. Once Dr. Strangelove's Doomesday Machine is triggered, no one could trigger it again, not even the agent who did it in the first place. We can claim that a freely-chosen action which renders all future freely-chosen actions impossible is self-contradictory. But this does not seem to apply to acts which ruin or degrade the material basis of human life without totally destroying human life. As the Lectures say, "Man is free to dispose of his condition but not of his person; he himself is an end and not a means; all else in the world is of value only as a means, but man is a person and not a thing and therefore not a means." (*Lectures* pg. 120)

A full exploration of the moral significance of our groundedness in the world would require making certain changes in the Kantian programme. For instance it would call into question the disjunction between freedom and nature, in order to fully understand the relationship between a human moral agent and the world in which she lives. It would have to acknowledge that a relationship of some kind is in play. It would not begin by first postulating the agent as a given self who possesses a will and a capacity of autonomous reason in a theoretically 'original position' logically prior to encountering the world. Nor would it begin by postulating a world wholly determined by given laws of nature which only thereafter serves as the "stage" of human activity. It would have to show that we develop ourselves into moral beings not only through the use of freedom, but also in response to the other things in the world, including the natural environment. In short, it would have to be much less strict about the disjunction between the duties we owe to ourselves, and the surroundings in which we find ourselves. It shall be my argument in chapters 4 and 5 that Virtue theory is capable of making these claims. For his part, Burch attempted to point the way towards resolving the tension between the practical and theoretical directions of Kant's geography using Fichte's readjustment of the Kantian system. But as he claimed in his concluding remarks, "the notion of an ethical determination of geography properly makes sense, only if we understand it in an existential, ontological way."[74] Philosophy is not to obtain a strong grasp of this until the early twentieth century, with Husserl, Heidegger, and Lévinas, and it is not until Barbara Hardy, Alasdair MacIntyre and Paul Ricoeur, in the late twentieth century, that philosophy obtains a sophisticated theory of narrative, one capable of supporting robust conclusions about selfhood and ethics. It seems, then that the 'ontological' understanding which Burch calls for is something like Virtue theory. As shall be shown, there is an Aristotelian way of expressing the moral significance of groundedness, and of humanity, which may be able to resolve the tensions Burch described. And Virtue theory is capable of claiming that an act is wrong even if is not self-defeating as a law for all, and even if no one's humanity is disrespected. However, it is still too soon to close this chapter. We must now turn more directly to the matter of future generations.

§ 5. Future Generations and the Appeal to Rights.

We can claim, as a working hypothesis, that to pollute the environment and deplete its resources is to violate future people's right to possess their fair share of the world's resources and to live in a world that is fit for the pursuit of their interests. I shall here define rights as specific interests of sufficient importance that one can place others under a duty to have them fulfilled. This is a loosely Kantian notion of rights, for as we have seen, Kant would claim that we are duty-bound to respect beings that have interests, especially interests generated from autonomy and autonomous reason. This notion of rights presupposes that the only rights-holders are beings who can articulate a complaint against those who violate their rights by thwarting their pursuit of specific interests. Thus we are not considering whether non human animals or plants possess rights. Although Utilitarians since Bentham have been willing to include animals in their calculations of happiness and suffering, Parfit's discussion of Conservation and Depletion is exclusively limited to the harms and benefits for people, and he makes no mention at all of animals, non-sentient living beings, or ecosystems. Taylor, who rejects the idea of human superiority, nevertheless claims that only human beings possess moral rights. Plants and animals, in his view, do not.[75] The inconclusiveness of the extension of the Practical Imperative to plants and to non human animals is avoided.

I shall claim, as a working hypothesis for this section, that the reason to avoid the Repugnant Conclusion, and the reason to initiate a practice of Just Savings and Virtual Reciprocity (the issues left over from the previous study), is that it violates the rights of future people to have a clean and bountiful environment, and to a share of the world's resources. Where Parfit claims that future people can not complain about acts that brought them their existence, even if they exist in bad conditions, other writers asserted that they can: Doran Smolkin, for instance, argued that "a future person has a complaint if and only if some act that was a necessary condition for her coming into being also resulted in her being unable to acquire to a sufficient degree one or more of the elements needed for well-being in a particular stage of life".[76] This is the claim that, although the alternative for such people is non-existence, they still have specific interests which were violated by the actions that brought them into existence. If future people possess rights which Depletion would violate, that would be a reason for choosing Conservation as our preferred environmental policy, and for initiating a practice of intergenerational just savings, or virtual reciprocity, as was left suspended from the previous study.

James Woodward's treatment of the Non-Identity Problem employs painstaking precision in properly reporting it, not only through a close interpretation of Parfit's text but also personal correspondence with Parfit himself. The two authors also shared a short-lived conversation in the journal *Ethics*. Woodward is primarily arguing against the interpretation that Parfit's argument precludes an appeal to rights and fairness and forces an entirely consequentialist approach upon us when dealing with population policy and future generations. This comes mainly from other philosophers who have joined the debate, not from Parfit's text. Parfit claims only that future people can not have an objection to any policy we choose today, and that they are "no worse off", because they would owe their existence to it. Parfit also claims that his problems cannot wholly be solved by an appeal to non-consequentialist principles. He claims only that the principle of beneficence must figure into the solution somehow. However,

Woodward charges Parfit with an omission serious enough to be described as 'failure':

> While Parfit certainly allows for the abstract
> possibility that non-consequentialist considerations
> will play some role in the problems he discusses in
> part 4 [of *Reasons and Persons*] his actual practice is
> to attempt to deal with these problems just by
> exploring various versions of the principle of
> beneficence; when he encounters difficulties in
> formulating such a principle he does not attempt to
> deal with these by introducing non-consequentialist
> considerations but, rather, by complicating his version
> of the principle of beneficence...[77]

Woodward begins quite energetically to tackle the "no worse off" view that he observes at the core of Parfit's problem, which I have already described. As Woodward reports it, it is the view that an action cannot be objectionable in the morally relevant sense if the bad effects it has on other people leave them no worse off than they would have been if another action had been taken. Woodward then offers several examples in which harms imposed on people can leave them no worse off than they would otherwise be, and may even leave their lives much richer for it, but are still objectionable. I will here describe two of them.

Imagine the case of the Black man who is unable to buy an airline ticket because the ticket counter agent is a racist bigot, but subsequently the plane on which he would have travelled crashes, killing everyone. As the man is still alive after the crash, he is no worse off than he would have been if the airline sold him the ticket. Indeed he is better off. The 'no-worse-off' view would have us believe that the man was not harmed by the racist insult served to him by the ticket agent. Yet something still seems unsatisfactory about it. We should still be able to say that the ticket agent's act was wrong. Another example is that of the author Viktor Frankl, who suggested in his memoirs that he developed a refined sense of insight into life and humanity as a result of being imprisoned in a Nazi concentration camp. It is possible to claim that had he not been oppressed by the Nazis, his later life would not have had this quality. The "no worse off" view holds that because of this fact, we can have no objection to what the Nazis did to him while he was imprisoned. And this seems grievously wrongheaded. Woodward answers these problems by appealing to rights, grounded in 'specific interests', which were violated. In the case of Frankl, it must additionally be asserted that the good life Frankl enjoyed afterwards is entirely his own creation, and he is to be credited for it, not the Nazis. Woodward emphasises the strength of this case by adding to the no-worse-off view the hypothetical possibility that a person may be able to predict that others will be left no worse off by what is done to them, or even that the harm may be 'for their own good', knowing that at the end of the day, they will be better for it. In doing so Woodward finds that it does not erase or cancel out the damage done to their rights or the other sufferings inflicted on them. The harm done to them may be a necessary condition for the benefits that accrue to them, but people can still be blamed for what they did.

Parfit agrees that our objection to harming someone can still be strong even if the harm done to that person would not render that person 'worse' in the long run. Thus, he says: "We can deserve to be blamed for harming others, even when this is not worse for them. Suppose that I drive carelessly, and in the resulting crash cause you to lose a leg. One year later, war breaks out. If you had not lost this leg, you would have been conscripted, and killed. My careless driving therefore saves your life. But I am still morally to blame." (R&P pg. 372)[78] Under normal circumstances we have no way of knowing whether or how a crime will lead to some long-term benefit for the victim. But in the case of the impact of environmental policy on future generations, such as a policy concerning pollution, nuclear energy, waste disposal, land planning, or transport, we can know in general terms, and well in advance, what will be the consequences for them not only in terms of their quality of life but also in terms of their identities.

This leads to Woodward's treatment of one of Parfit's own examples: the case of the Risky Policy. This example is different from the others in that we can, in fact, predict the disaster that will occur (as is stipulated by the case). It is not like the example of the man who loses a leg in a car accident, and is spared from military conscription a year later. In that case, the harm is a necessary condition for a later benefit. But this cannot be predicted at the time the harm occurs. In the case of Risky Policy, we can predict that, when the earthquake damages the nuclear waste storage facility it will kill thousands of people. We can also predict that those people will have lived worthwhile lives. Moreover, we also know that the choice of burying the nuclear waste in one place instead of another choice like burying it elsewhere or not burying it at all, is a necessary condition of those people being born. Parfit then asks, if people lead lives that are worth living, even though they are killed by some catastrophe, is this worse for these people than if they had never existed? His conclusion is "No", because since we know that their lives will be worth living, and that they would not have been born otherwise, it is not worse for them.

Against this, Woodward repeats a point that he raised with the other examples and which is still relevant: he distinguishes between that which was necessary for the situation to occur, and that to which credit for the situation can be properly given. I read this as a distinction between two kinds of causality: the causality of results and of achievements. The worth of these people's lives is a *result* of the planner's choice but it is not *achieved* by the planners. The worth of the lives of the nuclear-accident people is achieved by the many distinct actions and choices made by themselves, their associates, and nearest ancestors. He says,

> The fact of the planner's choice of the Risky Policy is a necessary condition for a certain couple deciding to marry and to have a child and their bringing up that child in such a way that it has a worthwhile life does not mean that the character of that life is properly credited to the planners' choices. We thus cannot

appeal to the worthwhile character of that life as
somehow cancelling the wrongfulness of the
planner's choice of the Risky Policy.[79]

All that is morally important to Woodward, here, is whether rights
were violated or fairness was breached, not whether the person was
affected just as favourably as she would have been had other choices
been made, and not whether the harmful action was a necessary
condition of the victim's existence. Otherwise, one could easily
imagine the scenario envisioned by Woodward in which a couple
whose child develops cancer proceed to sue their employer, a
chemical factory, for compensation. But the philosopher in the
company's legal department argues that had the company not
employed them they would never have met, and they would have
conceived different children with different people, and thus their
child is actually benefited by the company, or at least left him no
worse off.[80]

The analogy with environmental ethics here is as follows. If
we choose an environmentally destructive energy and pollution
policy, and as a result a future is created in which people suffer from
skin cancer, asthma, food shortages, weather disasters, and so on, a
philosopher today could argue that we have benefited those people,
or at least left them no worse off. For if we had chosen differently,
circumstances would be such that different people would marry,
conceive different children, and so on. Consider:

The Derrybrian Landslide. In the fall of 2003,
construction works on a wind turbine development in
unstable soil of the hills above the town of
Derrybrian, county Galway, caused a land slide.
Mud, stone, trees, and earth obstructed access to the
town for many days. A national moratorium on the
construction of wind turbines in the Irish Republic
was called as a result, which lasted for almost six
months.[81]

Suppose that as another result of the blocked road, different people met each other than who would have met otherwise, and a few different people were born. They would owe their existence to the poor land planning decision that permitted the wind turbines to be built on the unstable hilltop. If the moratorium on the construction of wind turbines had been permanent, and Irish people relied exclusively on carbon intensive fuels like oil and peat to produce electricity in the future, these different people might have a lower quality of life due to air pollution. But they would be benefited by the land slide and the moratorium, or at least made "no worse off". Such a conclusion clearly cannot be called an adequate environmental ethic. On the theoretical plane, it gives us no guidance for our environment-affecting choices. On the practical plane, it gives no reason to initiate or participate in a practice of intergenerational virtual reciprocity or intergenerational just savings, and it cannot explain what is morally wrong with causing environmental destruction.

To help overcome this situation, Woodward argues that we should claim the act was wrong on the basis of the rights that were violated, even if the results of the action produce a net balance of positive utility. He says we should compare the situation of Non-Identity people not to non-existence but to "unattainable baseline situations". Considering the case of Risky Policy, he writes,

> ...the sort of analysis I have been exploring explains the wrongfulness of the choice of the nuclear policy by focusing on the difference between the situation of the nuclear people under the choice of the nuclear policy (when they are killed, injured, etc.) and an (unattainable) baseline situation in which the nuclear people exist and these violations of their rights do not occur. This difference represents a loss which, arguably, one can coherently think of as happening *to* the nuclear people.[82]

These unattainable baseline situations are, as Woodward explains, the situations in which people's rights, and the specific interests in which they are grounded, are completely fulfilled. Parfit admits that if this view is defensible, it would be the complete solution to the Non-Identity problem. His reply is to suggest a new case example in which this argument does not seem to apply. Suppose you have an accident in which you become unconscious. Suppose that in order to save your life, it is necessary for a surgeon to amputate your arm. This is better for you than the alternative. The unattainable baseline situation is one in which you both live and keep your arm. Yet if we appealed to unattainable baseline situations, we would have to condemn the surgeon's act.[83] Parfit appears to be claiming that so long as such baseline ideal situations are indeed unattainable, then no action that an agent can perform is right. It may be objected that the surgeon example presents a different moral dilemma than Risky Policy or Depletion. But what is that difference? To tell them apart, Parfit suggests that Woodward is assuming a particular thesis, which he designates as "Thesis T" and describes as follows:

> Suppose (1) that an act predictably violates one of a person's "specific interests," though (2) the agent knows that, because this act will have some other effect, it will not be worse for this person. Clause 2 provides an excuse only if (3) this other effect is both intended and directly caused.[84]

But Woodward does not assert anything like this in his paper, and at several points he even repudiates it.[85] For instance, in his analysis of the case of Viktor Frankl, it would still not have been justifiable for the Nazis to have imprisoned and tortured him even if they knew in advance that he would benefit from the experience later in his life. Thesis T is still a thesis to do with effects and consequences: but Woodward has already departed from that realm somewhat. As Woodward says, "The general point, then, is that the difference which explains why the amputation but not the choice of the Risky Policy is permissible is supplied by the different structure of rights in these two cases. There is no right which is violated in the amputation case, but the nuclear people do have rights which would be violated by the choice of the Risky Policy."[86] Woodward's emphasis all along is on the rights of future people, which is a non-consequentialist ethical theory. However, it is still a person-affecting theory. Close to the end of his second paper, he admits "although I lack the space to argue the point in any detail here, I think there are good reasons, generated by the desire to give a plausibly naturalistic account of the status of moral requirements, for wanting to keep the role of non-person-affecting considerations to a minimum."[87] Thus Woodward is not completely ready to "let go" of consequentialist reasoning.

Like Woodward, Edward Page proposed a rights-based approach to handle the Non-Identity problem. According to Page, an action is wrong not if it harms people directly, it is more important if an action violates a person's right(s). Page defines rights the same way I do: they are interests that are important enough to justify imposing on others a duty to fulfil them. The adoption of the Depletion policy becomes objectionable because it would bring into being a population of people with interests that could not be protected. The unprotected interests are, in his view, sufficiently important that we are morally compelled to fulfil them. On such a view, it would be totally unimportant if the Depletion people were not the same as the Conservation people. Indeed he argues, as does Woodward, that it may be wrong to bring into being people who will have rights that cannot be protected.

> The upshot of this line of argument is that some future persons' interests, and the rights they ground, confer obligations upon their predecessors not only to refrain from harming these interests once they have come into existence, but in addition to refrain from adopting courses of action which result in bringing persons into the world whose specific interests will thereby be unavoidably harmed.[88]

As we saw with Woodward, Page's introduction of specific rights is the introduction of a non-consequentialist element in the approach to the Non-Identity problem. Page increases the power of the rights approach by asserting that certain rights might be inalienable, impossible to suspend. This replies to Parfit's claim that the Depletion people might "waive their right not to be born" because they are grateful to be alive regardless of the quality of their life. (*R&P* pg. 365) Page's reply is plausible, but he does not supply much of an argument for it. I'll not describe his account of the rights-based solution, as it is similar enough to Woodward's approach. What is innovative about Page's argument is his claim that specific rights can be grounded in *group* interests or the interests of *collectivities*. In his words:

> So it seems that the idea of the specific rights (or interests) of *individuals* will need to be supplemented by some appeal to the specific rights (or interests) of *collectivities* if we are to make sense of the idea of rights to environmental public goods such as clean air… What the Non-Identity Problem renders implausible, I think, are objections to Depletion which focus on the rights and interests of *particular persons* as central to the moral wrongness of choosing Depletion over Conservation.[89]

Thus Page was also led by the intuition that person-affecting consequentialist principles by themselves cannot supply us with the grounding reason for our intuition that it is wrong to choose Depletion. However, Page retains the person-affecting approach, substituting 'groups' instead of 'individuals' as the basic kind of rights-holder. "The Non-Identity Problem appears to undermine any account which takes the relevant, value-bearing token to be a particular person. But rather than abandon a token affecting approach altogether, this result might rather suggest that we ought to appeal to the interests or rights of a different token…"[90] This leads him to a discovery of the "group affecting approach", and finally to the "group affecting version" of the Non-Identity Problem. Page argues that Depletion is objectionable because it violates the rights of future groups of persons. Imagine a community of islanders in the south Pacific ocean, like Tuvalu, whose territory is being flooded by rising ocean levels as a result of global warming. Page says that their community is harmed, and as a community they may have an objection to the Depletion policy that caused the global warming effects that threaten their community.

> ...communities which future people belong to are deserving of concern and respect in their own right. And if present actions have the result either that these communities die out altogether, or are damaged in the sense that various communal practices are undermined, they are morally objectionable at least in this one important respect. Thus, despite the fact that no future individual islander will be harmed by the depletion Policy's adoption—they all lead lives which are at least worth living and owe their existence to it —the islanders *as a collectivity* are harmed.[91]

Page believes that this view is compatible with contractualist and specific-rights approaches, and with person-affecting utilitarian principles even though it is not concerned with particular persons. However, he found that he accidentally invented a new variation of the problem, the "group-affecting version of the Non-Identity Problem". Entire communities may owe their existence to tragedies experienced by their ancestors. The Irish Famine of 1847 was, as I believe all readers would agree, a terrible disaster. Yet communities of the Irish Diaspora across the world owe their existence to that tragedy. The group-affecting version of the Non-Identity problem suggests that those communities were not harmed, or made worse off, by the famine. If there was no famine, there would be Irish people in Canada from "normal" immigration, but there would not be the same rich, diverse, and 150-year old heritage of Irish culture which is arguably distinct from the Irish culture that stayed in

Ireland, or that emigrated to other parts of the world, and was, until recently, the largest minority ethnic group in the province of Quebec.

The group-affecting approach to the rights of future generations turned out to be a variation of the utilitarian principle, as it sought the to locate moral value on an action's consequences rather than on the action itself or its agent. It was different only in its token. It failed to find a solution to the problem; indeed it lead to a new variation of the problem. I think this adds further weight to the case that it cannot be solved with person-affecting principles, or at any rate, it cannot be solved with principles that place the emphasis of concern on the very individuals or groups who owe their existence to the situation that generates the problem in the first place. It is not merely a matter of substituting something new for the theory's token: for instance, as Page found, substituting "groups" instead of "people" leads to the group-affecting version of the Non-Identity problem. Parfit allows for moral principles that are not stated in person-affecting terms, in which an action may be objectionable even if it has no bad effect on anyone, but he merely substitutes a new token for consequentialism to take care of, such as "future standard of living" or "human well-being".[92] This is one way how, as Woodward put it, he "complicates his principle of beneficence". Although Parfit claimed that these are not person-affecting principles, one can always ask 'Whose standard of living?' and 'Whose human well-being' is to be taken care of? They are therefore disguised person-affecting principles. So long as one remains within the realm of such principles, one will always be confronted with something like the Non-Identity Problem. The Non-Identity Problem confronts us in situations that not only generate problems for people, but which also generate the people for whom the problems arise.

§ 6. Summary remarks for Chapter Three

We have seen how, as a practical matter, we can easily put policy choices like Conservation and Depletion to the test. However, Kant's own writings offer us no reason to prefer one over the other.

We discovered a promising hidden principle within Kant's conception of geography, which I named 'groundedness in the world'. Yet we found that it too possesses an internal tension, and that it has limits. As a holistic, all-encompassing idea, groundedness enables us to affirm that it can be self-defeating to degrade or ruin the qualities of the world which make it a suitable home and place for us. However, we also found that Kant's strict separation between a person's moral condition and the material condition of his surroundings makes it impossible for us to find definitive answers for the general questions of this thesis. The most we can say is that we should lean in the direction of Conservation where possible, to avoid disrespecting others who wish to use or enjoy the world. But this does not seem to be sufficiently authoritative.

However, I believe it was not a waste of time to explore these principles. The idea that beings require the right environment in which to develop their capacities to their fullest is, it seems to me, the seed from which a stronger, more robust principle of environmental ethics may grow. The idea is remarkably Aristotelian; Kant seems to share with Aristotle the idea that reason is the highest human faculty, and in his writings on history he also seems to share the idea that the good life, or in Kant's terms the 'evolution of his capacities', depends on the right kind of social environment. This is a seed that may yet grow strong if there is a way to show that what has been said of the social environment can also apply to the ecological. Furthermore, Kant's claim to the effect that refraining from harming animals and landscapes can make us better persons (for one who harms animals may "become hard also in his treatment of men") is, as seen, a very Aristotelian point of view. But in the discussion of future generations, an important impediment to the growth of our seed was found in the form of a Deontological version of the Non-Identity Problem. It appears that an acceptable statement of environmental ethics is possible only for a theory that can overcome these issues. It must be capable of claiming that an act can be wrong even if it is not self-defeating as a law for everyone, and even if no one's rights are infringed. Alternatively, it could be a theory which makes an appropriate connection between a person's dignity and freedom, on one hand, and the material conditions in which she finds herself, on the other hand.

With regard to future generations and the Non-Identity Problem, we find ourselves in the same position we were in at the close of the first study. We can agree that the Repugnant Conclusion is intrinsically repugnant. It would be a future characterised by resource scarcity and heavy pollution. It would also be characterised by serious social and political problems which can be started, or worsened, by environmental problems. The United Nations Security Council in 1992 included environmental resource scarcity among the causes of social stress leading to political violence in the form of border conflicts, civil strife, and war.[93] In the words of researcher Richard Kaplan, "it is time to understand the environment for what it is: *the* national security issue of the twenty-first century. The political and strategic impact of surging populations, spreading disease, deforestation and soil erosion, water depletion, air pollution, and, possibly, rising sea levels in critical, overcrowded regions like the Nile Delta and Bangladesh, will be the core foreign-political challenge."[94] Although we can know in advance that environmental degradation will create a seriously troubled future for humanity, person-affecting moral principles are unable to explain why it would be wrong to choose it. The solution to the Non-Identity Problem, and the discovery of a satisfactory environmental ethic, will require moral principles which locate the right and the good on some place other than the harms, benefits, or rights of the people affected by the action. All that remains, after the studies of Utilitarianism, Justice, and Deontology, is Virtue theory. We have seen how several aporias in the Kantian system, and in the Rawlsian system, already suggest this move. It is time, now, to delve into Virtue theory directly.

---

[1] Kant, Immanuel Groundwork of the Metaphysics of Morals, pg. 60. References to his text shall hereafter be abbreviated as *Groundwork.*

[2] "For since reason is not sufficiently serviceable for guiding the will safely as regards its objects and the satisfactions of all our needs (which it in part even multiplies)—a purpose for which an implanted natural instinct would have led us much more surely; and since none the less reason has been imparted to us as a practical power—that is, as one which is to have influence on the *will*, its true function must be to produce a will which is good, not as a means to some further end, but in itself; and for this function reason was absolutely necessary in a world where nature, in distributing her aptitudes, has everywhere else gone to work in a purposive manner." (*Groundwork*, pg. 64).

[3] "Thus the moral worth of an action does not depend on the result expected from it, and so too does not depend on any principle of action that needs to borrow its motive from this expected result. For all these results (agreeable states and even the promotion of happiness in others) could have been brought about by other causes as well, and consequently their production did not require the will of a rational being, in which, however, the highest and unconditioned good alone can be found. Therefore nothing but the *idea of the law* in itself, *which admittedly is present only in a rational being*—so far as it, and not an expected result, is the ground determining the well—can constitute that pre-eminent good which we call moral, a good which is already present in the person acting on this idea and has not to be awaited merely from the result." (*Groundwork*, pg. 69.)

[4] The paragraph continues, clarifying with an example what it means to act from duty as distinct from doing the same act from inclination: "When on the contrary, disappointments and hopeless misery have quite taken away the taste for life; when a wretched man, strong in soul and more angered at his fate than faint-hearted or cast down, longs for death and still preserves his life without loving it— not from inclination or fear but from duty; then indeed his maxim has a moral content." (*Groundwork* pg. 66)

[5] "…imperatives of prudence, strictly speaking, do not command at all—that is, cannot exhibit actions objectively as practically *necessary*; that they are rather to be taken as recommendations, than as commands, of reason; that the problem of determining certainly and universally what action will promote happiness of a rational being is completely insoluble…" (*Groundwork* pg. 86.)

[6] "An action done from duty has its moral worth, *not in the purpose* to be attained by it, but in the maxim in accordance with which it is decided upon; it depends, therefore, not on the realisation of the object of the action, but solely on the *principle of volition* in accordance with which, irrespective of all objects of the faculty of desire, the action has been performed." *Groundwork*, pg. 67-8).

[7] The word *Achtung*, here translated as "reverence", is also translatable as "respect".

[8] "For duty has to be a practical, unconditioned necessity of action; it must therefore hold for all rational beings (to whom alone an imperative can apply at all), and *only because of this* can it also be a law for all human wills. Whatever, on the other hand, is derived from the special predisposition of humanity, from certain feelings and propensities and even, if this were possible, from some special bent peculiar to human reason and not holding necessarily for the will of every rational being—all this can indeed supply a personal maxim, but not a law…" (*Groundwork* pg. 92-3).

[9] Thus Kant says, "Suppose, however, there were something whose existence has in itself an absolute value, something which as an end in itself could be a ground of determinate laws; then in it, and in it alone, would there be the ground of a possible categorical imperative—that is, of a practical law." (*Groundwork* pg. 95.)

[10] Onora O'Neill, Towards Justice and Virtue, pg. 176.

[11] Joe Humphries, "Rise in cigarette butt litter after smoking ban" *The Irish times* 10 May 2004.

[12] "Two illegal dumps found in county Meath" *RTÉ News* 23 February 2005.

[13] "Rubbish from Cork found on illegal dump in Fermamagh" *Northern Leader*, 6 March 2004.

[14] Niall O'Connor, "Waste firm owner gets suspended jail sentence for illegal dumping" *The Irish Times* 14 May 2004.

[15] Vincent P. Bantz, et.al., The European Parliament and the Environment Policy of the European Union, pg. 17.

[16] "Car culture causing transport crisis, forum told" *The Irish Times* 12 April 2005.

[17] Sabine Scalla, et.al., European Parliament Briefing No.2: Air Traffic and the Environment Pg. 7.

[18] Joanna Walters, "Save the Planet: Stay on the Ground" *The Observer* 12 May 2002. Is this a misleading statistic? For trans-atlantic aircraft carry hundreds of passengers, not just one. Dividing the number of years in a person's life in which she possesses a valid driver's license (let us say 50 years), by the number of passengers on a trans-atlantic flight (an Airbus A353 carries about 300 passengers), we can claim that one trans-atlantic flight produces about as much pollution as each passenger produces with her private car every six years. We can therefore still claim that air travel produces more per-passenger pollution than private car travel.

[19] Lorna Siggins, "Council go-ahead for Corrib gas land terminal" *The Irish Times* 1 May 2004, pg. 2.

[20] In that example the maxim to be tested was whether it is right to commit suicide when one's life is of such poor quality that shortening or ending it may appear as an improvement. (C.f. *Groundwork* pg. 89)

[21] Frank McDonald, "Hydrogen power for Vancouver Olympics" *The Irish Times* 15 April 2004, pg. 13.

[22] "Sun, Wind, Fuel Cells Power Cargo Ship of the Future" *Environmental News Service* 6 April 2005

[23] "For the universality of a law that every one believing himself to be in need can make any promise he pleases with the intention not to keep it would make promising, and the very purpose of promising, itself impossible, since no one would believe he was being promised anything, but would laugh at utterances of this kind as empty shams." (*Groundwork* pg. 90)

[24] "Air Pollution Raises Cancer Risk" *Environmental News Service* 3 October 2002.

[25] "This concept [of the will as good in itself, apart from any further end], which is already present in a sound natural understanding and requires not so much to be taught as merely to be clarified, always holds the highest place in estimating the total worth of our actions and constitutes the condition of all the rest." (*Groundwork*, pg. 64-5.)

[26] Christina Hoff, "Kant's Invidious Humanism"; John Passmore Man's Responsibility for Nature pg. 210.

[27] Kant, Lectures on Ethics pg. 240, emphasis added. References to this text shall be abbreviated as *Lectures*.

[28] Hoff, "Kant's Invidious Humanism", pg. 63.

[29] Tim Hayward, "Kant and the Moral Considerability of Non-Rational Beings" in Attfield and Belsey, eds. Philosophy and the Natural Environment pg. 131.

[30] As Hayward explains, "For Kant, rational beings can know their own ends subjectively, but cannot know other beings' ends in this way. On the one hand, such natural ends as are posited or inferred by biological sciences are known, if at all, *objectively*; on the other hand, positing subjective ends in nature, on analogy with our own, not only proceeds without any assurance that the analogy holds, but, furthermore, may introduce a more insidious anthropomorphism through the projecting of human characteristics, needs, and interests on to other beings which may in fact be radically different from what humans imagine." Hayward, "Kant and the Moral Considerability of Non-Rational Beings", pg. 137.

[31] Note that what is impossible to accept here is any claim about whether or not non-rational beings have ends, *not* the claim that non-rational beings do not have ends—the very point here is that it is impossible to confirm or deny that they consciously pursue ends.

[32] "material philosophy [distinguished from logic] which has to do with determinate objects and with the laws to which they are subject, is in turn divided into two, since the laws in question are laws either of *nature* or of *freedom*. The science of the first is called *physics*, that of the second *ethics*. The former is also called natural philosophy, the latter moral philosophy" (*Groundwork* pg. 55).

[33] "'Nature' taken adjectivally (*formaliter*) signifies the connection of determinations of a thing in accordance with an inner principle of causality. Conversely, by 'nature' taken substantively (*materialiter*) is understood the sum total of appearances insofar as these are in thoroughgoing connection through an inner principle of causality. In the first sense one speaks of the 'nature' of fluid matter, of fire, etc., and employs this word adjectivally; conversely, if one talks about the 'things of nature,' then one has in mind a subsisting whole." Kant, Critique of Pure Reason, A418/B446, pg. 466

[34] Tim Radford, "Two-thirds of world's resources 'used up'" *The Guardian* 30 March 2005.

[35] David Adam, "Oil firms fund climate change 'denial'" *The Guardian* 27 January 2005.

[36] For a more detailed treatment of the corporate driven subversion of the environmental movement, consult Andrew Rowell, Green Backlash, chapter 3.

[37] C.f. McMurtry, Unequal Freedoms pg. 289; Rowell, Green Backlash, pg. 205-9.

[38] MacIntyre, Dependent Rational Animals, pp. 11-52

[39] "Something can be in a being's interest and so benefit it, but the being itself might have no interest in it. Indeed, it might not even be the kind of entity that can have interests at all. In order to know whether something is (truly) in X's interests, we do not find out whether X has an interest in it. We inquire whether the thing in question will in fact further X's overall well-being. We ask, 'Does this promote or protect the good of X?' This is an objective matter because it is not determined by the beliefs, desires, feelings, or conscious interests of X." Taylor, Respect for Nature, pg. 63. This text shall be referenced from now on as *RN*.

[40] "Disputes about the applicability of *subjective* value concepts to nonhuman animals are simply not relevant to the ethics of respect for nature. It is the *objective* value concept of a being's good which is presupposed by this theory, not the various subjective concepts that have been mentioned." *RN* pg. 65.

[41] "An important implication of the condition of universal applicability is that a whole system of valid moral rules and standards must be such that it is possible for everyone (all moral agents) to live in accordance with it. No rule prescribing conduct that annuls or defeats itself when everyone attempts to comply with it can be included." (*RN* pg. 28).

[42] "If inherent worth is attributed to any wild creature just in virtue of its being a member of the biotic community of a natural ecosystem, then each wild animal or plant is understood to have the same status as a moral subject to which duties are owed by moral agents." (*RN* pg. 78-9)

[43] Further on, Taylor elaborates this conception of virtue in the light of the environmental ethic he defends: "the attitude of respect for nature is expressed in one's character when one has developed firm, steady, permanent dispositions that enable one to deliberate and act consistently with the four rules of duty: Nonmaleficence, Noninterference, Fidelity, and Restitutive Justice." (*RN* pg. 199.)

[44] "The general virtues are those traits of good character needed for deliberating and acting in the right way, no matter what particular moral rules and principles are being applied and followed... the special virtues, on the other hand, are the specific character traits associated with each of the four types of duty." (*RN* pg. 199-200.)

[45] Kant, Lectures on Ethics, pg. 241.

[46] "Ireland's Environmental NGO's support Pollardstown Fen Concerns" Press release by the Irish Peatland Conservation Council, 25 February 2001.

[47] Friedrich Paulson, Immanuel Kant: His Life and Doctrine pg. 60.

[48] Robert Burch, "On the Ethical Determination of Geography: A Kantian Prolegomenon" in Andrew Light and Jonathan M. Smith, eds. Space, Place, and Environmental Ethics, pg. 19.

[49] Kant, Critique of Pure Reason, pg. 691, 692. [A832/B860, A834/B861].

[50] Kant, "Physiche Geographie", as cited by Burch, "On the Ethical Determination of Geography", pg. 21. [At this time, an English-language edition of Kant's Gesammelte Shriften (in which the "Physiche Geographie" lectures appear) is not available.]

[51] Burch, "On the Ethical Determination of Geography", pg. 22.

[52] "The possibility of experience is therefore that which gives all of our cognitions *a priori* objective reality. Now experience rests on the synthetic unity of appearances, i.e., on a synthesis according to concepts of the object of appearances in general, without which it would not even be cognition but rather a rhapsody of perceptions, which would not fit together in any context in accordance with rules of a thoroughly connected (possible) consciousness, thus not into the transcendental and necessary unity of apperception. Experience therefore has principles of its form which ground it *a priori*, namely the general rules of unity in the synthesis of appearances, whose objective reality, as necessarily conditions, can always be shown in experience, indeed in its possibility." Kant, Critique of Pure Reason, A157/B196 (pg. 282)

[53] Kant, <u>Critique of Pure Reason</u>, A197/B158 (pg. 283) Emphasis added.

[54] As Burch explains, "He [Kant] makes this move by demonstrating that the latter conception of nature [the existence of things in accordance with laws] is a necessary condition for the very possibility of experience in general, and hence that, along with the conformity of things to law, this conception is required too by natural science proper. In strictly theoretical terms, then, the science of geography as an empirical doctrine of nature, and Newtonian physics, as Kant's paradigmatic natural science, *both* treat nature as 'objects of experience' understood as a 'conceptual complex of appearances.'" Burch, "On the Ethical Determination of Geography", pg. 32.

[55] Burch, "Ethical Determination of Geography", pg. 33.

[56] May, <u>Kant's Concept of Geography</u>, pg. 64.

[57] Kant, <u>Physical Geography</u>, as cited in May, <u>Kant's Concept of Geography</u>, pg. 65

[58] Kant, <u>Physical Geography</u>, as cited by Burch, "Ethical Determination of Geography", pg. 28-9.

[59] "…the preceding account of the place of geography points to a fundamental tension in Kant's thought. On the one hand, insofar as Kant's turn to geography subtends the perspective of the positive sciences, in which the world is simply the object of knowledge, with the more original pragmatic account of the world as the object of our life, 'it discovers in principle an entirely new foundation of science, just as it discovers a new horizon of philosophy'. On the other hand, the requirements of the critical system preclude Kant himself from realising the full implications of this discovery." Burch, "Ethical Determination of Geography", pg. 34-5.

[60] Kant, <u>Critique of Pure Reason</u>, A5/B9 (pg. 140)

[61] "I call all cognition transcendental that is occupied not so much with objects but rather with our mode of cognition of objects, insofar as this is to be possible *a priori*." Kant, <u>Critique of Pure Reason</u>, A11/B25 (pg. 149)

[62] "Albeit, then, between the realm of the natural concept, as the sensible, and the realm of the concept of freedom, as the supersensible, there is a great gulf fixed, so that it is not possible to pass from the former to the latter (by means of the theoretical employment of reason) just as if there were so many separate worlds, the first of which is powerless to exercise influence over the second: still the latter is *meant* to influence the former—that is to say, the concept of freedom is meant to actualize in the sensible world the end proposed by its laws; and nature must consequently also be capable of being regarded in such a way that in the conformity to law of its form it at least harmonises with the possibility of the ends to be effectuated in it according to the laws of freedom." Kant, "Introduction", <u>Critique of Judgement</u>, ii (176), pg. 14.

[63] Burch, "Ethical Determination of Geography", pg. 39.

[64] "Space is not an empirical concept that has been drawn from outer experiences. For in order for certain sensations to be related to something outside me... [and] in order for me to represent them as outside (and next to) one another, thus not merely as different but as in different places, the representation of space must already be their ground. Thus the representation of space cannot be obtained from the relations of outer experience through experiences, but this outer experience is itself first possible only through this representation." Kant, Critique of Pure Reason, A24/B39 (pg. 175)

[65] May, Kant's Concept of Geography, pg. 67-8.

[66] C.f. May, Kant's Concept of Geography, pg. 69.

[67] Kant, Anthropology, as cited in May, Kant's Concept of Geography, pg. 118.

[68] Kant, "History and Physiography of the most remarkable cases of the Earthquake which, towards the end of 1755 shook a great part of the Earth" in Essays and Treatises Vol 2., pg. 139-140.

[69] Kant, "The ultimate end of nature as a teleological system" Part 2, § 83 in The Critique of Judgement pg. 93.

[70] Kant, "The teleological system in the extrinsic relations of organisms" Part 2, § 82 in The Critique of Judgement, pg. 88.

[71] Kant, ibid, part 2, § 83, pp. 93-4.

[72] Kant, "Idea for a Universal History from A Cosmopolitan Point of View", in On History, pg. 12, 16,, & 21.

[73] Kant, "Earthquakes", in Essays and Treatises, pg. 140-1.

[74] Burch, "Ethical Determination of Geography", pg. 41.

[75] It is important to Taylor's view of moral rights that the bearers of rights are members of a community of moral agents, possessors of conscious self-respect, able to choose and enjoy the exercise of its rights, and possesses certain second-order entitlements in virtue of possessing moral rights. (C.f. RN pp. 245-251.)

[76] Doran Smolkin, "Towards a Rights-Based Solution to the Non-Identity Problem", pg. 206.

[77] James Woodward, "The Non-Identity Problem", pg. 808

78   It is worth noting again that Parfit claims we should still find Non-Identity choices objectionable. "Does the fact of Non-Identity make a moral difference? When we see that our choice of Depletion will be worse for no one, we may believe that there is less objection to our choice. But I believe that the objection is just as strong." (*R&P* pg. 378.) This summarises why the Non-Identity problem is still a problem, even for Parfit.

79   Woodward, *ibid*, pg. 812.

80   Woodward, *ibid*, pg. 813. Smolkin confirmed Woodward's opinion here: "the reason there is still a rights-based complaint in these cases even though a person is not on balance worse off as a result of the act is because rights protect highly specific interests which cannot (always) be justifiably violated by some overall gain in welfare." Smolkin, "The Non-Identity Problem and the Appeal to Future People's Rights", pg. 318.

81   Emmet Oliver, "Wind farm moratorium is lifted" *The Irish Times* 12 May 2004, pg. 21.

82   Woodward, "The Non-Identity Problem", pg. 817.

83   This example may be found in Parfit, "Comments", pg. 855.

84   Parfit, "Comments", pg. 857.

85   Woodward, "Reply to Parfit" pg. 805-6.

86   Woodward, "Reply to Parfit" pg. 807.

87   Woodward, "Reply to Parfit" pg. 814.

88   Page, "Global Warming and the Non Identity Problem", in Self and Future Generations pg. 116.

89   Page, *ibid*, pg. 118.

90   Page, *ibid*, pg. 119.

91   Page, *ibid*, pg. 123.

92   "We shall thus conclude that this part of morality, the part concerned with beneficence and human well-being, cannot be explained in person-affecting terms. Its fundamental principles will not be concerned with whether our acts will be good or bad for those people whom they affect. Theory X will imply that an effect is bad if it is bad for people. But this will not be *why* this effect is bad." (*R&P* pg. 370-1). Note that although he admits the possibility of moving away from the person-affecting view here, the presence of the words 'affect' and 'effects' indicates that he is still within the realm of consequentialism.

93   Peter Gizewski, "Environmental Scarcity and Conflict", pg. 1

[94] R. D. Kaplan, "The Coming Anarchy" <u>The Atlantic Monthly</u> (February 1994) pp. 44.

Chapter Four: The "Excellent" In Ancient Times
Aristotelian and Classical Virtue

The results of the previous studies were only partially successful. In various ways, all three theories previously studied were person-affecting theories, which left them unable to solve the Non-Identity Problem and therefore unable to provide an acceptable environmental ethic that fulfils both the theoretical and practical criterion. In various ways, each theory here studied called upon the philosophical resources of Virtue theory to resolve certain aporias which arose in the problems of the environment and future generations. I now turn to Virtue theory directly, the last of the four major moral theories in the Western philosophical tradition. This theory places the location of moral concern not on the results of the agent's actions, nor on the agent's actions themselves, but on the agent's character. Virtue theory is not person-affecting, as the term has come to be understood. It may be objected that by abandoning person-affecting principles, one is also "throwing out the baby with the bath water", that is, one is also abandoning the idea that happiness, duty, and beneficence matter, or that we are abdicating our moral responsibilities to others. But this is a straw man. There is no serious moral theory which claims that responsibility and benefiting others is not what matters. There are only different ways of conceiving and justifying what our responsibilities (to them) are.

A preliminary statement of the basic principle of Virtue theory is that the right thing to do is the action which manifests excellent character, or which helps to develop and sustain excellent character. Because of this emphasis, the theory could appropriately be called 'areteology', the *logos* (logic, reason, account, etc.) of what is *arete* (excellent) in human affairs. This of course demands an explanation of what excellent character is. The term 'character' has many meanings. Aristotle defined it in The Poetics this way: "Character is that in virtue of which we say that the personages are of such and such a quality" (*Poetics,* 5084). Here I shall take it to mean the collection of a person's general habits, attitudes, and dispositions by which a person constitutes her own sense of selfhood, and by which others recognise her as being who she is. Character, it seems to me, stands at the intersection between the phenomenology of selfhood, that is to say the first-person experience of being a self, and the externally presented face by which others identify someone as being the same person over time. "The unity of character", said Stephen Hudson, "is extremely labyrinthine. It couples systematically a person's values, choices, desires, strength or weakness of will, emotions, feelings, perceptions, interests, expectations and sensibilities."[1] The definition I have offered here may seem to require more explanation, however it is sufficient for the present purpose. What is at stake here is what constitutes *good* character, and what a person of good character would do when faced with certain environmental problems. In the chapter to follow, I will produce a precise principle of good character using an Aristotelian basis and apply it to the contemporary environmental ethics question: what way of interacting with the environment is approved by Virtue theory as the morally right way? To explore this question, I shall examine Aristotle's account of Virtue theory as expressed in The Nicomachean Ethics, as well as the work of some more recent theorists of virtue ethics. Parfit's Non-Identity Problem will continue to be used as the test case. Virtue theory potentially offers a rational ground for conservation and stewardship that does not rely upon rights, harms, interests, consequences, criterion for moral standing, and other concepts which have been troublesome for the theories previously studied, and which rendered them unable to overcome the Non-Identity Problem.

In this first of two parts to the enquiry into the ethics of environmental conservation, I shall examine how a Virtuous person understands the value of the environment. I shall argue that to a Virtuous person, the environment counts as an important, irreplaceable good for one's flourishing, and the flourishing of human communities, for the reason that it is the ground on which all human flourishing is based. This I take to be only a subtle variation or refinement of the claim that as a social being the virtuous person aims to be happy with and among his friends and in the *polis* of which he is a member. The following chapter shall consist in a critique of conservation and depletion from the Virtue ethics perspective.

§ 1. Aristotle's account of the virtues.

Aristotle begins his account of the virtues with the question of the *telos*, the aim or the purpose, of man. The normal way of setting up the question is through an analogy, as follows: each of the professions, like medicine, law, architecture, music, and so on, has its own special aim and all of its practices and skills are directed at this aim. Every profession has a certain body of skills the possession of which enables one to succeed at achieving the particular good for that profession. If I am a medical doctor, I aim to heal the diseases and injuries of patients in my care, for health is the aim of the profession of medicine. That aim is bound into what it means to be a doctor. If my skills as a doctor are developed to the level of excellence, which of course includes the knowledge of when, how, and to whom to apply those skills properly, then it can be said that I am a good doctor. The analogy is applied to morality in this way: living a complete life as a moral human being is a kind of practice as well. As a human being, I aim to flourish and be happy; this Aristotle takes to be an unquestionable given. Although he admits that there is much dispute about exactly what flourishing and happiness is, still he postulates that it is the supreme good. This is so because it is both final and self-sufficient. It is final because it is always chosen for its own sake and never for the sake of something else (*NE,* 1089b5), and self-sufficientficient because it is "a thing which merely standing by itself alone renders life desirable and lacking in nothing". (*NE,*1097b13). It requires no extra props or externalities; performing such an action is its own reward. Thus Aristotle establishes as one of his initial claims the proposition that everyone, through their actions either directly or indirectly, aims towards what she thinks will bring her happiness.

The word that Aristotle uses here is *eudaimonia*, and although it is frequently rendered in English as 'happiness', it has a number of other possible translations. Rosalind Hursthouse, whose modern theory of practical virtue is the most widely cited, noted that a standard criticism of Virtue theory is the claim that the term is obscure and complicated enough to render Virtue theory itself unwieldy and implausible. Certainly, it is a difficult and multi-faceted concept. But, as she argues, it is not more difficult than Utilitarianism's concept of harm or Deontology's concept of rationality; both of which have difficulties of their own.[2] Hursthouse prefers 'flourishing' as a standard translation of *eudaimonia* since it is less subjective than 'happiness': it is possible to be mistaken about whether one is flourishing, and possible to have the wrong conception of what it means to flourish.[3] For this thesis I too shall use 'flourishing' as a standard translation of *eudaimonia*. I shall take that to mean 'a good or favourable fortune obtained by means of habitual actions which develop and express the best parts of one's nature as fully as possible'. I take this definition from a precedent set by one of Heraclitus' fragments: *ethos anthropoi daimon* ("Man's character is his fate").[4] According to translator and editor Charles Kahn, this fragment is best interpreted as saying that:

> ...a man's own character, not some external power, assigns to him the quality of his life, his fortune for good or ill. His lot is determined by the kind of person he is, by the kind of choices he habitually makes, and by the psychophysical consequences they entail or to which they correspond.[5]

Eudaimonia, for Heraclitus, is a good or favourable fortune (*daimon*) which someone creates for himself through his habitual actions. This is Aristotle's meaning as well, for Aristotle claims that a person is made happy primarily by his actions and his character: in his words, we are made happy by "the active exercise of our faculties in conformity with virtue" (*NE*, 1100b8).

Aristotle's next question is whether a human being as such has a function peculiar to itself, in a way analogous to the purposes and functions of particular practices and skilled trades, or of our body parts.[6] It is his contention that human happiness will be bound together with the performance of a human being's own particular function: we will be happiest when we are fulfilling our specific function. He uses an elimination-strategy to identify this function: if there exists a human function in body and mind that is also possessed by animals or plants, then it is eliminated as a candidate for the special purpose of man. The particular purpose of a human being cannot be simply to live, to grow and to consume food, for that function is shared by plants. Neither can it be sentience, for that function is shared by animals. All that remains, according to Aristotle, is the exercise of reason. Aristotle expresses the elimination-strategy as follows:

> The mere act of living appears to be shared even by plants, whereas we are looking for the function peculiar to man; we must therefore set aside the vital activity of nutrition and growth. Next in the scale will come some form of sentient life; but this too appears to be shared by horses, oxen, and animals generally. There remains therefore what may be called the practical life of the rational part of man. (*NE*, 1098a1-4)

The exercise of reason is, for Aristotle, the one function not shared by other living beings and thus all that remains among possible candidates for the purpose of a human being. On this basis, Aristotle concludes that the good of man is "the active exercise of his soul's faculties in conformity with excellence or virtue, or if there be several excellences or virtues, in conformity with the best and most perfect among them." (*NE*, 1098a20) The practical exercise of reason, as the highest part of ourselves, is for Aristotle the most noble kind of action.

The logical sequence by means of which a person becomes virtuous has the following three stages. (1) At the first stage, we are born with several capacities and endowments of nature, such as the ability to move, grow, think, and speak. These Aristotle called the faculties, although among them Aristotle privileged the social and intellectual faculties as being higher and more noble than others, because they appear to be specific to humanity. Reason (*nous*), in his system, is the highest faculty we have, the "spark of the divine within us". (2) At the second stage, the person is thrust into social situations which require him to respond appropriately; that is, with the right faculty. We become virtuous (or un-virtuous) through the ways in which we interact with other people. The process of 'moral education', which is the development of the virtues and the exercise our faculties and capacities with virtues, is for Aristotle a social or a public affair, and not a private matter (*NE*, 1103b12). It is also a social matter for other philosophers who have advanced a theory of the virtues, especially including Alasdair MacIntyre.[7] (3) The third and final stage obtains in the way in which we regularly and repeatedly respond to and interact with other people. That is the practice, so to speak, that will produce virtue or vice. If we respond to a situation by acting upon that faculty within us which is highest and most noble, or in Aristotle's words 'closest to the divine', and with just the right application of it, neither too much nor too little, then we act rightly. To continue to respond the same way is habit forming. If we make a habit of responding to other people in this way, we will have installed within our character a virtue. A person whose actions are habitually virtuous flourishes and lives well.

While any endowment of nature can be developed and expressed to the level of the excellent, even a capacity for gratuitous cruelty and violence, not all of our endowments of nature are virtuous. How shall we separate the virtues from the vices? Aristotle's answer is the "doctrine of the mean". A disposition is a virtue if it manifests the actions and feelings that were needed for the occasion, no more and no less, as determined by reason. The mean is the application of some action or feeling which is "just right"; it is the amount which is appropriate for the situation. Vice is defined as the wrong amount of that disposition: it is too much, or it is not enough, of the action or emotion required. This enables Aristotle to finally articulate a precise definition of virtue:

> Virtue then is a settled disposition of the mind
> [*psyche*] determining the choice of actions and
> emotions, consisting essentially in the observance of
> the mean relative to us, this being determined by
> principle, that is, as the prudent man would determine
> it. And it is a mean state between two vices, one of
> excess and one of defect. Furthermore, it is a mean
> state in that whereas the vices either fall short of or
> exceed what is right in feelings and in actions, virtue
> ascertains and adopts the mean. (*NE*, 1107a1)

This passage introduced the notion of 'the prudent man' and 'right reason'. It is introduced because, as Aristotle says at the top of Book Six, it is often not enough to say that the virtuous person is one who aims at the mark between deficiency and excess. "This bare statement however, although true, is not at all enlightening", he says, because it is true of "all departments of human endeavour that have been reduced to a science." Therefore "a person knowing this truth will be no wiser than before." An act must also be "in conformity with the right principle" to be completely virtuous. (*NE*, 1138b24) Prudence, or 'right reason', therefore holds an important place in his system as the virtue associated with choice, with truth-attainment, and with mature decision-making. Here are Aristotle's words on prudence in the context of determining ethical choices:

> Now it is held to be the mark of a prudent man to be
> able to deliberate well about what is good and
> advantageous for himself, not in some one
> department, for instance what is good for his health or
> strength, but what is advantageous as a means to the
> good life in general. (*NE*, 1140a24)

Prudence, it may be inferred, is the ability to discern what is and what is not conducive to the good life. It is concerned not with short-term gain, but with broad, long-term, and constructive contributions to the person's overall happiness. Furthermore it is not concerned only with the virtuous person's own good life, but is also concerned with the good life of others as well. This is in part because of Aristotle's claim that "Man is by nature a social being" (*NE*, 1097b10), a famous statement about which more will be said elsewhere. But this is mainly because prudence discerns what is good for human beings in general. Aristotle is quite emphatic about this in the discussion: he observes in several places how prudence is "commonly understood to mean especially that kind of wisdom which is concerned with oneself, the individual" (*NE*, 1141b5) but that this understanding is wrong: For "a man cannot pursue his own welfare without domestic economy and even politics" (*NE*, 1142a6), and so when he chooses something in pursuit of his own happiness, he does so in reference to what is good for all people, and not just in reference to narrow personal or egotistical interests. When Aristotle writes that a Virtuous action is not only one which strikes the mean, but which is also in conformity with right reason, it is this faculty of prudence which enables one to evaluate one's reasons. It helps him find whether his reasons are right, and so enables one to evaluate whether one's actions do, or do not, in fact strike the mean.

This summarises Aristotle's theory in very broad strokes, but not in fine detail, for it is not the purpose of this study to provide a fully detailed and comprehensive account. There are several conceptual problems in Aristotle's account of the virtues which I have not addressed, for instance the question of what it is to have a habit, what it may mean to choose something we are habituated to do, or why Aristotle says that reason is the 'divine spark' within a human being. It should be possible to articulate and to defend a theory of environmental virtue without resolving these issues. It is sufficient for this purpose to present a schematic of the theory which can answer questions like, What does the environment mean to a Virtuous person? How would the Virtuous person understand the environment to be valuable, if at all? And, How would a Virtuous person respond to it or act towards it?

§ 2. The Significance of the Environment for Virtue Theory

      Environmental philosophy is a philosophy of nature. But the
word 'Nature' often appears to mean one thing to environmental
philosophers and another thing to other kinds of philosophers,
especially Aristotle scholars. In Aristotle's *Physics*,
'Nature' (*phusis*) is defined as an internal source of motion or rest,
and a 'life property' found only in things that are 'self-movers', i.e.
things which possess souls.[8] (*Physics* 192b13-33). Similarly in *De
Anima*, the soul is held to be a moving force.[9] In the *Metaphysics*
Aristotle provides six definitions of Nature, rather like a dictionary
entry, showing the many different meanings of the word which were
current at the time. He sums them up as follows:

> …primary nature, in the fundamental account, is the
> substance of those things with a principle of process
> within themselves *qua* themselves. Matter is then
> said to be nature by dint of its being receptive of the
> above, and it is because they are processes from it
> that productions and growth are said to be natural.
> And it is such nature that is the principle of process
> for things having natural being, in some way dwelling
> in such things either potentially or actually.
> (*Metaphysics* 1015a)

Clearly, therefore, Nature is for Aristotle something internal to a
being, something akin to the soul: a principle of order that is
constitutive of its identity or its being, as well as that which enables
it to be a self-mover.   This is the classical definition which obtains
in philosophy at least until Rousseau. A law-like variation of it is
used by Kant, as we have already seen. Yet it is normally the case
that to an environmental philosopher, 'nature' means the material
and ecological world we live in, or that part of the planet which is
dominated by non-human life and by the elements, or at any rate is
mostly untouched by human hands. The 'world of nature', a term
often used by environmental philosophers, can mean the world

where living beings dwell, i.e. the world of plants and animals, distinct from (but not exclusive of) humans. This is partially interchangeable with the term 'The environment', although this latter term is often preferred since it is not so narrow. It includes atmospheres, oceans, landforms, and non-living ecological processes where both humans and non-human life forms dwell. 'The environment' can also include developed landscapes and urban areas, the 'built' environment. Although this has been specified already, it is worth mentioning again that 'Environmental philosophy' is concerned with this broader, post-Rousseau definition of Nature and the Environment. Under an Aristotelian scheme, this is not 'nature', and it would be absurd to speak of a 'world' of nature. But as we shall see, there is a place in Aristotelian thought for that which is denoted by the contemporary meaning of 'nature' and 'the environment'. We find it in one of the categories of his ethical system.

In the *Nicomachean Ethics*, Aristotle placed the highest value on self-sufficient and noble activity. This means activity that engages our highest and specific functions, and is always chosen for its own sake and never for the sake of anything else. Yet any discussion of virtuous environmentalism must discuss the value of things which are 'external' to the virtuous person's pursuit of *eudaimonia*. The division of goods in Aristotle's theory is threefold: there are external goods, and two kinds of internal goods. Internal goods are those which are part of the performance of a virtuous action, of which one kind has to do with the agent's body, and another kind has to do with his mind or soul (*psyche*). External goods are, for the most part, his possessions and assets, and are not directly a part of the performance of virtuous actions. They can include the social and material rewards that Virtuous action produces for the agent and his associates, the props and instruments that help the virtuous person to perform noble actions, the agent's social relations, as well as material possessions and circumstances, all insofar as they figure into the agent's pursuit of *eudaimonia*.

The environment, it would seem at first, falls into the category of an external good. For the environment is a physical thing: it is the land, sea, and sky of our planet. It is the source of all the material resources which we use, and aside from the sun it is the source of all of our energy as well. There are very few things we do in and with natural settings (settings unaltered or mostly unaltered by human hands) that are performed for their own sake. Most which come to my mind are recreational and artistic activities like country walking, sailing, camping, mountain climbing, and landscape painting. Insofar as science is undertaken for its own sake, it could be claimed that environmental sciences are self-sufficient practices. There are some people for whom hunting, fishing, and forestry are similar self-rewarding activities, benefiting the practitioner with more than just food, trophies, fuel and building materials. But for the most part, the environment-affecting activities we do are done for the sake of something else: farming to produce food, mining to produce raw materials for industry, and so on. Although these activities are not 'self sufficient' in the Aristotelian sense given earlier, it would be wrong to say that it is un-excellent to do them. We need to eat, to build, to clear land, and do all the other things involved in survival and civilisation. We need to produce energy to power our industries, to transport us around, to heat our homes and cook our food, and so on. We have no choice about this—it is part of what we must do to have and to sustain our lives. We can, however, discuss how we go about these activities. Any theory of virtuous environmentalism cannot avoid discussing how we satisfy our needs for energy and material goods, even if it is claimed that to dwell on these needs is to dwell on our 'lower' faculties. For what is at issue in environmental ethics is precisely the ways in which we produce material goods and energy in fulfilment of our physical needs. Environmental ethics is (among other things) the ethics of the use of the resources of the planet.

Aristotle's claim that the highest *eudaimonia* is self-sufficient and noble activity is not an absolute position, like the Stoic view that someone could theoretically be self-sufficiently happy even while being tortured on the rack. He says that to fully flourish one must still have certain external goods which serve as instrumental aids. Aristotle says,

...it is manifest that happiness [*eudaimonia*] also
requires external goods in addition, as we have said;
for it is impossible, or at least not easy, to play a
noble part unless furnished with the necessary
equipment. For many noble actions require
instruments for their performance, in the shape of
friends or wealth or political power; also there are
certain external advantages, the lack of which sullies
supreme felicity, such as good birth, satisfactory
children, and personal beauty... (*NE*, 1099b1)

In this passage, it seems clear that external goods are useful to the
virtuous person as instruments with which to "play a noble part".
Elsewhere Aristotle says there are some virtues which cannot be
practiced without certain kinds of external goods, for instance one
must possess good health to practice the physical virtues like
strength and courage, sufficient money in order to demonstrate
charity and generosity, and so on. He also claims that a life without
friends, a unique kind of external good, may not be worth living:
"For no one would choose to live without friends, but possessing all
other good things." (*NE*, 1155a4)

A healthy and stable environment is not mentioned on this
list of necessary external goods from the *Nicomachean Ethics*.
There are several straightforward reasons for this. One is that the
ancient Greek language did not have a word for 'the environment'
which captured quite the same meaning of our modern English word.
'Nature' was something internal to a being. The nature of a thing is
its qualities, properties, characteristic habits, and whatever else
internal to itself which makes it what it is. 'Nature' as that part of
the world which is unoccupied by human civilisation, 'out there'
beyond the cities and farms, was unthinkable (at least until
Rousseau). That was 'wilderness', not 'nature'. But the more
principled reason for this omission may be simply that Aristotle
focuses on the external advantages that would be useful to the sons
of Athenian aristocrats with careers in politics, commerce, or the

military ahead of them. Such people formed the bulk of his students at the *Lyceum*. All of the things cited by Aristotle as examples of useful instruments for flourishing are social in nature: they concern the possessor's ability to interact with others, find a place in society (especially Athenian society), and succeed in it. This is one of several reasons why he says one's friends are the greatest of one's external advantages. (*NE*, 1169b12) The list of external advantages cited in this passage need not be exhaustive. Aristotle's explanation continues as follows:

> A man of very ugly appearance or low birth, or childless and alone in the world, is not our idea of a happy man, and still less so perhaps is one who has children or friends that are worthless, or who has had good ones but lost them by death. As we said therefore, happiness does require the addition of external prosperity, and this is why some people identify it with good fortune, though some identify it with virtue. (*NE*, 1099b4)

In the *Politics*, Aristotle describes the best kind of city-state for the encouragement of human flourishing, and describes in detail how territory at land and at sea, the location of the city, and even its climate, affects the ability of the city-state to succeed. It is worth exploring this portrait of the ideal city: it shows that the eco-physical world can count as an important external good to the flourishing of the members of a *polis*. This portrait of an ideal city lists the things which help a *polis* to fulfil its function of providing to the citizens the things they need for the good life.[10]

The best kind of city, according to Aristotle, should be easy to access from both land and sea. It should be easy to get raw materials and other goods into the city. It should be easy to survey the territory controlled by the state, for instance to see if the city is being invaded. It should also be easy for the army to defend.[11] Aristotle discusses how climate has an effect upon the character of the inhabitants, and that certain climates tend to produce the people who are unsuited for the kind of character he has in mind.

> We must now ask what kind of natural qualities they [the citizens of the *polis*] should have… The nations that live in cold regions and those of Europe are full of spirit, but somewhat lacking in skill and intellect: for this reason, while remaining relatively free, they lack political cohesion and the ability to rule over their neighbours. On the other hand the Asiatic nations have in their souls both intellect and skill, but are lacking in spirit; so they remain enslaved and subject. The Hellenic race, occupying a mid-position geographically, has a measure of both, being both spirited and intelligent. (*Politics*, 1327b18)

Aristotle's remarks here could be taken as mere stereotypes, possibly even as racist stereotypes, especially given that he upholds his homeland of Greece as the environment which tends to produce the best sort of people. But let us not loose sight of the philosophical point which is being expressed here. Climate and geography has an effect on people's character. The kinds of character traits which are most useful for survival and flourishing in a given environment tend to become dominant in people's lives. This is an empirical point, not a moral point, but it has moral significance. If there are particular character traits which we want to uphold as morally excellent, then we can look for, or create, the kind of environment in which those traits will be useful and appropriately rewarded.

As Aristotle describes, the site of the city should be chosen with consideration for the health of the citizens, for instance it should be sheltered from cold winter winds.[12] Half of the territory controlled by the city should be privately owned and the other half communally owned. Half of the communally owned land should "support the public service of the gods"; this apparently means to use it for the location of temples and religious festivals, otherwise to leave it alone, as land that 'belongs to the gods'. The other half should "meet the expenses of the communal feeding." (*Politics*, 1130a13) Certain areas of the city must be reserved for certain functions and kept apart from each other although easily accessible to each other, for instance the marketplace must be easily reached from the roads and the harbour, and the *agora* (the public square) should look down on it. No economic transactions are allowed in the *agora*, as it is a site dedicated to leisure and to publicly debating the governance of the city. Farmers and tradespeople are not even allowed to enter it unless summoned by the civil authorities, apparently because their livelihoods are too strongly rooted in material production and practical affairs. (*Politics*, 1331a30) Similar public meeting places should be provided in the surrounding countryside for the administrators responsible for farms and forests (*Politics*, 1131b10).

It would seem that Aristotle is here influenced by the Hippocratic Writings, especially the discussion of the effect of climate upon human health in the piece entitled "Airs, Waters, Places". Hippocrates states assertively that a physician must study the climate, water supply, and other factors of the earth and sky in order to understand medicine:

> Being familiar with the progress of the seasons and the dates of rising and setting of the stars, he could foretell the progress of the year. Thus he would know what changes to expect in the weather and not only would he enjoy good health himself for the most part but he would be very successful in the practice of medicine. If it should be thought that this is more the business of the meteorologist, then learn that astronomy plays a very important part in medicine since the changes of the seasons produce changes in diseases.[13]

Hippocrates describes the kind of diseases that tend to arise in areas where the dominant winds come from certain directions, where the water comes from certain sources, when and how the seasons change, what region of the world the people live in, and what customs and lifestyles they have. His concluding remarks are concise: "The chief controlling factors, then, are the variability of the weather, the type of country and the sort of water which is drunk. You will find, as a general rule, that the constitutions and the habits of a people follow the nature of the land where they live."[14] This should not be taken as a kind of environmental determinism. As noted by David Hume, the character of a community is also a product of the moral choices its members made in the past, for instance "the accidents of battles, negotiations, and marriages".[15] This is Kant's point as well, as we have previously seen. But we must concede that climate, geography, and environment is hugely influential in people's lives.[16]

This picture of the ideal environment, even with its seemingly peripheral matters like the arrangement of a city's facilities relative to each other, is ethically significant because it is intimately connected with an idea of what constitutes the worthwhile life. It also describes how we should arrange ourselves in and with the environment to maximise the possibilities for flourishing. It is an early recognition of the idea that the world is the field and stage of our life and our flourishing. This relation to the worthwhile life is provides the principle of Groundedness with the ethical significance that was found to be lacking in the Kantian treatment of the principle. Aristotle and Hippocrates may have seen the environmental problems associated with urban areas such as sanitation and waste disposal. But they would not have had to face the kind of health crisis which climate change and industrial pollution creates today:

> *Air pollution and health.* The European Union
> Environment commission recently released a report
> on air pollution, focusing on the health effects of
> ground-level ozone, nitrogen dioxide, and fine dust
> particles small enough to penetrate the human
> respiratory tract, most of which comes from
> automobile emissions. The report found that air

> pollution kills 310,000 people every year, reduces
> life-expectancy by an average of nine months, and
> costs the European economy 80 billion euros per year
> in sick-leave time.[17]

Aristotle and Hippocrates would not have seen health-affecting environmental problems manifesting on this huge scale. But it is clear they would both agree that a poisoned environment affects people's health negatively and so thwarts human flourishing, and that a clean and bountiful environment is an asset to flourishing. Since we can now see that a picture of the ideal environment was indeed on the ancient Greek list of external goods for human flourishing, we can ask whether a similar picture should be on our list.

§ 3. The External Goods Argument.

The argument that the environment is a necessary external good to one's virtue can now be stated quite straightforwardly. The virtuous person chooses self-rewarding actions, springing from the highest and most noble parts of human nature, with which to flourish and be happy. But certain possessions, circumstances, and the like can be valued as external goods to the project of living well. Life is desirable to the Virtuous person, for life itself is just such a self-rewarding action. It follows that the Virtuous person would value the external goods which are necessary to life, and to the self-rewarding project of living well, lest his flourishing be incomplete for the lack of them.[18]

What can we make of the claim that life is desirable to the Virtuous person? What is meant by 'life' here? A contemporary environmentalist may claim that life is corporeal embodiment in an ecologically organised physical world. We are embodied beings who exist in and with the embodied world, in various ways related and connected to it, and as such we flourish or we fail to flourish. As life is desirable to the Virtuous person, he will desire the stable and healthy environment from which he obtains the external goods required for the continuation of his life; goods like living space, food, water, air, building materials, fuel, and waste disposal. A landscape's aesthetic qualities could be included here, as Aristotle says that the Virtuous person likes to surround himself with beautiful things (*NE*, 1125a15). Someone who lives in an environment of degraded quality, for instance someone who lives close to waste dumps or factories that poison the local air or water, would suffer bad health-effects which make it hard to flourish. Moreover, the project of living a flourishing life through sensation and thought, the uniquely human faculties as Aristotle saw them, is rather moot to someone who, because the air, water, or food quality is very poor, is weakened by hunger and disease. If one cannot eat or breathe, one cannot flourish. The overall point is that we seek *eudaimonia* in specific contexts of social and environmental life; and as seen in the picture of Aristotle's ideal *Polis* and in the Hippocratic Writings, some environments are better suited for the pursuit of *eudaimonia* than others. The condition of these social and environmental contexts figures into the person's flourishing insofar as they assist or thwart that which the moral agent must do in pursuit of *eudaimonia*. And in this respect Aristotle himself would agree. He says, "the philosopher being a man will also need external well-being, since man's nature is not self-sufficient for the activity of contemplation, but he must also have bodily health and a supply of food and other requirements." (*NE*, 1179a2)[19] But there is more to this point than that, as shall be explained shortly. A well-known example of this principle in Irish life today is:

> *Mobile phone mast radiation.* Dún Laoghaire-Rathdown County Council recently rejected a planning application to place a mobile phone transmitter mast next to a primary school on such grounds.[20] A farmer in county Tipperary with a transmitter mast on his land experienced severe headaches, dizziness, and cramps which he attributed to the radiation from the mast, and he took to wearing a silver-plated protective net over his head while outdoors. A doctor

certified that his symptoms are real (without, apparently, attributing them to the radiation).[21] Scientific studies of the health effects of radiation from mobile phones and from transmitter masts is still inconclusive, and there is evidence both for and against the case. A report by the British government called The Stewart Report found that "the balance of evidence to date suggests that exposure to RF [radio frequency] radiation below... ICNIRP [International Commission on Non-Ionizing Radiation Protection] guidelines do not cause adverse health effects to the general population. There is now scientific evidence, however, which suggests that there may be biological effects occurring at exposures below these guidelines."[22]

The philosophical point here is that adverse environmental conditions, like intense radio frequency radiation, are detrimental to human health and thus an obstacle to the good life, and that this is a well known and commonly accepted social fact.

A stable and healthy ecosystem is a condition for the possibility of life, health, and well-being, and thus a condition for the possibility of virtue. Without the external goods which are to be found in the environment, we would not live long nor well enough to develop the uniquely human social and intellectual virtues and to perform noble deeds. It follows that we must develop in our characters certain environmental virtues. What are those virtues? On the basis of the forgoing discussion, I assert that the environmental virtues are those character traits which are useful and/ or necessary for preserving and cultivating the environmental conditions that are well suited for human life and flourishing. An environmental vice would be a disposition to act in ways that render the environment less favourable, or even unfavourable, for human life and flourishing. At this stage it is not necessary to list specific virtues.

This version of the external goods argument is simple enough and may be useful for most purposes, but it is not without its own theoretical problems. Here are three of them. First, as observed by Ronald Sandler, most early versions of the external goods argument were not strong enough to make environmental virtue theory more than merely a supplement to other moral theories. The argument as it stands here allows for the possibility that someone who lacks the environmental virtues is not necessarily lacking in virtue altogether. What Sandler observed about this position is that someone might still be a virtuous person, achieving a life of at least partial, if not complete, happiness and fulfilment, even if he can be criticised for lacking environmental virtues. Against this position, Sandler says,

> ...if a virtue ethic is to support an adequate environmental ethic—that is, if it is to be an alternative and not just a supplement to rights-based, consequentialist, pragmatic and intuitionist approaches—then the virtue ethic must provide the theoretical underpinnings of the environmental ethic. The traits and/or conditions that are required for being an environmentally virtuous person cannot be any different from the traits and/or conditions that are required to be virtuous *simpliciter*. An environmental virtue ethic will lack the normative force requisite for adequacy if environmentally degradative practices betray a lack of environmental virtue, but not a lack of virtue *simpliciter*.[23]

Philosophers who are aiming to do no more than show that environmental virtues are part of a complete and fulfilling life, but not a necessary and essential part of that life, are not seeking to establish Sandler's strong claim, and should not be criticised for failing to do so. However I agree with Sandler that this is a weak position because it does not aim to provide a strong alternative or a rival to consequentialism, deontology, or justice theory. Is this simply begging the question? Does Sandler not presuppose an intuition that the environment is valuable and should be conserved and respected, and then simply find that early attempts to articulate an environmental Virtue theory fail to fulfil his expectation? In this situation, I think not. Sandler is asserting the need for a Virtue theory that is robust enough to stand on its own. If Virtue was a mere supplement to other theories, it would be unable to succeed where other theories fail. It is not 'begging the question' that an acceptable environmental ethic should not condone acts which cause (unnecessary) environmental destruction. This is stated explicitly in his paper in the form of the "general adequacy condition", which he claims most environmental ethicists would accept, and which reads as follows:

> If an environmental ethic is an adequate environmental ethic then it provides a theoretical platform for censure of environmentally unsustainable practices, policies, and life styles and promotion of environmentally sustainable practices, policies, and life styles.[24]

With reference to the Non-Identity Problem, the need for an adequacy condition like this is clearly apparent. If Utilitarianism cannot explain what is morally problematic about choosing the Repugnant Conclusion, and therefore cannot provide a satisfactory environmental ethic, then a Virtue theory that aspires to do no more than supplement Utilitarianism will be at a loss as well.

Here is a second theoretical problem with the external goods argument as it stands so far. There is more than one way to conceive the idea of an external good. Alasdair MacIntyre, in his discussion of practices, emphasises a slightly different aspect to the meaning of the external good. On his argument, any practice, including the various kinds which Aristotle cited as examples, will have particular skills, standards of excellence, and goals which the people who undertake the practice seek to achieve, and if they are successful they are rewarded in many ways. The social and material rewards and benefits received by someone who undertakes a practice well are the external goods. It is characteristic of the Virtuous person that in his various practices and pursuits he aims for the internal goods, which benefit and reward everyone who is involved in the practice. MacIntyre says,

> It is characteristic of what I have called external goods that when achieved they are always some individual's property and possession. Moreover characteristically they are such that the more someone has them, the less there is for other people... Internal goods are indeed the outcome of competition to excel, but it is characteristic of them that their achievement is a good for the whole community who participate in the practice. (*AV* pg. 190-1)

For MacIntyre, this distinction is crucial in the first of his three definitions of virtue.[25] It is slightly different from Aristotle's definition as it emphasises that external goods are won for the agent and associates by his actions, rather than prerequisites for his actions, although the difference is only a matter of emphasis. They are not mutually exclusive positions. MacIntyre emphasises that external goods are such that the more there is for one person, the less there is for others. Certain kinds of environmental resources certainly count as that kind of a good: clean water, nutritious food, building materials, fuel, and so on—all of which exist in limited supply (even if some of them are renewable). The more oil is bought by one country, the less there is for other countries. This, to my mind, seems to demand some account of distributive justice. Aristotle does provide such an account, although he provides it on a personal rather than a social scale. But if such an account is demanded here, then the problem which appeared in the study of Rawls, that distributive justice by itself offers no reason to initiate a practice of conserving for the future, could appear here as well.

The third and most difficult theoretical problem, already introduced briefly, is that when Aristotle says life is desirable to the Virtuous person, he does not mean just the continuation of an organism's metabolic functions, nor does he refer to all organic life generally, thus to include non-human life and the ecosystems in which they exist. His claim can not be equated with eco-centrism or bio-centrism as a contemporary environmental philosopher would understand the terms. The life of a being, Aristotle says, is grounded in the being's specific and 'highest' faculties, whatever they may be. The life of plants is grounded in the capacity of growth and nutrition, of animals sensation, and of man sensation and also reason (*nous*) and intellectual thought (*phronesis* or 'practical wisdom'). Aristotle's own words on this matter are:

> ...that which is essentially good is good and pleasing
> in itself to the virtuous man. And life is defined, in
> the case of animals, by the capacity for sensation; in
> the case of man, by the capacity for sensation and
> thought. But a capacity is referred to its activity, and
> in this its full reality consists. It appears therefore
> that life in the full sense is sensation or thought. (*NE*,
> 1170a18)

This contrasts sharply with the aforementioned contemporary-environmentalist claim that life is corporeal embodiment in an ecologically organised physical world. Where the environmentalist locates the value of life in the qualities that are common to other living beings, Aristotle locates it in the qualities which are specific to each (type of) being, and so human life 'in the fullest sense' is in the use of the qualities that are specific to humankind.

What makes this 'life' desirable to the Virtuous person? Aristotle's claim is bound into the argument for the value of friendship, and it is subtle: it is "the *consciousness of oneself as good* that makes existence desirable, and such consciousness is pleasant in itself" (*NE*, 1170b5). The value of life, then, is something the Virtuous person finds within himself *qua* Virtuous person. Thus Aristotle would never say that life is valuable to a person in a coma. Nor would he claim that a vicious man (that is, a man whose character is dominated by vices) would find his life desirable.

Vicious people love wealth or pleasure because "they are eager for life, but not for the good life" (*Politics*, 1257b41). We also cannot fit this claim into the contemporary debate on whether intrinsic value is to be discovered in the world, apart from our intentions and practices, or if it is an anthropomorphic projection. Certainly, a Virtuous person discovers within himself the intrinsic value of his own life; he does not project it there with an act of will, nor does he declare it to be valuable on the basis of some sequence of theoretical reasoning. It is a first-order insight, a phenomenological discovery. Within our experience of living there is, if we are Virtuous, a consciousness that living is good. It is because he has made this discovery within himself that he is able to discover the intrinsic value of other beings, especially his friends. Someone who has not made this discovery in himself is liable to be mistaken about the nature of the flourishing life and the virtues needed to achieve it.

Reason is humanity's highest faculty in Aristotle's system. As Singer, MacIntyre, Taylor, and others have shown, many of the properties which Aristotle claimed were specific to humanity are in fact found throughout the animal kingdom. We have more in common with the animals than we normally like to believe. Could we, therefore, locate the desirability of life in life's common properties, instead of each being's specific properties? Aristotle's case is in part theological. Although practical reason (*phronesis*) was isolated by Aristotle as properly belonging to humanity, he also says in Book 10 that theoretical reason (*nous*) is of divine origin, as it is the activity of the gods.[26] In Book 6 we are told that *nous* is excellence in the field of knowledge of things necessary and unchanging. We are also told that the only object for theoretical reason is reason itself: indeed Aristotle even says that God is theoretical reason contemplating itself. A human being has "something within him that is divine" (*NE*, 1177a1), a limited capacity for theoretical reason, which enables him to contemplate, as do the gods. It is limited by the material and practical needs of living in a mortal body. These functions enable us to transcend our embodied existence by contemplating that which is necessary, eternal, and unchanging, and therefore (as Aristotle claims) immaterial, and so we are enabled to participate in the society of the gods and obtain a kind of immortality. Note that Aristotle does not say that we have something in us that resembles or is like the divine, but that we have something within us that *is* divine. It is the 'highest' thing within us. Aristotle says that living in accordance with reason will obtain for the practitioner the best quality *eudaimonia* possible. In his words, "The activity of God, which is transcendent in blessedness, is the activity of contemplation; and therefore among human activities that which is most akin to the divine activity of contemplation will be the greatest source of happiness." (*NE*, 1178b21). Theoretical contemplation is also the only activity that is purely and perfectly a *praxis*, for "it produces no result beyond the actual act of contemplation, whereas from practical pursuits we look to secure some advantage, greater or smaller, beyond the action itself". (*NE*, 1177b1) In practical pursuits, we seek external goods (here as rewards, rather than as instrumental aids for the performance of the action); in purely virtuous pursuits, the pursuit itself is its own reward.

The claim that the value of a being's existence is a function of a being's specific faculties and qualities should not be circumvented or countered, but rather should be invited into the case for the value of the environment as an external good. I shall now construct a stronger version of the external goods approach. The first premise is the claim that although Aristotle privileges man's own 'higher' faculties, all of our faculties exist in relation to, and dependence on, the world in which they function. Even practical wisdom (*phronesis*), the one faculty Aristotle claimed was uniquely human and therefore especially connected to human flourishing, obtains a dimension of what I have previously called *Groundedness in the world*. As defined in the previous study, groundedness refers to the various ways in which we necessarily live in and with the world, and are inseparable from the world. The Kantian explanation left several difficulties to be resolved, especially including a tension between a phenomenological and an objective conception of the world in which we are all grounded. But there is an Aristotelian way of stating this principle which avoids this tension, as I shall now explain.

§ 4. Groundedness in the World.

To explain this principle in an Aristotelian way, let us look again at the faculties Aristotle considered while seeking for the uniquely human good. As argued by Susanne Foster, the animal and plant faculties have their part to play in the aim for *eudaimonia*. Even if it is admitted that it is mainly the exercise of the uniquely human faculties which constitutes happiness, still Foster argues that healthy and functioning animal and plant faculties are the prerequisites for happiness. She claims that the animal and vegetative faculties have certain roles to play in the pursuit of *eudaimonia*, and in their contribution to human flourishing they too can be elevated to the level of human excellence. To be specific, each higher faculty in Aristotle's hierarchy serves to "perfect" the lower ones. "Reason supervenes on the lower faculties and perfects them (makes them more reliable). It is served by lower faculties." [27] Likewise the other faculties have an important role to play in the human pursuit of *eudaimonia*. Foster says,

> Reason plays roles in shaping our conception of the good and ordering our desires. It helps strengthen or weaken our desires. Hence, the activities initiated by the desiderative part of the soul are human activities. Moving and its virtues (e.g. speed and strength) as well as the vegetative capacities and their virtues (e.g. good digestion) are influenced by other activities. Those who choose better diets and exercise regularly are generally healthier. Hence, at least to some extent, vegetative excellences like health are important prerequisites for higher functions. At the very least, sensitive and vegetative activities are still activities, ways of actualising one's nature.[28]

A similar point was argued by D. S. Hutchinson, who wrote that all of humanity's special faculties are extensions, improvements, or refinements of faculties and excellences already present in the rest of the animal world:

> For Aristotle, human goal-directed behaviour, human excellence, and the connection between these ideas and the distinctive activity of human beings are simply instances of the corresponding truths which hold quite generally for all of the animal world (some versions of which hold for plants and for the natural world in general). It is true that there are distinctively human categories of evaluation (the noble, *to kalon*, is the most prominent); but nevertheless the general connection between excellence and what is natural holds for human beings because it holds for animals generally.[29]

Hutchinson studied Aristotle's comments on animals in his scientific writings to demonstrate this point. A passage in Aristotle's <u>Politics</u> seems to confirm this as well: "there are three ingredients which must all be present to make us blessed—our bodily existence, our intellectual and moral qualities, and all that is external." (*Politics*, 1323a22) To this I add that the various faculties and endowments of nature which are possessed by all of the animal kingdom correspond to various dimensions of groundedness in the world. Sensation, an animal faculty which Aristotle ranked among the highest of human faculties, is a form of groundedness: for it is the world which we take in and experience with our physical senses. We are also grounded in the world through the plant faculties of growth and nutrition, and they too are shared by all living things. Our bodies are living organisms which require food, water, air, a certain amount of sunlight, and so on, for continued health and survival. Man is a corporeal animal (as well as a political animal) whose existence inhabits not only a social world but also a physical and material world organised into ecosystems, in which relations necessary for

244

health and survival are established with the animals, plants, and natural habitats from which are derived the material resources necessary for life. I claim that groundedness in the world is an irreducible condition of human existence, however much we may overlook or aspire to transcend this condition.

Is groundedness also an irreducible condition of human virtuous flourishing as well? As we have seen, the Aristotelian tradition places reason in the place of honour as the highest specific human faculty, and therefore the basis of our flourishing. We do establish necessary relations with other beings with whom to share and enlarge our existence, but in the case of man this means, in Aristotle's words, "conversing and communicating their thoughts to [other people]… it does not mean merely feeding in the same place, as it does when applied to cattle" (*NE*, 1170b9). This assertion may be handled as follows. Whereas our animal and plant faculties correspond to their own ways of existing in the world, the faculty of practical reason corresponds to the condition of being a political animal: itself a way of existing in the world. Aristotle says,

> Nobody would choose to have all possible good things on the condition that he must enjoy them alone; for man is a social being; and designed by nature to live with others; accordingly the happy man must have society, for he has everything that is naturally good. (*NE*, 1169b16)

Our sociability creates relationships and bonds with our fellow human beings, and I take that to be a valid form of groundedness in the world. For the various ways in which people relate to other people and create social bonds require shared landscapes and physical settings: houses, public streets and town squares, market places, sports fields, theatres and concert halls, farm fields, forests, and all the different kinds of landscapes we inhabit together and utilise for social purposes.

Groundedness provides each of our faculties with the materials necessary for proper functioning. It provides our animal and plant faculties with materials to power our growth, movement, and sensation. It provides our social and intellectual faculties with a sense of home, place, and belonging. One's groundedness figures into one's identity, by providing one with a sense of having a home, a sense of belonging to a place. Groundedness creates a means of reaching out to others by offering a space for meetings to "take place", a space to share. I have corresponded sociability with the rational and intellectual faculties. It is appropriate to do so because like reason it appears to be specifically human: although many species of animals live in families and packs, it seems that only human beings have elevated sociability to the level of culture and civilisation. Aristotle would have claimed that the human social faculties require the right social surroundings in which to develop to the level of excellence. And for Aristotle, the right social environment in which to develop into a complete human being is a *polis*—a politically organised society. That is what is implied by Aristotle's claim that man is a political being. I am adding only that social environments are also simultaneously and necessarily physical environments, and that all human relations "take place" in physical surroundings which sometimes configure, and sometimes are configured by, the human relations which are realised in them.

It may be noted as a short aside that for Aristotle, the social environment he had in mind in which human beings flourish best was not just any social environment but a Greek city-state; and among Greek city-states he had in mind an *Athenian* city-state, and among the citizens of the Athenian city-state he had in mind the educated aristocratic gentleman. Slaves, foreigners, certain kinds of manual labourers, and those who are not members of a Greek *polis* are not counted as full or complete human beings in his system.[30] We may object (as MacIntyre did) to Aristotle's wholesale dismissal of slaves, barbarians, and non-Greeks as not just lacking a *polis* but as incapable of possessing one, and thus incapable of being fully human. According to MacIntyre, Aristotle is able to hold that position partly because it was "part of the general, although not universal, blindness of his culture" (*AV* pg. 159), and partly because "Aristotle did not understand the transience of the *polis* because he had little or no understanding of historicity in general." (*AV*, pg. 159-60).[31] The point, however, is that our intellectual faculties correspond to a particular environment, the socially and/or politically organised community, and that the flourishing or non-flourishing of our intellectual faculties happens in the context of that relationship. MacIntyre asserts that Aristotle was able to see this for only his own society and no other, and in his own society he saw this only for his own class and not for any other. This may be somewhat overstated: in the *Politics* Aristotle indicates that he studied 158 different kinds of constitutions, which he took to be 158 different ways of living in a community. However even if MacIntyre's criticism is correct, it does not diminish the philosophical point at stake here. Furthermore, a historical perspective (which MacIntyre claims Aristotle lacks) makes it clear that there are many kinds of human community other than the classical Greek city-state, and more than one kind of human society in which human flourishing is possible and supported. This may imply that there are many different kinds of human flourishing as well—a problem MacIntyre faces directly, in his consideration of five different lists of the virtues from five different societies separated by wide gulfs of time and space.[32] But that possibility I shall set aside for now.

The general claim of this version of Groundedness is that each faculty we possess corresponds to a particular and appropriate kind of surrounding in which it is meant to function, and each faculty is able to develop best when the 'external goods' of its appropriate environment are 'excellent'. I have previously defined excellence as a specifically moral term, having to do with excellence of character, which we do not apply to material objects and resources. Material excellence is the degree to which something is well suited to support the exercise of moral excellence, excellent of character, and aid one's aspiration to flourish.[33] As our capacity for sociability requires that we live in a social environment, it is reasonable to claim that humanity's animal and plant faculties require the right physical environment in which to develop properly as well. We do not flourish, or we do not flourish as well as we could, if the environment in which we are grounded is not supportive or conducive of that aspiration. Our social faculties correspond to the community of which we are a part, and our corporeal faculties correspond to the world as "our home and stage", as was previously seen in the discussion of Kant's geography.[34] The world as our home and stage is both the integral world of our experiences, which we sense, and the physical world which we inhabit as corporeal beings, in which we grow, move, eat, drink, sense and experience things, and do everything involved in having and continuing their embodied life. The condition of groundedness thus underlies and figures into all of our pursuits and projects, including the aim for *eudaimonia*. For we do not aim for *eudaimonia* in abstraction. We aim for *eudaimonia* within specific social and environmental contexts.

Such is the general shape of the external-goods approach to the theory of environmental virtue. It must be noted that this is not a disguised version of Utilitarianism. The value of an external good, as was shown by Aristotle in his own description of that value category, is not merely that external goods are *useful* to the moral agent, but that external goods *figure into the Virtuous person's flourishing*, and for humanity that means they figure into the development and excellent exercise of the 'high' and 'divine' faculties, as well as the capacity for sociability.

The environment is an external good of a very peculiar kind. Like other external goods, many of the benefits we gain from it are such that the more one person has, the less there is for others. Material resources like food, building materials, and fuel are the obvious examples. But unlike most other external goods, many of its benefits are common to all, and can benefit someone *only* if they are common to all: clean air, for instance. The good of clean air can only be mine if it also belongs to everyone. In this way it is like the *polis*. It is also like the *polis* in that it is the setting in which our faculties are exercised and expressed. It is that on which we stand, that through which we move and travel, that in response to which we become what we have in us to become. But it is also unlike the *polis* in that it is not something which can reciprocate the value, care, and 'friendship' invested in it, in the manner of one rational and virtuous moral agent to another. The environment is not a social or political body. It is also unlike the *polis* in that no one can live apart from a physical environment, although it is conceivable that someone could live apart from all social relations. (This latter claim is inconceivable for Aristotle, since "man is a political animal", but it is certainly conceivable for *us*.) Environmental relations are an unavoidable part of life. There is no category in Aristotle's own writings which quite captures the meaning and the value of groundedness in the world. Nor does it easily fit into contemporary categories of moral value either, for it is both an intrinsic and an instrumental good, and a good which can be pursued both with self-interest and with benevolent altruism. It is also the kind of good which requires what MacIntyre would call the virtues of 'acknowledged dependence'; I shall have more to say of this in the next study, where I look at modern (i.e. practical) virtue.

Although any Virtue theorist would agree that external possessions and surroundings of good quality (i.e. possessing material excellence, possessing suitability for their purpose) are useful for one's flourishing, none would claim that human flourishing is entirely contingent upon them. The Virtuous person flourishes in and through her actions, emotions, and the way she relates to them, and not her circumstances or possessions but for the way she relates to them. Someone living in a polluted environment, then, may still be able to flourish. It is for this reason that Sandler observed that most early attempts at Virtue theory could do no more than offer a set of environmentally connected virtues the possession of which is desirable, but the lack of which is not necessarily an obstacle to flourishing in general. This is also affirmed by Aristotle, where he says:

> …great and frequent reverses can crush and mar our
> bliss both by the pain they cause and by the hindrance
> they offer to many activities. Yet nevertheless even in
> adversity nobility shines through, when a man
> endures repeated and severe misfortune with patience,
> not owing to insensibility but from generosity and
> greatness of soul… (*NE*, 1101a2)

From this passage it appears Aristotle would claim that someone could persevere in bad environmental conditions and flourish as a human being anyway. Aristotle might locate the condition of one's environment among the "accidents of fortune" rather than among the instruments necessary for the performance of virtue, for although global warming and climate change is largely the result of human activity, no one can predict that he will be born into this situation. One may be able to flourish in its midst through virtues like endurance, patience, resourcefulness, and "greatness of soul". A self-sufficiently happy person already has within his character all the resources he needs to flourish and be happy. *Eudaimonia* is a self-sufficient activity; it is activity the performance of which is its own reward, and such activity may require few material possessions or property. How is that position to be reconciled with the position that some external goods are necessary to one's flourishing, especially including friends?

As explained by Aristotelian scholar J. O. Urmson, the dilemma concerning friends is easily solved. There are several different kinds of friends, some of whom we have no substantial need for, others are indispensable. Specifically, there are three kinds of friendship, each based on three different qualities for which things are worthy of being liked or loved: the useful, the pleasurable, and the good. [35] Correspondingly, the three kinds of friendship are friendships based on utility, on pleasure, and on virtue. This correspondence obtains because "when men love each other, they wish each other well in respect of the quality which is the ground of their friendship." (*NE*, 1156a12) The first two kinds of friendship, those based on utility and on pleasure, Aristotle claims do not constitute true friendship because the friends do not love each other for who they are, but rather for what they can get from each other. Such friendships, he says, are easily broken off.[36] Those lesser types of friends are the types for which, as Urmson says, the virtuous person has little need. Urmson says, "The life of the contemplative man needs few external goods, so such a man will have little need of 'friendships of utility', of business associations; the life of such a man is also intrinsically pleasant, so he will not need companions to keep him amused."[37] His virtuous friends are not a mere supplement to his *eudaimonia*, but are positively bound together with his practice of virtue, for the reason that 'man is a social animal' and good friends excellently satisfy the natural need for social relations.[38]

Knowing that other people, in the form of one's society and the best of one's friends, are an integral part of one's aim for *eudaimonia* in that virtuous sense, is the relation with the environment in any way analogous? Can the external good of environmental resources be loved for itself and thus become a similarly integral part of one's flourishing? Many contemporary environmentalists say 'yes'. Wensveen claims that for courage to function as an ecological virtue, it must be "mediated through the experience of love".[39] Someone motivated by love of the natural world, love of the Earth, love of life, would acquire sufficient courage to "shake familiar, but unsustainable habits and to challenge ecologically harmful practices, institutions, and structures of power."[40] Wensveen appears to be arguing that it is *politically useful* to love the Earth because of the way it can motivate people to take action, and not arguing that loving the Earth can be justified in its own terms. Similarly, in the social ecology of Bookchin, as shown by Wensveen, love is one of the most prominent virtues in his extensive catalogue.[41] Love of nature as a primary virtue is also found in the writings of various eco-centrists and theologians, such as Thoreau, Muir, and Naess, who believe that the act of loving the Earth is self-rewarding, and they place less emphasis on the political usefulness of love. In describing the Virtuousness of love for the land these authors usually turn to aesthetic virtues: they claim that appreciation of beauty, and of one's place in, and relationship with, the ecological world, motivates respect for the land, and they argue that a lack of respect for the environment is connected to vices such as cold-heartedness, ignorance and self-importance.

In strictly Aristotelian terms, however, the answer is 'no'. We cannot love the Earth the same way we love other people. For like the friendships of utility and of pleasure, we value the environment largely for the sake of what we can get from it. Without meaning to diminish the importance of the aesthetic qualities just mentioned, we normally wish that a forest should be an 'excellent' forest (in the sense of possessing diversity, integrity, suitability for its inhabitants, and so on) because we will use it to obtain food, building materials, and fuel. We wish for a field of crops to grow well because we will eventually want to eat them. We also find that however much we may love a forest, a lake, a river, and so on, it does not love us back. For Aristotle, love and friendship is genuine and virtuous when it involves a "return of affection". In his words:

> ...the term friendship is not applied to love for inanimate objects, since there is no return of affection, and no wish for the good of the object—for instance, it would be ridiculous to wish well to a bottle of wine: at the most one wishes that it may keep well in order that one may have it oneself; whereas we are told that we ought to wish our friend well for his own sake. (*NE*, 1155b28)

These are the Aristotelian reasons why we cannot regard the Earth the same way we regard a friend. I cannot see how these reasons can be avoided unless complex and controversial theological principles are brought into play, for instance the claim sometimes attributed to Plato that the world is an intelligent living being, or the claim some Pantheists assert that the love of God is discernable in and through the environment. Moreover, a defence of an idea's political usefulness cannot be the whole of its rational justification.

Remaining with Aristotle, however, we are not at a loss. We find that while we cannot expect a return of affection from the Earth, still we cannot dismiss the world as we can dismiss un-virtuous friends. Groundedness in the world is an irreducible property of life. The thesis of the external goods approach is that even if we can still flourish and be happy in areas of environmental instability and degradation, such flourishing can never be as complete and as perfect as it would in areas that are well suited to the project of human flourishing. Just as the company of virtuous friends and one's membership in a social community is an asset to the development and excellent exercise of one's social and intellectual qualities for the reason that a human being is a political animal, the excellent environment is an asset to the development and excellent exercise of one's potentials for the human being is also a corporeal animal. Notice that it is material or functional excellence that is attributed to the environment here, rather than virtuous excellence which exists within a moral agent's character and not in his external goods. Just as each of the professions has its own set of skills which enable a practitioner to be an excellent practitioner, each profession is best practised in surroundings and circumstances appropriate to them; and just as the professions are corresponded by Aristotle with the 'practice' of living a worthwhile life, the best setting in which to practice living well is 'the world'—when so arranged that its qualities and properties are well suited to the enterprise of living well. A professional theatre is a well-suited place to perform a Shakespearean play; a well-equipped workshop is a well-suited place to build the set pieces and costumes; well trained and experienced actors and technicians are excellent people with whom to perform; and likewise a fertile, prosperous, and beautiful world is an excellent place to live a worthwhile life. Without the right kind of environment, our aim for *eudaimonia* can have only limited success. Note also that there is more than one right kind of environment, just as there is more than one excellent place to perform Shakespearean plays.

If the alternative view is emphasised, the view that the world is unlike the *polis*, we find we still cannot dismiss the importance of the environment for human flourishing. Life itself is surely necessary for flourishing. Life depends on various environmental goods: air, water, food, building materials, energy, and of course spaces and places to call home. The absence of these necessary goods is a threat to health and survival. As we have seen, Aristotle provides that health and survival is an indispensable external good to human flourishing. The point about the value of an external good, here, is that although happiness does not depend on one's possessions, the absence of external goods is an obstacle to complete flourishing. As Aristotle says:

> The truly good and wise man will bear all kinds of
> fortune in a seemly way, and will always act in the
> noblest manner that the circumstances allow; even as
> a good general makes the most effective use of the
> forces at his disposal, and a good shoemaker makes
> the finest shoe possible out of the leather supplied
> him, and so on with all the other crafts and
> professions. And this being so, the happy man can
> never become miserable, though it is true he will not
> be supremely blessed if he encounters the misfortunes
> of a Priam. (*NE*, 1101a4)

It seems to follow that an excellent environment must be an indispensable external good as well, and its absence is effectively an obstacle to flourishing. However, this way of looking at the ethical significance of our Groundedness may be insufficient for various purposes. Life is impossible if our biological needs are unsatisfied, but it is conceivable that a life that never lacked for food, shelter, warmth, and so on, and which never knew injury and disease, might lack other things also connected to the environment without which life is less worthwhile. As observed by Lincoln Alison, we also need to live in a world that has a special magic for us. The beauty of the world, the great joy and wonder we often experience when travelling and discovering it, the many ways we find it to be our home and place, also figure into human flourishing. A purely materialistic view of the external argument, while it is an undeniable part of the fully acceptable environmental ethic, cannot be the whole of it.

This completes the preliminary case for why a Virtuous person should desire an environment that is well suited for flourishing, and to do things which contribute towards creating and sustaining such an environment. I claim, provisionally, that so far Virtue theory has proven to be well able to provide a satisfactory environmental ethic. The right way to treat the environment is "as the field and stage of action" (we have seen this already in Kant) with the attending implication that it can be wrong to undermine the qualities which make it well suited to be the field and stage of action. It would be wrong to cause environmental disasters because it would be contrary to the pursuit of the flourishing life, and a failure of the virtues necessary for the maintenance of the social and ecological environment in which the flourishing life is possible and supported. This provisional conclusion is encouraging, but it does not yet answer the Non-Identity Problem, nor does it provide a reason to initiate or participate in a practice of inter-generational just savings and/or virtual reciprocity. Also, certain other details remain to be filled in, including a clarification of Aristotle's value theory, and these shall be undertaken in the discourse to come.

In an essay entitled "Ecosystem Sustainability as a Criterion for Genuine Virtue", Wensveen argued that "genuine" virtue must entail the goal of environmental sustainability. Her argument took the form of a standard three-term syllogism, as follows: (1) Ecosystem sustainability is a necessary condition for the cultivation of a virtue. (2) A genuine virtue includes the goal of ensuring necessary conditions for the cultivation of virtue. (3) A genuine virtue includes the goal of ensuring ecosystem sustainability.[42] The first point affirms the premise that flourishing depends upon possessing a healthy living physical body, and supplying it with the material resources which it needs to function well.[43] The second point in the syllogism is "a simple consistency requirement."[44] Any catalogue of the virtues will include at least one 'meta-virtue', required to sustain other virtues. For Aristotle, *phronesis* is the virtue which enables one to discern the mean state between vices of deficiency and excess. Wensveen here argues that a disposition towards environmental sustainability is another meta-virtue. Environmental health and stability, she claims, is a condition for the possibility of living a virtuous life, therefore a virtuous person must do that which is necessary or required to sustain the healthy and stable environment. Other philosophers have recognised this on social and political dimensions: for instance, MacIntyre explained that:

> The catalogue of the virtues will therefore include the virtues required to sustain the kind of households and the kind of political communities in which men and women can seek for the good together and the virtues necessary for philosophical enquiry about the character of the good. (*AV* pg. 219)

MacIntyre's point is entirely concerned with social environments. In order to be able to quest for the good, one must sustain the surroundings and conditions in which the quest is possible. This point is obviously central to MacIntyre's thought, since it is re-affirmed in several of his books which followed After Virtue. For instance, in a discussion of the virtues of family life which was published in 1999, MacIntyre writes "The family flourishes only if its social environment also flourishes. And since the social environments of families vary a great deal, so do the modes of flourishing of families."[45] It is no great leap to include the physical and ecological environment here as well, for the reasons already seen. Concerning the concluding step of her syllogism, "a genuine virtue [therefore] includes the goal of ensuring ecosystem sustainability", Wensveen emphasises that genuine virtue "includes" eco-sustainability. Virtue is not simply 'compatible' with it, which would be too weak a claim, nor is it genuine virtue's primary goal, which would be too strong. Eco-sustainability is claimed by Wensveen to be an integral part of the pursuit of virtue, and neither more nor less than an integral part of that pursuit.[46]

Sandler takes the position of a sympathetic critic of environmental virtue theory. He agreed that although no one can live long enough or well enough to develop and exercise virtue without the food, water, air, and other essentials which come from ecosystems. But that by itself, he argued, does not establish that ecosystem sustainability is a necessary condition for the cultivation of virtue. As he explains, the external goods approach can have the implication that someone who lives in an ecologically unfit environment could not fully flourish, or would find it very much harder to flourish.[47] But this is the very point that environmental virtue theorists wish to make. It is the reason that the external goods approach offers for why a virtuous person should be interested in the environment. If one's environment is in such a condition that one cannot flourish, or finds it hard to flourish, Virtue theory would require that one do those things which improve the quality of the environment and its ability to support and sustain the good life. As Wensveen claims Virtue theory does not have eco-sustainability as its *primary* goal, but as a goal integrated with its other goals, a person in a degraded or unstable environment may be able to flourish in other ways, making the best of his own dwelling-place and immediate neighbourhood if he cannot affect larger regions or territories. Living in an unsuitable environment can be a barrier to living a worthwhile life, but not an insurmountable one if it can be changed. I have previously claimed that the virtues are the traits of character one needs to sustain the aim for *eudaimonia* in specific social and environmental circumstances. This claim need not imply that the contexts in which we aim for the worthwhile life are fixed and unchanging, or that we are not permitted to change them. The aim for *eudaimonia* may, from time to time, demand that we change our environment. Building settlements, clearing land for agriculture, pushing back the sea with dykes, and so on, are all examples of how we change our environment in order to improve our quality of life and thus assist the aim for *eudaimonia*.

Someone living in a degraded and unfit-for-life environment may flourish by doing precisely those things which will aim towards improving the quality of his world. Insofar as our potentials are grounded in the environment, when we transform our environment we indirectly transform our own opportunities and potentials for flourishing. In other words, we transform *ourselves* in the course of transforming our environment as well. We can claim that when we make changes to the environment, we do so in pursuit of a particular conception of *eudaimonia*, and indeed in pursuit of a particular conception of who we are and what we wish to be. We observe something like this in other animals as well, for humans are not the only animals on the Earth which make changes in the environment to suit their purposes. Some animals dig burrows, others build barrows and nests. Some animals, like beavers, create whole habitats for themselves by blocking up rivers with dams. Some insects like bees and termites build large and complicated structures with temperature-controlled internal environments. These are all examples of changes made to the environment to enable the species to develop and express its potentials to the greatest possible level. The scientist Jonas Salk, discoverer of the vaccine for polio, expressed this principle as follows:

> I believe that the fundamental relationship in all living things is the relationship between the organism's biological potential and its environment. The organism's potential is revealed and developed only under environmental influence. The environment educes, draws out, causes the potential to be expressed—if the relationship is appropriate.[48]

What Salk claims here for the physical environment, Aristotle also claimed for the *polis*, and to some extent the household as well. For Aristotle, a person's virtues exist in a necessary relation to her surroundings, for it is in responding to those surroundings that a person becomes virtuous. I claim that this principle obtains with the physical and ecological environment as well. When we make changes to those surroundings, we also open up new possibilities for flourishing.

Of course we also build motorways, burn fossil fuels, dig deep mines, and do many other kinds of environmentally destructive things, all in pursuit of the new possibilities for flourishing which we hope they will open up. The various different ways in which our society undertakes Depletion are pursued for the sake of the improved quality of life which we hope to realise in doing so. The point being asserted here, then, is that when we make changes to the environment, we also change the circumstances in which people do or do not become virtuous and flourish. Since that is the case, it is also the case that we are morally accountable for the way we change the environment, as judged by whether or not it is conducive to the *eudaimonia* for which we aim. There may be environment-altering actions which reduce, rather than increase, our opportunities for flourishing. There may be other choices which create new opportunities while permanently foreclosing others. When a dual-carriageway road is built, for instance, it is generally held that it will make it easier for people to travel. There is an ancient connection between the feeling of freedom and the ability to move unhindered through space. Yet we also find that new motorways do not simply make easier those journeys which would have happened anyway. They also create new journeys, as people travel more than they would have otherwise. When the M25 "Orbital" motorway was built around London, traffic flows in many places were found to be very much more than was predicted, in some cases more than double.[49] The choice to build a new road is therefore not a choice between traffic congestion and de-congestion. It is a choice between different scales of the same kind of congestion.[50] The decision, then, should not have been made entirely on the basis of projected traffic flows and the cost of purchasing the land and building the road. It should also be made on the basis of what alternative modes and levels of transport are available and which of them would contribute best to the creation of a social and ecological environment well suited for the pursuit of the flourishing life. The lesson of London's M25 must be learned by Ireland as it completes a circular motorway around its own capital, the Dublin M50, and as it embarks on numerous new motorways around the country. A total of 17 new national primary roads are planned by Ireland's National Roads Authority, most of them bypasses, with 9 to be initiated in 2004. Eleven of these new roads will be toll roads.[51]

Moral education (that is, the process of developing the virtues; the process of becoming habituated to be moral) begins when the agent is thrust into situations that call for a moral response. Of course Aristotle privileges the social environment: "It is by taking part in transactions with our fellow-men that some of us become just and others unjust." (*NE*, 1103b12) One of the qualities of the suitable environment, we can say, is that it challenges us to be moral. The right kind of environment for flourishing is the one in which the qualities of character which we need for survival and success, and which are most rewarded, are our most excellent and most noble qualities. Less suitable environments for flourishing do not reward our noble qualities so well, and may even reward our vices. Living in a *polis* is for Aristotle the paradigm case of an environment well suited for excellence. Indeed it is a basic presupposition for Aristotle that people can attain a worthwhile life *if and only if* they are habituated to be moral by a *polis*. In the <u>Politics</u> he says that man reaches full development only within the surroundings of a politically organised society (i.e. a state), and is "not fully self sufficient" when separated from it. The statement appears in his claim that the household and the state has a 'natural priority' over the individual:

> Separate hand or foot from the whole body, and they will no longer be hand or foot except in name, as one might speak of a 'hand' or 'foot' sculpted in stone. That will be the condition of the spoilt hand, which no longer has the capacity and the function which define it… For if an individual is not fully self-sufficient after separation, he will stand in the same relationship to the whole as the parts in the other case do… For as man is the best of all animals when he has reached his full development, so he is worst of all when divorced from law and justice. (*Politics* 1253a18)

Just as a hand or foot separated from the whole body is unable to function according to its proper purpose, an individual separated from the society is unable to fully flourish as a human being. Anyone who lives without any need for a society is "either too bad or too good, either subhuman or superhuman". (*Politics* 1253a1) MacIntyre explains that the indispensable thing which the *polis* provides is *dikaiosune* (justice), and so to be separated from the *polis* is to be without *dikaiosune*.[52] Without the *polis*, then, one's various natural talents and abilities would go undeveloped, or would be developed to serve unjust ends, and "what could have been a human being becomes instead a wild animal."[53]

Note that Aristotle's *polis* is not at all like our idea of a nation-state. For Aristotle, the *polis* combines two ideas which modern political theorists tend to separate carefully: the state on one hand, and civil society on the other. 'Civil society' includes all the different ways in which people associate with one another, and all the different reasons for which they form ordinary relationships. The associations of civil society can be formal or informal, private or public, voluntary or involuntary. They include families, friendships, trading partners, and special purpose associations like theatre groups, service clubs, and sports teams. The state, by contrast, is a formal institution responsible for the provision of various public functions within a specific territory, such as a system of justice, and of protection against criminals and military attack. When Aristotle claims, then, that people flourish best only in the right kind of *polis*, it is this holistic, inclusive sense of the whole of society, including but not limited to a specific set of political relationships, which he has in mind.[54]

What Aristotle claims for the social environment here, I claim also holds for one's ecological environment as well. Separated from the physical environment, a human being also becomes unable to develop various natural talents and abilities in the service of a worthwhile life. Here, it is not the absence of *dikaiosune*, but the absence of *groundedness*, which prevents flourishing. There is, first of all, the obvious point that the Earth provides the material and energy resources which make organic life possible. Separated from these resources, we die. Even in a space craft we do not leave the Earth entirely behind: we must bring food, water, air, and so on, which is effectively to take a piece of the Earth with us, and we must return to the Earth when supplies run out. There is also the phenomenological point which is that to be deprived of groundedness is to be deprived of a home and place, and therefore deprived of all of the possibilities for thought, feeling, and action which the possession of a home and place makes possible. To live in and with a certain environment, to react and respond to its challenges, and indeed to make changes to it, is part of one's flourishing. This latter point deserves special emphasis. Aristotle claims that in the *polis*, we become moral human beings through 'transactions with our fellow-men'. The corresponding point with reference to groundedness is that we become moral human beings, capable of *eudaimonia*, by responding and reacting to the environment in which we find ourselves. We do not, of course, respond and react to mountains, rivers, the wind, and so on, the same way we react and respond to other people. Rather, the normal way in which we respond to the environment is by changing it in various ways: building roads to make mountains and rivers passable, building houses to shut out the weather. Insofar as we transform or re-create our own environment, (and that is how conservation and depletion arise as problems) we also transform the environment's suitability as an external good for its flourishing. We thus indirectly transform and re-create the way(s) in which our own potentials and natural talents can be expressed. This claim brings out the full significance of the external-goods approach to environmental virtue, and the principle of groundedness. The world figures into our flourishing as the field and stage for the performance of excellence, and we extend the range of our potential to achieve excellence by transforming the world into a field and stage better suited for such aspirations. By transforming the environment, we transform it into an expression of our flourishing.

We may well ask, then, what possibilities for flourishing are being opened up, or foreclosed, by the creation of a heritage park, a dual-carriage toll road, a sustainable organic farm, a landfill site. We may well ask what possibilities for flourishing are created by making Conservation or Depletion our overall way of living in and with the environment, using it, and transforming it for our purposes. As if in recognition of this principle, governments create laws for themselves and sign treaties among one another to protect the environment from undue destruction. For example:

European Union Environmental Directives. Protection of the environment is listed among the aims of the European Union in various articles of its Constitution.[55] But most EU environmental laws come in the form of Directives, enacted by the Commission and the Parliament, which bind all member states to implement certain orders within the national law within a specific time, usually two years, and achieve the objectives they describe within another specified time, usually three to five years. There are hundreds of EU directives concerning the treatment of the environment. The first dates back to 1967, and concerns the classification, packaging and labelling of dangerous substances (Directive 67/548). The main ones presently in force include a directive to control automobile emissions for the sake of air quality (70/220); the Birds Directive, on the protection of habitats for avian life (79/409); Minimum Standards for Drinking Water (80/778); Directive on Environmental Impact Assessments (85/337); several directives to limit the use of genetically modified organisms (90/219 and 90/220); and the Habitats Directive on the conservation of habitats for wild flora and fauna (92/43).[56] On 22 December 2000, the Water Framework Directive (2000/60) came into force, which was the most comprehensive directive on environmental matters ever handed to EU member states. It requires member states to monitor water quality, produce sustainable use and management plans, prevent deterioration of water quality, prevent toxic discharges into lakes, rivers, and coastal waters, and restore 'heavily modified' or 'artificial' waters to their original condition (although states are entitled to designate 'artificial' waters which it would be against their socio-economic interest to restore).[57] The 10 new countries which joined the European Union on 1st May 2004 are required to comply with existing EU directives, although for environmental directives requiring significant investment for compliance, extended periods of transition were granted.[58]

The philosophical point here is that environmental laws such as these do not merely create legal regimes. They have practical effects upon the planet, with the result that a different environment is created. The effect is similar to that which Parfit claims is the consequence of various Non-Identity choices for future human generations. Practical implementation and enforcement of these and other environmental policies can, and sometimes do, reshape the environment: they alter the course of rivers, the habitats of animals and insects, the shape and size of fields and meadows, the chemical composition of soils, waters, and airs, and so on, with related effects on temperature, cloud cover, rainfall, animal and plant populations, and other effects. Environmental policies can transform the environment into something other than it would have been had different policies been enacted, with the result that a different environment is created. Even to preserve the environment is to 'transform' it, insofar as changes are *not* made which otherwise would be made, with the result that the condition of the environment is different than it would otherwise be. We may ask, then, whether the environment which is created by such policies is suitable for flourishing. It is not enough, then, that the debate concerning such laws should be restricted to the language of economics and politics. We should also ask the more general, comprehensive question of what kind of world we want to live in, and whether the kind of *eudaimonia* we are aiming for is achievable in the world as it presently exists and as we are shaping it to be.

To work out the precise application of such a question, it would seem that a principle of practical virtue is required. I defer this necessary study to the next chapter, in order to discuss several important remaining theoretical issues.

§ 5. The Use and Misuse of Eunoia as an Environmental Virtue.

What would an example of an environmental virtue be, and what kind of life would be lived by someone who possessed environmental virtues? As Wensveen has shown, a literary proto-Virtue theory has been a part of environmental ethics from the beginning, although never explicitly presented as such. Some of the earliest papers to discuss environmental virtue theory directly proposed special variations on the virtue of *eunoia,* the faculty which enables the possessor to recognise the value of other beings or other things. It is normally translated as "benevolence" or "good will", and it underlies much of Aristotle's discussion of friendship.

In 1983 Thomas Hill published "Ideals of Human Excellence and Preserving Natural Environments",[59] which was the first professional philosophy paper to overtly and directly discuss environmental ethics using Virtue theory. He claimed that the cardinal virtue of environmentalism is 'humility', which involves recognition and awareness of one's place in the world. Those who feel free to destroy a part of nature, or even those who value it purely instrumentally, lack this awareness. Hill clarifies that this awareness has nothing to do with data, information, or a body of facts: a person who feels himself free to cover his garden with asphalt might have perfect information about the plants and habitats he destroys. Rather, environmental virtue is an attitude and a perspective. Hill's argument is that someone who possessed the right perspective about one's place in the world would normally or naturally acquire a sense of humility, and so be motivated to respect the world. In his own words:

> ...the argument appeals to the common idea that
> awareness of nature typically has, and should have, a
> humbling effect. The Alps, a storm at sea, the Grand
> Canyon, towering redwoods, and "the starry heavens
> above" move many a person to remark on the
> comparative insignificance of our daily concerns and

even of our species, and this is generally taken to be quite a fitting response. What seems to be missing, then, in those who understand nature but remain unmoved is a proper humility.[60]

Wensveen has shown how 'humility' had been treated as an appropriate environmental attitude by a number of forerunners to the present environmental ethics debate, especially those inspired by Christianity. 'Humility' as an environmental virtue regards the environment as a source of numinous wonder, possessing a certain authority and integrity, participating in the goodness of God. Hill, in this sense, is participating in an established tradition.[61]

Another similar contribution to the debate was Geoffrey Frasz's, "Environmental Virtue Ethics: A New Direction for Environmental Ethics",[62] which appeared ten years after Hill's paper. Frasz, commenting on Hill's description of humility, re-cast it as 'openness' and placed it in an Aristotelian framework as a mean between vices of deficiency and excess: 'arrogance' and 'self-importance' at one possible extreme, and 'false modesty' at the other. Frasz' summary comment about openness as an environmental virtue reads:

> In a positive sense, openness is an environmental
> virtue that establishes an awareness of oneself as part
> of the natural environment, as one natural thing
> among many others. A person who manifests this
> trait is neither someone who is closed off to the
> humbling effects of nature nor someone who has lost
> all sense of individuality when confronted with the
> vastness and sublimity of nature. [63]

The notion that anthropocentric arrogance is an environmental vice goes back to the beginning of environmental philosophy. Its most direct statement is Lynn White Jr.'s essay, "The Historical Roots of the Ecological Crisis", in which Christianity's acclaimation of the superiority of human beings over animals and plants is blamed for creating an intellectual and cultural climate of disdain towards nature. She claimed that "Especially in its Western form, Christianity is the most anthropocentric religion the world has ever known."[64] The 1994 edition of the Catechism of the Catholic Church places limits on humankind's dominion over nature, but does not deny that dominion: It says, "Man is at the summit of the Creator's work" and "Animals, like plants and inanimate beings, are by nature destined for the common good of past, present, and future humanity". Man's dominion is limited by "concern for the quality of life of his neighbour, including generations to come; it requires a religious respect for the integrity of creation."[65]

One more recent contributor to the debate to mention is Jason Kawall, who proposed 'Reverence for Life' as a comprehensive virtue.[66] Kawall claims that it is a virtue to respect all living things *qua* living things, regardless of whatever other qualities various living things may possess, including sentience, capacity for intentionality, or for suffering. Rather than provide a defence for this position, he defers to other authors who have articulated justifications for the intrinsic value of non-human life, and also claims that it is already a part of everyday moral reasoning.[67] Kawall claims that life is an intrinsic value, and while some beings may possess certain properties which are also intrinsically valuable, just the property of being alive demands respect, and it is virtuous to respect things just insofar as they are alive.[68]

The strategy of grounding environmental Virtue ethics in particular qualities of the environment and of living beings individually is certainly something I personally appreciate, having walked some of the most scenic mountains, islands, and landscapes of Ireland and several other countries. On those occasions I too felt the awe-inspiring, sublime effect that Frasz, Hill, and Kawall say should make people feel humble and motivated to care for and respect the world. I certainly agree that these experiences are important and valuable. Philosophically, however, I find this kind of argument incomplete. A Virtuous person does find that certain things are intrinsically valuable, like his friends, but that value always exists in reference to the value he attributes to his own life.

We are able to find things to be intrinsically valuable if we already find intrinsic value in our own lives. Virtue theory is not a matter of claiming that we are to respond with appropriate respect to some special quality or property, whatever it may be and wherever it is found. Therefore environmental virtue theory is not a matter of claiming that the special quality or property is to be found in the environment. This is the logic of Kant's Practical Imperative, for whom 'humanity' was the special quality or property to which we are morally obliged to respond appropriately. To dress this up as Virtue theory is to miss the point of Virtue theory. To a Virtuous person, something is valuable if it "resembles him in virtue", and so it edifies and uplifts him to respect it. A Virtuous person respects or cares for others primarily because she flourishes by doing so, not because, like Deontology, the other being possesses a special quality or characteristic that one is duty-bound to respect. In his discussion of 'reverence for life', Kawall presupposed this logic from the beginning.

This should not, however, be taken to imply that to a Virtuous person, all value is instrumental value. *Eunoia*, as Aristotle uses it, is in part the capacity to see the excellences of people and things, yet it is also the honour and respect due to such people and things. *Eunoia* is thus not only a faculty of intellectual perception, but also something that we do. It is the appropriate way of responding to excellence. But one is only capable of seeing the excellences of things and responding appropriately if one already possesses *eunoia*. How could these three modern authors have mistaken the faculty of *eunoia* this way? One possible answer is because between Aristotle's time and our own there is the edifice of Christianity. Christian theology, as observed by MacIntyre, changed the way we think about the virtues. "What Christianity requires is a conception not merely of defects of character, or vices, but of breaches of divine law, of sins." (*AV* pg. 168) This point was raised by Anscombe as well: in her words, "between Aristotle and us came Christianity, with its *law* conception of ethics. For Christianity derived its ethical notions from the Torah… In consequence of the dominance of Christianity for many centuries, the concepts of being bound, permitted, or excused became deeply embedded in our language and thought.'[69] For Hill, Frasz, and Kawall, the environment possesses a duty-generating quality, and virtue consists in the propensity to respond to that quality properly, rather like the way the presence of God stands over the agent and motivates or commands him to respond in certain ways. If we do not respond properly it is because we are arrogant, insufficiently humble, or lacking in proper openness, in their view. I am not claiming that this is essentially wrong. I claim only that that is not an *Aristotelian* approach to ethics. 'Humility' and 'Openness' are not easy counterparts or substitutes for *eunoia*. The active part is missing. *Eunoia* is only partly a matter of open-ness to the qualities of the other. It is also the excellence of character which is habituated within us when we respond to such qualities properly. The point of virtue theory is to respect something for reasons to do with the qualities of one's own character as a moral agent, not the qualities of something else. Aristotle does claim we must respect others, and that *eunoia* enables one to do so, but *eunoia* is bound together with the Virtuous person's own aim for *eudaimonia*. It is not the special qualities possessed by other people and things, but the value he assigns to his own life, which commands the moral action.

 Eunoia was applied to environmental ethics in a more recognisably Aristotelian fashion by Susanne Foster, in her 2002 paper, "Aristotle and the Environment".[70] The principle that stands out in her paper is a general correspondence between goodness and *ousia*, the Aristotelian concept of "substance", which *eunoia* empowers someone to recognise. As she explained it, a thing's substance is its intrinsic nature, consisting in not only its distinct shape and structure but also its forms of behaviour.[71] Substance is not to be likened to a material 'stuff', but to its intrinsic potentialities for action and behaviour: specifically, its potential to actualise itself by performing functions natural to it. A living being's nature, on Foster's interpretation of Aristotle, consists in the ideal which the thing is striving to actualise. In various places, Aristotle claims that things are good insofar as they are able to perform their function and actualise their nature excellently. The more a being actualises its nature with excellence, Foster explains, the more it possesses being, and hence the more it possesses goodness.

Some philosophers, such as by Bill Shaw,[72] Kent Peacock,[73] Lawrence Johnson,[74] and others, argue that ecosystems and species appear to exhibit a teleological 'way of being' in the Aristotelian sense, and therefore they are living beings. They argue that the function of an ecosystem to support life constitutes teleological behaviour, and hence an interest. Possessing interests, so this school of thought goes, ecosystems therefore possess moral standing and are worthy of our respect. We have seen this way of doing ethics in Taylor's Biocentric Attitude, although Taylor discusses only individual entities and not holistic systems like ecosystems. If the aim of life-support was the reason for the existence of the biosphere, then it would be a teleological system.[75] Interestingly, James Lovelock's *Gaia Hypothesis*, on whom some of these authors rely, does *not* claim that the Earth is a teleological system. Lovelock uses a thought experiment called "Daisyworld" to show how a planet can regulate temperature entirely through automatic thermodynamic processes.[76] Foster also denies the teleological thesis and claims it is better to liken ecosystems to artefacts. What distinguishes a teleological being from an artefact, according to Foster's interpretation of Aristotle, is that teleological beings generate their own *telos* with an "internal principle of motion and rest", whereas artefacts have theirs imposed on them by external forces—by craftsmen or artisans, for example. Ecosystems have no internal principle of motion and rest; their function of life support is, in Foster's view, a natural by-product of the normal activity of its living inhabitants. The function of a natural body such as an animal is always internal to itself: the eagle's function is to sense and to move, to eat and reproduce, and so on, and not to control rodent populations and balance the ecosystem (even if that is a natural by-product of its activity).[77] Thus it is better to think of ecosystems as artefacts. As artefacts, they may still possess a kind of moral standing: they are good insofar as they possess *suitability* for their function,[78] and this stands in the place of flourishing-potential as the root of the object's being, and the root of its goodness. On Foster's view, the more complex a being is, the greater and more excellent its capacities will be if allowed to flourish, and the more substance, and therefore goodness, it will possess. For an artefact, the category in which she classifies ecosystems, the strictly instrumental-value concept of 'suitability' for a function or a purpose applied to it by another being can be substituted for the flourishing-potential of a living being as the root of its substance and hence its goodness. This accords with my claim that a Virtuous person values the environment as an external good, materially well suited for the performance of its function, rather than as a fellow being which resembles him in virtue.

Foster's treatment of *eunoia* in all of this can be summarised in the following four steps. (1) When we direct our capacity of *eunoia* towards artefacts, we find they are good to the degree that they possess this kind of substance: they are good to the degree that they are excellently suited for performing their function, in a way that is loosely analogous to the way that a living being can be esteemed for expressing its potentialities with excellence. (2) The goodness of both the intrinsic 'flourishing-capacity' value of a living being, and the instrumental 'suitability-value' of artefacts, can be recognised by humanity's rational capacity for *eunoia*. (3) The environment, as an artefact, can be valued for the extent to which it is suitable for its function of sustaining the lives of the beings who inhabit it. (4) On her interpretation of Aristotle, "obligation or care for others is based on a perception of their goodness or being."[79] To 'senselessly' destroy an artefact, by ruining its suitability or by using it for a different purpose than that for which it was made, is a failure of *eunoia* and thus a mark of flawed character.

There is beauty to a philosophical system that equates being with goodness, as Foster observed. Similar arguments can be found in the work of other contemporary Virtue theorists. Elisabeth Anscombe argued that 'goodness' is an attributive quality which is the same for objects, plants, and animals as it is for people, and does not mysteriously become an evaluative term when human morality is under discussion. One can also find versions of this argument in the 'naturalistic' Virtue Theory of Philippa Foot, and in the practical virtue of Rosalind Hursthouse, for both of whom it is one step in the larger argument that the virtues benefit whosoever possesses them. The virtues are the qualities which makes an X a characteristically *good* X, whether we are speaking of tables, flowers, tigers, or people.[80] Foster has created a place for *eunoia* in this system, which is a constructive contribution but it creates a certain difficulty. The correspondence between being and goodness as Foster presents it seems to distract from the point of Virtue theory. Strictly speaking, the claim that something has a special quality which entitles it to receive moral respect is Deontology and not Virtue Ethics. The question of whether something has moral standing is for Virtue theory subordinate to the question of whether the moral agent's character and nature is excellent and conducive to his or her flourishing. The argument that flourishing is good is of course classically Aristotelian (and Foster might be forgiven for assuming that the reader of a professional philosophy journal is already familiar with it). But there is something wrong with simply transferring this correspondence from flourishing-potential to generalised being. *Eudaimonia* (flourishing and/or happiness) is the good which we choose for its own sake and not for the sake of another good, as Aristotle claims, and we achieve it through living our lives in such a way that our highest and most divine capacities and potentialities in us are developed to the level of excellence. It is *Arête*, excellence and/or virtue, not 'being', which in the <u>Nicomachean Ethics</u> Aristotle corresponds most directly and clearly with goodness.

This criticism is not meant to be a hostile counter-argument. Rather, I think Foster is inadvertently pointing the way to a possible meeting place between Deontology and Virtue Theory. A complete description of this meeting place may be very complex. It would still be *arête*, 'excellence' or 'virtue', and not *ousia*, 'substance' or 'being', which matters, but *arête* is related to *ousia* in subtle ways. One becomes a good human being, capable of *eudaimonia*, by making *arête* a property of her *ousia*. We can interpret Foster as having simply used "suitability" as a special kind of *arête*. Aristotle allows for the possibility that objects can have (or can lack) *arête* in the service of performing the function for which they were made. In Aristotle's own words:

> ...all excellence has a twofold effect on the thing to which it belongs: it not only renders the thing itself good, but also causes it to perform its function well. For example, the effect of excellence in the eye is that the eye is good *and* functions well; since having good eyes means having good sight. Similarly excellence in a horse makes it a good horse, and also good at galloping, at carrying its rider, and at facing the enemy. If therefore this is true of all things, excellence or virtue in a man will be the disposition which renders him a good man and also which will cause him to perform his function well. (*NE*, 1106a1)

This passage, it seems to me, proposes that goodness is to be associated with *arête*, and not with *ousia*. Yet it is, evidently, Foster's position that a being is worthy of esteem precisely for its capacity to flourish, and only to the extent that it both potentially can, and actually does, flourish. It also appears to be Foster's position that, similarly, artefacts deserve to be 'respected' insofar as they are suitable for their purpose. Foster uses the example of a carpenter who drives nails with a level instead of a hammer. Although the level would do the job, it is not suitable for the job, and it would be "senseless" to use it instead of the hammer.[81] But a moral agent living in terms of Virtue theory does not analyse the moral status and standing of the people and things he is dealing with the way that Foster suggests. His primary interest is in whether what he is doing is conducive to sustaining a worthwhile life. It is not a question of extending moral status to non-natural or non-living substances, but a question of whether the agent is manifesting good character in what she does. This is something Foster herself recognises where she writes: "I am arguing that the implausibility of extending consideration to non-natural substances disappears if we switch the focus to the agent, and make the central ethical question, 'am I doing good or ill?'." But the very next statement after that one reads, "The way to answer this question is to consider the value and goodness of the things we destroy or protect."[82] By retaining the notion of the value or goodness of the things we destroy or protect, she appears to miss her own point. The value or goodness of other things is not what matters to a virtuous moral agent, or it is not what matters *primarily*: What matters is what she does, as a moral agent, to aim at the good life. If a Virtuous person chooses to do something to contribute to the conservation of the environment, she does it not because she thinks that the environment has moral standing, even if it can be shown that it does. She does it because it is excellent to do so. *Eunoia* is "good will" directed towards that which is valuable in reference to the agent's actions, personal qualities, and her aim for the flourishing life. In Aristotle's words:

> The perfect form of friendship is that between the good, and those who resemble each other in virtue. For these friends wish each alike the other's good in respect of their goodness, and they are good in themselves; but it is those who wish the good of their friends for their friend's sake who are friends in the fullest sense, since they love each other for themselves and not accidentally. (*NE*, 1156b11)

Eunoia, here, is the agent's wish for the good of his friend, because the two have similarly excellent characters. Can the environment resemble me in virtue? As we have seen, the answer in strict Aristotelian terms is "no". *Eunoia* can only be properly applied to a being who is himself capable of *eunoia* as well, and not to inanimate objects like bottles of wine, for the reason that the object to which *eunoia* is directed is valuable for the way it figures into the agent's own flourishing. The contemporary distinction between 'intrinsic' and 'instrumental' value does not quite capture the meaning of *eunoia;* something which "resembles the moral agent in virtue" is treated as an intrinsically good thing, or person, but the virtuous person is able to see it that way only because he already finds his own life intrinsically good.

It is certainly possible to recognise the value of things that are not people. A collector of fine paintings may love art and in particular his own collection. Families may love their houses, sailors love theirs ships, musicians their instruments, and so on. All of these things may have loveable qualities: they may be well built or aesthetically pleasing. Children may be taught by their parents not to scratch the dinner-table with their knives and forks because of qualities to do with the table: it is as-yet unblemished, for instance. Someone with sufficient imaginative vision could love a forest, a mountain, an island or coastline, the sea, or the sky, in a way similar to how mariners love their ships and musicians love their instruments. Most people have at least a nostalgic fondness for the landscapes of their own region or country, especially the area where they grew up. Many artists, musicians, poets, writers, and philosophers have praised the aesthetic qualities of the land, sea, and sky that make it loveable. Aristotle's point about friendship is that one cannot be "friends" with inanimate objects, for "there is no return of affection". No inanimate object can love you back. In Aristotle's view, the love and goodwill of friendship must be mutual and reciprocated to count as friendship at all.[83] It follows that if an Aristotelian recognises the value of artefacts and inanimate objects, or non-human systems like the environment, he does not do so in the same way that he recognises the value of a friend. We only assess whether an ecosystem is able to perform its material function with *arete*, just as we assess good eyes, good horses, and so on.

This, however, does not mean the environment has no value at all to a Virtuous person. He might value the environment in another way or for another reason. If we accepted the argument that ecosystems and species can have teleological virtues in the service of their functions and hence can flourish, then one would have to question whether 'flourishing' can function in the Aristotelian system the way 'humanity' and 'reason' functioned in the Kantian system—as a quality or attribute which renders the possessor worthy of moral consideration. Alternatively, if we follow Foster's argument and think of ecosystems as artefacts instead of as living beings, then we must concede that they do not 'flourish' in the sense that they do not strive for *eudaimonia*. We only assess whether an ecosystem is able to perform its material function with *arete*, just as we assess good eyes, good horses, and so on. This second claim is the stronger of the two. Things can possess 'virtues' of a non-teleological sort. They can possess qualities which enable them to fulfil their functions. These qualities may be poor or excellent, and if they are excellent we say that the object is good. The environment, conceived as an artefact in this way, has the function of sustaining the lives of its inhabitants. It has various qualities like the oxygen content of the air, pH balance of the water, species biodiversity, constancy of temperature, regularity of seasonal changes, availability of food, capacity to absorb toxins, and so on. If these and other qualities are at a state where they serve the function of life-support excellently, then we affirm the ecosystem as good. But it is a material or a functional excellence, rather than a virtuous excellence, that is affirmed here.

The role of *eunoia* can now be properly stated. This faculty, normally used to recognise the value of one's friends, can indeed be used to recognise the value of the world, although not quite the way Foster claimed it would. It does not recognise a value which is entirely or completely external to the moral agent. *Eunoia* recognises the value of things in reference to, or in relation to, the value one assigns or attributes to one's own life and one's own practice of living well. It is in relation to the quality of one's own life that *eunoia* is able to reveal the value of other beings, and it enables the virtuous person to invite those other beings into his practice of living well, with and for other people, in and with the world.

This completes the statement of Virtuous environmental ethics, as articulated on the theoretical plane. This argument is flexible in that it allows for the possibility that there is not one single kind of right environment—an important flexibility, since the human race lives in many different kinds of environments. A sub-tropical island region like the Caribbean might be just as good for flourishing as an inland temperate forest like central Europe or a cold mountain plateau like Tibet. The environmentalist in me would like to leap to the conclusion that the right kind of environment for flourishing is necessarily a natural one; an ecosystem of some kind. But that would be premature. If there are many kinds of surroundings which are well suited for human flourishing, could a completely engineered, artificial enclosure be one of them?

§ 6. Artificial environments?

Artificial environments can enter the discourse here as a critical thought experiment with which to put this principle of environmental virtue to the test. What if we accept that a person flourishes best in the right kind of environment, but an artificial environment might be similarly right for human flourishing? The kind that Aristotle would have preferred is the *polis*, a community organised to promote human flourishing. A *polis* is primarily defined by its constitution, which outlines the structure of the human social world. But it is also a special type of physical world: a town or a city, and in Aristotle's meaning of the term it also included the surrounding villages, farms, and landscape. The thought experiment here is, What if it is entirely possible to fully flourish in urban settings, and ignore the 'natural' environments of the fields, forests, rivers, and oceans that exist outside the city wards? The surroundings that a lifetime city dweller responded to as he developed his virtues were the streets, houses, shops, factories, offices, and parks of his city. Perhaps in the course of his life he never leaves the city. Thus he might think he has no reason to seek the conservation and improvement of distant forests and lakes, even if he does seek the conservation of his city's parks, trees, and architectural landmarks.

One answer to this critical objection can run like this. Cities are just as much a part of the world as are fields and forests, and moreover the reverse is also true: the (rest of the) world is just as much a part of the city and the life of its citizens as are its streets, buildings, and built infrastructure. It is now commonly understood in the social sciences and among urban planners that a city occupies more land than is inside its boundaries. A city is also defined by its "ecological footprint", the land area required to feed its inhabitants, supply its industrial and commercial activities with energy and raw materials, and receive its waste. The idea of the 'ecological footprint' for cities was initially put forward by environmental economists M. Wackernagel and W. Rees as an analysis tool for government agencies and local authorities for use in planning the sustainable development strategies required by various domestic laws and international agreements. [84] The World Wildlife Federation defines it concisely as follows:

> The footprint expresses the land area that is required
> to feed, provide resources, produce energy, assimilate
> waste, and to re-absorb its CO_2 output from fossil
> fuels through photosynthesis. This approach uses
> land as its 'currency', and provides a notional figure
> for the land area required, wherever and however
> located on the planet, that is necessary to support an
> individual, a community or a nation's population at its
> present standard of living.[85]

This ecological footprint of a city is very much larger than the land occupied by the roads and buildings, and of course can overlap with the ecological footprint of other cities. For instance the ecological footprint of London, England, is nearly 50 million acres, or approximately the size of the whole of Britain. Herbert Girardet, professor of environmental planning at Middlesex University, put this figure into perspective this way: "Although [London] contains only 12 per cent of Britain's population, it requires an area equivalent to all the country's productive land to service it—though this extends to the wheat prairies of Kansas, the tea gardens of Assam, the copper mines of Zambia and other far-flung places."[86] Thus a lifetime city dweller should seek the improvement of the quality of the natural environment surrounding his city, at least as much of it as is covered by the city's ecological footprint. In this way, it is not possible for a Virtuous urbanite to cut the ecological environment entirely out of the range of his concern. He may also seek the improvement of the global ecosystems which support his life and the life of his city from all over the Earth, for instance by recycling water and oxygen or by regulating climate and temperature. Even if he never leaves his city, he should be concerned about issues like:

> *The Earth's Regeneration Capacity.* The World Wildlife Federation reported in 2000 that "while the size of our remaining natural ecosystems has declined by over 33% over the last 30 years, human demands on natural resources (natural capital) have increased by 50% in the same period, and now exceeds the biosphere's regeneration rate... Current estimates suggest that we have overshot our global 'carrying capacity' by over 30%".[87] The world ecological footprint, at this time, is thus $1/3$ larger than the surface area of the Earth. While this may appear as a mathematical absurdity, what it represents is the degree to which human demand for natural resources exceeds by over 30% the capacity of the planetary biosphere to regenerate itself (assuming the WWF's figures are correct).

There is another possible kind of artificial environment that we could use to test the environmental virtue theory I have here outlined. Suppose that a Virtuous person finds that a totally engineered, self-contained structure is for him the right kind of environment in which to flourish. *Eudaimonia* might be possible for someone living in a space capsule, or in something like "Biosphere-2", the self-contained and fully enclosed ecosystem constructed in a greenhouse in the desert near Tucson, Arizona, USA. Biosphere-2 was built to experiment with and to demonstrate certain principles of eco-sustainability and the possibilities for human survival in colonies on other planets. Suppose a Virtuous person claimed that it was entirely possible for him to flourish and be completely happy inside a perfectly engineered and entirely self-contained Biosphere-2, one which provided all of our bodily needs like food and water, as well as other luxuries and benefits typically associated with good living. Another variation of this thought experiment is the techno-fantasy world. Might *eudaimonia* be possible for a lifetime dweller of a holographic simulation room, or 'within' a computer-generated simulation electronically fed directly into his brain? In the techno-fantasy, not only is the ecological environment suspended, but one's very groundedness in the world is suspended as well. If this variation of the basic thought experiment succeeds, then the external goods argument that I have defended, that people are most likely to flourish best when their surroundings are well suited for them to do so, would not necessarily defend a reason to conserve natural ecosystems. The question, "wouldn't it be possible to flourish in an artificial environment?" asks whether an artificial environment could do all that an ecological environment could do. If the answer is "yes", the implication is that the type of environment a Virtuous person lives in is irrelevant to his flourishing, so long as it supplies him with the physical, intellectual, aesthetic and social goods that he needs. If people develop and adapt in response to the natural environment, they would presumably develop and adapt in response to a man-made environment custom-built to suit them as well, developing the skills and virtues needed for success and happiness in that situation.

My reply is to ask, what kind of happiness would the inhabitants of a theoretical Biosphere-2 or a theoretical computer-generated world be able to enjoy? A Virtuous person values the world not simply as the supplier of material goods, even if it supplies his material goods in abundance. He values it as the field of his actions, the physical dimension of the social environment of which he is inherently a part, and he values it insofar as it is involved in his actions, which are the source of his happiness. Therefore the question is, what kind of actions are possible in such a world? I claim that an artificial environment has properties which make it inherently unsuited for the kind of flourishing Aristotle has in mind, and these properties have nothing to do with the environment's utility-value, as I shall here explain. It is a necessary property of all artificial environments, including the kind hypothetically postulated here, that they are planned, ordered, and especially *controlled* environments. As controlled environments, they would be in principle limited in what they can provide in a way that natural ecologies are not: they are limited by the design specifications of the architects, whereas natural ecologies are limited only by the availability of organic compounds, mineral resources, solar energy, and by the inherent potentialities of the inhabitant organisms, including those of humankind. To be happy in an artificial environment, a person would have to want only what is offered by the artificial world, and nothing more, nor anything different. But that is precisely *not* the kind of person Aristotle would uphold as virtuous. Aristotle's own ideal type of Virtuous person is the "Magnanimous Man" or the "Great Souled Man". Two qualities of the great souled man stand out in relation to life in a hypothetical artificial world: that he prefers to confer benefits on others, and does not like to receive them (*NE*, 1124b9); and that he is incapable of living at the will of another (*NE*, 1124b31). These are not passive nor docile qualities. But if an artificial world is to be the perfect place that it is here theorised to be, an inhabitant would have to possess passive and docile qualities: he would have to accept that he is the inhabitant of an artificial world, happily receiving its benefits, living at the will of its designers and managers. He would have to be modest and temperate, in order to desire nothing more nor anything different than what the artificial world provides to him—and while Aristotle claims that those qualities are virtues in some circumstances, they are normally qualities of the small souled man (*NE*, 1123b8).

The great-souled man does not simply accept his place in the world as it is, but rather aims to make something noble of himself within it. Initiative is his virtue. The objection might be raised, then, that if he is placed in an artificial world, he might adapt to it and make something noble of himself within it. That might satisfy the great souled man's sense of initiative and his will to be the giver and not the receiver of benefits. This is not precisely the claim that he would want to control the artificial world himself. Aristotle does not claim that a person can flourish and be happy only if he rules the world. It is enough that he rules his own life. But in an artificial environment, this he could not do, for the control provisions of the artificial environment would not just supply to him his physical needs. It would have been built with certain presuppositions in the architect's mind concerning what an inhabitant's needs actually are, and thus it would dictate to an inhabitant those presuppositions. To passively accept the rules of the artificial environment's control system is a quality necessary for success and happiness in that environment, and this is not a quality of the Aristotelian great souled man. The control system of the artificial environment is not a substitute for the irreducible property of groundedness in the world. Groundedness is the existential basis of human life, the platform from which all our projects for *eudaimonia* are launched, including the project of transcending our groundedness. The control system of an artificial world, by contrast, imposes boundary conditions for existence and flourishing within the artificial environment it constitutes, and to go beyond them is to go beyond the confines of the artificial environment itself.

The environment in which we flourish best must have the property that it can *challenge* us and surprise us: it must present us with obstacles and difficulties for survival and for flourishing. We respond by rising to the challenge, and in so doing, we develop to the level of excellence the skills and virtues we need to succeed and flourish as human beings living in that environment. A completely controlled environment, even if controlled by the inhabitants, would offer insufficient challenge, making us lethargic and complacent. We would not fully flourish; we would not become all that we have within us to become. We could become only what the control system of the artificial environment allows. Again, these are not the qualities of the great souled man. Does this mean that the features of the natural ecological world which make it well suited for human flourishing include the ones normally taken to be negative, like natural disasters? For such events do surprise and challenge us. We might assume that an artificial world would not replicate them: the very point of creating an artificial world would be to protect ourselves from them. However, I do not claim that all ecological environments, and only ecological environments, are the right kind for flourishing. Here I claim only that artificial environments are not the right kind. The right kind of environment for flourishing is not necessarily the biblical Garden of Eden, whether a natural ecological one, or an artificial one. For a computer generated environment to be the right kind for flourishing, the inhabitants would have to believe that they are living in a real world, and could not be allowed to know they are living in a computer generated falsehood.[88] The problem here for environmental virtue theory lies in the prospect that the life might be worthwhile for the inhabitants of a computer generated version of Plato's Cave. Plato did not precisely claim that we are morally obligated to escape the cave and to liberate the other prisoners. Rather, he argued that it is the natural and proper inclination of the philosophical person, who both Plato and Aristotle upheld as the best and most noble sort of person, to want to know what is real. Aristotle confirmed this in the first line of his Metaphysics: "All men by nature desire to know". Precisely because it is unreal, a computer generated techno-fantasy world is unable to support the Virtuous person's desire for knowledge of the real, and thus unable to support that aspect of his aim to flourish. For the great-souled man, as for the Platonic philosopher, the life of blissful ignorance in the cave is not as good as life in the blessed sunlight, however difficult and challenging such life might be.

I am not, however, arguing that we ought never to create artificial environments, and that the world should always to some degree remain mysterious, constantly challenging, and forever beyond our power to control. In the study to follow I shall argue that one of the ways in which we flourish is precisely by 'artificialising' our environment. The kind of environment in which human excellence is possible and supported will have, among other properties, the property of being at least partially, if not fully, accessible to human intelligence and at least partially, if not fully, available to human labour. For one of the ways we respond to the world and thus become virtuous is by changing it. We develop into virtuous people not only by responding to the environment, but by involving ourselves in it. A city is an artificial environment in the sense that it is an environment of artifice, the product of human design, craftsmanship, and labour. Human communities are likewise environments of human artifice, and yet they certainly possesses the property of being able to challenge us. An artificial environment of the kind envisioned by science-fiction style hypothetical scenarios is already formed, already finished; no prospects remain for further development and involvement by the inhabitants. To a strict happiness-maximising Utilitarian, happiness might be maximised by getting everyone to in holographic projection rooms or plugged into computers that feed them happy experiences, but to a great-souled man, for whom happiness consists in excellence and not in utility, the very idea would be horrifying. A great-souled man living in such a place would be like the mythological Celtic hero Oisin, who was brought to the land of Tir Na n-Og and given everything he could want, and who eventually felt the need to return to the mortal world. For all of its hardships and imperfections, the mortal world was the only world where he could be completely happy.

§ 7. Summary Remarks for Chapter Four.

To summarise the case so far: the Virtuous person desires an environment that supports his aim to flourish and be happy. He has a wish for a world in which flourishing is possible, and indeed a world which maximises the possibilities for flourishing. He wishes for this world not as a possession to be owned, nor as the material output of his actions. He desires it for three reasons: as a condition for the possibility of performing noble and self-rewarding actions including but not limited to life itself; as an instrument that enhances or assists such actions without which the action would be difficult or impossible to do; and as the field and the stage where our lives are lived, our actions performed, and our potentials developed (or not developed) to the level of excellence. The right kind of environment, the one which offers to each of our faculties and potentials the right surroundings in which to develop and flourish, is a valid and indispensable external good to the moral agent's flourishing. We develop and flourish in response to the environment; therefore we develop and flourish best when the environment is excellently suited for that purpose. We therefore find that it is Virtuous to have a wish for a world in which flourishing is possible, and to do that which will contribute to bringing that world into being.

The recent announcement by Irish communications minister Noel Dempsey that the wind energy industry will in future receive a guaranteed price for their contribution to Ireland's electricity supply, counts as an example of such an act. At present, wind energy companies compete with each other for 15-year contracts with ESB, and the lowest bidder normally wins. It is hoped that this new policy will act as an incentive to wind energy developers, and in the long run reduce our dependence on fossil fuels. The target for energy production from renewable sources is 13.2% of total production by the year 2010.[89] Reducing dependency on fossil fuels helps aim for a world in which flourishing is possible in a variety of ways, most of them related to reducing impediments to flourishing. For instance, it reduces the danger to human health from pollution, and reduces resource scarcity which is a major cause of political and economic conflict. An American national security advisory group, the Energy Future Coalition, recently recommended that the world should make itself much less dependent on oil in order to avoid the problems of political and economic instability, climate change, and the lack of access to energy for the world's poor. The report was signed by some of America's highest ranking military and political officials, including R. James Woolsey, former Director of Central Intelligence.[90]

What remains now is to apply this principle of environmental Virtue to the practical plane, and find how a person committed to this kind of thinking would choose between Preservation, Conservation, and Depletion.

[1] Hudson, Human Character and Morality, as quoted in Hursthouse, On Virtue Ethics, pg. 12.

[2] Rosalind Hursthouse, "Virtue Theory and Abortion", *ibid*, pg. 219-20.

[3] Hursthouse, On Virtue Ethics, pg. 10.

[4] Fragment CXIV (Kahn); 119 (Diels); 94 (Marcovich). The translation used here is Kahn, The Art and thought of Heraclitus, pg. 80-1. Kahn translates *ethos* as 'custom, habit', and in the context of this fragment as "the customary pattern of choice and behaviour distinctive of an individual or a given type". Pg. 335, fn. 376.

[5] Kahn, The Art and Thought of Heraclitus, pg. 261.

[6] "Are we then to suppose that, while the carpenter and the shoemaker have definite functions of businesses belonging to them, man as such has none, and is not designed by nature to fulfill any function? Must we not rather assume that, just as the eye, the hand, the foot and each of the various members of the body manifestly has a certain function of its own, so a human being also has a certain function over and above all the functions of his particular members?" (*NE*, 1098a1)

[7] MacIntyre says, "One of the features of the concept of a virtue which has emerged with some clarity from the argument so far is that it always requires for its application the acceptance for some prior account of certain features of social and moral life in terms of which it has to be defined and explained." (*AV* pg. 186).

[8] For a fuller treatment of this premise, especially as it appears in the *Physics*, see Furley, J. *Self-Movers* in Rorty, A. Essays on Aristotle's Ethics pg. 55-65.

[9] "All those therefore who have regarded life from the point of view of movement have held soul to be pre-eminently a moving force." Aristotle, *De Anima* 1.ii.42 (pg. 62)

[10] "…as our object is to find the *best* constitution, and that means the one whereby a state will be best ordered, and since we call that state best ordered in which the possibilities of happiness are greatest, it is clear that we must keep constantly in mind what happiness is." (*Politics* 7.xiii, 1332a6, pg. 428)

[11] "The general configuration of the land is not difficult to state (though there are some points on which we must also take the opinion of those who have experience of conducting operations of war): it ought to be hard for a hostile force to invade, easy for an expeditionary force to depart from. Apart from that, just as we remarked that the population ought to be easily surveyed, so we can say the same of the territory; in a country that can easily be surveyed it is easy to bring up assistance at any point. Next the position of the state: if we are to put it exactly where we would like best, it should be conveniently situated for both sea and land. One definitive requirement, mentioned above, is that it should be well placed for sending assistance in all directions: a second is that it should form a centre for the easy receipt of crops as well as of timbre, and of any other similar raw material for whatever manufacturing processes the land may possess." (*Politics* 7.v, 1326b29, pg. 406.)

[12] "First, it is essential that the situation be a healthy one. A slope facing east, with winds blowing from the direction of sunrise, gives a healthier site, but second-best is one on the lee side of north, which gives more shelter in winter..." (*Politics*, 1330a34)

[13] Hippocrates, "Airs, Waters, Places" in Hippocratic Writings pg. 149.

[14] Hippocrates, *ibid*, pg. 168.

[15] Hume, "Of National Characters", as cited in May, Kant's Concept of Geography pg. 41.

[16] Even Hume conceded this point: "If we consider the face of the globe, Europe, of all the four parts of the world, is the most broken by seas, rivers, and mountains, and Greece of all countries of Europe. Hence these regions were naturally divided into several distinct governments; and hence the sciences arose in Greece, and Europe has been hitherto the most constant habitation of them." Hume, "Of National Characters", as cited in May, Kant's Concept of Geography pg. 42.

[17] Frank McDonald, "EU report finds air pollution kills 310,000 Europeans annually" *The Irish Times* 21 February 2005.

[18] This statement that life is desirable to the Virtuous person comes from Aristotle's argument for why the Virtuous person values friends: "If then to the supremely happy man existence is desirable in itself, being good and pleasant essentially, and if his friend's existence is almost equally desirable to him, it follows that a friend is one of the things to be desired. But that which is desirable to him he is bound to have, or else his condition will be incomplete in that particular. Therefore to be happy a man needs virtuous friends." (*NE*, 1170b10).

[19] Aristotle qualifies this statement only to say that happiness does not demand excessive or abundant possessions: "it is possible to perform noble deeds even without being a ruler of land and sea; one can do virtuous acts with quite modest resources." *NE*, 1179a6

20 Joe Humphreys, "Council rejects application for mast beside school in Stillorgan" *The Irish Times* 9 July 2004, pg. 12.

21 Joe Humphreys, "Farm bodies may prohibit phone masts" *The Irish Times* 9 July 2004, pg. 12.

22 Joe Humphreys, "Monitoring the masts: who is responsible?" *The Irish Times* 9 July 2004, pg. 12.

23 Ronald Sandler, "The External-Goods Approach" pg. 283

24 Sandler, "The External Goods Approach", pg. 280. This general adequacy condition creates two more conditions: a "theoretical" condition in which an adequate environmental ethic does not condone unsustainable or degradative practices, and also a "practical" condition in which an adequate environmental ethic "effectively engages social and political discourse regarding the environment in order to promote implementation of environmentally sustainable resolutions to concrete environmental problems and issues." *Ibid*, pp. 281-2.

25 The first definition runs as follows: "A virtue is an acquired human quality the possession and exercise of which tends to enable us to achieve those goods which are internal to practices and the lack of which effectively prevents us from achieving any such goods." (*AV* pg. 191)

26 Aristotle is philosophically a monotheist, although in the text the plural term 'the gods' appears frequently, presumably because he lived in a polytheistic society. Pure reason, and not practical reason, is the activity of the gods; as they are immortal and have no material needs about which to deliberate or to come into conflict, they have no need for practical reason. (*NE*, 1178b11)

27 Foster, "Aristotle and the Environment", pg. 419.

28 Foster, "Aristotle and the Environment", pg. 419.

29 D. S. Hutchinson, The Virtues of Aristotle pg. 26.

30 As MacIntyre says, "It is crucial to the structure of Aristotle's extended argument that the virtues are unavailable to slaves or to barbarians and so therefore is the good for man. What is a barbarian? Not merely a non-Greek (whose language sounds to Hellenic ears like 'ba, ba, ba') but someone who lacks a *polis* and thereby shows—on Aristotle's view—that he is incapable of political relationships." (*AV* pp. 158-9)

31 The passage continues: "Thus a whole range of questions cannot arise for him including those which concern the ways in which men might pass from being slaves or barbarians to being citizens of a *polis*. Some men just *are* slaves 'by nature', on Aristotle's view."

[32] The five different cultures which MacIntyre considers are Homeric Greece, Aristotle's Athens, the Christian culture of the New Testament, Jane Austin's England and Benjamin Franklin's America, all of which produced different lists of virtues and had different ideas about just what a virtue is. Concerning this disparity, MacIntyre says, "If different writers in different times and places, but all within the history of Western culture, include such different sets and types of items in their lists, what grounds have we for supposing that they do indeed aspire to list items of one and the same kind, that there is any shared concept at all? A second kind of consideration reinforces the presumption of a negative answer to this question. It is not just that each of these five writers lists different differing kinds of items; it is also that each of these lists embodies, is the expression of a different theory about what a virtue is." (*AV* pg. 183).

[33] Susanne Foster's use of the term *suitability* as a substitute for *being* with reference to non-living objects captures the meaning of 'material excellence' here. In her words, "By suitability, I men that an object is suited to its function. A well-designed home should be not only beautiful, but also efficient and comfortable. Houses with oddly shaped rooms and many hallways may be beautiful, but they are not 'suitable' for their purpose. Notice that suitability derives from the artefact's function, its nature. Its function gives it its being. Hence suitability adds to the being of an artefact." Foster, "Aristotle and the Environment", pp. 413-4.

[34] It might be added here that our intellectual faculties can also correspond with the society of the gods, the divine 'realm' of pure thought-thinking-itself, or the Platonic realm of the eternal forms. But it is unnecessary to explore this possibility for the current purpose, so I leave it to others.

[35] "It seems that not everything is loved, but only what is loveable, and that this is either what is good, or pleasant, or useful. But useful may be taken to mean productive of some good or of pleasure, so that the class of things loveable as ends is reduced to the good and the pleasant." (*NE*, 1155b23)

[36] "Hence in a friendship based on utility or on pleasure men love their friend for their own good or their own pleasure, and not as being the person loved, but as useful or agreeable. And therefore these friendships are based on an accident, since the friend is not loved for being what he is, but as affording some benefit or pleasure as the case may be. Consequently friendships of this kind are easily broken off, in the event of the parties themselves changing, for if no longer pleasant or useful to each other, they cease to love each other. And utility is not a permanent quality; it differs at different times. Hence when the motive of the friendship has passed away, the friendship itself is dissolved, having existed merely as a means to that end." (*NE*, 1156a16)

[37] Urmson, <u>Aristotle's Ethics</u>, pg. 116.

[38] "Nobody would choose to have all possible good things on the condition that he must enjoy them alone; for man is a social being, and designed by nature to live with others; accordingly the happy man must have society, for he has everything that is naturally good. And it is obviously desirable to associate with friends and with good men than with strangers and chance companions. Therefore the happy man requires friends." (*NE*, 1169b15)

[39] Wensveen, <u>Dirty Virtues</u>, pg. 140.

[40] Wensveen, <u>Dirty Virtues</u>, pg. 131.

[41] Wensveen, <u>Dirty Virtues</u>, pg. 48-9.

[42] Wensveen, "Ecosystem Sustainability as a Criterion for Genuine Virtue" *Environmental Ethics* 23 (Fall 2001) pp. 232-3.

[43] "The cultivation of a virtue involves a person's ability to feel, think, and act in certain ways. Any feeling, thought, or action is made possible thanks to physical conditions that sustain the person as a living being. Many of these essential physical conditions—such as oxygen, water, food, and fiber—derive from ecosystems. (By contrast, many of the physical conditions that may impede virtuousness, such as pollution and lack of food, can be linked to ecosystem stress.)" Wensveen, *ibid*, pg. 233.

[44] Wensveen, *ibid*, pg. 233.

[45] MacIntyre, <u>Dependent Rational Animals</u> (London: Duckworth, 1999) pg. 134.

[46] Wensveen, *ibid*, pp. 236-8.

[47] "Moreover, there is the problematic implication that if ecosystem sustainability is a necessary condition for virtue then it is impossible for those who live in sufficiently environmentally degraded areas to be genuinely virtuous." Sandler, "The External Goods Approach", pg. 287.

[48] Richard Carter, <u>Breakthrough: The Saga of Jonas Salk</u> pg. 117.

[49] Steve Platt, "Did we really need the M25?" pp. 20-22.

[50] This is a point which could have been raised in the discussion of applying Kant's Categorical Imperative to the choice of whether to prefer private or public transportation. It was there suggested that building new roads might mitigate the self-defeating character of private transport as a law for everyone. I concluded that while it can be wrong, on Kantian grounds, to damage the environment, no practical example of an environmentally destructive activity could be found which fails the test of universalisation. Here it is claimed that building new roads to mitigate traffic congestion actually doesn't change much at all. Perhaps this disconfirms my conclusion? I think not. If everyone chose to buy and to drive a private car, that would not make it impossible to buy and to drive a private car, even if there might be no way to eliminate traffic congestion with new roads.

[51] Tim O'Brien, "NRA chief promises some more money for roads in BMW region" *The Irish Times* 14 May 2004.

[52] "*Dike* is the ordering of the *polis*, declares Aristotle, but he understands this In a way that relates his claim to the Homeric use if *Dike*. For the *polis* is human community perfected and completed by achieving its *telos*, and the essential nature of each thing is what it is when it achieves its *telos*. So it is in the forms of the *polis* that human nature as such is expressed, and human nature is the highest kind of animal nature. The Homeric view of *dike* as the order of the cosmos thus re-appears in the Aristotelian view of *dike* as the ordering of what is highest in nature. *Dike* orders by the giving of just judgements, and justice (*dikaiosune*) is the norm by which the *polis* is ordered, a norm which lacks application apart from the *polis*. So the first answer to the question of what it is that a human being separated from the *polis* is deprived is: *dikaiosune*. But to be deprived of *dikaiosune* involves certain other depravations." MacIntyre, Whose Justice? Which Rationality? Pg. 97.

[53] MacIntyre, Whose Justice? Which Rationality? Pg. 98.

[54] See the discussion of 'community' in Fred D. Miller, Jr., Nature, Justice and Rights in Aristotle's *Politics* pg. 358. According to Miller, Aristotle's claim that the *polis* exists by nature can only make sense when society and the state are identified in this way.

[55] For instance Articles I.3.3, II.37, III.4, III.65, and III.129-131 of the Draft Treaty establishing a Constitution for Europe (CONV 850/03) Brussels, 18 July 2003.

[56] European Commission, Choices for a Greener Future (Luxembourg: Office for Official Publication by the European Communities, 2002) pg. 8; see also Vincent P. Bantz, et.al., The European Parliament and the Environment Policy of the European Union Working Paper ENVI 101 (Luxembourg: European Parliament, 1999).

[57] "First Consultation Paper on the Implementation of the EC Water Framework Directive in Northern Ireland" UK/NI Department of the Environment, March 2002, pp. 10-11.

[58] Milieu Ltd. (Brussels) The Enlargement of the EU: Consequences in the Field of the Environment, pg. iii.

[59] Hill, "Ideals of Human Excellence and Preserving Natural Environments" pp. 211-224

[60] Hill, *ibid*, pp. 219.

[61] "When we still believed that the Earth could, with the right technology, produce enough food for all people, our moral focus was on technological creativity, redistribution, and development. Virtues like simplicity and responsibility predominated in environmental discourse (this ethic was primarily addressed to rich elites). Now that many of us can no longer support this belief, and now that we are developing a greater interest in the plight of nonhuman life as well, our moral focus is shifting to the challenges of fashioning integrated forms of existence. As a result, virtues like humility, vulnerability, and feeling kinship are becoming increasingly prevalent in ecoliterature." Wensveen, Dirty Virtues, pg. 16.

[62] Geoffrey Frasz, "Environmental Virtue Ethics" pp. 259-274.

[63] Frasz, "Environmental Virtue Ethics", pg. 274.

[64] Lynn White, Jr., "The Historical Roots of our Ecological Crisis" in Environmental Ethics: Divergence and Convergence pg. 207.

[65] As cited in Sean McDonagh, Passion for the Earth, pg. 108. The Catechism titles here cited are nos. 343 and 2415.

[66] Jason Kawall, "Reverence for Life" pp. 229-358.

[67] "...our moral intuitions seem to be grounded simply in the fact that this is a living creature that we would be destroying. Of course, I do not claim that everyone will share this reaction to the insect example. But at the very least, it seems a very common reaction—and shows that a virtue of reverence for life may not be as foreign to common Western moral intuition as we might initially expect. It is important to show that there is a plausible virtue and value at stake here." Kawall, "Reverence for Life", pg. 341.

[68] "...we need to recognise that attributing intrinsic value to life does not require us to treat every living thing in the same way, as there may be other properties of living beings that have intrinsic value. Thus, while life may be intrinsically valuable, so too is love... more generally, we can and do attribute value to rationality, compassion, creativity, the capacity for morality, and so on. Life may have intrinsic value, but it does not follow that it is the only property of living beings with such value." Kawall, "Reverence for Life", pg. 343.

[69] Anscome, "Modern Moral Philosophy" in Crisp and Slote, eds. Virtue Ethics, pg. 30

[70] Foster, "Aristotle and the Environment" pp. 409-428.

[71] "Aristotle's analysis of human beings and what constitutes their good relies on several elements from his biological works. The first is that human beings and, indeed, all natural bodies (and to a limited extent artefacts) are substances. A substance is a thing which has a nature. The nature is both the characteristic activities carried out by the body and the shape or the structure of the body. For example, the characteristic activities of plants include resistance to corruption, growth, reproduction, and taking in nutrients." Foster, *ibid*, pg. 411-2.

[72] Bill Shaw, "A Virtue Ethics Approach to Aldo Leopold's Land Ethic", pp. 53-67.

[73] Kent Peacock, "Symbiosis and the Ecological Role of Philosophy", pg. 704

[74] Lawrence E. Johnson, "Toward the Moral Considerability of Species and Ecosystems" pp. 145-57.

[75] Here is a definition of teleology in environmental or biological systems. "Teleological explanations account for the existence of a certain feature in a system by demonstrating the feature's contribution to a specific property or state of the system. Teleological explanations require that the feature or behaviour contribute to the existence or maintenance of a certain state or property of the system. Moreover, and this is the essential component of the concept, the contribution must be the reason why the feature or behaviour exists at all." Francisco J. Ayala, "Teleological Explanations" in Michael Ruse, ed. Philosophy of Biology pg. 188.

[76] See "Exploring Daisyworld", in The Ages of Gaia, chapter 3.

[77] "…a distinction must be made between goal-directed behaviour and by-products. A behaviour is goal-directed just in case (1) the behaviour tends to bring about the goal, and (2) the behaviour occurs because it tends to bring about the goal. The stability, resilience, and unity of an ecosystem, like those of an artefact, are merely by-products of the goal directed behaviour of its inhabitants. The eagle eats to nourish itself. As a result, the rodent population is held in check. That is, unlike organisms, ecosystems have no internal principle of motion or rest. They are more like artefacts." Foster, "Aristotle and the Environment", pg. 414.

[78] "By suitability, I mean that an object is suited to its function. A well-designed home should be not only beautiful, but also efficient and comfortable. Houses with oddly shaped rooms and many hallways may be beautiful, but they are not 'suitable' for their purpose. Notice that suitability derives from the artefact's function, its nature. Its function gives it its being. Hence suitability adds to the being of an artefact." Foster, *ibid*, pp. 413-4.

[79] Foster, *ibid*, pg. 422.

[80] See Hursthouse's discussion of Naturalism in chapters 9 and 10 of On Virtue Ethics pp. 192-238.

[81] Foster, "Aristotle and the Environment", pg. 425.

[82]   Foster, "Aristotle and the Environment", pg. 425.

[83]   Thus Aristotle also says, "…liking can be felt even for inanimate things, but reciprocal liking involves deliberate choice, and this springs from a fixed disposition". (*NE*, 1157b28)

[84]   M. Wackernagel and W. Rees, Our Ecological Footprint: Reducing Human Impact on the Earth, pg. 3

[85]   Stuart Bond, Ecological Footprints, pg. 7.

[86]   Quoted in Richard Rogers, Cities for a Small Planet, pg. 111-2.

[87]   Bond, Ecological Footprints, pg. 4.

[88]   As an aside, note that the really important question in this case is not the ethical question of whether it would be better to live in such a world, but the epistemological question of how do we justify our belief that we are not already living in one. If such computer technology is theoretically possible, the question is not whether we will some day invent it, but whether an advanced civilisation possessing enormous computer power has not already done so, and is using it right now to simulate our world and our lives. How do we know that we are not already part of a simulation, or that we are not ourselves simulated? For the computer simulation might be so good that it can simulate consciousness itself. This is not merely the question of whether the world is real, but is also the question of whether *we* are real.

[89]   Emmet Oliver, "Guaranteed price for wind energy sector – Dempsey" *The Irish Times* 9 April 2005.

[90]   "Avoid Oil Crisis with Renewables, Security Leaders Advise" *Environmental News Service* 30 March 2005.

Chapter Five: The "Excellent" In Modern Times
Anscombe, Hursthouse, MacIntyre, etc.

The preceding study ended on an encouraging note. I concluded that the environment is valuable to a Virtuous person as an external good of a special kind: it serves as the field and stage of his life and all the different ways in which he aims for *eudaimonia*. It is therefore virtuous to have a wish for a world in which flourishing is possible. However, that is not the last word. We have not yet addressed the Non-Identity Problem and the case of future generations.

As a starting place, it can be claimed that a Virtuous person living among the Depletion people, in the situation of environmental degradation and suffering it entails, might 'flourish' only just enough to make life barely worth living, or in Parfit's terminology, to make life "not worse than death" (which casts doubt upon whether such a life can properly be called a 'flourishing' life at all). The Virtuous person in that situation would find it morally right to seek the improvement of the qualities of the world which figure into her own flourishing. But the question for Virtue theory is not primarily whether Parfit's Depletion People can or can not flourish. The question is whether a Virtuous person would choose Conservation or Depletion. Having explored the external goods approach, I can now make a provisional statement about how a Virtuous person would choose. I claim that a Virtuous person, who values other people, the community, and the environment for the reasons explained, would find the Repugnant Conclusion just as repugnant as Parfit did. He would want a good environment in which to flourish, and he would want it sustained throughout his lifetime. He would make the choice that sustains the social and ecological environment in which the greatest excellence is possible for himself and his friends, children, associates, regardless of their numbers or their identities.

Even though we can conclude that Parfit's Depletion People would find it hard or impossible to flourish, and we can conclude that the Virtuous person would want to sustain the conditions in which flourishing is possible and supported, for himself and at least his nearest associates, it remains possible to ask, Would a present person's *eudaimonia* be any less if the people of the far distant future do not flourish? The *prima facia* answer is "no", because non-flourishing of people in the distant future, to whom present people have no direct causal connection, need not be an obstacle to a present person's flourishing. A Virtuous person is responsible primarily for his own flourishing, and he cares for the welfare of his friends, his *polis*, and his world because his flourishing is interconnected with theirs (which does not mean he is using them merely as a means to his own ends). It may be possible for a present person to lead a worthwhile, happy life without any care or concern for people of the far distant future, beyond the next two or three generations. This may represent a limit to what Virtue theory can do, and a reason why a Virtuous person might find it neither virtuous nor vicious to choose a policy that leads to the Repugnant Conclusion. If this limitation stands, Virtue theory may not, after all, provide an acceptable environmental ethic. Modern Virtue theory, to which I now turn, is able to go further than ancient Virtue theory and provide a solution to the problem this limitation creates.

§ 1. A Theory of Practical Environmental Virtue

In the last study, it was argued that Aristotle's claim that human beings need the *polis* to flourish can also apply to the ecological environment. It was found that as we change and re-create the environment, we also change and re-create the circumstances and opportunities for our own flourishing. Consider, as an example of this:

> *Electric wind turbines.* As many as 85 electric wind
> turbines are planned to be built at Tunes Plateau, an
> offshore area of shallow water roughly five
> kilometres north of Portstewart, co. Derry. However,
> the place where the land connection is to be built,
> Portstewart Strand, is designated as the North Derry
> Area of Natural Beauty, the Portstewart Strand Area

of Special Scientific Interest, and the Lower Bann
Estuary Area of Scenic Quality. It is asserted by the
UK National Trust, which maintains several heritage
properties in the area, that the wind turbines would
disrupt some of the aesthetic and scientifically
valuable qualities of the area. [1] An Bord Pleanála
recently rejected plans to build 15 wind turbines on a
farm in the foothills of the Ox Mountains, which lie
on the border between the counties of Sligo and
Mayo. According to the report, the wind farm plan
was contrary to "the objective of the planning
authority, as set out in the Mayo Development Plan,
to recognise and facilitate development in a manner
that had regard to the character and sensitivity of the
landscape". [2]

What kind of environment, and what kind of flourishing, is being
sought by those who support and those who oppose the construction
of wind farms to generate electricity? The placement of these wind
turbines contributes to the creation of a world fit for human
flourishing by reducing society's dependence on high-polluting, non-
renewable fossil fuels for the production of electricity. But on the
basis of the possible threat to the scenic character of the landscape
where the land connection will be built, it can be claimed that to *not*
build the wind turbines on the Tunes Plateau would *also* contribute
to the maintenance of a world that is well suited for human
flourishing. Much of the opposition to wind farm development is
driven by the oil, gas, and nuclear energy industries. Britain's two
nuclear power companies receive £2 million in subsidies from the
UK government each day,[3] which it stands to loose if renewable
alternative energy sources become the norm. It is also the case that
wind power is enormously more popular than nuclear energy, and
that more people find the turbines themselves aesthetically pleasing,
than find them obtrusive and ugly. I observed wind turbines almost
everywhere while travelling through Germany in the summer of
2004, and found the gentle turning of their massive sails quite

elegant and majestic. It should be added that the engineers know that their windmills will be prominent structures and it is important to them that their appearance is appealing, or at least not seriously repelling. But we should not hang the solution to this conflict entirely on aesthetic matters. Philosophy would have to provide a complete and sophisticated theory of aesthetics, which includes a theory of the ethical value of aesthetic values, and not just alternative opinions, to seriously object to the person who regards wind turbines as eyesores.

Consider, as another example, the case of:

The Mutton Island Sewage Treatment Plant. This sewage treatment plant, built on an island just one kilometre from the harbour of Galway City and linked to the land by a purpose-built causeway, became operational on the 7th of May 2004. Before construction of the treatment plant and causeway to the island began, the island was a candidate for designation as an Special Area of Conservation under the EU Habitats Directive, mainly because of the variety of sea birds which roost there. The EU was prepared to supply partial funding for the project if it was located at an alternative site in Renmore (another district of Galway City). Galway City Council chose to place the plant on the island anyway, and it was built without EU funding.[4]

The construction of a sewage treatment plant in Galway can be a contribution to the creation of world fit for human flourishing; it is generally hoped that "blue flag" status will be restored to Salthill beaches. If the plant had been constructed at the alternative site in Renmore, the bird habitats on Mutton Island would not have been destroyed and the city would still have benefited from a sewage treatment plant, and at less cost. Bird watchers and amateur astronomers would have been able to use the Mutton Island lighthouse. In this example, the conflict between two conceptions of a flourishing-suitable world is fairly easy to sort out. The goal of building a sewage treatment plant and that of protecting a bird habitat were not mutually exclusive goals. And the goal of protecting property values in Renmore should not have been mistaken for the aim for a worthwhile life. It would therefore have been better to build the plant in Renmore. But there may be other examples that are less easy to solve. If each of these cases were also treated as Non-Identity cases, creating different future populations and different environmental landscapes, how would they be worked out? It would seem that we require a principle of practical environmental virtue. It shall be the aim of this study to develop such a principle.

Kant, Rawls, and Taylor all described a theory of the virtues, although in each of their accounts the virtues were subordinate to the deontological rules they were primarily interested in expressing. Rawls says "the virtues are sentiments, that is, related families of dispositions and propensities regulated by a higher-order desire, in this case a desire to act from the corresponding moral principles" (*TJ* pg. 167). Kant's conception of virtue is that virtue is a kind of substitute for happiness. He claims that happiness consists in "holiness of morals", but no human being can ever attain this condition; the most we can hope for is to be virtuous, which is to possess "a disposition conformed with law from respect for law", and this disposition will make us not so much happy but rather "worthy of happiness".[5] This conception of the virtues also appears in Taylor's theory of environmental ethics. He claims that the virtues are the "the firm, steady, and permanent dispositions that enable one to deliberate and act consistently with the four rules of duty: Nonmaleficence, Noninterference, Fidelity, and Restitutive Justice." (*RN* pg. 199) James Wallace, who published on the topic of the Virtues just before MacIntyre, also wrote that virtues are "attitudes toward moral requirements or rules".[6] For these four authors, then, virtue consists in a propensity to respect and to obey a moral duty. All four authors in their own way missed the point. A tendency or propensity to act in accordance with a rule, for the sake of the rule, is not the Aristotelian concept of a virtue. It has to be a rule which a person possessing *phronesis*, practical wisdom, would follow. Wallace's conception of the virtues was more subtle than the others, for he agued that the virtues are "forms of conscientiousness", that person who lacks the virtues "is incapacitated in crucial ways", and that for some virtues, "one who lacks them is not necessarily handicapped [but] you or I could not live well if most other people lacked these virtues."[7] Nevertheless, by defining the virtues from the outset as "forms of conscientiousness", he is lead to the conclusion that they serve only as the psychological motivators to observe generally beneficial forms of behaviour. In his words: the virtues are "commitments to forms of behaviour that we, as a community, reasonably require of one another."[8] Wallace's text may be seen as forming a transition between rule-based deontology and proper Virtue theory. As we shall see, MacIntyre goes on to endorse the idea that the virtues are immersed in communities and are always connected to rules which maintain the cohesion and stability of community (although he never cited Wallace while building this argument). But with Wallace, the virtues are still subordinate to deontological considerations.

Many critics of Virtue theory and a few Virtue theorists themselves have claimed that there is a deep disjunction between the virtues and any conception of moral law, and therefore Virtue theory is not well suited to handling practical ethics problems.[9] Robert Louden identified Virtue theory's emphasis on the general character of the agent as the cause of this difficulty. In his words:

> The virtue theorist is committed to the claim that the primary object of moral evaluation is not the act or its consequences but rather the agent—specifically, those character traits of the agent which are judged morally relevant. This is not to say that virtue ethics does not ever address the issue of right and wrong actions, but rather that it can only do so in a derivative manner. Sometimes, however, it is clearly acts rather than agents which ought to be the primary focus of moral evaluation.[10]

To overcome this problem, among other problems like it, Louden suggested that virtue theory needs to be co-ordinated with a practical principle that addresses actions. A statement that crafts Virtue theory as a principle applicable to specific acts, without at the same time compromising the special emphasis on the agent's overall character, would be able to achieve that co-ordination. This preparatory task may be contrary to Aristotle's philosophical purpose, since for him a single good action by itself does not make someone virtuous: a habitual practice of good actions over the course of a lifetime does (*NE*, 1098a20). However, Aristotle also claims that for ethics to be practical, ethical decision-making must eventually give way to action, and cannot remain forever in the theoretical realm of intellectual speculation. In his discussion of the process of moral deliberation in the Nicomachean Ethics, he says "a man is the origin of his actions, and that the province of deliberation is to discover actions within one's own power to perform... For a man stops enquiring how he shall act as soon as he has carried back the origin of action to himself, and to the dominant part of himself, for it is this part that chooses." (*NE*, 1113a1). When likening deliberation to investigating geometrical figures, Aristotle says "the last step in the analysis seems to be the first step in the execution of the design." (*NE*, 1112b22). In the Politics this point is re-affirmed: "it should be remembered that virtue in itself is not enough: there must also be the power to translate it into action" (*Politics*, 1325b13). Thus for Aristotle, the question of "what kind of a person should I be?" eventually leads to the question of "what should I do?", which opens the possibility for a practical ethic that can judge an action as right or wrong. I believe such a judgement can be made without removing the action from its context in the agent's life, and without undermining the special emphasis on the agent's character.

Elisabeth Anscombe, one of the first philosophers in the 20th century to look at Virtue theory, argued that the concept of 'moral ought' and various concepts like it are anachronistic remainders from a law-like view of ethics. The theoretical groundwork of this, she says, is no longer taken seriously, as modern philosophy has for the most part lost belief in a divine law-giver and in principles of rational self-legislation. She claims, therefore, we are better off without the term 'morally wrong', and should use more specific evaluative terms for immoral acts like 'unjust', 'uncharitable', and so on.[11] But as shown by Hursthouse, some decades later, this does not expunge the notion of the moral law altogether. Hursthouse shows that the virtues, once they are enumerated, generate many clear and specific moral rules, which she calls the "V-rules". She says, "Not only does each virtue generate a prescription—do what is honest, charitable, generous—but each vice a prohibition—do not do what is dishonest, uncharitable, mean."[12] The point here is that, instead of following Anscombe's recommendation to dispense altogether with the concept of 'moral ought', we should find the proper place for that concept within a sufficiently strong theory of the virtues. It should be noted, however, that the specific evaluative terms which Anscombe recommends as replacements for 'morally right' and 'morally wrong' exactly parallel the moral rules which Hursthouse says are generated by every virtue and vice. These two authors are not so opposed to each other as it may seem.

A Virtuous person may answer the question 'Why did you do that?' by saying that it was an instance of a virtue: it was 'courageous', or 'honourable', or even 'what a Virtuous person would do'. On the practical level, this is normally enough. But on the theoretical level, we must ask what makes this a satisfactory answer. We could answer quite simply, as MacIntyre does in Dependent Rational Animals, that "what makes it a sufficient answer is that it is only through the acquisition and exercise of the virtues that individuals and communities can flourish in a specifically human mode."[13] In other texts MacIntyre's discourse is more detailed. In After Virtue and in Whose Justice? Which Rationality? he argues that every conception of the virtues is necessarily connected in various ways to some conception of moral law, and therefore any adequate account of the virtues would require an adequate account of the morality of laws, especially of justice, as its counterpart (AV pg. 150-2).[14] He claims that for any theory of the virtues, there will be a set of moral laws which are the laws of some community. They identify the actions which stress or break the bonds of that society. Virtue is not simply a propensity to obey them, but the knowledge of how to apply them properly. "Knowing how to apply the law is itself possible only for someone who possesses the virtue of justice" (*AV*, pg. 152). An agent's violation of such rules constitute the agent's failure as a member of that community. Such laws (provided, of course, that they are good laws!) are necessary because the bonds of community are, for MacIntyre as for Aristotle, that which makes the Virtuous person's aim for *eudaimonia* possible. As we have seen in the preceding study, it is only as a member of a community that someone is able to become a Virtuous person at all, for "man is a social animal"; it is in and with a community that one may learn to be a Virtuous person and practice a worthwhile life.[15] According to MacIntyre, Aristotle too had to grapple with the concept of right action. His account of the good life for man had to include at least a short account of actions which are strictly prohibited. It seems that these laws are civic laws, and that they are the same everywhere although the punishments meted out by the authorities for breaking them are different from place to place.[16] But Aristotle's words are obscure here. Moreover, in the <u>Politics</u> Aristotle asserts that the virtues of a citizen might not always be the same as the virtues of a human being. A good citizen is someone whose virtues contribute positively to the *polis*. There are many kinds of *polis,* and there are many different functions which someone may fulfil to contribute to it, so there may be many kinds of good citizen, but there can only be one kind of good human being (*Politics*, 1276b20). But some of Aristotle's remarks here indicate that this conclusion does not so much force a wedge between civic virtue and human virtue, but rather becomes the impetus for the search for the type of *polis* in which one can be both good citizen and good human being at the same time. For instance, he asks whether there are any virtues that can exist in the good man and the good citizen at the same time (*Politics*, 1277a12). He concludes that the ability to govern free men, or as he puts it, the knowledge and ability to rule and be ruled, can be a virtue for both the good citizen and the good human being

(*Politics*, 1277b7). But this is possible only if the *polis* is organised in a way that allows and supports the development and exercise of that very virtue. In other words, the virtues of the human being and the citizen can coincide if one is living in the right kind of *polis*. But as mentioned, Aristotle's argument here is very vague, and at any rate it is not necessary for the present purpose to go into this aspect of Aristotle's thought in detail.

(As an aside, we may note that Kant made a similar statement in the Critique of Judgement. There he said that "the greatest development of humankind's natural tendencies" requires a national constitution in which "the abuse of freedom by individuals striving one against another is opposed by a lawful authority centred in a whole, called a *civil community*." Moreover, this is the situation in which "the end pursued by nature itself, though it be not our end, is thereby attained."[17])

In general, we can claim that for MacIntyre, the rules of morality which we find in Virtue theory are those which are intended to create, sustain, and protect the social environment in which the life of *eudaimonia* is possible and supported. We can make a similar claim for Aristotle, who devoted the <u>Politics</u> to the search for the kind of *polis* in which we can be both good human beings and good citizens simultaneously, or to put it another way, the kind of *polis* in which we may flourish best as human beings. For as we have seen in the previous study, the happy and flourishing life is only possible if the social surroundings are well suited for that aim; and we have seen how this can be rationally extended so as to include the landscape in which we dwell. As a first candidate for a principle of practical environmental virtue, I propose the following: *an action (affecting the environment) is right if it contributes the creation, development, maintenance, and protection of the social or ecological circumstances in which the good life is possible and supported, or at least if it does not damage, destroy or degrade those circumstances.*

This principle does not collapse into the deontological virtue discussed earlier. On this principle, we do not develop virtue in order to be better rule-followers, which is how Kant, Taylor, and Wallace conceived the virtues. Rather, we follow rules because it will help create the conditions in which we can be virtuous people and pursue *eudaimonia* with some expectation of success. This, I believe, is what McDowell means when he says that virtue theory grasps right conduct "from the inside out", as opposed to deontology which, characterising the virtues as dispositions to follow moral duty, grasp right conduct "from the outside in".[18] However, this candidate principle of practical environmental virtue does not seem to be completely correct. It looses sight of the virtues themselves, for it says nothing about the agent's character. It provides the external and/or bodily goods which the pursuit of the good life needs, but says nothing about what the good life actually is; it affirms actions which contribute to the development of the virtues but says nothing about what the virtues actually are. Therefore while this may be adequate to handle certain practical problems including environmental issues, it may be criticised for missing the point of Virtue theory altogether. Moreover, it may not after all provide much help sorting out a practical solution to the example of the wind turbine farms with which I set out this study. It is possible to argue that building and also *not* building the wind turbines on the Tunes Plateau contributes to the creation of the environment in which the good life is possible and supported. If they are built, we would reduce our dependence on fossil fuels, and so reduce pollution. If they are not built, an area of natural scenic beauty would be preserved. It would be wrong to assume that aesthetic matters are irrelevant to the flourishing life, even if it is hard to be precise and systematic about them. Some obvious answers present themselves already. For instance, the valuable scientific and aesthetic qualities of North Derry may be obscured if, in the future, smog obstructs the view and pollution kills the local flora. However, the principle of practical virtue as here stated says nothing about future generations.

Rosalind Hursthouse provided the first and still most widely cited theory of practical virtue in a 1991 essay entitled "Virtue Theory and Abortion". In this article she claimed "an action is right if and only if it is what a virtuous agent would do in the circumstances" and "a virtuous agent is one who acts virtuously, that is, one who has and exercises the virtues". The virtues themselves she defined as "a character trait that a human being needs to flourish or live well",[19] thus adding a teleological element to a principle which would otherwise be circular. Hursthouse modified her principle when she published <u>On Virtue Ethics</u> in 1999, to read: "An action is right iff it is what a virtuous agent would characteristically (i.e. acting in character) do in the circumstances."[20] This revision of the basic principle has a number of advantages. It allows for more than one way to conceive of the Virtuous person, which makes it flexible for different kinds of social and ecological environments. It excludes acts which may be out of character for a Virtuous person. It allows the possibility of doing the right thing for the wrong reason. Most importantly, it allows character to be at the centre of the ethicist's attention without sacrificing practicality. It has been praised even by its critics for being a desirable alternative to the standard utilitarian and deontological theories.[21] Note that for Hursthouse, unlike for MacIntyre and Aristotle, the ground for the practical rule is not the bonds of community which make the flourishing life possible, but just the character of the virtuous person herself.

Hursthouse's position has been criticised on several grounds. The most prominent criticism has been that if right action is what a Virtuous person would do, then who is this virtuous person? Should we be looking for actual people who exemplify completely Virtuous character, or is the completely Virtuous person an abstraction, or even an impossible ideal to which we are asked to strive even if we tacitly know we will never succeed? Christina Swanton asked, how can we know whether a Virtuous person really is qualified to make the moral judgements she is called up on to make? In her words, "the rightness of an act is criterially determined by a qualified agent, but how qualified is a virtuous agent?".[22] In her view, it is a deep truth that we are limited, fallible and finite beings, and so no matter how practically wise an agent is, he may also be ignorant about some important end of virtue, and thus unqualified to make certain kinds of moral decisions. Swanton cites the virtue of 'environmental friendliness' as an example. We might not have enough information to know what has caused climate change, and what to do about it.[23]

Similarly, Robert Johnson worried that Hursthouse's principle, by itself, "can deliver no determinate answer to the question of what to do, because the very concept of a 'virtuous person' is indeterminate, and so, in turn, it is indeterminate which action in any given circumstance would be characteristic of that person."[24]

This criticism appears frequently in the literature. However, it is a straw man. Most philosophers who articulate a theory of Virtue ethics also provide a very detailed picture of the virtuous person, either explicitly or implicitly. Aristotle's concept is that of someone who possesses the virtues necessary to sustain the aim for *eudaimonia*, and who finds life desirable because he is conscious of himself as good. This conception is elaborated in the long and poetic description of the "magnanimous man" or "great-souled man".[25] MacIntyre examines not one but five separate conceptions of the virtuous person bequeathed to us by various Western cultures in the form of different rival theories of what the virtues are and what list of virtues should be preferred.[26] Hursthouse summarises the concept of the Virtuous person in an elegant, if open-ended way: a virtuous person is "one who has, and exercises, certain character traits, namely the virtues".[27] Of course this demands an explanation of what the virtues are, and Hursthouse recognises this. The very enterprise of Virtue ethics is in part the sustained enquiry into that very question. Other moral theories are in a similar position; they must explain for instance what duty is, what utility is, what is someone's due.[28] Johnson conceded that this objection "loses force once an account of the virtues and vices is provided. Hence, while what a virtuous person would do in a given circumstance is indeterminate, what a kind, courageous, just, and so on, person would do is not."[29] The principle of groundedness, as I have derived it from the work of Aristotle, provides the account of the virtues and vices which Johnson claims is required. The virtues are those character traits which a person must have to achieve *eudaimonia* in specific social and environmental surroundings.

Here is one final common objection to the concept of a Virtuous person to consider. Johnson claimed Hursthouse fails to account for the possibility that we may have moral obligations as

Virtuous agents to better ourselves. In support of this, he claims that this argument is vulnerable "merely if there are actions producing the virtues that one morally ought to perform, and these actions are not part of the characteristic behaviour of virtuous persons". [30] Finally he argues that there may be things which are right to do which are not characteristic of the completely virtuous person. Such things would be characteristic of the non-virtuous person in his process of becoming virtuous. As examples he claims the non-virtuous person would have to keep track of his "progress toward becoming a better person", "control himself in many ways", and occasionally "seek guidance and try to improve one's perceptual capacities". [31] Johnson's argument here hangs on the appearance of the word 'completely' in the phrase 'completely Virtuous person'. [32] Apparently for Johnson, a 'completely' Virtuous person is finished his moral education, and has nothing left to do in the process of becoming a Virtuous person. However, no Virtue theorist characterises the Virtuous person as 'complete' in this sense. Hursthouse accepts the thought that the Virtuous person occasionally seeks the advice and guidance of others. She says, "we do not always act as 'autonomous', utterly self-determining agents, but quite often seek moral guidance from people we think are morally better than ourselves." [33] MacIntyre's conception of the good life as "the life spent in seeking for the good life", and the virtues as the qualities of character which "enable us to understand what more and what else the good life for man is" (*AV* pg. 219), necessarily implies that the virtuous person is never 'complete', if by 'complete' we mean 'finished, 'ended', or 'done'. It is, indeed, one of MacIntyre's central theses in a 1999 work entitled <u>Dependent Rational Animals</u> that we are always in need of help from others, that no moral agent is ever fully or totally autonomous, even after the virtues are fully acquired. The virtues he calls for in this work are the virtues of acknowledged dependence. "We may go astray in our practical reasoning because of intellectual error" or because of "moral error", and from both types of error "the best protections are friendship and collegiality". [34] The condition of being a Virtuous person is an ongoing, continuous occupation. It is complete the way a fire is complete: it may be bright and warm, but still requires fuel and tending. We take our bearings in this ongoing process from the consistency of the direction of the aim.

It is characteristic of the non-virtuous person on Aristotle's view not just that he lacks the virtues, but is mistaken about what the worthwhile life is and mistaken about the virtues are. Moreover, even the non-virtuous person wants to be happy, and has the worthwhile life as his *telos*, even if he is mistaken about what that worthwhile life entails. The non-virtuous person may not understand why it is important to possess the virtues precisely because he does not possess them; for the rational justification for developing the virtues in large measure is visible only to those who are already living the virtuous life.[35] The not-yet-completely virtuous person who strives to acquire the virtues is still acting virtuously even if he is not acting "as the completely Virtuous person" would act, because he is doing that which is required by the quest for *eudaimonia*, which includes seeking the council and guidance of others, as even the 'completely' Virtuous person sometimes does.

There are some notable alternative Virtue theories which do not rely on an account of the Virtuous person. Two prominent examples are Michael Slote's 'agent based' theory'[36] and Christine Swanton's 'target based' theory.[37] It is not necessary to go into these two theories in detail, but it is sufficient to say that neither of them rely on a comprehensive *telos* for man like *eudaimonia*. For Slote, it is enough that the moral agent has the right motivations; for Swanton, it is enough that the agent's actions "hit the target of virtue" even if the agent has no particular habits or qualities of character which predispose her to do so. However, a Virtue theory that lacks a comprehensive *telos* for man like *eudaimonia* would be vulnerable to Johnson's criticism concerning moral development. It would fail to account for why it can be rational to acquire the virtues and how we may have an obligation to better ourselves. It would also fail to provide a way of judging worthwhile lives as a whole. But with a conception of the *telos* of man like *eudaimonia*, we can see exactly why it is desirable to possess the virtues. Furthermore, there is a deep weakness in any Virtue theory that lacks a conception of the *telos* of humankind. As MacIntyre explains, it is that:

> ...unless there is a *telos* which transcends the limited goods of practices by constituting the good of a whole human life, the good of human life conceived as a unity, it will *both* be the case that a certain subversive arbitrariness will invade the moral life *and* that we shall be unable to specify the context of certain virtues adequately. (*AV,* pg. 203, emphasis his.)

It appears that whatever problems may be associated with the development of the conception of the Virtuous Person, we still need an account of the *telos* of human life in any practical principle of Virtuous right action. This account must allow that self-improvement is virtuous, and that the process of acquiring the virtues is itself virtuous. Indeed, MacIntyre adds that "there is at least one virtue recognised by the tradition which cannot be specified at all except with reference to the wholeness of a human life—the virtue of integrity or constancy." (*AV* pg. 203)

There is a specific reason for this requirement in my own project. In the previous study, it was claimed that when one lives in a degraded or unsuitable environment, it is virtuous to try to improve its quality, because we are grounded in the world and so the conditions of the world figures into the agent's flourishing. Improving the living conditions of one's environment is an indirect form of self-improvement, for it opens up new possibilities for flourishing. A practical principle of Virtuous right action, for my purpose, cannot be such that self-improvement is logically impossible. MacIntyre, whose theory of the virtues retains an account of the character of the Virtuous person, finds it impossible that there could *not* be virtues associated with self-improvement. Neither Hursthouse nor MacIntyre require that virtuous people be 'completely' Virtuous. MacIntyre requires, however, that whatever virtues are on one's list, they must include the virtues which are necessary for discovering what more and what else constitutes the good life for man. "The catalogue of the virtues will therefore include the virtues required to sustain the kind of households and the kind of political communities in which men and women can seek for the good together and the virtues necessary for philosophical enquiry about the character of the good." (*AV* pg. 219). Since MacIntyre's theory is heavily indebted to his account of the historical development of the virtues and the various ways in which different catalogues of virtues compete with each other, it is the case for him that the concept of a Virtuous person is contestable and able to change to suit different circumstances; but that does not mean it is indeterminate.

Following Hursthouse, I am now prepared to state a second candidate for the principle of practical virtue. *An action is right if it is a manifestation of, or contributes to the development of, the virtues.* This claim demands a definition of the virtues, which in accord with Hursthouse, MacIntyre, and Aristotle, I define as *the qualities of character which we need in order to act in ways that sustain the aim for eudaimonia in practice.* What relation does this have to the first candidate principle of practical virtue? First of all, it restores the personal dimension which the first candidate principle lacked. Secondly, we can claim that actions which create, protect, etc. the environment that is fit for flourishing is in itself a contribution to the development of the virtues. The first candidate principle is thus contained within the second. On this definition the action is still judged in terms of the agent's character, and therefore is still placed in the context of the whole of the agent's life, and yet it becomes possible to ask specific questions about actions like, 'Does this action manifest good character?' In an Aristotelian way, we can ask 'Is the action excellent?', which as we have previously seen, means, 'Does it act upon humankind's specific and highest faculties? Is it self-rewarding? Does it hit the mean?' This much may be found within the action itself. Acknowledging MacIntyre, I shall claim that what constitutes the Virtuous person in specific detail can change over time and across different historical, geographical, or cultural circumstances, although it will normally be the case that 'classic' virtues like justice, prudence, courage, and so on, will somehow be involved. Acknowledging Aristotle I shall also claim that whatever it may entail from one place and time to another, it shall still entail that the Virtuous person is one who has attained, or who is on track towards attaining, *eudaimonia*.

As an example of an act which aims to re-make the world into a condition better suited for flourishing, consider:

> *Ireland's plastic shopping bag tax.* The tax was intended to reduce litter in public places and also protect the lives of some marine mammals: sea turtles, for instance, would eat them, and the bags would fill their stomachs. When the tax was first enacted in 2002, the initial public reaction was scepticism and mild annoyance at the inconvenience. Yet in the first week alone, the tax reduced demand for plastic bags at Tesco and Superquinn by 90% and at Londis and Supervalue by 95%. And this was the point of the tax: Mr. Martin Cullen, the Minister for the Environment at the time, said that "the primary purpose of this levy is not to generate revenue, but to change consumer behaviour."[38] All the revenue generated by the tax goes toward environmental projects.

As I finish writing this thesis, roughly three years later, everyone I know now considers it perfectly natural to carry re-usable bags to the grocery stores. Given enough time and education, the people of Ireland may have made this change on their own, without the need for government intervention. But it would be too harsh to claim that as an incentive to change consumer behaviour the tax was 'patronising'. Moreover, it cannot reasonably be denied that the tax contributed to the creation of a world with less litter, less reliance on non-renewable resources (plastic is a petroleum product), and more environmentally aware people. In those ways the tax contributed to the creation of a world more fit for human flourishing, and must count as a virtuous environmental policy choice.

§ 2. Virtue and Utilitarianism.

Having cast Virtue theory in this practical way, the
differences between Virtue theory and Utilitarianism, and the way in
which Virtue theory represents a genuine alternative to
Utilitarianism, can be clarified. This is important not only because
the Non-Identity Problem began as a problem for Utilitarianism, but
also because the 20th century revival of Virtue theory was in part
driven by the perceived problems and failings of Utilitarianism.
Anscombe argued for its revival in order to help straighten out
certain problems that troubled the English-language consequentialist
ethics of her time, which she famously called "shallow
philosophy".[39] One of the problems she considered was the way in
which strict Utilitarianism can be shown to force unjust or otherwise
morally unpalatable decisions upon us. An example of this is the
case of a law enforcement agent who contemplates framing and
executing an innocent person in order to prevent a situation which
would result in the deaths of many more innocent people, like a riot
or a war. Someone able to countenance this thought in her view
"shows a corrupt mind".[40] The peculiar difficulty of the Non-
Identity Problem is precisely that it is a situation in which strict
Utilitarianism forces an unpalatable decision upon us, and that is
exactly why Parfit, a Utilitarian himself, called one of its conclusions
"repugnant". He claimed that it was inherently repugnant, but also
found that Utilitarianism could not explain why it would be wrong to
choose it.

The primary structural difference between Utilitarianism and
Virtue theory is that the utility which results from an action is not
what makes that action virtuous or un-virtuous. It is right if it is
noble (*kalon*) and excellent (*arete*) to do it; it is noble and excellent
if it springs from the exercise of a specific faculty of humankind, yet
hits the mark between deficiency and excess, and so promotes and
sustains the aim for *eudaimonia*. This does not mean that harm to
people is irrelevant to a Virtuous person. A character disposition to
harm people is not in Aristotle's view a virtue. A Virtuous person

and a Utility-maximiser might often do the same thing, with more or less the same consequences, but they do it for different reasons. As illustrated by Greg Pence, "Take almost anyone regarded as having admirable moral character. Next ask about the explanation of why this person's approach to life should be a model for others. The answer is never that the person has a personal goal of maximising utility."[41] Since a Virtuous person's reasoning is different from that of a Utility-maximiser, what a Virtuous person does may not always coincide with what a Utility-maximiser does. When he does something that is the same or similar to what a Utility-maximiser does, he does it for different reasons. A virtuous person may wish to do something not because of its contribution to the general utility, but instead because it is excellent and noble to do it, an expression of the best part of human nature. He might be unwilling to trade it for some other action that contributes as much or more to the general utility. I may choose to be a classical pianist instead of a medical doctor, even if I can accurately predict that as a doctor I would benefit more people. Virtue theory allows that the choice to be a classical pianist instead of a doctor is morally permissible, even praiseworthy. For maximisation of utility is not what matters to a Virtuous person. One implication of this position is that *it is not necessarily wrong to choose the lesser total utility*. It is therefore not a valid objection to a Virtuous person's action that there is some other action she could have done instead which would have resulted in a greater total or average utility (although this may be a way to compare the two theories). It would be a valid criticism of the action if the action was base rather than excellent, or if it thwarted instead of assisted the aim for *eudaimonia*. Likewise, it is possible that acts which harm no one, or which infringe no one's rights, are nonetheless vicious. Virtue theory can thus easily accommodate 'harmless wrongs'. For instance, no one is harmed if I secretly post someone's photograph on a dartboard and throw darts at it. Yet the action may be an expression of an intemperate, cold hearted, or resentful disposition. If I enjoy gratuitously breaking things or take pleasure in burning things to ashes, I manifest the vice of desiring excessive and unnecessary pleasures. Even if it is stipulated that the

314

things I gratuitously destroy are my own property and so no one's rights are infringed, the impulse to gratuitously destroy things is one which should be countered with the virtue of self-restraint (i.e. temperance), rather than released with the vice of unrestraint.[42] It can be added that I display the extraordinary vice of 'bestial character', which is a propensity to do that which is fitting only for animals.[43]

Someone may object that the possibility is thus opened to do something that is characteristically excellent but which produces a very great amount of dis-utility, disrespects people's rights, or is otherwise seriously wrong according to some other prominent moral principle. A powerful political leader might manifest excellences like strength, courage, and forthright determination by starting terrible wars or oppressing his people. But this objection is weak. It is normally only in war propaganda that we find the capacity for destruction and terror associated with virtues like strength and courage. While it is true that conflict and competition often spurs us to excel, and also true that we have an extraordinary capability to be cruel and destructive, nevertheless someone who is the cause of large amounts of suffering and pain is not, on the view of every Virtue theorist here studied, a fine example of a Virtuous person. In causing great suffering to other people, or committing great crimes against peace and humanity, he acts upon his lower, base faculties, and not on his higher faculties. He is thus what we might properly call an evil man. Furthermore, the virtues have moral laws as their counterparts, and we could refer to them for reasons why extraordinary acts of evil must be condemned. As seen, such laws tend to be the laws which are necessary to prevent the weakening or breaking of community bonds which make the Virtuous person's flourishing possible. MacIntyre asserts that an evil man excludes himself from normal human relationships like friendship and love. He thus excludes himself from the possibility of attaining a sustainable *eudaimonia*. And so, according to the practical virtue principle offered earlier, such an action must count as morally wrong.[44]

In Aristotle's system, consequences are not the criteria for right and wrong because consequences are excluded from the domain of deliberation and practical reason. To be precise, Aristotle's claim is that we deliberate only about the means to our ends, but not about the ends themselves. This may seem strange, for surely we do deliberate about what ends we should be aiming for, as well as the best strategy to reach them. Aristotle's own words are:

> ...we deliberate not about ends, but about means. A doctor does not deliberate whether he is to cure his patient, nor an orator whether he is to convince his audience, nor a statesman whether he is to secure a good government, nor does anyone else debate about the end of his profession or calling; they take some end for granted, and consider how and by what means it can be achieved. (*NE* 1112b14)

Aristotle's point here, it seems to me, is that we do not deliberate about what the *outcomes* of our actions actually will be. The final outcome, such as whether we are successful in achieving the aim we have set for ourselves, is not always within the range of one's agency, and thus is not a proper object for *phronesis* (practical reason). If I choose to become a doctor, then as a doctor I deliberate about how best to treat the patients in my care. I choose to be a doctor, but I do not choose that being a doctor involves aiming to heal other people—that is already bound together with what it means to be a doctor. With regard to outcomes: as a doctor I aim to heal people, but the outcome is that I am successful in this aim or I am not. Success at healing patients depends on some factors beyond my control, such as the strength and stamina of the patient, the side-effects of the treatment, and so on. If I am a runner, then as a runner I aim to run the race as fast as I can, and I train myself so that I become the best runner I can be. But the outcome of the race, i.e. the winner, is a matter of chance, which Aristotle claimed we do not deliberate about. Aristotle makes a similar point about being a human being: he assumes from the beginning that being human

316

involves aiming to flourish and be happy, although he admits that there is much dispute about exactly what flourishing and happiness is. (*NE*, 1095a22) To aim at *eudaimonia* is for Aristotle inescapably bound together with what it means to be human.

In the absence of a direct statement from Aristotle's text on the significance of consequences, I claim that what stands in the place for consequences in the Aristotelian system is in the rational wish for success in achieving the aim of one's activities. For while we do not deliberate about ends and consequences, we can "wish" for them. As Aristotle says, "Wishes, on the contrary, as we said above, are for ends." (*NE*, 1113a12). I can wish to heal my patients, or to win the race, or to flourish and be happy. Consequences and outcomes are things for which we may have a "rational wish" or a "rational aim", and thus they are not entirely irrelevant to Virtue theory, but their place is not front-and-centre. Consequences can figure into deliberations about what can count as a proper object of a rational wish, but they do not figure into deliberations about what to do. The rational wish for success is virtuous when we wish for success in activities bound to our highest and specific faculties. This claim about the proper relevance of consequences for Virtue theory is nowhere stated in Aristotle's text. In fact Aristotle claims that we do not deliberate about any of the objects of our striving—not even our striving towards *eudaimonia*. Aristotle claims rather that we strive to flourish and be happy because it is natural for human beings to do so. What distinguishes a *rational* wish from any other kind of wishful thinking is that a rational wish is the aim that is appropriate to one's function: a doctor wishes to heal his patients, an athlete wishes to win the competition, and a human being wishes for *eudaimonia*. For someone in each of those positions to wish otherwise, for instance if the runner wished lose the race, would be irrational (unless, perhaps, there was some special external circumstance relevant to the race). In pursuit of that rational wish I deliberate about what to do to achieve it. But the actual achievement of that aim is in the unknowable future, outside the proper realm of *phronesis*. For the aim of happiness, the virtuous person may wish that his actions produce for him and his friends the most happiness, but as happiness is a self-sufficient noble activity, and performing such an action itself accomplishes the end that is sought by the action, it is not the Utilitarian happiness of 'pleasure' or 'benefit'.

Finally, Virtue theory contrasts most sharply with Utilitarianism in its conception of happiness. It was shown in the first study that to a Utilitarian, happiness can consist in pleasure, benefit, well being, or the satisfaction of preferences, and that the notion of 'utility' can accommodate all of these conceptions. In the fourth study we saw that a virtuous person's happiness is the exercise with excellence of humankind's specific and highest faculties. Yet it was also shown that the Virtuous person needs various external goods, which were defined as the bodily, material, or social benefits which aid a person's aim for *eudaimonia*, the aim to flourish and be happy. The lack of such goods is effectively an obstacle to his flourishing, and the possession of which an asset. Could we say, as a Utilitarian might, that to possess more of these external goods is better than to possess less, and that one flourishes better if one possesses more of them? If someone is working to provide or maintain certain useful environmental external goods, is he not aiming for a particular set of material consequences of his actions? Is he not aiming to benefit people? If the answer to these questions is 'yes', then this part of Virtue theory may be reducible to a special variety of Utilitarianism. However, this cannot be so. The Virtuous person pursues *arete*, excellence, for its own sake and does not pursue pleasure, happiness, or benefit for its own sake as a Utilitarian would typically understand the terms. Happiness, for a Virtuous person, is the pursuit of excellence itself; it is an internal good to the pursuit of excellence. It supervenes on the pursuit of excellence in such a way that to aim at one is to aim at the other as well.[45] Happiness involves that every good thing you need for it is present, yet any addition of a good does not make one happier. Happiness is neither a part of a sum of goods, nor the sum total. (*NE*, 1097b15), On MacIntyre's view, this pursuit of excellence should be undertaken in a way that has no concern for consequences:

It is of the character of a virtue that in order that it be
effective in producing the internal goods which are
the rewards of the virtues it should be exercised
without regard to consequences... cultivation of the
virtues always may and often does hinder the
achievement of those external goods which are the
mark of worldly success." (*AV* pg. 128)

It is not the external goods which bring the Virtuous person
happiness, and however much they may be an asset to his
flourishing, no amount of them will make him happy or unhappy
tout court. The Virtuous Person makes himself happy, or not, by the
way he conducts his life and by the kind of person he is. This
important point MacIntyre claims cannot be accommodated by
Utilitarianism. One "crucial difficulty for *any* version of
Utilitarianism", he says, is that:

Utilitarianism cannot accommodate the distinction
between goods internal to and goods external to a
practice. Not only is that distinction marked by none
of the classical utilitarians—it cannot be found in
Bentham's writings nor in those of either of the Mills
or of Sidgwick—but internal goods and external
goods are not commensurable with each other. Hence
the notion of summing goods... in terms of one single
formula or conception of utility, whether it is
Franklin's or Bentham's or Mill's, makes no sense.
(*AV* pg. 198-9)[46]

This is an important distinction. For Aristotle, there are some
'external goods' which one can possess without depriving others of a
chance to possess them as well: friendship, for instance. But for the
most part internal and external goods are indeed incommensurable.
From this premise it follows that we can not treat the distribution of
internal and external goods in a Utilitarian way. It may be the case
that to give someone more of that which is an asset to his flourishing

is to benefit that person, but it is not the case that doing so will make that person flourish more. Only the Virtuous person himself can make himself happy. Indeed Aristotle wrote in The Politics that the citizens of the ideal society should not have too much material wealth. "External goods, being like a collection of tools each useful for some purpose, have a limit: one can have too many of them, and that is bound to be of no benefit, or even a positive injury, to their possessors." (*Politics*, 1323a38). Similarly, Plato wrote in The Republic that when the people of a city desire too much material wealth, they become like a 'city of pigs' or a 'city with a fever', a city full of people so accustomed to material luxury that they are prone to start wars with their neighbours to seize more land and wealth.[47]

If, however, the Virtuous person knows that benefiting others will not necessarily make them happy, that should not be a reason for her to refuse to benefit them. To benefit someone by providing her with the external goods she needs for flourishing is a consequence of one's actions, yet as we have seen it is not the consequences of one's actions that makes one's actions right or wrong. Each Virtuous person's flourishing is her own responsibility. But it is part of each Virtuous person's flourishing to have a rational wish for a world in which flourishing is possible. A person working to provide environmental external goods, and so create and sustain that world, is acting on that rational wish. She is thus is acting Virtuously, whether she successfully benefits others or not; although it is normally the case that in order to pursue that wish, it is necessary and unavoidable that one should benefit other people, especially one's friends. Indeed there are some virtues which cannot be practiced without benefiting others.

How much benefit-provision of this kind is enough, and how much is too much? Given that the environment is the field and stage of a Virtuous person's flourishing, and that as such the Virtuous person desires a world in which *eudaimonia* is possible and supported, how much attention and effort should be put towards environmental conservation and sustainability? Should one improve the quality of the environment as much as possible, taking as many of its goods as the limits of sustainability may allow, and getting it to produce for us the most benefit that it can, in order to attain the greatest possible *eudaimonia*? Does the principle of groundedness in the world require the agent to always work on improving his well-being through a never-ending upward progression of improvement to the qualities of his world? Could this requirement exclude the pursuit of other things like art, athletics, scientific discovery, philosophy, or even the excellence of his own character? This would be the position a Virtuous person would take if the virtues were nothing more than propensities to aim for the greatest utility. But to a Virtuous person, for whom the greatest *eudaimonia* does not necessarily coincide with the greatest utility, maximising one's external goods is not what matters. As with all Virtuous actions, it is excellence which matters, not the maximisation of utility. It is 'hitting the target of the mean' which makes an action excellent. This applies also in the pursuit of external goods. Thus in some situations, the production of the greatest utility might constitute a vice of excess.

The Doctrine of the Mean translates into environmentally-directed actions as follows. The right kind of environment for human flourishing is the one which *obtains a parity between what one aims to do as a virtuous person,* on the one hand, and *what actions are supported and enabled by the world in which one lives,* on the other. Excellence in environmental conservation here is the balance between what one aims to do and what the environmental external goods which are available offer the power and opportunity to do. I shall call this variation of the doctrine of the mean, the 'principle of parity'. This represents the completion of the principle of practical virtue discussed earlier. Note that it is a principle of parity for what one aims to do *as a virtuous person* that is stipulated here. There may be some situation in which a parity exists between someone's aim to terrorise people and destroy things on the one hand, and the world's resources and opportunities to do so on the other. But a virtuous person would not aim for evil acts like terror and wanton destruction. Note also that there is no suggestion here that one's choice is between having everything one could ever want and having to make do with very little. The principle of parity limits our use of environmental resources in two related ways: it licences us to take what we need to flourish, neither more nor less, yet within the bounds of what the environment can sustainably supply. It allows us to develop and exploit valuable ecological resources which might be more productive than they presently are, but only insofar as doing so will help us pursue the human good more successfully. It grants no sanction to conspicuous consumption and the maximisation of material wealth, nor does it demand that we live in Eamonn De Valera's "frugal comfort", while intervening as little as possible, or not at all, in the environment.

As we have seen, the Virtuous person does not require many possessions or great political power to obtain the flourishing life. Conspicuous consumption is a vice for Aristotle, just as it is a great dis-utility for Singer (as seen in chapter 1). Large scale projects of environmental development and resource depletion may create great wealth, but may be more than what he needs to flourish, and thus a vice of excess. This is an ancient wisdom, taught even by Socrates during his trial.[48] Most of the time, environmental issues will not arise until and unless the environment becomes sufficiently poisoned, polluted, or unstable as to be an obstacle to one's own flourishing, or the flourishing of one's *polis*. On other occasions, as when the virtue of 'magnificence' compels one to make public benefactions (*NE*, 1123a3), he may wish to contribute to an environmental development or improvement project that increases the quality of the environment's external goods, be they aesthetic, health-related, or economic. A wildlife protection fund, a pollution clean-up programme, a reforestation effort, might be examples of such projects. The general idea is that the Virtuous person refrains from acts which degrade or destroy the qualities of the environment which make it suited for the kind of *eudaimonia* for which he aims. When he aims for a kind of *eudaimonia* that is greater than that which the world in which he lives can support, as when for instance he finds himself in an impoverished, polluted, or disaster-stricken area, then acts which aim to develop or improve the world to the point where it can support that aspiration will be a part of the aim for that kind of *eudaimonia*.

Having obtained a principle of practical virtue, contrasted it with Utilitarianism, and placed the discoveries of the previous study in its terms using the 'principle of parity', we can now proceed to the task of putting environmental virtue theory to the test of future generations, the practical criterion of the acceptable environmental ethic, and the Non-Identity Problem. Since a Virtuous person's choices are not primarily directed by the consequences of his actions, it is possible that a Virtuous person would not find himself forced to choose the Repugnant Conclusion, as Parfit claimed a Utilitarian would, even knowing that the case brings about more total benefit than harm in the final calculation of utility. From this, however, it does not follow that a Virtuous person would automatically choose Conservation. It follows only that a Virtuous person is not forced by the consequences to choose one way or the other. How should he choose? We shall continue from here, examining the Virtuous person's responsibilities in reference to other people and to the future.

§ 3. People and *Pleonexia.*

If a Virtuous person is not necessarily bound to promote the most utility for the greatest number of people, then what value, if any, does a virtuous person assign to or recognise in other people? Notwithstanding that Virtue theory places emphasis on the quality or excellence of the agent's character, still it is, according to Aristotle, more excellent to promote the flourishing of groups of people than that of one person alone. A critic of the theory might read this as just another way of saying that one ought to maximise utility for the greatest number of people. Here is a statement from the <u>Nicomachean Ethics</u> which exemplifies this position.

> For even though it be the case that the good is the
> same for the individual and for the state, nevertheless,
> the good of the state is manifestly a greater and more

> perfect good, both to attain and to preserve. To
> secure the good of one person only is better than
> nothing; but to secure the good of a nation or a state is
> a nobler and more divine achievement. (*NE*, 1094b1)

Why is it more noble to secure the good of many people than it is to secure only one's own, if the reason has nothing to do with consequences? Aristotle argues that one's own flourishing is bound together with that of others, and to the community in which one lives. We may infer this from Aristotle's claim that man is a political being. Parents pursue the good of their children because the children are 'their product' and in helping them to flourish, the parents themselves flourish. Also, Aristotle claims that the complete friend is another self: friends "resemble each other in virtue" and help each other to achieve noble deeds. Aristotle says that happiness is a self-sufficient good, because it is chosen for its own sake, but it is not just one's own happiness which is chosen for its own sake:

> The same conclusion also appears to follow from a
> consideration of the self-sufficiency of happiness—
> for it is felt that the final good must be a thing
> sufficient in itself. The term self-sufficient, however,
> we employ with reference not to oneself alone, living
> a life of isolation, but also to one's parents and
> children and wife, and one's friends and fellow
> citizens in general, *since man is by nature a social
> being*. (*NE*, 1097b10)

'Self-sufficient' here means that, as seen, flourishing (*eudaimonia*) is chosen for its own sake, and not for the sake of some additional or external aim. The appearance of the term in reference to the community means that the condition of self-sufficient *eudaimonia* can apply to a community as well as to an individual. A community can be self-sufficiently happy. Alternatively it can mean that we choose self-sufficient happiness for others as well as just ourselves.

I have highlighted the phrase, 'man is by nature a social being'. The phrase should be translated as 'a political being'. In the Politics, Aristotle similarly claims that a human being is "a political animal" (*Politics*, 1253a1). This means that it is natural for people to be social beings, to live in communities organised for the promotion of the good life, and that a capacity for sociability is among the potentialities and endowments of nature with which a person is born. If people are by nature social animals, then it will be natural for them to possess and develop the characteristics which enable them to live socially. An example of this is language. We are not born immediately able to speak: language is something we must learn to do. But it is natural for us to learn it: we have an endowment of nature that enables us to do so. Moreover, it is in the company of others that we learn it. We are taught to speak by others, and with others we practice speaking. Like the virtues, the possession of language and of any qualities required for successful sociability must be trained and developed, or in Aristotle's words, "brought to maturity by habit" (*NE*1103a20). Other people are invaluable for the assistance they give to this process. From this it may be inferred that for Aristotle, the flourishing of a person as a social being is intertwined with the human community of which he is a member, especially the community of his friends. It cannot be the case, therefore, that the Virtuous person neither attributes nor recognises intrinsic value in others.

Holmes Rolston III, the noted environmental ethicist, claimed that by benefiting another being, a Virtuous person is aiming at his own flourishing and thus the act has nothing to do with the beneficiary. This he takes to be a form of fraud. Rolston put the objection in a discussion of the preservation or protection of inland fish species which have no instrumental value to humankind. In his words:

> …it seems unexcellent—cheap and philistine, in fact
> —to say that excellence of human character is what
> we are after when we preserve these fishes. We want
> virtue in the beholder; is value in the fishes only

tributary to that?… Excellence of human character
does indeed result from a concern for these fishes, but
if this excellence of character really comes from
appreciating otherness, then why not value that
otherness in wild nature first? Let the human virtue
come tributary to that.[49]

This argument, however, is a straw man. There are certain virtues
such as justice, charity, magnanimity, and so on, which simply
cannot be practiced without benefiting others. Moreover, Aristotle's
discussion of social relations shows that a Virtuous person does
indeed attribute intrinsic value to others, especially his friends and
associates who, resembling himself in virtue, he loves for their own
sake, and he finds it is un-virtuous to love others for the sake of what
can be gained from them.[50] The Virtuous person aims for the good
life *with and for others*. There is no hint of egotism in the aim for
eudaimonia. We have seen this in the preceding chapter's discussion
of the faculty of *eunoia*. While it is the habits created by one's
actions themselves, more than the other beings with and for whom
they are performed, that makes one virtuous, still it is not a
contradiction to edify oneself and to benefit others at the same time.
If it is virtuous to conserve a rare or endangered species, or a
sensitive ecosystem, there is nothing fraudulent about doing so.
There is, however, an ambiguity in Aristotle's text concerning how
far a Virtuous person is willing to go for the sake of other people,
which I shall here explore for the sake of completeness. The passage
of the text where this ambiguity appears, which must be quoted at
length, is located where Aristotle discusses the virtue of self-love. It
reads:

But it is also true that the virtuous man's conduct is
often guided by the interests of his friends and of his
country, and that he will if necessary lay down his life
in their behalf. For he will surrender wealth and
power and all the goods that men struggle to win, if
he can secure nobility for himself; since he would

prefer an hour of rapture to a long period of mild enjoyment, a year of noble life to many years of ordinary existence, one great and glorious exploit to many small successes. And this is doubtless the case with those who give their lives for others; thus they choose great nobility for themselves. Also the virtuous man is ready to forgo money if by that means his friends may gain more money; for thus, through his friends get money, he himself achieves nobility, and so he assigns the greater good to his own share. And he behaves in the same manner as regards honours and offices also: all these things he will relinquish to his friend, for this is noble and praiseworthy for himself. (*NE* 1169a19)

The ambiguity here is in the tension between a sacrifice for the sake of another, and a sacrifice for the sake of the honour and nobility that one will attain for oneself in the sacrificial act. If one makes a sacrifice that benefits another, but this sacrifice is performed ultimately for the sake of one's own honour, then one has not truly made a sacrifice for another. Aristotelian scholar J. O. Urmson claims that Aristotle himself never resolves this ambiguity. "If this line of argument is correct," says Urmson, "[then] Aristotle has failed to reconcile his view of friendship as involving disinterested care for the friend's welfare with his general view that men seek what they take to be their highest good."[51]

The most that Aristotle says about this tension is that "…it is right to be a lover of self, though self-love of an ordinary sort is wrong" (*NE*, 1169b4) and that "the bad man ought not to be a lover of self, since he will follow his base passions, and so injure both himself and his neighbours. (*NE*, 1168b10) This ordinary sort of self love is called *pleonexia*, and is characterised by the desire to maximise material wealth and public honours. I shall have more to say about this soon. Urmson's own attempt to resolve this tension on his own engaged an exploration of what exactly is "the greater good" that the agent secures for himself, and what it really means to act for the sake of what is noble. Here are his words on the matter:

> The Greek word *kalon*, which is regularly translated 'fine' or 'noble' in ethical contexts is also regularly translated 'beautiful' in other contexts; it is thus used of scenery and people; its opposite, translated 'base' in ethical contexts, is also the regular word for what is ugly… if we attempt to draw conclusions from these data, it would seem that *kalon* is an aesthetic or (in ethical contexts) a quasi-aesthetic term and thus 'fine' may well be the best translation to employ.[52]

The word *kalon* also appears in the Rhetoric where it is translated as "the praiseworthy good in itself" or as "the pleasant because of good", and in the Topics as "the fitting".[53] This will help us understand the several places where Aristotle claims that it is noble (*kalon*) to face death for one's friends,[54] for one who dies for the sake of one's friends surely cannot receive any benefit of honours or public recognition. If *kalon* is a matter of publicly bestowed honour, an immaterial benefit external to the act itself, then it is a reward that the agent cannot gain by a noble death. Such a reward might be attached to one's posthumous legacy, but the dead person himself would be unable to enjoy it. As a quasi-aesthetic term, 'noble' is a way of describing one's actions, and is perfectly applicable to someone who sacrifices his life for another. Such an act represents or reveals human nature at its finest: it is representative of the most excellent, beautiful, and even divine aspects of our nature. The virtuous person who sacrifices for another "assigns the greater good to his own share"; that greater good he assigns to himself is *the virtuous action itself* which is its own reward. The "lesser good" is the aim external to the action itself. The goodness of a Virtuous action is internal to itself, the "lesser good" of the same action is its practical consequences: money, opportunity, or whatever externally obtained material or immaterial benefit the action has among its consequences for the agent and/or his associates and beneficiaries.

The noble action is self-sufficient, concerned not with external aims nor with outcomes and results.

This again re-affirms the structural difference between Virtue theory and Utilitarianism—for *eudaimonia* is not a 'consequence' of the noble action in an ordinary Utilitarian sense. To choose moral nobility for its own sake *and* for the sake of *eudaimonia* is not a contradiction. For Aristotle, the performance of noble actions is *eudaimonia* itself, and the possession of the virtues gives the agent the fixed disposition of character from which noble actions spring. Thus Aristotle says, at the close of the discussion of self-love, that the Virtuous person "…chooses moral nobility in preference to all other things. It may even happen that he will surrender to his friend the performance of some achievement, and that it may be nobler for him to be the cause of his friend's performing it than to perform it himself." (*NE* 1169b1)

It can be objected that a self-sacrificing action cannot be noble, because death puts an end to the agent's flourishing. I think that Aristotle accepts sacrifice as a noble action for several reasons. For Aristotle, it is the action itself, not its consequences, which is counted as noble or base (even if the agent's death is one of the consequences). A noble death can be a culmination and completion of a well-lived life and thus it may be possible to say of a self-sacrificing person that 'even in death, he did well'. This may be behind Aristotle's statement that someone who sacrifices himself for others "chooses great nobility for himself" (*NE*, 1169a26). Note also that Socrates was not warned by his *daimon*, his inner divine voice, to flee from his trial and save his life. Socrates chose to do what he thought was right even though the consequence for him was to die.[55] The point I wish to emphasise here is this: one implication of the claim that utility is not what matters is that *it can be Virtuous to do something even if death precludes the agent from enjoying any of the material benefits and consequences of the action*. This is why the great-souled man, although he regards life as desirable, does not treat it as the highest good. "He will face danger in a great cause, and when so doing will be ready to sacrifice his life, since he holds that life is not worth having at every price." (*NE* 1124b5) The Virtuous

Person is prepared to sacrifice himself for the sake of honour or for the benefit of friends. This point shall be important in the discussion of time and the future.

Such is the nature of noble and virtuous self-love. Is it enough to simply say that 'ordinary' self-love, which Aristotle claimed was wrong, is just the opposite of this? Actually, Aristotle is very specific about what constitutes ordinary self-love. It is the vice of *pleonexia*, which is the self-love of those who:

> ...assign to themselves the larger share of money,
> honours, or bodily pleasures; since these are the
> things which most men desire and set their hearts on
> as being the greatest goods, and which accordingly
> they compete with each other to obtain. Now those
> who take more than their share of these things are
> men who indulge their appetites, and generally their
> passions and the irrational part of their souls... Hence
> self-love is rightly censured in those who are lovers
> of self in this sense. (*NE*, 1168b10)

We can thus characterise this kind of self-love as the desire to maximise material wealth and public honours for oneself, possibly at the expense of others. *Pleonexia* is the vice of excess connected to the virtue of *dikaiosune*, "justice" (*NE*, 1129b9), and according to MacIntyre its appropriate English-language translation has had a history of its own. Hobbes translated it as a desire for more than one's proper share.[56] Today it is normally translated as "greed", and although this is not mistaken, it is misleading: to the Greek mind it would have designated a tendency to engage in material acquisitiveness for its own sake, rather than a particular kind of desire.[57] Thus an alternative translation for today could be "narrow self-centredness" or a disposition to be "materialistic". Clearly, it is the kind of self-centredness Aristotle associated with the (un-Virtuous) pursuit of pleasure or wealth, and so is distinguished from the Virtuous self-love of someone who pursues *eudaimonia*. MacIntyre explains:

What such translations of '*pleonexia*' conceal from us
is the extent of the difference between Aristotle's
standpoint on the virtues and vices, and more
especially his standpoint on justice and the dominant
standpoint of peculiarly modern societies. For the
adherents of that [modern] standpoint recognise that
acquisitiveness is a character trait indispensable to
continuous and limitless economic growth, and one of
their central beliefs is that continuous and limitless
economic growth is a fundamental good.[58]

While to Aristotle, and to Hobbes as well, it is a vice, to modern
people it is not a vice but the driving engine of capitalism.
Furthermore it is also the root of the environmental crisis. The
cultivation of *pleonexia* on a social scale has created enormous
volumes of wealth, material goods, and energy, but has also resulted
in the wide spread loss of landscape, biodiversity, wildlife and plant
habitat, in the quest for resources to satisfy the demand, and the
search for new sinks to absorb the waste. Conspicuous consumption
has depleted invaluable resources across the planet, and created and
pollution-induced health hazards and climate change. *Pleonexia* is
now not only a social issue, but also an environmental issue.

MacIntyre believes that the transformation of *pleonexia* from
vice to "the driving force of modern productive work" happened
when productive work was moved out of the household and into
separate locations where it was "made to serve impersonal capital",
instead of households and communities, and thus productive work
was "expelled from the realm of practices with goods internal to
themselves" (*AV* pg. 227). This is not a mere caricature of modern
economic principle. If the moment when this idea entered the
Western intellectual tradition could be fixed, it would be the year
1776, when Adam Smith published The Wealth of Nations (also,
coincidentally, the year the United States of America was founded).
In Smith's view, everyone is "constantly exerting himself" to
maximise his own wealth by finding "the most advantageous

employment for whatever capital he can command". In so doing, everyone seeks his own gain, not that of society, but this "necessarily leads him to prefer that employment which is most advantageous to society", although he "neither intends to promote the public interest, nor knows how much he is promoting it".[59] Almost all economists and political theorists in modern Western countries have followed this principle ever since, with or without believing in Smith's 'invisible hand'.[60] Certainly, the basic message of all consumer advertising in the mass media is for consumers to indulge in *pleonexia* and maximise their good or pleasure through conspicuous consumption. *Pleonexia* is to be found in philosophy as well: as I have already shown, Rawls presupposed that self-interest is the standard of reason and rationality, "familiar in social theory", with which men behind the veil of ignorance bargain with each other for a just social distribution. (*TJ* pp. 111, 123-4). Rawls cites four other scholars in support of this claim, all of whom are economists.

It is beyond doubt that *pleonexia* is a vice for Aristotle, and a virtue for modern capitalism. Which should it be for contemporary environmental virtue theory? The way to answer this question is to put it to the test of practical Virtue which I developed earlier in this study. Would a *pleonexia*-manifesting act be noble, self-rewarding? Would it assist or frustrate the aim for *eudaimonia*, and the aim for a world that is well suited for the pursuit of *eudaimonia*? I find that the answer is "no". A life dedicated to the maximisation of material wealth for oneself, without just principles of distribution, misses the mark of environmental virtue established by the principle of parity. *Pleonexia* as a personal quality compels its possessor to strive after more material goods than may be necessary to assist the aim to flourish and live well. *Pleonexia* as a principle of economic organisation has the effect of creating extra demands on the environmental resource base, depleting them quicker or sooner, increasing the volume of waste, and thereby degrading the qualities of the environment which make it a suitable stage for human flourishing. I therefore side with Aristotle and MacIntyre here, and claim that it should still be regarded as a vice, especially if not balanced by social, political, and economic justice. The Virtuous person does not necessarily seek to always increase his material standard of living. We do not need conspicuous wealth to be happy. While poverty and depravation is clearly an obstacle to flourishing, conspicuous consumption is not necessarily an asset. Why own an expensive sport-utility-vehicle when a compact car with a fuel efficient engine, or even a hybrid engine, will do? Why own a private car at all when public transportation will do? This obtains on a public level as well. If public transportation is not sufficient to meet one's needs, then seeking after its improvement may be more virtuous than obtaining a private car, since public transport (other than jet aircraft) tends to produce less pollution. Why build a dual-carriageway when an improvement to existing road and rail networks will do? This may not sit well with the land planners, business leaders, industrialists, and politicians who make the environment-affecting decisions about which this thesis is concerned. As MacIntyre says, "That a systematically lower standard of living ought to be preferred to a systematically higher standard of living is a thought incompatible with either the economics or the politics of peculiarly modern societies." [61] But it should not be surprising that the pursuit of virtue is often incompatible with the pursuit of material wealth.

In the light of the discussion of *kalon* and *pleonexia*, it might be claimed that the Non-Identity choice of Depletion would be rejected on the grounds that it is not noble to choose it: to destroy a landscape, a marine, a forest, in order to satisfy the desire of *pleonexia* is un-virtuous, un-excellent, and thus wrong. To do so mistakes material prosperity for the human good. But the Non-Identity problem is not only a problem concerning environmental resource use: it is also a problem concerning future generations. I shall now explore the value of the future to a Virtuous person.

§ 4. The Temporal Continuity of Virtue

It can seem hard, at first, to construct a theory of Virtue ethics that encompasses the claims of, or our responsibilities to, future generations. Although we now know what is noble in a Virtuous agent's actions, and why the human community is important to him, and indeed why it can be a vice to damage the environment, we do not yet know if that argument carries into future generations. Yet as we have seen, Deontology and Justice theory relied on Virtue-concepts in order to construct their own theories of ethics to future generations.

We can take as one starting place Aristotle's claim that the cultivation of virtue takes time. Based on this premise, Wensveen claims:

> The cultivation of virtue also requires that a person can *continue* to feel, think, and act in certain ways over an indefinite period of time. Therefore, it implies that the supporting ecosystems must also *endure* over time, which is exactly what the notion of sustainability conveys. [62]

Thus, as one aims to flourish and be happy through the course of a complete life, the health of the environment in which this aim is sought must be sustained throughout the whole course of that complete life. It follows that acts which contribute to environmental conservation are, on her view, virtuous. Sandler's objection to Wensveen's claim, which usefully describes the problem of the future for Virtue theory, runs as follows. A virtuous person might not need a healthy and stable environment for the whole duration of his life. He might need it only long enough to complete his moral education (i.e. his process of becoming virtuous), after which he might act in environmentally unsustainable ways and never see the bad ecological consequences of his actions in his lifetime. The environment might degrade to the point of unsuitability for human flourishing many generations after he is dead. [63] The choice to take from the environment in an exploitative way might set the environment on an ecological course of decline, leading to the Repugnant Conclusion, but that might happen in the far distant future, and not in the lifetime of the agent or agents responsible for initiating that decline, nor in their children's or grandchildren's lifetime. Therefore environmental stability or instability might not be an issue to a Virtuous person who already lives in a supportive and stable environment. Additionally, if, as a result of his actions, the future environment is unstable and unhealthy, and his distant descendants find themselves less able or even unable to flourish, that might not be a barrier to the agent's flourishing in the here-and-now. In Sandler's words: "Why should one be incapable of flourishing just because after you are dead the environmental conditions will be so degraded that it can no longer produce these goods? How could that be a constituent of *your* flourishing?"[64]

This I consider to be very nearly a new form of the Non-Identity Problem. If people alive today find that the world in which they flourish best is made possible by the exploitative depletion of environmental resources, with the result that far distant future people suffer from the pollution and waste that life-style creates, that may not be a barrier to people's flourishing here and now. The flourishing or non-flourishing of far distant future people is their own responsibility, not the responsibility of any present people. If the Virtuous person cares only for the flourishing of his friends, children, community, nearest descendants, and himself, then he might choose Depletion, knowing that Depletion would sustain the kind of surroundings in which it is possible for himself and his contemporaries or near-contemporaries to live well throughout the whole of their natural lives. Conservation may also sustain the desirable surroundings, but possibly not as well as Depletion would in the short term of the agent's own life-span, due to the limits or restrictions it would impose on the availability of goods and resources derived from ecosystems. An environment on a decline towards near-total unsuitability for the function of supporting life might be able to continue providing the necessary external goods for human life for one or two generations, and for at least the lifetime of the agent in the place of making a Non-Identity choice. The question now is whether Depletion or Conservation, as a future that could be created by the choices of someone alive today, is the future that a virtuous person would choose.

To answer this question, I find Aristotle's lectures in the *Nicomachean Ethics* almost completely unhelpful. Statements and arguments concerning time and the future in his ethical writings are few and far between, and also intertwined with his other concerns and commitments. For example, in the discussion of "the wisdom of Solon", the claim that no one is to be counted as happy until after he is dead, Aristotle says:

> ...suppose a man to have lived in perfect happiness
> until old age, and to have come to a correspondingly
> happy end; he may have many vicissitudes befall his
> descendants, some of whom may be good and meet
> with the fortune they deserve, and others the opposite;
> and moreover these descendants may clearly stand in
> every possible degree of remoteness from the
> ancestors in question. Now it would be a strange
> thing if the dead man also were to change with the
> fortunes of his family, and were to become a happy
> man at one time and then miserable at another; yet on
> the other hand it would also be strange if ancestors
> were not affected at all, even over a limited period, by
> the fortunes of their descendants. (*NE*, 1100a20)

Aristotle does *not* claim, as the wording of this translation may suggest, that the dead man is made happy or unhappy by the fortunes of his descendants after his death. It is, rather, our estimate of his life as having been happy or unhappy that changes.[65] But Aristotle's reason for bringing this matter into the discourse is not to discuss future generations. It is his purpose here to defeat Solon's 'wisdom', by showing how it is possible to be self-sufficiently happy in the here-and-now, and not wait until after death to be counted as happy by one's peers. One's happiness is not contingent upon the description of one's life made by others.

MacIntyre discusses the relevance of time and the future more directly than Aristotle does, especially in the discussion of the practices with which the case for Virtue Theory was initiated in both of their accounts. Starting with the relevance of the past, MacIntyre claims that whenever and wherever the virtues appear, they always do so within the context of a historical tradition sustained by a community, of which practices are one way in which historical continuities are transmitted.[66] Each of the practices, of which the 'practice' of being a human being is the analogous extension, has a history, which is theoretically distinct from the biography and habits of any particular practitioner. Insofar as one takes on the role of a carpenter, a musician, a doctor, and so forth one also takes on the history of that profession as well. Thus, a person's happiness as a social being, intertwined with the community of which he is a member, is also intertwined with that community's history. This is importantly unlike other moral theories in the Western tradition, especially the Kantian position, for it does not begin by first postulating that an individual moral agent is already formed and defined 'prior' (logically prior) to entering the world and taking a place in it. Rather, a person emerges from the world, and comes into the world possessing a package of inheritances from it. As we saw in the discussion of Kant and the philosophical significance of geography, the tension between the conception of the world as "our home and place, the stage of our actions" on one hand, and the world as the totally internalised *a priori* category of space on the other, had to be resolved by changing the Kantian programme such that the human person is not a *tabula rasa*, possessing only autonomous reason and a collection of *a priori* categories of logic, but is a product of his world, already engaged in various relations with it. This is precisely the situation MacIntyre claims is the moral agent's original position. As MacIntyre says: "I am born with a past; and to try to cut myself off from that past, in an individualist mode, is to deform my present relationships. The possession of an historical identity and the possession of a social identity coincide." (*AV* pg. 221) In MacIntyre's view, a person doesn't have to accept the limitations of his historical and social inheritances; for instance he can choose to rebel. But a person's inheritances are his starting place in the quest for the good. The quest moves forward from them. MacIntyre illustrates this relation as follows:

What I am, therefore, is in key part what I inherit, a
specific past that is present to some degree in my
present. I find myself part of a history and that is
generally to say, whether I like it or not, whether I
recognise it or not, one of the bearers of a tradition. It
was important when I characterised that at any given
moment what a practice is depends on a mode of
understanding it which has been transmitted often
through many generations. And thus insofar as the
virtues sustain the relationships required for practices,
they have to sustain relationships to the past—and to
the future—as well as in the present. (*AV* pg. 221)

The past, on this account of a Virtuous person, is the inheritance
which figures into his present identity. An awareness of the past
strengthens and fortifies his present social relations. It is what
provides him with role models from whom to learn what *eudaimonia*
is and what to do to achieve it. This idea of the past, it must be
noted, is a function of the present: it is what we inherit and possess
in the present. As shall soon be shown, the future is also a function
of the present. What is established here is that we have a means of
assessing the ethical significance of history, and a means of asserting
why history should figure into some of our moral decisions. The
decision by Limerick City Council, and the county councils of
Limerick and of Leitrim, to discontinue the position of heritage
officer, could be looked upon as partial failures to recognise this
significance. In the year 2003, Dublin City's heritage officer went
on sabbatical for six months and was not replaced while he was
away.[67]

For both Aristotle and MacIntyre, the analogy with practices
is only the launching platform for Virtue theory, not the destination.
For Aristotle, the destination is *eudaimonia* (although perhaps the
'destination' metaphor does not fit well, since *eudaimonia* is not a
'final' destination). For MacIntyre, there really is no destination.
There is only an ongoing quest: "The good life for man is the life

spent in seeking the good life for man, and the virtues necessary for the seeking are those which will enable us to understand what more and what else the good life for man is." (*AV* pg. 219). But MacIntyre does supply a map with which to chart one's direction in the quest. That map is the concept of *narrative*. To describe it as briefly as possible: narrative is the structure of storytelling, in which things are linked together by being a part of the same plot progression. Narrative enables one to identify a person as being the same person over time, and having the same virtues over time. MacIntyre argues that narrative is the best way of understanding human identity for two reasons. One is that narrative makes action intelligible.[68] The other is that human life is structured in a way that naturally lends itself to representation in dramatic storytelling.[69] In the <u>Poetics</u>, Aristotle argued that tragic drama is possible because it represents the structure of the lives and events that the plot structure narrates.[70] The narrative connection to the past is obtained through history-telling, and the only relevant difference between a historical narrative and a human life is that unlike the characters of storytelling, real human beings are the authors of their stories.[71]

The connection to the future is obtained as follows. "At any given point in an enacted dramatic narrative", says MacIntyre, "we do not know what will happen next." (*AV* pg. 215). The future is that part of the narrative which is unknown because it has not yet been told. It appears as the element of surprise and unpredictability. We may know the past and we may know why it has led to the present in which we live, but we do not know what the future will be. But the time-embedded quality of narrative, which is common to human life, carries with it a pressure to move towards the future.

We have already seen how the justice theorists T'Hooft and de-Shalit appropriated this part of MacIntyre's theory for their purposes, and so stepped out of the realm of justice theory proper. T'Hooft explicitly states that this has an existential significance. "Man is a being that lives in time, whose life indeed is temporal through and through, and for whom the future consequently is a constitutive dimension of his existence, as much as his remembrance of the past." (*JFGE*, pg. 113). For T'Hooft, it therefore follows that

"Concern for the welfare of future generations first raises an issue for our understanding of the self." (*JFGE* pg. 119). This, as I asserted earlier, is the vocabulary of Virtue theory. The passage from MacIntyre which best expresses this quality of the virtuous act, which both T'Hooft and de-Shalit cite with approval, reads as follows:

> We live our lives, both individually and in our relationships with each other, in the light of certain conceptions of a possible shared future, a future in which certain possibilities beckon us forward and others repel us, some seem already foreclosed and others perhaps inevitable. There is no present which is not informed by some image of some future and an image of the future which always presents itself in the form of a *telos*—or of a variety of ends or goals—towards which we are either moving or failing to move in the present. Unpredictability and teleology therefore coexist as part of our lives; like characters in a fictional narrative we do not know what will happen next, but nonetheless our lives have a certain form which projects itself towards our future. (*AV* pg. 215-6)

In the structure of action as interpreted in the teleological way Aristotle and MacIntyre do, we not only obtain a unique way to think about our "original position" of being grounded in social relations and in the world, but also a new way to think about time and the future. Virtue theory requires us to think of the future as a function of the present, rather than as that which must come to be as the result of material cause and effect.

This notion of time has a history (so to speak) which should be briefly described. For most of the ancient philosophers, time exists in some relation to a fact about the world, especially the stars in the sky. For example, Plato, in <u>The Timeus</u>, described a model of the universe comprising a series of concentric crystal spheres on which are attached the sun and moon, the five visible planets, and the 'fixed stars' on the outermost sphere. He claimed that time itself is nothing other than the movement of the stars on their spheres. The first philosopher to disconnect time completely from references to cosmology or to movement in space was the 4th century Christian theologian Saint Augustine, in the 11th chapter of The Confessions. For him, time is completely internalised as a function of intentionality. In the Critique of Pure Reason, Kant placed time alongside space as one of the *A Priori* concepts of understanding. The most prominent recent philosophers to articulate this conception of time are almost all Continental philosophers working in the fields of phenomenology and hermeneutics, such as Edmund Husserl, Martin Heidegger, Emmanuel Lévinas, and Paul Ricoeur. In 1984 Ricoeur published a three-volume masterwork entitled Time and Narrative which binds time to the hermeneutics of narrative as did MacIntyre, although with considerably more sophistication and attention to detail. For Ricoeur, time is 'humanised' by the act of narrating events, and narrative 'attains its full meaning' when treated as a condition of temporal existence.[72]

To state this conception of time more directly, without using the hermeneutics of narrative: the future, for the most part, appears to the Virtuous person in the *telos,* the aim, of his actions. It appears in the rational wish for success in whatever activity he might be engaged in. The future in the *telos* of virtuous and noble action is not the future which will come to be as a result of temporally-sequenced chains of cause and effect from events and actions performed in the past and present. The future in the *telos* of action is the future which actions in the present are driving towards. The future, to a Virtuous person, as a property or a function of action in the present, might be called the 'envisioned' future, the 'desired' future, the future we wish for and aim for. The role of narrative in this process, according to MacIntyre, is only to forge links of intelligibility and continuity between the past, the present, and the future.

Aristotle would not claim that the *telos* of a virtuous and noble action is postponed to the future. It is achieved in the performance of the action itself that aims for that *telos*; that is part of what it means for an action to be self-sufficient. Other kinds of virtuous actions achieve their aim in the material results of the action which serve as external goods to the general project of living well. In this sense a virtuous person is primarily interested in the present moment, and the future is of related but secondary interest to him insofar as he is interested in the security of the external goods throughout the course of his lifetime, and possibly also in the lifetime of his children and nearest descendants. As we have seen, the Virtuous person's concern with the present moment, and the concern with expressing good character instead of with consequences, is such that if there are benefits which his action produces which he cannot participate in, that is not a reason to refrain from the action. What, then, does it mean to say that the future appears in the *telos* of the virtuous and noble act? MacIntyre's insight can be expressed in Aristotelian terms by claiming that the distinguishing mark of a virtuous and noble aim, a "rational wish", is that the *telos* at which it aims at is a perpetual *telos*. The activity of aiming at a self-sufficient end like *eudaimonia* continues throughout one's life, in all of one's other projects and activities, and it never really ends. It is a continuous, unfinished and never-ending goal. This does not mean that we are committed to believing that the actual achievement of *eudaimonia* is impossible, as Schopenhauer believed that the universal Will to Life strives for a satisfaction it is doomed to never possess. Rather, this is the claim that the achievement of *eudaimonia*, an achievable goal in the present, is a time-inscribed achievement that also drives the agent into the future as an eternally renewable, ongoing action. On the practical plane, there are several kinds of future-directed, time-inscribed actions that aim towards the future by being ongoing and continuous. The perpetuation of the *polis* is one of them, as is maintenance of one's friendships. Raising a family is another example: parents stand in a special relationship to their children, and this relation is the microcosm of the more larger social relation between two generations. The family relationship has continuity as the children grow up and become parents to a new generation of children. Education is a future-directed activity *par excellence*, as one of its many aims is the transmission of knowledge and skill to an upcoming generation and thus the provision of intergenerational continuity on the public level. The institutionalisation of education provides that continuity through the teacher to student relationship, which is distinct from but related to the family relationship of parent to child, and which is necessarily a public relationship insofar as it is constituted by public bodies such as governments, churches, and schools themselves. The right of third parties to have a say in it also constitutes the public dimension of these relations. The conservation of heritage monuments, the treasures of art, architecture, and culture, and the establishment of museums to protect them and interpret them for each new generation is another fine example. Environmental conservation and sustainability is another: as Wensveen observed, the very notion of sustainability already implies a temporal continuity, and a projection into the future. To conserve something means to hold it in its present state for an indefinite but long span of time. The goal of environmental conservation is not accomplished in any single act, but like *eudaimonia* itself it must be constantly re-accomplished, constantly maintained by a series of acts. To aim at living well through good environmental practice is to act not only for the sake of the agent's own flourishing, but also at the maintenance over time of the conditions in which flourishing is possible, for oneself and for others as well.

One of the best practical examples of this connection between time and virtue is in the conservation and preservation of heritage monuments. And of all Irish heritage monuments, the best example is:

> *The Hill of Tara.* Tara, in county Meath, is the ancient cultural centre of Ireland. It provides an outstanding example of an ecologically sensitive area, being close to the sea and sky, centrally located in Ireland, and having the biodiversity of most of the whole of Ireland represented in and around it. Tara was the centre of religious and political power in Ireland for approximately four thousand years. In mythological

times, the kingship of Ireland was established here by Partholan, the leader of Ireland's pseudo-historical first colonists. Some of the Old Gods of Irish mythology ruled here as kings. Saint Patrick lit his 'illegal' bonfire here to inaugurate the arrival of Christianity (circa 430 AD). Four thousand pikemen who died in the Battle of the Boyne (1690) are buried on its northern slope. Thousands of people attended a meeting called by Daniel O'Connell on 15th August 1843 to support his demand that the Act of Union with Great Britain should be repealed. Some of Ireland's most well known cultural figures, including Arthur Griffith, W.B. Yeats, and Maude Gonne, protected Tara from being excavated by the British Isrealite Association, who thought the Arc of the Covenant was buried there. And in 1916, the Declaration of the Republic was read out on Tara before it was read out at the GPO on O'Connell Street, in Dublin. The Hill of Tara is for Ireland what the Acropolis of Athens is for Greece, what the Coliseum of Rome is for Italy, and the Great Pyramid is for Egypt. It embodies the continuity of Irish history, the beauty of the Irish landscape, and the national pride of the Irish people.

The heritage monument stands at the intersection of a person's social and historical identity. It embodies the very past which informs one's present social identity and relations, being either a commemoration of certain people or events, or in the case of a landscape monument like Tara, embodying the physical remnants of the commemorated people or events. A monument embodies in art, architecture, landscape, and historical commemoration the values and shared cultural commitments that in large measure makes a community what it is. Tara might not appear as physically impressive as other Irish monuments like Newgrange, or other monuments in Europe. The hill itself is a grassy knoll rising only 500 feet above a flat plain, with a collection of earthwork circles and ancient burial mounds at its summit. Still, it affords connection and continuity between the present time and the ancient historical or semi-mythological events that decisively shaped the culture we today have inherited. To recognise something as a monument means to recognise in the art, architecture, landscape, or inaugural event, the values and cultural commitments which one both calls one's own and also shares with a community. I have visited Tara many times in the last four years, and always find myself spiritually uplifted by the palpable history in its ancient man-made features and in the extraordinary scenery that surrounds it. It is one of the great treasures of Ireland's landscape and heritage.

On this basis, it would be un-virtuous to damage, destroy, or undermine the dignity of heritage monuments like Tara, for the reason that it would represent a failure of the consistency requirement of Virtue theory, the requirement that whatever one's conception of the good, one must possess the virtues required for the maintenance of one's social and community context in which one's quest for the good is possible. To damage Tara would also be a failure of virtue because the link with the past that Tara makes possible, which is also a necessary part of the well-lived life, might be irretrievably severed. Two specific issues of this nature concern Tara. One is a tourist development plan. At the time of writing, it is not yet known what decisions have been made by the landscape engineering consultants hired to create a development plan for Tara. (The company acknowledged receiving my enquiry but did not answer any of my questions.) Residents local to Tara are concerned that the Hill will be commercialised, rather like Newgrange.[73] The other issue is the construction of a dual-carriageway toll road a short distance away, within sight of the hill. In the eyes of local residents, prominent Irish archaeologists, and thousands of activists around Ireland and the world, this new motorway will destroy the landscape character around Tara and dozens of archaeological sites along its path. In a letter of protest against this motorway signed by numerous academics from Ireland and abroad, it was claimed that:

The Hill of Tara constitutes the heart and soul of
Ireland. Its very name invokes the spirit and mystique
of our people and is instantly recognisable worldwide.
The plan approved recently by An Bord Pleanála for
the M3 motorway to dissect the Tara-Skryne valley,
Ireland's premier national monument, spells out a
massive national and international tragedy that must
be averted.[74]

Another position statement released two years later, and endorsed by
85 scholars and academics from around the world, including Dr. Pat
Wallace, director of Ireland's National Museum, said: "If the
motorway is constructed as currently planned, what does that say to
the world about the cultural sensitivity of the Government?"[75] Note
the implied Virtue language in their complaint: cultural sensitivity is
presented here like a quality of character which a society, not just an
individual, can possess, and which the government would lack if the
motorway plan went through. But despite the international protest,
and the presentation of alternatives, the government's plans remain
unchanged.

The debate about the M3 motorway concerns not only
whether it should go through, but also concerns what Tara essentially
is. Land planners and developers are satisfied that Tara is just the
area scheduled as a national monument, which is about 100 acres.
The opposition regard the whole landscape context surrounding the
hill itself to be part of Tara. Certainly the latter opinion is supported
by the translation of the name: *Teamhair*, its original Irish name,
means 'spectacle' or 'wide view', since it affords an impressive view
over the landscape of Ireland. As suggested by Dáithí Ó h-Ógáin,
professor of folklore at UCD, that impressive view may very well
have been the reason the hill was selected as the seat of Ireland's
mythological and historical high kings.[76] What matters in the
philosophical debate is that the choice to build or not build the
motorway according to the present plan may be indicative of the
value that is placed on the aesthetic experiences and historical
continuities which Tara makes possible. The choice may also be

precedent-setting for similar monuments in other parts of the country. The quality of a visit to Tara, the 'spectacle' of the landscape for which it was named, will certainly be very much less than it is now if the motorway is built where it is planned to go. The public debate is also about whether the hoped-for economic benefits of the new motorway will be greater or lesser than the heritage and landscape value of Tara and its surrounding area. An alternative plan proposed by the activist group, in which the new motorway runs on the other side of the nearby Skryne Hill, would allow the motorway's economic benefits to be realised without the potential loss to Tara.

What we have here, it must be noted, is an argument for why a Virtuous person would find it morally excellent to contribute to conservation projects through the course of his life. Indeed we have a way of using Virtue theory to say what Singer said about 'irretrievable loss'. The motorway planned for Tara may well cause an irretrievable loss of heritage continuity, aesthetic experience, and landscape qualities. However, this is not by itself an argument for why the Virtuous person would prefer the Non-Identity choice of Conservation over Depletion. If the generation affected by the Non-Identity Choice between Conservation and Depletion is immediately subsequent to the agent's own, then it may seem fairly clear that the agent would choose Conservation. To do so would be an example of 'wishing well' to one's progeny, friends, and the *polis* of which one is a member. But what of far distant future generations? The further distant and more anonymous a future person becomes, the less of an issue their flourishing or non-flourishing becomes for the Virtuous agent in the present. A Virtuous person might have a rational wish that his progeny will prosper. As we have seen, children were included in Aristotle's list of external goods. That wish may be justified if he acts today in ways that prepare for them a world fit for flourishing, or at least does not act in ways that contribute to the degradation of the world. This claim was suggested by Sandler, although only in a preliminary way.[77] But it has not been shown how, if at all, a Virtuous person's interest in the future beyond his own death extends much further than the nearest few generations of descendants. Insofar as the future appears to the Virtuous person as a

347

function of the present, the actual future disappears. Virtue theory is unable to claim that the non-flourishing of future people is an obstacle to the present person's flourishing. But it does not follow from this, as Sandler claimed, that the Virtuous person would therefore find it Virtuous to do things which contribute to a general decline in environmental quality. There is yet one more dimension of the temporally-inscribed, future directed action which remains to be explored.

§ 5. The Gift of the Future

Insofar as the future appears to the virtuous person as a function of the "now", the actual or real future itself disappears. What remains, however, is the future to which a person's actions are driving at any present moment. The Non-Identity Choice of Conservation versus Depletion draws out this special dimension of Virtue theory particularly sharply. What makes Non-Identity Choices so philosophically interesting and difficult is precisely that they are choices with definitive effects upon the future, especially for the people who will live in the future. For every time that a Virtuous person is confronted with a Non-Identity choice, he is also confronted with a potential future that the choice is driving at. The Non-Identity Choices of Conservation and Depletion draw out the present-moment orientation of the Virtuous person's attitude towards the future because Non-Identity choices create different futures: the options are between two or more non-identical futures. Knowing that the identities, numbers, and the quality of life is not what directs a Virtuous person's decisions, and that the actual future is not a moral issue for him, it would not occur to him to pose the Non-Identity Problem in the form of an enquiry into which world is better for its inhabitants. He would pose the question in the form of an enquiry into which future it is better for him to drive at with his present actions.

There is one passage in Aristotle's text that can be interpreted as expressing a principle that can help answer this question. It concerns the claim that aiming for immortality is a part of *eudaimonia*:

> Nor ought we to obey those who enjoin that a man
> should have man's thoughts, and a mortal the
> thoughts of mortality, but we ought so far as possible
> to achieve immortality, and do all that man may to
> live in accordance with the highest thing in him; for
> though this be small in bulk, in power and in value it
> far surpasses all the rest. (*NE*, 1177b26)

The kind of immortality which Aristotle has in mind here is not unending embodied life, but is the kind that can be obtained by doing things which act upon the divine element within human nature, which in his view is the capacity for theoretical reason. The life in accord with 'the highest thing in him' enables him to connect with, participate in, and identify himself with the divine thought-thinking-itself, the theoretical reason contemplating that which is necessary, eternal, and unchanging.[78] This immortality has to do with participating in the timeless and eternal things which theoretical reason contemplates. These things are ideas, and so they are not temporally-bound, not located in any particular past, present, or future.[79] They are also immaterial; the activity of contemplating them produces no material effect, for which reason Aristotle claimed it is the most completely self-sufficient, most perfect and fulfilling kind of activity.[80] If that is the kind of immortality Aristotle has in mind, it has nothing to do with the 'actual' future or 'real' future, the future which will in fact come to be, and which may or may not be what we expect it to be. But it can be translated to the practical plane.

There is another kind of immortality which a Virtuous person may find it fitting and noble (*kalon*) to strive for: the 'legacy'. It may be virtuous to do something today which will out-last one's own life-span, to leave something for the people of the future, and in that respect gain a kind of immortality, or at least gain an extension of one's presence into the future beyond the limit of one's embodied life. People who know that they are about to die sometimes prepare a gift for those who survive them: a legally notarised "Last Will and Testament" is an example of this, in which one's possessions are re-distributed among one's friends and relations. People with terminal diseases, life-threatening injuries, or people about to attempt suicide usually leave letters for their friends and family to find and read, and collect their most treasured possessions together in one place as if assembling them into a shrine. Prisoners on "death row", who we do not normally regard as models of moral excellence, sometimes spend their final hours cleaning up their cells, washing and folding their clothes, and talking with family members or with religious councillors to make peace with them, with themselves, or with their God, before facing death. In the ancient world, Herodotus wrote that the Spartan soldiers at Thermopylae combed their hair before entering battle; thus they faced possible death with a certain finesse and elegance.[81] 'Last acts' like these are *kalon*, "fitting", for the people in such circumstances. Most people leave as a legacy nothing more than the story of their lives, but let us not underestimate the value and importance of that legacy. For it is precisely the legacy of one generation's stories which is received by the subsequent generation as the heritage with which they understand their present relationships to each other. It may also be the legacy of the story of one's life which, as Aristotle said, is affected by the fortunes of one's descendants.[82] The desire to leave a legacy obtains on a social level as well. There are certain social goods which are constructed in order to provide intergenerational continuity, and to secure the preservation of certain social values into the future. As T'Hooft pointed out, "large libraries or monuments are not built in order to be torn down the next day". (*JFGE*, pg. 128)

It is worth noting that the fitting-ness of last acts has nothing to do with consequences. Last acts are future-directed acts in which the agent himself is mostly untouched by the consequences of his own act. The bad consequences for failure, if any exist, are not normally "worse than death", and there would be little or no incentive for another agent to punish him for failure. The rewards or honours which might normally benefit the agent in return also would not obtain, as they could not continue to benefit the agent after death. We have already seen how self-sacrificing actions remain Virtuous even if the agent dies in the act, and so cannot participate in any material benefits produced by his action. With the action's benefit to himself, as a motivation for performing the action, stripped away, the agent is motivated by his own sense of self-worth (here I am presupposing Aristotle's claim that life is desirable to the Virtuous person). 'Last acts' constitute a resolution or completion of a well-lived life, allowing someone to maintain a sense of dignity and pride even to the end. The consequences for others may not be entirely irrelevant: as described earlier, Aristotle claimed that it is noble to benefit others even if one faces death in doing so. But it is not the benefit to others which, primarily, makes the act noble. There is one sense in which the act benefits others and is noble therefore; it sets a precedent, it shows others what it looks like to excel as a human being. But for the most part, it is the maintenance of the virtues that sustained one's practice of *eudaimonia* throughout one's life, even as one departs it, that makes the act noble.

I claim that if it is noble to aim towards a certain future, as when one aims for continuous and ongoing ends like environmental conservation or even *eudaimonia* itself, then it remains noble to aim for that future *even if the agent personally will never share in it.* Such acts I shall call the agent's legacy. To aim to leave such a legacy is how the aim for immortality, which for Aristotle is an activity of theoretical reason, may be translated onto the practical plane. Since what matters to a Virtuous person is the quality of his character, a Virtuous person will desire to leave a legacy if he regards his life as having been worthwhile and noble enough to merit being preserved into the future. Just as he is able to have friends because he believes himself worthy of having them, he prepares a legacy for the future, however small, because he believes himself worthy of being remembered and honoured by others through the legacy left for them. When one's future-directed choices have definitive effects on what future comes to be, as happens when one makes Non-Identity choices, one is in effect giving a gift. It is a selfless gift because one cannot partake in it, and yet it is a gift only someone possessing the noble self-love of the great soul could give. I shall call the legacy that is nobly given, which definitively brings into being a future which may be non-identical to the future brought into being by another choice, and in which the agent himself cannot partake, 'the gift of the future'.

A 'gift' is something that one person gives to another, or something done for the benefit or pleasure of another. It is an act of kindness, friendship, charity, and well-meaning. Gifts are not reciprocal exchanges, and so the giver of a gift does not normally expect anything in return, except perhaps the recipient's gratitude (and some gift-givers do not want even that). One philosophical problem that arises here is that we do not normally regard 'the future' as the sort of thing that can be given as a gift. The future is immaterial: it is precisely what does not (yet) exist, even if there are hints or trends in the present that lead to it, and so cannot be a possession that someone could offer to others. In the case of Non-Identity Choices, it is not just the decision of the land planner, or energy planner, or policy-maker that causes a particular future to manifest. It is also created by the choices of the hundreds or thousands of unrelated others. The future is always brought into being by many people and many causes, some made together, some made separately. What then can it mean to call this a Non-Identity future a 'gift'?

I believe it is appropriate to use the word 'gift' in this context for this reason. The future circumstance about which we are concerned is a product of a person's choices and actions. The hundreds or thousands of others who contribute to the creation of that Non-Identity future are put into the position of making the choices they made due to that first person's original Non-Identity choice, as stipulated by Parfit's case. That person, it may be presumed, planned for the future, and did things which will create the future he wants. That which is his to 'give' are the orders, the money or material resources, the professional expertise, or the like, which is ultimately responsible for the future situation that comes into being. Admittedly this may seem to bend the notion of 'giving' somewhat. But I believe it is not wildly implausible; certainly, each person 'possesses' his or her choices, and these choices can be 'given' to others in the form of the material products and consequences they create or make possible.

A second question about the notion of 'the gift' is whether the Virtuous Person as Aristotle describes him is capable of giving such a gift. Aristotle's portrait of the Great Soul appears like an extraordinarily egotistical man, by our standards. He is not exactly selfish, but he is certainly not humble nor modest, and not normally inclined to be self-sacrificing except in special circumstances. Aristotle even claims that he is "justified in despising other people" (*NE*, 1124b4). The great-souled person prefers to be the giver of gifts rather than the receiver, as already mentioned; but he has this preference because in giving gifts he expects to receive honour in return. If he is the beneficiary of some gift, he will soon give something else in return that is greater, in order to put the giver of the first gift in his debt.[83] The quality of desiring honour above all things, and of being worthy of the highest honours, characterizes the great-souled man above all other qualities: for honour is "most coveted by men of high station, and is the prize awarded for the noblest deeds". (*NE* 1123b17) If he gives things to others in order to be rewarded with honour, then it is questionable whether they really are 'gifts' in the proper sense of the word.

This is a serious and substantial criticism, similar to the objection raised earlier that in benefiting others the Virtuous person is really aiming only for his own flourishing. Much of what was said there also applies here. Some virtues cannot be practiced without benefiting others in the course of practicing them, and the pursuit of *eudaimonia* is not an exercise in egotistical self-promotion. I believe this criticism rests on a narrow interpretation of the great souled man's desire for honour. Indubitably, Aristotle affirms that the great soul is concerned with honour above all else: "Honour and dishonour then are the objects with which the great-souled man is especially concerned." (*NE* 1124a6). But in the Aristotelian scheme of values, honour counts as an *external* good: it is a reward bestowed upon someone for performing noble deeds. Of all external goods it is the highest; but it is still an external good nonetheless. The great souled man, however, is concerned with the noble deeds themselves more than with the external rewards which they earn, however high they may be. As Aristotle says:

> The great souled man, then, as has been said, is especially concerned with honour; but he will also observe due measure in respect to wealth, power, and good and bad fortune in general, as they may befall him; he will not rejoice overmuch in prosperity, nor grieve overmuch at adversity. For he does not care much even about honour, which is the greatest of external goods… he therefore to whom even honour is a small thing will be indifferent to other things as well. (*NE* 1124a14)

The point of the Virtuous Person's concern with honour is that of all the external goods it is the best and the most desirable; but it is still an external good, and not the same as virtue itself. Furthermore, there are occasions when the great souled person will benefit others without an interest in being rewarded with honour, for instance, when benefiting a friend. He will often prefer to be the cause of his friend's performance of a noble action, in which case the friend receives the honour instead of him. The Virtuous Person receives "moral nobility" (*kalon*) for his part (*NE* 1169b1) which is the internal good of simply knowing that one acted well and rightly in the circumstances. So concerned with moral nobility is the Virtuous person that he would prefer to give up his own life, if preserving it might mean forgoing moral nobility. As already seen, the Virtuous person values his life but finds that it is "not worth having at every price" (*NE* 1124b5) and so is prepared to act nobly even if his own death is a consequence of the act. Clearly, then, the great souled man can be a gift-giver without gaining more in return for himself than was given to others. Finally, in the discussion of prudence, Aristotle asserts that the right reason for an action is that the action is in pursuit for what is good for human beings in general—not just what is good for oneself alone. "Men like Pericles are deemed prudent," he says, "because they possess a faculty for discerning what things are good for themselves *and for mankind*." (*NE*, 1140b10; emphasis added). It follows that the Virtuous Person is abundantly capable of selfless giving, and that prudence sometimes seems to demand it.

As most of the consequences of Non-Identity choices appear in the future (as stipulated), possibly well after the person's death, the honour earned for such an act may go to the virtuous person's posthumous legacy, not to the person himself in his lifetime. For others may not learn of his action, or of his role in the coming-about of events, until long after his death. But this is not an obstacle to him, nor a reason to shirk from taking action. Guided by prudence to find what is good for all humankind and not just for himself alone, he makes his choice. This gives us good cause to claim that the giving of a future can be largely selfless, and intended for the benefit of others with little or no thought of an outstanding reward in return.

It should not be hard to see how this principle translates into practical environmental problems. Land planning serves as an excellent example:

> *Land Planning and Forest Cover.* A lecturer at the Dublin Institute of Technology lamented that a change in the way rural land is owned and controlled is causing forests to re-cover the land: "For the first time since the late stone age the tree canopy will close out the sun and the sky from the ancient fields and meadows."[84] Ireland already has the smallest forest cover in Europe as a percentage of its territory. According to a 1997 Working Document of the European Parliament, only 5% of Ireland's territory is forest. (Contrary to this figure, the Irish Times reported in 1999 that less than 1% of Ireland is forest.[85]) Other countries with less total land than Ireland have more forest cover: Austria has 39%, for instance. The European average is 27.7%. [86]

When we build houses, roads, other infrastructure, or when we plant forests or clear forests away, we re-shape the land in more or less permanent ways. The growing forest cover, which is changing the "ancient fields and meadows" of Ireland, changes the landscape, in effect creating a new landscape, which is then passed on to the people of the future as the gift we effectively give to them. If Ireland's forest cover were to increase up to the European average, it would change the landscape, and this may indeed result in a loss of continuity with the recent past. Yet this may be more than compensated for by the benefits of food, shelter, building materials, fuel, atmospheric cleansing, recreational opportunity, and aesthetic satisfaction, which forests provide. And the loss of forests may be similarly permanent. Another land planning example which has a similar effect on the future is:

> *"One-off" Housing.* In county Kerry, hundreds of "Section 140" (of the Local Government Act, 2001) motions in the county council required the county manager to grant planning permission for "one-off" housing developments in the county, all of which were refused or likely to be refused by planners. On 19th April 2004, sixty of these motions were passed in a single session.[87] Planners had to cancel two weeks of public meetings to deal with them, with the result that many of the proposals did not go through the regular planning process at all.[88] County planners, including the county manager, complained that these development decisions would disrupt traffic flows, ecology, and heritage. An academic group for the promotion of heritage in Ireland described this process as "corrupt and careless".[89]

This pattern of land planning can re-shape the appearance of the landscape irreversibly, or nearly irreversibly, more so than changing the forests and fields, with the effective result that a different landscape is created in the future than that which would have been created otherwise. Kerry County Council's endorsement of hundreds of one-off planning applications thus counts as a legacy— and possibly also as a gift of the future, depending on one's judgement of the virtuousness of the gift.

How shall we decide which of these ways of changing the landscape we should prefer? Which is the better legacy for us to leave as a gift to the people of the future? In terms of the Non-Identity problem, our theoretical test case, which of two or more non-identical futures should we strive for? The claim here is that if it is noble to aim for a certain future, it remains noble to aim for it even if one cannot partake in it. We have seen this already in the discussion of *phronesis* and the rational wish. To a Virtuous person, it is the aim towards a certain future, undertaken in the present, which matters, and not the manifestation of that future. The future that matters to a Virtuous person is not the one he can predict, but the one he can wish for. It is the means of attaining a certain future which can be an object for *phronesis*, practical reason; what will in fact transpire when that wished-for future arrives (or does not arrive) may be subject to other occurrences, accidents, and influences which are beyond our abilities to predict or control. What kind of future is it noble to aim for? If the activities involved in aiming towards a certain future are temporally continuous, and which tend to call upon, develop, and bring out the agent's best qualities of character, then it is noble to aim for it. In this way *eudaimonia* becomes configured as a temporally continuous end. For it is the activity in itself, of striving for such a future, which matters to the Virtuous person. Again, the case of the continuity of human society is an outstanding practical example. It remains noble to aim for the continuity of the *polis* even for an agent who, because he is mortal, will not partake in its continuity. Aristotle's discussion of pleasure provides the foundation of this point: for the base or un-Virtuous pleasures are those which result from the agent's actions, while the noble and Virtuous pleasures are those which come from performing virtuous acts in themselves.

I claim *the virtuous person should choose the future which, in the act of striving for it, brings out his best and most noble qualities.*

Someone makes a gift of the future by partaking in temporally-continuous actions whose completion is to be found in a future in which the agent himself cannot partake. Such an act may or may not be a self-sacrificing action of the kind described earlier. A gift of the future is a virtuous gift if partaking in the actions which aim for that future tend to require, produce, develop, or otherwise demand the manifestation of virtuous human qualities. I do not claim that it is a *necessary* part of someone's flourishing to make a gift of the future, or that a Virtuous person's reasoning should always be directed towards the future in this way. I claim only that this principle is the way a Virtuous person understands his relationship to the future, and the means by which he may resolve future-directed moral dilemmas like Non-Identity choices, if and when they arise. The actual production of the aimed-at future may well depend on other unpredictable factors such as the actions of other people, the weather, and so on; and so it falls outside the range of the agent's own power, and thus outside the range of *phronesis*. The agent is responsible only for his own actions. I claim only that this is the reasoning which should guide a Virtuous person's thinking when a moral dilemma appears in his relationship to the future. Non-Identity choices are such situations. The moral dilemma which appears in such situations is the question of which future is it best to aim for. Which future will bring out the best in me by my strivings toward it? By stipulation, a person in the position of making a Non-Identity choice knows that he is required to choose among two or more non-identical futures, and that whichever future is chosen, he will not partake in it and neither will his nearest descendants. Between Parfit's cases of Conservation and Depletion, which future is it virtuous to give as a gift to future generations?

I claim that the Virtuous person would choose Conservation.

The Non-Identity choice of Conservation expresses several virtues. One is the virtue of 'temperance', in that it strives to take from the environment only what is necessary for the temporally-continuous maintenance of the agent and his social body, and to take it in a sustainable, non-excessive way, to ensure the continuity of the social body in a condition that remains fit for flourishing. It is also a choice which passes the test of Aristotle's Doctrine of the Mean: the Virtuous man in his economic affairs prefers to be liberal and magnificent, but "can discern what is suitable", and prefers to exercise "good taste" rather than be as liberal as possible (*NE* 1122a35). The Virtuous person does not necessarily seek to maximise his wealth and power. Rather, he seeks the optimal amount, which I have defined as the principle of parity, the balance between what he aims for as a Virtuous agent and what actions the world in which he lives will support. This principle of parity is the application of the Doctrine of the Mean which answers the question of just how much material wealth, how many external goods, the Virtuous person needs to flourish. It would not be necessary for him to demand the short-term bonanza of material wealth and resources which the choice of Depletion would give him (as Parfit stipulated the case). Additionally, the Non-Identity choice of Conservation is Virtuous since it can be part of the rational wish that the social body of which one is a member should outlast one's life. To aim for the continuity of the *polis* is a future-directed, continuous and ongoing act, much like environmental conservation and *eudaimonia* themselves. To aim for its continuation even beyond one's own lifetime constitutes a valid 'gift of the future', and undoubtedly a possible part of a Virtuous person's *eudaimonia* in his present time and place. The choice that aims towards a future world in which flourishing is supported is an excellent legacy for a great-souled person, possessing morally appropriate sense of self-love, to create with his choices as a gift of the future. The choice which strives toward it tends to bring out of the agent his sense of Virtuous self-love: in holding himself in high esteem, worthy of transmitting his virtues into the future, he aims to create or sustain the conditions of the world in which his kind of *eudaimonia* is possible and supported.

What about Depletion? If the agent making the Non-Identity choice understood Parfit's claim that the alternative choice of Depletion would produce the greatest total happiness, the Virtuous person would counter that it is not the greatest utility which matters. If the agent understood the claim that Depletion would 'harm no-one', because it would also create a future population for whom the

359

alternative is non-existence, he may nevertheless find it un-Virtuous to choose it. An act which harms no-one may still be a manifestation of a vice. A Virtuous person would find that to choose Depletion is to manifest *pleonexia* if Depletion is representative of a desire to possess more, rather than less, of the world's resources, than is our fair share.

According to Parfit's description of the Depletion case, a generation which chooses Depletion continues to use the world's resources without restraint, and therefore enjoys a higher quality of life, even if only a slightly higher quality of life.[90] This stipulation presupposes a direct linear relationship between quality of life and bountifulness of material wealth, which Virtue theory calls into question. A Virtuous person, as seen, finds that it is not his possessions and the bounty of his society's wealth which makes him flourish. A Virtuous person would not choose Depletion because the choice which aims towards the Depletion future brings out of the agent a propensity for *pleonexia*. Depletion displays an un-virtuous interest in material wealth by taking from the environment more material resources than may be necessary for the flourishing of the members of his social body, and for his own flourishing. Someone who prefers Depletion is like the 'vulgar' man who exceeds the mean in economic affairs by spending more than what is right.[91] Depletion also displays an un-virtuous contempt for other people and the world in which one is grounded by leaving as a legacy for future generations a world in which the very flourishing one enjoyed in one's own life is hard to attain, or even impossible. If he is satisfied or undisturbed by the thought that he is leaving a legacy of depletion, or if he thinks that character traits like excess and vulgarity are worthy of being transmitted into the future, then he is not, in the Aristotelian view, a Virtuous man.

This is my final statement concerning the Non-Identity Problem and the Repugnant Conclusion in its application to environmental resource conservation and depletion. Parfit claimed that the theory which would solve the Non-Identity Problem, which in anticipation of its invention he called "Theory X", would be a theory of beneficence. In its own, non-utilitarian way, the Virtue theory I have here proposed *is* a theory of beneficence. It gives us reasons to benefit others. I will not, however, claim that Virtue theory is "Theory X", because in other respects what I have outlined here does not fulfil Parfit's expectations. For instance, I have said nothing about the Mere Addition Paradox. It is also not, strictly speaking, a theory of *person-affecting* beneficence. It is a theory of *Virtuous* beneficence. But it should not be an objection to the theory that the rationale for benefiting others is grounded in the moral agent's character and his intertwined relationship with the community and the environment, rather than on a principle of maximising total or average utility, as Parfit expected. The emphasis on the moral agent's character has enabled us to overcome the puzzles which, for Utilitarianism, are inherently insurmountable. For Virtue theory, maximising utility is not what matters, and therefore an action can be right even if it produces the lesser utility, wrong if it produces the greater utility, and wrong even if it harms no one and infringes no one's rights. No strict Utilitarian could make such a claim: one who did so would in effect be abandoning his Utilitarianism. Virtue Theory explains what is repugnant about choosing the Repugnant Conclusion by claiming that to choose it is to display the vice of *pleonexia*. This is an instance of *pleonexia* because such a person essentially prioritises the wealth and well-being of his own generation above that of the people living in the intrinsically repugnant future situation his choice will create. The Virtuous person, by contrast, confronted with a decisive future-affecting choice like this one, does not ask himself which option would result in the greatest benefit to himself and his own generation. He asks himself which option it is Virtuous for him to choose. If he finds that one choice is Virtuous, but that he personally will not be able to fully share in its benefits, because its realisation extends beyond the finite span of his life, that is not a reason for him to reject it. He chooses the option which brings out of him his best qualities. Excellence of character becomes his gift of the future.

[1] The National Trust (UK), <u>Tunes Plateau Offshore Wind Farm Proposal</u> Position Statement, February 2003.

[2] Tom Shiel, "Board rejects plans for Mayo wind farm" *The Irish times* 9 July 2004, pg. 2.

[3] Paula Toynbee, "Countryside Alliance", *The Guardian* 13 August 2004.

[4] Lorna Siggins, "€70m Galway Bay treatment plant opens" *The Irish Times* 7 May 2004, pg. 2.

[5] "The moral law is holy (inflexible) and demands holiness of morals, although all the moral perfection that a human being can attain is still only virtue, that is, a disposition conformed with law *from respect* for law…" Kant, <u>Critique of Practical Reason</u> 5:128, pg. 107.

[6] Wallace, <u>Virtues and Vices</u>, pg. 9.

[7] Wallace, *ibid*, pp. 10-1.

[8] Wallace, *ibid*, pg. 127.

[9] For example, Robert Louden wrote: "It has often been said that for virtue ethics the central question is not 'What ought I to *do*?' but rather 'What sort of person ought I to *be?*'. However, people have always expected ethical theory to tell them something about what they ought to do, and it seems to me that virtue ethics is structurally unable to say much of anything about this issue." Robert Louden, "On Some Vices of Virtue Ethics", cited in Crisp & Slote, <u>Virtue Ethics</u> pg. 205. Emphasis his.

[10] Louden, *ibid*, pg. 210.

[11] "I should judge that Hume and our present-day ethicists had done a considerable service by showing that no content could be found in the notion 'morally ought', if it were not that the latter philosophers try to find an alternative (very fishy) content and to retain the psychological force of the term. It would be most reasonable to drop it. It has no reasonable sense outside a law conception of ethics; they are not going to maintain such a conception; and you can do ethics without it, as is shown by the example of Aristotle. It would be a great improvement if, instead of 'morally wrong', one always named a genus such as 'untruthful', 'unchaste', 'unjust'. We should no longer ask whether doing something was 'wrong', passing directly from some description of an action to this notion; we should ask whether, e.g., it was unjust; and the answer would sometimes be clear at once." Anscombe, "Modern Moral Philosophy", in Crisp and Slote, eds. <u>Virtue Ethics</u> pg. 33-4.

[12] Hursthouse, <u>On Virtue Ethics</u>, pg. 36.

[13]   MacIntyre, <u>Dependant Rational Animals</u>, pg. 112.

[14]   Also, according to MacIntyre himself, critics of <u>After Virtue</u> interpreted him as defending a strict separation of the virtues from moral laws. For these critics he has written <u>Whose Justice? Which Rationality?</u>. That latter work, then, may be read as a sustained enquiry into the relation between the virtues and the various conceptions of justice and rationality which have obtained in the history of ideas.

[15]   The point concerning the relation of a virtuous person to her community is raised in several places in <u>After Virtue</u>. In reference to the relation of virtue to moral rules, MacIntyre says "An offence against the laws (of the community) destroys those relationships which make common pursuit of the good possible; defective character, while it may also render someone more liable to commit offences, makes one unable to contribute to the achievement of that good without which the community's common life has no point." (*AV* pg. 152). In general, he claims that "it is always as part of an ordered community that I have to seek the human good." (*AV* pg. 173).

[16]   "Aristotle takes that part of morality which is obedience to rules to be obedience to laws enacted by the city-state—if and when the city-state enacts as it ought... What he says about the law is very brief, although he does insist that there are natural and universal laws as well as conventional and local rules of justice. It seems likely that he means to insist that natural and universal justice absolutely prohibits certain types of act; but what penalties are assigned to which offence may vary from city to city. Nonetheless what he says on this topic is so brief as to be cryptic." (*AV*, pg. 150).

[17]   Kant, "The ultimate end of nature as a teleological system" part II, §22 (83) of *The Critique of Judgement*, pg.96, emphasis his.

[18]   John McDowell, "Virtue and Reason" in Crisp and Slote, eds. <u>Virtue Ethics</u> pg. 141.

[19]   Rosalind Hursthouse, "Virtue Theory and Abortion", pg. 235

[20]   Hursthouse, <u>On Virtue Ethics</u>, pg. 28. The word 'iff' is not a typo—it appears to designate the logical function 'if and only if'.

[21]   These and other advantages of Hursthouse's theory were described by Robert Johnson, "Virtue and Right", pp. 816.

[22]   Christine Swanton, "A Virtue Ethical Account of Right Action", pg. 34.

23 In Swanton's own words, "Actual human agents, no matter how virtuous and wise, are not omniscient. As a result, an important end of virtue may be something about which there is large scale ignorance and for which no blame can be attached to individuals, or even cultures. To illustrate the point I am making, consider the relatively newly discovered virtue, that of environmental friendliness... controversy rages about whether or not environmental friendliness requires various drastic measures to reduce a perceived threat—for example, global warming. The Aristotlelian virtuous agent possesses phronesis, but phronesis, with its connotations of fine sensibilities and discriminatory powers, is impotent in the face of massive ignorance of the entire human species." Swanton, *ibid*, pg. 35. I recognise the principle she has in mind here, but find that her example of global warming is a poor choice. For we do have enough information to know what global warming is, why humanity is responsible for it, and what can be done to prevent its continuance—what we lack is political will, not information.

24 Robert Johnson, "Virtue and Right" pg. 814.

25 The discussion of the desirability of life can be found in the *NE*, 1170b4; the discussion of the great soul can be found in the *NE* starting at 4.iii.1, 1123b1 (pg. 93-8)

26 Those five different conceptions of the virtues are those from ancient heroic Greece, from Aristotle's Athens, from Augustine's Christianity, from the novels of Jane Austin and from the writings of Benjamin Franklin. MacIntyre then discusses at length what, if anything, they may all have in common. ("The Nature of the Virtues" *AV* pp. 181-203)

27 Hursthouse, On Virtue Ethics, pg. 29. This forms the second premise in her general theory of Virtuously right action.

28 "Act utilitarianism must specify what are to count as the best consequences, and deontology what is to count as a correct moral rule, producing a second premise, before any guidance is given... so far, the three are in the same position". Therefore, "why not direct similar scorn at the first premises of act utilitarianism and deontology...?" Hursthouse, On Virtue Ethics, pg. 28.

29 Robert Johnson, "Virtue and Right" pg. 814.

30 Robert Johnson, "Virtue and Right" pg. 818.

31 Johnson, *ibid*, pg. 817-821.

32 The version of Hurstouse's principle in my copy of the 1999 edition of On Virtue Ethics does *not* have the word 'completely' in it. It is as I quoted it earlier. Johnson quotes a 2000 edition in which the principle does include the word 'completely'. I assume that a referencing error has taken place somewhere. I shall use Hursthouse's principle as it appears in the 1999 edition, without the word 'completely'.

33 Hursthouse, On Virtue Ethics, pg. 35.

[34] MacIntyre, Dependent Rational Animals pg. 96.

[35] "It follows that for those who have not yet been educated into the virtues the life of the virtues will necessarily seem to lack rational justification; the rational justification of the life of virtue within the community of the *polis* is available only to those who already participate more or less fully in that life." MacIntyre, Whose Justice? Which Rationality? Pg. 110. This may seem a convenient excuse for not providing a rationale for becoming virtuous which a non-virtuous person would accept.

[36] Slote, "Agent Based Virtue Ethics" in Crisp and Slote, eds. Virtue Ethics, pp. 239-262.

[37] Christine Swanton, "A Virtue Ethical Account of Right Action", pg. 34.

[38] Earth Summit Ireland, Telling It Like It Is: 10 years of unsustainable development in Ireland, pg. 17.

[39] Anscombe, "Modern Moral Philosophy", in Crisp and Slote, eds. Virtue Ethics, pg. 37.

[40] Anscombe, *ibid,* pg. 42.

[41] Greg Pence, "Virtue Theory" in Peter Singer, ed. Companion to Ethics, pg. 250.

[42] C.f. the discussion of pleasure in Book 7 of the *Nicomachean Ethics*.

[43] The vice of bestial character ("bestiality" in the translation I consulted) is discussed in the *NE* at 1148b18, and in contrast with its corresponding vice of morbidity at 1149a12.

[44] MacIntyre also considered a similar objection. In the first stage of his argument, he defined the virtues in terms of their relation to practices, and then considered the possibility that some practices are evil (*AV*, pp. 199-202). My reply to this problem here is similar to his own. It may also be useful to consult MacIntyre's discussion of Nietzsche and the 'great man' who, in 'transcending' morality, cuts himself off from any possibility for true friendship and even from the possibility of discovering any value outside himself. (*AV*, pp. 256-9).

[45] "the enjoyment of the activity and the enjoyment of achievement are not the ends at which the agent aims, but the enjoyment supervenes upon the successful activity in such a way that the activity achieved and the activity enjoyed are one and the same state. Hence to aim at the one is to aim at the other; and hence also it is easy to confuse the pursuit of excellence with the pursuit of enjoyment *in this specific sense*. This particular confusion is harmless enough; what is not harmless is the confusion of enjoyment *in this specific sense* with other forms of pleasure." (*AV* pg. 197).

[46] MacIntyre considers the possibility that it was 'something like' this distinction that J.S. Mill was driving at in his distinction between higher and lower pleasures. The above-quoted passage continues, explaining this point about Mill: "…it is plausible and in no way patronising to suppose that something like this is the distinction which he was trying to make in *Utilitarianism* when he distinguished between 'higher' and 'lower' pleasures. At the most we can say 'something like this', for J.S. Mill's upbringing had given him a limited view of human life and powers, had unfitted him, for example, for appreciating games just because of the way it had fitted him for appreciating philosophy. Nonetheless the notion that the pursuit of excellence in a way that extends human powers is at the heart of human life is instantly recognisable as at home in not only J.S. Mill's political and social thought, but also in his and Mrs. Taylor's life." (*AV* pg. 199.)

[47] "Then we'll have to seize some of our neighbours' land if we're to have enough pasture and ploughland. And won't our neighbours want to seize part of ours as well, if they too have surrendered themselves to the endless acquisition of money and have overstepped the limit of their necessities?" Plato, The Republic, 373d, pg. 48.

[48] "Wealth does not bring about excellence, but excellence brings about wealth and all other public and private blessings for men." Plato, The Apology 30b.

[49] H. Rolston III, "Fishes in the desert: Paradox and Responsibility", in W.L. Minckley and James E. Deacon, eds. Battle Against Extinction, pp. 99-100. This objection is also raised by Geoffrey Frasz, "Environmental Virtue Ethics: A New Direction for Environmental Ethics" pp. 259-274.

[50] "Friendship being divided into these species, inferior people will make friends for pleasure or for use, if they are alike in that respect, while good men will be friends for each other's own sake, since they are alike in being good". (*NE*, 1157a34)

[51] J. O. Urmson, Aristotle's Ethics, pg. 114. We may question whether the Virtuous person's care for his friend really is 'disinterested'. A virtuous person is genuinely interested in the well being of his friends. I think, however, that by 'disinterested' he means that the act of benefiting the friend is genuinely for the sake of the friend, rather than for the sake of being rewarded for the act by anything more than the satisfaction of having done it.

[52] Urmson, *Ibid,* pg. 115.

[53] *Rhetoric* 136a33, *Topics* 145a22; as cited in Urmson, *ibid*, pg. 115.

[54] "The courageous man, therefore, in the proper sense of the term, will be he who fearlessly confronts a noble death, or some sudden peril that threatens death." (*NE*, 1115b5)

[55] Plato, The Apology, 40a-c.

[56] Hobbes' own words are in reference to a 'law of nature' to the effect that "at the entrance into conditions of peace, no man require to reserve to himself any right, which he is not content should be reserved to every one of the rest... the observers of this law are those we call *modest*, and the breakers *arrogant* men. The Greeks call the violation of this law *pleonexia*, that is, a desire of more than their share." Hobbes, Leviathan ch. 15, pg. 102.

[57] MacIntyre, Whose Justice? Which Rationality? pg. 111-2.

[58] MacIntyre, Whose Justice? Which Rationality? pg. 112.

[59] Smith's own words are: "Every individual is continually exerting himself to find out the most advantageous employment for whatever capital he can command. It is his own advantage, indeed, and not that of society, which he has in view. But the study of his own advantage naturally, or rather necessarily leads him to prefer that employment which is most advantageous to society... He generally, indeed, neither intends to promote the public interest, nor knows how much he is promoting it... [But] by directing that industry in such a manner as its produce may be of the greatest value, he intends only his own gain, and in this, as in many other cases, led by an invisible hand to promote an end which was no part of his intention." Smith, The Wealth of Nations, pp. 351-2.

[60] For a discussion of the principle of self-interest as standard of rationality and a guiding principle of modern economics, see John McMurtry, Unequal Freedoms, pp. 46-53.

[61] MacIntyre, Whose Justice? Which Rationality? Pg. 112.

[62] Wensveen, Dirty Virtues, pg. 233, emphasis hers.

[63] "A person's moral education takes less than a human lifetime, but an unhealthy and unsustainable ecosystem can supply those essentials and the requisite opportunities for several human lifetimes before it becomes so sickened that it can no longer produce them." Sandler, "The External Goods Approach", pg. 287.

[64] Sandler, "The External Goods Approach", pg. 289, emphasis his.

[65] *NE,* translator's note 63, pg. 29.

[66] On MacIntyre's definition, a practice is: "any coherent and complex form of socially established co-operative human activity through which goods internal to that form of activity are realised in the course of trying to achieve those standards of excellence which are appropriate to, and partially definitive of, that form of activity, with the result that human powers to achieve excellence, and human conceptions of the ends and goods involved, are systematically extended. Tic-tac-toe is not an example of a practice in this sense, nor is throwing a football with skill, but the game of football is, and so is chess. Bricklaying is not a practice; architecture is. So are the enquiries of physics, chemistry, and biology, and so is the work of the historian, and so are painting and music." (*AV* pg. 187)

[67] "Heritage Protection in Ruins" *The Irish Times* 27 December 2003.

[68] Narrative makes life intelligible because "…the concept of an intelligible action is a more fundamental concept than that of an action as such." (*AV*, pg. 209)

[69] "…we render the actions of others intelligible in this way because action itself has a basically historical character. It is because we all live out narratives in our lives and because we understand our own lives in terms of the narratives that we live out that the form of narrative is appropriate for understanding the actions of others." (*AV*, pg. 211-2).

[70] "…tragedy is not an imitation of men but of actions and of life". *Poetics* 50a16

[71] MacIntyre says, "What I have called a history is an enacted dramatic narrative in which the characters are also the authors. The characters of course never start out literally *ab initio*; they plunge *in media res*, the beginnings of their story already made for them by what and who has gone before… the difference between imaginary characters and real ones is not in the narrative form of what they do; it is in the degree of their authorship of that form and of their own deeds." (*AV*, pg. 215).

[72] "…between the act of narrating a story and the temporal character of human experience there exists a correlation that is not merely accidental but that presents a transcultural form of necessity. To put it another way: time becomes human to the extent that it is articulated through a narrative mode, and narrative attains its full meaning when it becomes a condition of temporal existence." Paul Ricoeur, Time and Narrative Volume 1, pg. 52

[73] See, for instance, the position paper released by *The Friends of Tara*, a local activist group: see also John Donohoe, "The Friends of Tara Finalises Submission", *Meath Chronicle Extra* 17th May 2003, pg. 4.

[74] "Do not destroy the Hill of Tara" *The Irish Independent* 20 Nov 2003

[75] "Minister to press ahead with Tara route for motorway" *The Irish Times* 31 March 2005

[76] "The most famous and prestigious site in Celtic Ireland was the Hill of Tara (*Teamhair*) in co. Meath. The meaning of this placename seems to have been 'spectacle'. There is a wide view from there over a large area of Ireland, and it was doubtlessly for this reason that it was celebrated and revered for a very long time. There are signs of habitation at Tara dating from around 4,000 BC… As if to underlie the ceremonial importance of Tara from remote antiquity, two magnificent gold torcs have been found there, dating to the end of the 2nd millennium BC." Dáithí Ó h-Ógáin, The Sacred Isle, pg. 129.

[77] Sandler wrote, "One possible response to this criticism would be to argue that it is part of my good now that I have a justified belief (or something else suitably psychological) that my distant progeny will flourish. That belief would in turn only be justified if I had reason to believe that the requisite external goods for flourishing would be present in their generation, and perhaps I could only be justified in that belief if there were ecosystem sustainability. In this way, ecosystem sustainability would be a necessary condition of my flourishing now, and would not require that my distant progeny actually flourish." (Sandler, "The External Goods Approach", pg. 290.) Sandler did not follow up this possibility in great detail because he believed that the external goods approach could not support it.

[78] I interpret Aristotle's meaning this way since this would enable a reconciliation between the claim that we ought to strive for immortality, with the claim that "…we can wish for things that are impossible, for instance immortality". (*NE*, 111b19)

[79] "An object of scientific knowledge, therefore, exists of necessity. It is therefore eternal; and what is eternal does not come into existence or perish." (*NE*, 1139b26)

[80] "Also the activity of contemplation may be held to be the only activity that is loved for its own sake: it produces no result beyond the actual act of contemplation…" (*NE*, 1177b1)

[81] Herodotus VII, 207; as cited in MacIntyre, Whose Justice? Which Rationality? Pg. 113.

[82] "…it would also be strange if ancestors were not affected at all, even over a limited period, by the fortunes of their descendants." (*NE*, 1100a20)

[83] "He is fond of conferring benefits, but ashamed to receive them, because the former is a mark of superiority and the latter inferiority. He returns a service done to him with interest, since this will put the original benefactor into his debt in turn, and make him the party benefited." (*NE* 1124b9)

[84] Gordon Deegan, "Lecturer warns of collapse of Irish agriculture" *The Irish Times* 4 May 2004.

[85] Mary Carolan, "Annihilation of woodland feared" *The Irish Times* 27 February 1999.

[86] Kraus, H.H. (ed.) The European Parliament and the Environment Policy of the European Union pg. 11. The figure for the European average is my own calculation, based on figures provided in this source, and excludes the ten accession states of May 2004.

[87] Anne Lucey, "Manager warns of threat to Kerry tourism" *The Irish Times* 20 April 2004, pg. 2.

[88] Anne Lucey, "Kerry planners, county council at loggerheads" *The Irish Times* 16 May 2004.

[89] Fiona Tyrrell, "New Academy for Heritage aims to protect historical environment" *The Irish Times* 23 May 2004

[90] Parfit's description of the case reads as follows: "As a community, we must choose whether to deplete or conserve certain kinds of resources. If we choose Depletion, the quality of life over the next two centuries would be slightly higher than it would have been if we had chosen Conservation." (*R&P*, pg. 361-2).

[91] The vulgar man "spends a great deal and makes a tasteless display on unimportant occasions; for instance, he gives a dinner to his club on the scale of a wedding banquet, and when equipping a chorus at the comedies he brings it on in purple at its first entrance…" (*NE* 1123a20)

Overall Conclusion.

We have finally arrived at the end of this philosophical tour of the Good, the Just, the Right, and the Excellent. Of all the systems of ethics here studied, only Virtue theory proved capable of providing an acceptable environmental ethic on both theoretical and practical levels, and capable of defeating the primary test case, the Non-Identity Problem. The theoretical principle of environmental Virtue theory is that the worthwhile, flourishing life must include a wish for a world in which flourishing is possible, and the virtuous person must in various ways do things which aim for the creation of that world, or the prevention of its degradation, both now and in the future. On the practical plane, the Virtuous Person chooses Conservation, since she wants the environment of her flourishing to become a Gift of the Future, and because Depletion can manifest the vice of *pleonexia*. It remains only to show that success for Virtue theory need not imply defeat for Justice, Utilitarianism, and Deontology. Here I shall recap the details, with an emphasis on how Virtue theory's success was made possible partly through incorporating certain ideas from other moral systems.

§ 1. A World Fit for Human Flourishing.

There are five specific principles of environmental virtue theory. In the order that they were developed, they are:

(1) *Groundedness*. The flourishing life is bound together with the environment in which it takes place. Both the social and ecological environments are valid and irreplaceable goods to the agent's flourishing, as the field and the stage on which his potential for excellence is not only made possible, but also developed and expressed. The aim for the worthwhile human life includes the aim to create and sustain the social and environmental conditions in which the worthwhile human life is possible and supported.

(2) *Excellence*. To a Virtuous person, the maximisation of utility is not what matters. It is excellence of character which

matters, as it is excellence of character which is required to pursue and achieve *eudaimonia*. Such a person is not swayed by the total happiness to result from one choice or the other; nor on the claim that a bad consequence would 'not be worse' for those whom it affects. Virtue theory is therefore able to claim that an action can be wrong even if it produces the greatest utility, right even if it produces the lesser utility, and wrong even if it harms no one. The Non-Identity Problem is thereby avoided. Similarly it can claim that an act can be wrong even if no one's rights are infringed, no one is unjustly deprived of her fair share of some good, and no one's humanity is disrespected.

(3) *Parity*. The right amount of environmental resource development is that which obtains a parity between the aim for a flourishing life on one hand, and on the other the opportunities and abilities to succeed in that aim afforded by the environment in which one lives. On this principle, excessive depletion of the environment constitutes *pleonexia*, 'greed' or 'acquisitiveness', the vice of excess associated with *dikaiosune*, 'justice'.

(4) *Temporal Continuity*. The future appears to the Virtuous person as a function of the present, in the form of a *telos* the fulfilment of which is temporally continuous. The pursuit of *eudaimonia* is just such a temporally continuous end. A Virtuous person shows his concern for the future through aiming at ends which are, while achievable in the present, also temporally continuous and ongoing, possibly even beyond the agent's own lifetime. Environmental conservation is such a temporally continuous end.

(5) *The Gift of the Future*. Occasions such as Non-Identity Choices present the moral agent with decisions that have definitive effects upon the future. A choice which creates a different future than that which would be created after another choice, and which creates a future the moral agent himself cannot participate in, is a 'legacy'. The legacy which it is virtuous to aim for is the one which brings out the agent's best qualities in the course of striving for it. Such a legacy can be called a gift of the future. Again, environmental conservation counts as such a gift.

372

The importance of these conclusions is manifest in several ways. First and foremost, I have shown how the study of environmental ethics leads towards the study of the Virtues. Utilitarian environmentalism was unable to overcome the Non-Identity Problem, and the various utilitarian proposals for overcoming that problem called for an ethic capable of claiming that an act can be wrong even if it produces the greatest utility, or even if it harms no one. Utilitarianism thus calls for other moral theories to take over where its limits are reached. I did not show that Utilitarianism calls for the Virtues; only that Utilitarianism calls for something other than itself. Justice theory and Kantian Deontology both call upon the Virtues more directly. We found reasons for why competing claims between generations for access to certain resources could not count as a "circumstance of justice". T'Hooft and de-Shalit both appropriate MacIntyre to overcome this problem. The perspective of justice they presented in which the good of present people includes, as T'Hooft put it, the wish to give the things one values "a future they cannot do without", relied heavily upon MacIntyre's conception of the future as a function of the present. Only Virtue theory was able to develop this principle completely, allowing us to see its full significance. We also found an impetus to move to Virtue theory in the Deontology of Kant. Harm to the environment was found to be non-universalisable only at the theoretical level. The study of Kant's interest in geography introduced the principle of Groundedness, although it contained a logical tension which Kant never saw, and the possibilities for overcoming it point to phenomenological and existential regions which Kant's other philosophical commitments prevent him from exploring. An Aristotelian revision of the principle of Groundedness was called for. In the Deontology of future generations, we found reasons why the people of the future may have no rights, or that we may do no wrong if we do not respect their rights. It was thus necessary to look for a satisfactory environmental ethic in a moral theory capable of claiming that an action can be wrong even if no one's rights are infringed.

My proposal for a solution to the Non-Identity Problem, first glimpsed in the claim that the maximisation of utility is not what matters, and finally achieved in the principle of the Gift of the Future, should be of interest to the many philosophers who have found the problem so far impossible to solve. Utilitarians may find my solution difficult to accept, since it requires an abandonment of one of the central principles of Utilitarianism. Additionally, my claim that Utilitarianism's inability to solve this problem constitutes Utilitarianism's failure to provide an acceptable environmental ethic is bound to be controversial. However, even if this conclusion is disputable, I believe the impetus which directed me to it, which was the claim that a step outside of strict Utilitarianism is necessary if we wish to avoid the Non-Identity Problem, is indisputable. Person-affecting principles are simply incapable of solving the Non-Identity Problem. I have claimed that Virtue theory *is* capable of solving it, although there may be more sophisticated forms of Deontology than those which I studied which may be able to solve it in a different way.

This series of five principles of environmental virtue provide new conceptual tools with which policy makers, legislators, and philosophers may assess their decisions and the procedures with which they made them. For one of the implications of these conclusions is that it is not enough to assess environmental policy and planning proposals in a strictly economic way. One reason for this is because modern economic theory is dominated by *pleonexia*. It is ethically necessary to ask if and how certain kinds of economic, political, or other kind of social decisions affect our prospects for happiness and human flourishing, while bearing in mind that happiness and human flourishing is not contingent upon industrial production and economic growth. Aside from, or in addition to, any economic questions, we must also ask what kind of world we want to live in, and what kind of world we want to leave behind, and what kind of flourishing we want and so what kind of world we should create to make that kind of flourishing possible. These are not questions of economics. Nor are they questions of utility. As Allison writes, with a rather un-Utilitarian enthusiasm for things that are not easy to quantify: "The questions to be asked of a 'National Park' or 'Area of Outstanding Natural Beauty' should not be 'How can we improve access?' or 'What recreational facilities should we provide?', but 'What kind of special magic does the place have and for whom?'" (*E&U* pg. 145). We can ask these kinds of questions without delving into the metaphysical controversies of ecocentrism, religion, and deep ecology.

§ 2. What Synthesis In View?

I have claimed that Virtue theory is best able to provide an acceptable environmental ethic to and overcome the Non-Identity Problem. Yet none of these five conclusions, except possibly the second one (excellence), is *prima facia* contrary to the positions of Utilitarianism, Justice theory, or Kantian deontology. It is possible for the proponents of all moral theories to ask what human flourishing is, and what kind of world we should aim to create to make human flourishing possible. I believe we should find this discovery encouraging. It may be more important for us in the long run—more Virtuous, it could be said—for philosophers in different traditions to emphasise their similarities rather than their differences. Hursthouse expressed this wish as well, when she wrote of the reduced need for the supporters of Virtue theory to take a combatative stance:

> If Utilitarians and Deontologists disagree with what I say then of course I shall want to argue with them... if they were to agree, and their only protest was 'But we can say that too—that's a utilitarian (or a deontological) thesis', I should not be inclined to argue at all; I should be delighted. Let us by all means stop caring about how we distinguish ourselves and welcome our agreements.[1]

Like Hursthouse, I am more confident in the similarities between various moral theories than in their differences, and I believe that the most important contribution this study provides to modern philosophy is a platform on which to build a synthesis between them. The complete statement of that synthesis is probably a lifetime's work. But here I shall describe it in a tentative, exploratory way, through each of my five general statements of environmental virtue.

My first general conclusion, the principle of Groundedness in the World, requires that the flourishing life must include acts which create and sustain the environment in which the flourishing life is possible. It corresponds loosely with an insight derived from Kantian thought. It was in the study of Kant's geography that the idea of groundedness, which proved to be so important to the subsequent studies of Virtue theory, was first introduced. According to this idea, we should think of the world as our home and place, to which we are related and indeed inseparably connected in various different ways. What Aristotle and MacIntyre claim about the relation of the *polis* to human flourishing obtains also in relation to the physical and ecological environment. Acts which degrade or destroy the world tend to undermine themselves by harming those who perform them. To care for our home and place is thus to care for ourselves as well. The Aristotelian reading of the principle of groundedness resolved the theoretical and practical tensions in the Kantian reading by showing how the environmental connections and relations which constitute our Groundedness are obtained through the exercise of all the organic and human faculties which were important to Aristotle: the faculties for growth, movement, sensation, sociability and reason. The aporia discovered in the study of Kant's ethical system, that no particular environmentally destructive act fails the test of universalisation, is here overcome by the claim that some acts which are not self-negating as a law for everyone can nevertheless be wrong. They can be wrong if they 'damage the humanity with us', which for Kant is the same as saying that the act is irrational, and which for Aristotle is the same as saying that the act mistakes what humanity's *telos* is, and so fall short of *eudaimonia*.

The relation I have described as Groundedness was described by Allison as a kind of totemism. He describes the importance of land to people's identities as follows:

> The world is full of holy lands; most countries are
> God's own. Landscape is an important peg of
> identity, a rival and relation to language. In cultures
> as diverse as the Welsh, the Australian Aboriginal and
> the Jewish, the two come together to allocate meaning
> and spiritual significance to the relation between
> people, words and places. Less obviously, the
> American has his frontier, the National Parks being
> the 'cathedrals of America' as Daniel Boorstin saw it,
> the German his forest, the Englishman his
> 'countryside'. (*E&U* pg. 149)

I would like to add, as an Irish-Canadian and a citizen of both countries, that the Canadian has his Great White North, and the Irishman has his Four Green Fields, the four traditional provinces of Ireland with their distinctive hills, hedgerows, meadows, valleys, lakes, islands, and bogs. It was part of the purpose of several Irish Literary Revival authors, especially Lady Augusta Gregory, to re-populate the Irish landscape with gods, heroes, saints, ghosts, and monsters, thus to encourage the sense of wonder and magic Allison describes, and also to provide the Irish people with a narrative of their cultural identity, beginning in a mythological past and culminating in the modern present. For Gregory, the geography of Ireland itself forms the primary medium of narrative continuity. Allison is right to put these cultural and spiritual feelings shared by most people to the service of environmental protection and conservation. I have described Groundedness as "the quality, property, or condition of belonging to the world, living in and with it, and being inseparable from it". The spiritual and cultural commitments described by Allison as a form of totemism concurs with my description of Groundedness, as this quotation illustrates. Totemism is for him a source of enormous benefit to people's lives which Utilitarianism cannot rationally underestimate or ignore. These same spiritual and cultural commitments support the claim I made in the study of Aristotle's Virtue theory that the *polis* is both a social and also a physical environment: it is a landscape and an ecology as well as a system of social and political relations.

The second general conclusion, that the location of moral concern should be the excellence of the agent's character, and not on the consequences of an action, is most obviously contrary to the position of Utilitarianism. It was stated at the conclusion to chapter one that an acceptable environmental ethic would have to include the claim that maximising utility is not what matters. This is the case for Justice and for Deontology, however both of these principles are, like Utilitarianism, person-affecting: they depend upon the complaint of the other person, for instance the complaint that rights were infringed, to certify that a wrong has been done. This was found to be problematic for several reasons. One of them, presented by Narveson, was that as future people do not yet exist, they will have rights only if we grant that they do; and indeed that it may make no sense to say that they have rights at all. We were forced to conclude that an acceptable environmental ethic would have to have the property that it can judge an action wrong even if no one is harmed and no one's rights are infringed. Of all the moral theories here studied, only Virtue theory is capable of making that claim, because the location of moral concern is primarily on the moral agent himself. At this level, Virtue theory must stand its ground, and resist being synthesised with other principles.

There are certain forms of Utilitarianism which agree that the *maximisation* of utility should not be what matters, although of course no Utilitarian would ever claim that utility itself should not matter. Elijah Millgram, for instance, has argued for a 'utility-satisfying' principle, in which people aim for the 'very best' but usually settle for the 'good enough'.[2] This, Millgram claims, more accurately represents our actual decision-making procedures. But what would convince a utility-maximiser to become a utility-satisfyer? Such a person would have to be shown that the relevant differences between his various choices are not simply, nor only, differences to do with the utility that would result from each action. He would have to be shown that there are other relevant differences between his choices which have little or nothing to do with the utility involved. One of those relevant differences is the way each choice reflects the agent's character. There are certain virtues which can help here, for instance the virtue of 'temperance', which is normally associated with the moderation of pleasure. A utility-satisfyer must possess the virtue of temperance in order to know which among his choices will produce the most satisfactory result, to know when a choice that results in the greatest utility is nevertheless wrong, or to put it colloquially, to know "how much of a good thing is too much". Indeed the very notion of 'good enough' seems to invite a comparison with Aristotle's Doctrine of the Mean, although I lack the space to give this suggestion the full attention it deserves. By developing and manifesting temperance, the utility-satisfyer does not cease to be a Utilitarian. He might argue that possession of the Virtues positively increases his utility, and that to manifest a vice is a dis-utility. But someone could argue that the utility-value of the Virtues may not be enough to outweigh the Repugnant Conclusion, with its very high total utility and very low average utility. A utilitarian wishing to avoid this outcome might have to become a 'Virtuous Utilitarian' (if there is such a thing) and give due acknowledgement to the Virtues even if only to help him become a better Utilitarian. Given an environmental policy choice like that which Parfit described in the case of Depletion, such a person would choose an option that falls between the small population of blissful people, and the large population of miserable people, and thus avoid the Repugnant Conclusion. The virtue of Temperance may help him pinpoint the place where increasing total Utility crosses the path of declining average utility. However, I suggest this variation of Utilitarianism only tentatively. It seems to me that the only reason to become a Virtuous Utilitarian, or a Utility-Satisfyer, instead of a Utility-Maximiser, is to avoid the Repugnant Conclusion whilst remaining a Utilitarian. Otherwise, if there is some group of people whose happiness we could improve at minimal cost, then we should do so, and we may be morally blameworthy if we do not.

My third general conclusion, the principle of parity, was a variation of Aristotle's Doctrine of the Mean. It applies the doctrine to the acquisition and use of external goods, rather than the exercise of character traits: an Aristotelian move which Aristotle himself never made. As it concerns material goods, it invites a discussion of justice. It concerns what, and how much, of the resources of the environment we should take, or leave behind, or even return again. Some principle of distributive justice is implied here, with its range of concepts including shares, fairness, dues and entitlements, and so on. The principle of parity can serve as a basic statement of everyone's just entitlement. When environmental ethics is a question of how to distribute the material resources we procure from the environment, like food, building materials, waste dumping space, fuel and energy, and even the surface territory of the Earth, among contemporaries and among generations, then some conception of distributive justice seems to be demanded. Aristotle praised justice as "the whole of virtue" and as "virtue itself". I have shown how in the distribution of external goods, there is a mean to be struck between insufficiency and excess. Between extremes of Preservation and Depletion, the choice of Conservation strikes that mean. The argument for why a Virtuous person would not choose the Repugnant Conclusion relied heavily on a conception of the vice of *pleonexia*, the vice of habitual material acquisitiveness associated with *dikaiosune*, 'justice'. We can say, then, that a Virtuous person would find it not only un-Virtuous, but also unjust, to make Depletion his overall environmental resource policy, because it indulges *pleonexia*. An exploration of the relationship between Virtue theory and Justice theory would seem to be required. Such a synthesis may look like that which was offered by Onora O'Neil, in her recent book-length treatment of both subjects, <u>Towards Justice and Virtue</u>, in which she wrote:

> Refraining from destroying or damaging
> environments which provide the material basis for
> socially connected lives constitutes environmental
> justice. Yet lives and cultures will remain vulnerable
> if they depend on environments which, although not
> damaged, are also not cherished. Vulnerabilities
> multiply for those who find themselves drawing bare

subsistence and shelter from environments they do
not understand or care for. They are lessened and
limited for those who inhabit a natural and man-made
world that flourishes and supports them both
materially and spiritually. An ethically sound relation
to the environment must then go beyond avoiding
systematic and gratuitous damage that injures others'
lives; it must also be expressed in care and concern to
sustain and conserve at least some parts or aspects of
that environment in a flourishing condition.[3]

My fourth general conclusion, concerning the temporal continuity of
virtue, also originated in Deontology. In the study of justice theory,
my conclusion was that it can be just to participate in a practice of
intergenerational 'virtual' reciprocity in which each generation is
obligated to save resources for the future because it partakes in a
practice that enabled them to expect and demand that their
predecessors save for them. But the reason to initiate and to
continue to participate in such a practice was precisely because, as
T'Hooft said, the future "figures into the present meaning of things".
T'Hooft and de-Shalit both turned to Virtue theory, specifically
MacIntyre's principles of narrative identity and temporality, to
buttress their case for why future people share in our community,
and why we owe them a share of our wealth.

This depends on a conception of the future unlike that which
is usually preferred by other moral theories. Utilitarianism, Justice,
and Deontology all consider a future that could be called the 'actual'
future, the future which will in fact come into existence in time. It is
the rights and/or the harms and benefits possessed and/or
experienced by the people of the future which concerns these
theories. On the conception of the future which I have described for
Virtue theory, it is not the actual future which matters. It is the
future as a function of the present, the future as the *telos* of present-
moment activity rather than the consequences of present-moment
activity, which concerns a Virtuous person. This is the only
conception of the future which is consistent with the placement of

the location of our moral concern on the condition of the moral agent's own character.

In the fifth general conclusion, the Gift of the Future, several correlations to concepts in other moral theories present themselves. The principle was discovered in the exploration of Virtue Theory but it can be seen as a transformation of Parfit's Non-Identity Problem. A Gift of the Future emerges from a choice which creates a future that must be different than that which would be created if the moral agent chooses differently. Singer's principle of 'irretrievable loss' can count as a 'gift' of the future insofar as it makes permanent changes to landscape and culture—essentially a gift we ought *not* to give, because it entails such enormous dis-utility. The Gift of the Future is tied to the flourishing of present people, especially their sense of self-worth, and are manifestations of the qualities of character, both individual and social, which the gift-giver(s) possess. It is not, therefore, altogether necessary that a person must give a certain kind of gift to future people because he was the beneficiary of a practice of Virtual Reciprocity. What he received from his predecessors, and what future people may be entitled to claim from him, are not the primary factors in his reasoning. This satisfies the need for a reason to initiate a practice of Virtual Reciprocity, which Justice theory was unable to provide. One generation may choose to make some Just Savings schedule, some system of allocating social goods and natural resources from one generation to the next, into its Gift of the Future, and in so doing create a practice of Virtual Reciprocity.

The Gift of the Future is similar to another well known principle of intergenerational justice: Passmore's 'Chain of Love'. For one of the things which can motivate someone to want to create a Gift of the Future is the feelings of care and benevolence he has for his offspring. The Virtuous person's own sense of self-worth is the primary motivating force behind the Gift of the Future, not his sentiments for his offspring, although that does not mean he has no such sentiments. We saw in the discussion of Aristotle that a person is capable of friendship only if he finds his own life desirable and believes himself worthy of having friends. The same motivating force also applies here: a person is capable of creating a Gift of the Future if he already believes his values merit being passed on to future people, and is therefore able to have genuine feelings of love and benevolence toward them. The principle of the Gift of the Future is enriched if it is tied to our sentiments for our offspring but it is not essential to tie it so. One could give a Gift of the Future impartially, impersonally; that is, not to any particular person, but to people with whom one is totally anonymous—a necessary provision, given that the further into the future we look, the more faceless the people become. Like a philanthropist donating an art treasure to a museum or university, for the benefit of people with whom he has no relation, a virtuous person creating a Gift of the Future can intend to benefit people who are totally unknown to him. The Gift of the Future is thus immune to Barry's criticism of the Chain of Love, the criticism that it will not be wrong (that is, it will not be unjust) to leave nothing for the people of the future if we do not care about them. It is Virtuous person's sense of self-worth which motivates him here, coupled with the wish to share the kind of world in which he lived and found his life to be worthwhile. It follows that even if there are no particular people he cares for and wants to benefit, he still has reasons to give such a gift.

An objection can arise here: future generations may claim the right *not* to share in our own moral values. The people of the future might have their own values, which might not be the same as ours. They may choose to partially or completely break with the continuity of value from our past, through us, to them, in order to affirm their own, new and different values. Whatever gifts we may create to give to them, they should have the right to reject them in favour of something else. How, then, can this claim be advanced together with the claim that we should wish for future generations to carry forward our own values in and through the gifts we give to them? How can these two principles be affirmed at the same time? We concede to other contemporaries the right of moral autonomy, and we presently judge this concession to be a self-evident moral obligation. Kant claimed that this basic moral value needs only to be clarified, not argued for. How can we concede this to future generations as well, even while giving gifts to them in the hope that they will, in fact, share our values? There are two ways in which it is possible to respond to this dilemma.

First of all, in the case of the gift of environmental conservation, I find it impossible to believe that the people of the future might decide that an ecologically stable and bountiful world is of no value to them. It is, as we have seen, a basic prerequisite for life, survival, and civilisation. It is a deep contradiction to deny the value of life and at the same time to do that which is necessary to have and to preserve life: eating nutritious food, building safe homes and communities, avoiding harms and dangers, and so on. The condition of groundedness in the world is, I have argued, an irreducible condition, and to suspend it or deny it is to suspend or deny the basis of life itself as well. As was noted in the first study, the amount of interest in protecting the ecological world is increasing, and we have reason to believe this interest will continue to increase.

Secondly, we note that we are the recipients of various gifts from past generations, and that we have found many of them important enough to warrant respect and preservation. The great treasures of art, architecture, literature, philosophy, and the like, are among them. We find that the continuity with the past, the aesthetic and intellectual stimulation they provide, and so on, benefits us greatly. Our society *inherits* more values than it creates. We can therefore expect that future people will respond similarly to some of the gifts we leave for them precisely because that is how we have responded to some of the gifts that past generations have left for us. If we find ourselves obliged to respect what we inherit from our past, we can expect that future people will find themselves obliged to respect what they inherit as well. This second answer depends upon the presupposition that future people will be 'like us' enough to respond to their past in more or less the same way we have responded to our past. But is not our concession of future people's moral autonomy also the concession of the possibility that they may not be like us? It is, and yet it appears we concede to future people the right to decide their own values only with certain reservations.

Our own values oblige us to hope that they will be preserved into the future. Even our concession of future people's right to their own moral autonomy is an expression of the hope that they too will value moral autonomy, just as we do. Thus we do not, in fact, expect future generations to possess values which we do not ourselves possess as well. In the tension between the wish to project certain values into the future, and the wish to respect the moral autonomy of the people of the future, the latter tends to give way.

§ 3. The Gardener

What kind of comprehensive environmental morality can be distilled from these discoveries? Are there specific virtues which the five principles of environmental virtue call for? Even after this lengthy and fruitful discourse, it remains difficult to pin down specific character traits which we could call 'ecological virtues'. Although Wensveen produced a list of 189 virtues and 174 vices in her study of the literature,[4] nevertheless she claims that too much analytical scrutiny may be counterproductive. In her words:

> The biggest danger that threatens books on virtue is death by analysis. Life-giving habits and attitudes that flourish in an atmosphere of spontaneity have a proclivity to wither when subjected to the light of critical inquiry… Ecological virtues like respect for nature, attunement, frugality, compassion, courage, and care are ideally cultivated without too much self-awareness and theoretical hairsplitting.[5]

This position is not, as an uncharitable reading of it might imply, a request to overlook any ambiguities or logical weaknesses that may appear. It is, however, a request that a systematic and holistic understanding of environmental virtue should be emphasised. Such an understanding should be possible without sacrificing logical coherence and rigour. The most obvious place to find it may be in the analogy with professional occupations with which both Aristotle and MacIntyre initiated their study of the virtues.

There is at least one professional occupation which can help to explore the virtues of the environmentalist by standing as the general model of an environmentally virtuous person. Consider gardens and gardening. There are many virtues which would enable one to become a excellent gardener aside from possession of the relevant scientific knowledge. They might include patience, aesthetic sensibility, nurturing, protectiveness, industriousness, foresight, and imagination—virtues we also find admirable in many other contexts. Some of these are mentioned in Wensveen's long list as well. A gardener is a professional on par with builders, musicians, animal-handlers, and the others which Aristotle cited as examples when constructing his theory of the virtues. Someone who loves his garden and who manifests that love by treating it well, tending it, caring for its plants and features, and so on, is in some sense rewarded by the garden. The flowers bloom and the birds sing. It might not be right to say 'the garden rewards the gardener', in case that statement is interpreted to mean that the garden is a sentient being able to consciously respond to the gardener (a controversial claim which need not be advanced here). But it is undeniable that the gardener's work and care is rewarded. The work itself is not what Aristotle would call a self-sufficiently pleasurable activity, since it aims at producing a material result. Yet the activity of enjoying a well cared-for garden is undeniably self-rewarding. In that may lie the virtuousness of the work of creating and tending one. And surely to create and tend a garden can be at the same time to enjoy it! Moreover, the garden has needs and demands which a good gardener must understand if she wishes to tend it well and get it to be all that it can be, in much the same way that a musician must care for and understand the needs of her instrument in order to perform with it the most excellent music that she can. This is not a metaphysical "expanded self" understanding of the sort Arne Naess and the Deep Ecologists say is a precondition of environmental ethics. Nor is it an awareness of intrinsic values external to the agent, in the usual sense. This is a more practical kind of understanding, in which the gardener knows what he wants and knows how to use the organic properties and processes of the landscape he is tending in order to obtain it. A good gardener forms a relationship with his garden, and a kind of interaction develops between them. The gardener is rewarded for his work by the blossoming of the trees, flowers, and other plants, the singing of the birds, and the presence of other kinds of wildlife. Indeed the garden becomes loveable precisely because the gardener loves it, understands its needs, works with it, and respects it. If the gardener slackens his effort, the garden's loveable qualities diminish: weeds overrun the flowerbeds, litter spoils the view. The qualities that make a garden loveable are nurtured, developed, fortified and improved by the tending care of the gardener.

I take the case of the gardener as the model for human stewardship of the Earth in general, and the model for how plans for balancing environmental conservation with our economic development needs should proceed. The virtues of a land planner, conservation authority manager, park ranger, environmentalist, agriculture policy maker, or official in a public works office are the virtues of a gardener "writ large" upon much bigger territories. The profession of a gardener has a history, in landscape architecture traditions or in flower hybrid breeding for instance. Thus it is able to sustain the relevant webs of connection with the past and the future: the past we inherit from tradition, the future to which we aim in our present actions. The gardener's creation can be designed to outlast himself: he may have a rational wish that his children or some successors should take up responsibility for it after he is gone. More generally, the case of the gardener is the paradigm for a being or species, like humanity, which is able to alter and re-create its own environment. For the work of a gardener is in some sense an intervention into nature and an imposition of human values and labour power on to nature. No one would find in nature rows of manicured flowers, perfectly trimmed trees, symmetrically arranged hedges, and so on. These features are the product of the gardener's work. Likewise no one would find in the wilderness cities, motorways, housing estates, farms, and the like—even conservation areas, parks, heritage landscape monuments, and the like are human impositions on to the natural landscape. These impositions are successful when they are implemented with an understanding of the landscape on which they are placed. Success, in this case, I take to mean the creation and maintenance of a physical environment in which the aspiration to flourish and be happy is possible and supported.

My conception that the environmental virtues are the virtues of a gardener has certain advantages. Contained in the profession of the gardener, as the template for environmental virtue in general, is a recognition of our groundedness in the world, and that we live within the world and interact with it in a way that is comparable to the way we live in and with our social communities. Other conceptions of environmental virtue recognise this also, but not in quite the same way. Environmental conservation is sometimes taken to mean environmental non-intervention, and it is the often un-stated wish of environmentalists that the whole surface of the Earth should be left untouched as much as possible. This is implicit in the claim that it is virtuous for us to recognise the valuable qualities already present in the environment, and un-virtuous for us to interfere with them. But in fact all human activity in relation to the environment is an intervention. Good conservation practice must, in my view, be a matter of getting involved in the environment, working in it and with it to create a living space for humanity that is supportive of our physical, intellectual, social, and aesthetic needs, and in which the aspiration to flourish and be happy is possible and supported. This is why I chose the gardener as the model. The gardener's labour input makes it impossible that he is nothing more than a passive witness to the garden, keeping his hands off it, although there may well be some parts of the world which are so ecologically sensitive that they should be left entirely alone. A good garden can include 'wild' areas, left mostly untouched by human hands; it is the correct observation of Hill, Frasz, Alison, Singer, and others that some of us do find virgin landscapes beautiful and spiritually uplifting, and that aesthetic sensibility is a virtue. There are also some ecosystems and territories which are so sensitive and fragile, and so important for the recycling of the air, water, and other organic compounds necessary for life, that nothing less than a "hands off" policy will do. But in general, humankind must involve itself in the environment, and intervene in its processes, to obtain the things we need for life and survival and to create surroundings which are suited to the pursuit of a worthwhile life. For instance, a good gardener must also weed his garden: that is, he must remove unwanted plants. Land planning, conservation, sustainable development, and so on, can include a kind of weeding of unwanted elements, for instance to protect the human community from diseases and from flooding, to preserve the fertility of agricultural land, to prevent non-native plant and animal species from unbalancing an area's ecosystem. Some of the 'weeding' may need to be carried out on ourselves, to prevent human actions from severely disrupting an area's valuable qualities, be they aesthetic, economically productive, or of another character. The ethical choice is not between intervention and non-intervention, but between virtuous and un-virtuous forms of intervention. This is what is lost when the environmental virtues are passive virtues like humility and open-ness, or those which are required for success and happiness in totally controlled artificial environments.

The other advantage of this template of environmental virtue is that it is easy for us to apply it to specific practical examples and use it as a decision-making guide. For we already know what a garden is, how to make one and take care of one, and how to judge whether a garden is good or bad. We also know of many different kinds of gardens, some which require more maintenance and planning than others, some of which allow nature to take its course more than others. Some are meant to be decorative, and are planted with flowers and trees. Others are meant to be productive, and are planted with vegetables and fruit. It is thus a very flexible model, able to suit various situations and needs in different parts of the world. The creation of Alto Púrus National Park and Conservation Reserve, in the Peruvian Amazon, can count as an excellent example of good planetary gardening which conserves an existing green landscape. It combines the features of a national park with the features of a reserve for indigenous people, who co-manage the territory with the government of Peru. It strikes a remarkable compromise between conservation of biodiversity needs, the livelihoods of the tribal people who live there, and the farming and industrial interests which encroach the territory and which have an interest in preventing illegal logging. At 6.7 million acres, it is one of the largest national parks of its kind in the world.[6] We can also look to the creation of new garden-like landscapes. The city of Kabul, Afghanistan, is undertaking a massive tree-planting initiative to make its war-torn urban environment look brighter and less depressing, to cleanse the dusty air, and to mitigate the effects of droughts and soil erosion. Nearly 4.5 million saplings will be planted this year, most of them native fruit-bearing and decorative trees which have been growing in local nurseries for the past three years.[7] This too counts as an outstanding example of excellent planetary gardening. There are many more examples of this kind of land planning on larger and smaller scales. And there are signs that environmental efforts are having positive results. For instance, the well-publicised 'ozone hole' over Antarctica is showing signs of shrinking, and may be closed again within 50 years. One of the scientists who discovered this new trend said "I think this shows global protocols can work".[8]

May I say that I do not claim to have found the complete formulae to completely answer all ethical questions about the environment. Certainly, the model of the gardener will not be helpful for all of our environmental policy dilemmas. For instance, gardeners sometimes weed their gardens by applying chemical fertilisers and pesticides. On the level of larger-scale environmental policies, we may not want to count this as an example of good planetary caretaking. But the gardener model is only a model, and when it conflicts with the known needs and requirements of environmental conservation, we can still look directly at the underlying moral theory which is its foundation. The debate, after all, is about what environmental virtue is, not about what gardening is; I have raised it since it seems to be the most useful practical model with which to make the environmental virtue come alive for us, and render it familiar and workable. Aside from minor issues, I believe I have obtained a strong working hypothesis of what constitutes sound ethical practice relating to the environment. Why might it be virtuous for our species to take upon itself the role of the gardener of the Earth? It cannot be because the Earth somehow needs us. Life proliferated on Earth for millions of years without us, and would continue to proliferate if our species disappeared. The environment doesn't need sustainable development. People do. It may be possible to assert that human flourishing is bound to the health of the world for the reason that through the ecological reactions to human activities that affect the environment, the proliferation or non-proliferation of environmental life on Earth becomes *the indicator of the moral condition of human community.* Although the environment does not require human intervention to sustain itself, the non-proliferation of an ecosystem tends to be a direct or indirect result of human impact. Actions which contribute to the degradation or destruction of the environment represent a failure of the qualities and attributes of character Aristotle and MacIntyre claim we need to succeed as human beings. A destroyed landscape, a poisoned marine, an unbreathable atmosphere, or a territory rendered unfit for human habitation (or for habitation by anything) is surely a product of qualities like pleonexia, as well as 'traditional' environmental vices like short-sightedness or even ignorance, and not nobility nor excellence. A stable and clean environment, by contrast, furnishes us with the material resources we require to eat and be healthy, the space in which to have homes, playgrounds, industries, and all kinds of social relations. It is a nearly boundless field of play for our aesthetic sensibilities, just as it is also the pre-condition required to cultivate other "higher" virtues. Conservation of the field and stage of our flourishing is connected to our faculties of intellect, aesthetics, and sociability, to all the things within us which are uniquely human and which make us noble, and indeed to all the things around us which make life worth living.

Brendan Myers

[1]   Hursthouse, <u>On Virtue Ethics</u>, pf. 7.

[2]   Millgram, "What's the Use of Utility?", pg. 133.

[3]   O'Neil, <u>Towards Justice and Virtue</u>, pg. 203.

[4]   See Wensveen's <u>Dirty Virtues</u> pp. 163-7.

[5]   Wensveen, <u>Dirty Virtues</u>, pg. 161. The passage continues as follows: "Thus they will more likely involve authentic self-expression, uncalculated self-giving, and intuitive sensitivity to the situation at hand. As soon as they become objects of reflection, ecological virtues risk becoming part of some new 'program' that people 'ought' to follow, a program that introduces external rewards in the form of social acceptance for political correctness. Such a development not only spells the end of these virtues as virtues, carrying their own rewards, but also of their cultivators' unambiguous orientation toward nonhuman nature." (pg. 161.)

[6]   "Peru Preserves Biodiversity in Vast New Park" *Environmental News Service* 1 April 2005

[7]   Wahidullah Amani, "Afgan Government on a Treeplanting Mission" *Environmental News Service* 5 April 2005

[8]   Kathy Marks, "Ozone hole to start shrinking and will close in 50 years, say scientists" *The Independent* (UK) 18 September 2002.

Bibliography

Excluding newspaper articles, press releases,
and news wire service articles

Aiken, H.D. (ed.) Hume's Moral and Political Philosophy (New York USA: Hafner, 1949)

Allison, Lincoln. Ecology and Utility: The Philosophical Dilemmas of Planetary Management (Leicester University Press, 1991)

Anscombe, "Modern Moral Philosophy" *Philosophy* 33 (1958) pp. 1-19.

Armstrong, S. & Botzler, R. (eds.) Environmental Ethics: Divergence and Convergence 2nd edition (McGraw-Hill, 1998)

Attfield, R, & Belsey, A. (eds.) Philosophy and the Natural Environment *Royal Institute of Philosophy Supplement* 36 (Cambridge University Press, 1994)

Aristotle, De Anima trans. Foster, K, "in the version of William of Moerbeke and the Commentary of St. Thomas Aquinas". (New Haven USA: Yale University Press, 1951/1959)

Aristotle, The Metaphysics trans. Lawson-Tancred, H. (London UK: Penguin, 1998)

Aristotle, The Nichomachean Ethics trans. Rackham, H. (Ware, Hertfordshire, UK: Wordsworth Editions, 1996)

Aristotle, The Politics trans. Sinclair, T.A., revised Saunders, T. J. (London UK: Penguin, 1992)

Bantz, Vincent P, et.al., The European Parliament and the Environment Policy of the European Union Working Paper ENVI 101 (Luxembourg: European Parliament, 1999)

Boethius, The Consolation of Philosophy trans. Watts, V.E. (London UK: Penguin, 1969)

Bond, Stuart. Ecological Footprints: A Guide for Local Authorities (Godalming, Surrey, UK: World Wildlife Federation, 2002)

Buchanan, Brock, Daniels, and Wilker, From Chance to Choice (Cambridge UK: Cambridge University Press, 2000)

Cafaro, Philip. "Thoreau, Leopold, and Carson: Toward an Environmental Virtue Ethics" *Environmental Ethics* 23 (2001) pp. 3-18

Callicott, J. Baird, "Animal Liberation: A Triangular Affair" *Environmental Ethics* 2 (1980), pp. 311-338

Callicott, J. Baird, In Defense of the Land Ethic (Albany, New York USA, SUNY Press, 1989)

Callicott, J. Baird, "The Wilderness Idea Revisited: The Sustainable Development Alternative" *The Environmental Professional* 13 (1991a), pp. 235-244.

Carter, Alan. "In Defence of Radical Disobedience" *Journal of Applied Philosophy* Vol. 15, No. 1, 1998, pp. 29-47

Carter, Richard. Breakthrough: The Saga of Jonas Salk (New York: Pocket Books, 1967)

Crisp and Slote, eds. Virtue Ethics (Oxford UK: Oxford University Press, 1998)

Danielson, Peter. "Theories, Intuitions and the Problem of World-Wide Distributive Justice" in *Philosophy of the Social Sciences* Vol. 3 (1973) pp. 331-340

Department of the Environment (Northern Ireland), "First Consultation Paper on the Implementation of the EC Water Framework Directive in Northern Ireland" March 2002.

de-Shalit, Avner. Why Posterity Matters: Environmental Policies and Future Generations (London, UK: Routledge, 1995)

Earth Summit Ireland, Telling it like it is: 10 years of unsustainable development in Ireland (Dublin: Earth Summit Ireland, 2002)

Ellmann, R. Yeats: The Man and the Masks (London: Macmillan, 1949)

European Convention, Draft Treaty establishing a Constitution for Europe (CONV 850/03) Brussels, 18 July 2003.

European Commission, Choices for a Greener Future (Luxembourg: Office for Official Publication by the European Communities, 2002)

Feinberg, Joe. "Wrongful Life and the Counterfactual Element in Harming" in Freedom and Fullfillment (Princeton, New Jersey USA: Princeton University Press, 1992)

Foster, Susanne. "Aristotle and the Environment" *Environmental Ethics* 24 (Winter 2002) pp. 409-428.

Fotion, Nick and Heller, Jan C., eds. Contingent Future Persons (Dordrecht, Holland: Kluwer Academic Publishers, 1997)

Frasz, Geoffrey. "Environmental Virtue Ethics: A New Direction for Environmental Ethics" *Environmental Ethics* 15 (1993) pp. 259-74.

Gauthier, Practical Reasoning (Oxford: Clarendon Press, 1962)

Gizewski, Peter. "Environmental Scarcity and Conflict" *Commentary* No. 71 (Ottawa, Canada: Canadian Security Intelligence Service) Spring 1997.

Gregory, Lady Augusta, Gods and Fighting Men (Gerards Cross, Buckinghamshire: Colin Smyth, 1970 [first published 1904]).

Hanser, Matthew. "Harming Future People" *Philosophy and Public Affairs,* 19(1) Winter 1990, pp. 47-70

Hart, H.L.A. The Concept of Law (Oxford UK: Clarendon Press, 1961)

Hengeveld, H. "The Science" *Alternatives Journal* (University of Waterloo, Canada) Vol. 26 No 2, Spring 2000.

Hill, Thomas. "Ideals of Human Excellence and Preserving Natural Environments" *Environmental Ethics* 5 (1983), pp. 211-224.

Hobbes, Thomas. Leviathan (Oxford University Press, 1996)

Hoff, Christina. "Kant's Invidious Humanism" *Environmental Ethics* no. 5, 1983

Howlin, Brendan. (T.D.) Sustainable Development: A Strategy for Ireland (Dublin: Department of the Environment, 1997)

Hursthouse, Rosalind. On Virtue Ethics (Oxford: Oxford University Press, 2000)

Hursthouse, Rosalind. "Virtue Theory and Abortion" *Philosophy and Public Affairs* 20 (1991) 223-46.

Hutchinson, D.S. The Virtues of Aristotle (London and New York: Routledge & Kegan Paul, 1986)

Johnson, Robert. "Virtue and Right", *Ethics* 113 (July 2003) pp. 810-834

Kahn, Charles. The Art and thought of Heraclitus (Cambridge UK: Cambridge University Press, 1979)

Kamenka (ed.) <u>Justice: Ideas and Ideologies</u> (London: Arnold, 1979)

Kant, Immanuel <u>Groundwork of the Metaphysics of Morals</u> trans. H. J. Paton (New York USA: Harper Torchbooks, 1964)

Kant, Immanuel, <u>Critique of Judgement</u> trans. James Creed Meredith (Oxford: Oxford University Press / Clarendon Press, 1952)

Kant, Immanuel, <u>Critique of Pure Reason</u> Paul Guyer and Allen W. Wood, trans. (Cambridge: Cambridge University Press, 1997)

Kant, <u>Essays and Treatises</u>, Vol. 2. (Bristol, England: Thoemmes Press, 1993 [reprint of 1799 edition])

Kant, <u>Lectures on Ethics</u> trans. Louis Infield (New York USA: Harper Torchbooks, 1963)

Kant, <u>On History</u> ed. Lewis White Beck, (New York USA: Bobbs-Merrill, 1963)

Kaplan, R.D. "The Coming Anarchy" *The Atlantic Monthly* (February 1994) 44-76

Kawall, Jason. "Reverence for Life as a Viable Environmental Virtue" *Environmental Ethics* 25 (2003)

Kraus, Hans-Hermann (ed.) <u>The European Parliament and the Environment Policy of the European Union</u> (Brussels: European Parliament Director-General for Research, 1997)

Leopold, Aldo. <u>A Sand County Almanac: And Sketches Here and There</u> (New York USA: Ballantine Books, 1970 [first published 1949])

Light, A, & Smith, J. M., eds. <u>Space, Place, and Environmental Ethics</u> (New York USA & London UK: Rowman & Littlefield Publishers, 1997)

Hippocraties, <u>Hippocratic Writings</u> ed. Lloyd, G.E.R. (Pelican, 1978)

Locke, John. <u>The Second Treatise of Government</u> (Indianapolis USA: Bobbs-Merrill, 1952)

Lovelock, James. <u>The Ages of Gaia</u> (New York USA: Bantam New Age / W.W. Norton, 1990)

MacIntyre, Alasdair. <u>After Virtue: A Study in Moral Theory</u>, 2nd edition (London: Duckworth, 1985).

MacIntyre, Alasdair. <u>Dependent Rational Animals</u> (London: Duckworth, 1999)

MacIntyre, Alasdair. <u>Whose Justice? Which Rationality?</u> (London: Duckworth, 1988)

May, J.A. <u>Kant's Concept of Geography: and its relation to recent geographical thought</u> (Toronto Canada: University of Toronto Press / U. of T. Dept. of Geography Research Publications, 1970)

McDonagh, Sean. <u>Passion for the Earth: The Christian Vocation to promote Justice, Peace, and the Integrity of Creation</u> (London: Geoffrey Chapman, 1994)

McLeman and Barry, "Climate Change, Migration, and Security", *Commentary* no. 86, (Ottawa, Canada: Canadian Security Intelligence Service) 2 March 2004.

McMurtry, John. <u>Unequal Freedoms</u> (Toronto Canada: Garamond Press, 1998.)

Minckley, W.L., and Deacon, James E. (eds.) <u>Battle Against Extinction: Native Fish Management in the American West</u> (Tucson: University of Arizona Press, 1991)

Milieu Ltd., <u>The Enlargement of the EU: Consequences in the Field of the Environment</u> (Brussels, Belgium: EU Directorate-General for Research, 2003)

Mill, John Stewart. <u>On Liberty and Utilitarianism</u> (London UK: Everyman's Library, 1992); *On Liberty* first published 1859, *Utilitarianism* first published 1863

Miller, David. <u>Social Justice</u> (Oxford: Clarendon Press, 1979)

Miller, Fred D., Jr., <u>Nature, Justice and Rights in Aristotle's *Politics*</u> (Oxford: Clarendon Press, 1995.)

Millgram, "What's the Use of Utility?" *Philosophy and Public Affairs* Vol. 29, No. 2, (2000) pp. 113-136

National Trust (UK), <u>Tunes Plateau Offshore Wind Farm Proposal</u> Position Statement, February 2003.

Ó h-Ógáin, Dáithí, <u>The Sacred Isle: Belief and Religion in Pre-Christian Ireland</u> (Cork, Ireland: The Collins Press, 1999)

O'Neill, Onora. <u>Towards Justice and Virtue</u>, (Cambridge UK: Cambridge University Press, 1996)

Parfit, Derek. <u>Reasons and Persons</u> (Oxford: Oxford University Press, 1984)

Parfit, "Comments", *Ethics* Vol. 96 (July 1986) pp. 832-872

Passmore, John. Man's Responsibility for Nature 2nd edition (London UK: Duckworth, 1980)

Paulson, Friedrich. Immanuel Kant: His Life and Doctrine trans. J. E. Creighton and Albert Lefevre (New York USA: Ungar, 1963)

Peacock, Kent. "Symbiosis and the Ecological Role of Philosophy" *Dialogue* 38 (1999) pp. 699-717.

Plato, The Republic trans. G.M.A. Grube (Indianapolis USA: Hackett, 1992)

Platt, Steve. "Did we really need the M25?" *New Society*, 79: 5 (1986) pg. 48

Rachels, Stuart. "A Set of Solutions to Parfit's Problems" *Nous* Vol. 35 no 2: (2001) pp. 214-238

Rachels, Stuart, "Review Essay: Contingent Future Persons" *Bioethics* Vol. 13 No. 2, 1999, pp. 160-167.

Rawls, John. A Theory of Justice Revised Edition (Oxford UK: Oxford University Press, 1999)

Rawls, John. Political Liberalism, (New York USA: Columbia University Press, 1993)

Ricoeur, Paul. Time and Narrative Volume 1, trans. K. McLaughlin and D. Pellauer (Chicago USA: University of Chicago Press, 1984)

Roberts, Paul. The End of Oil (London UK: Bloomsbury, 2004)

Rogers, Richard. Cities for a Small Planet (London UK: Faber and Faber, 1997)

Rorty, Amélie Oksenberg, ed. Essays on Aristotle's Ethics (Los Angeles, USA: University of California Press, 1980).

Rousseau, J. J. The Confessions, (Penguin, 1966 [first published 1782])

Routley, Richard. "Is there a need for a new, an environmental ethic?" *Proceedings of the XV World Congress of Philosophy*, No. 1., Varna, Bulgaria, 1973, pp. 205-210.

Rowell, Andrew. Green Backlash (London: Routledge, 1996)

Ruse, Michael (ed.) Philosophy of Biology (NY USA: MacMillan / London UK: Collier MacMIllan, 1989)

Russell, George ("A.E."), The Candle of Vision (London: MacMillan and Co., Ltd. 1931)

Sandler, Ronald. "The External-Goods Approach to Environmental Virtue Ethics" *Ethics* Vol. 25 No. 3 (Fall 2003), pp. 279-293

Scalla, Sabine, et.al., European Parliament Briefing No.2: Air Traffic and the Environment (Luxembourg: Division for the Environment, Energy and Research, European Parliament, 1998)

Shaw, William H. Taking Account of Utilitarianism (London: Blackwell, 1999)

Shaw, Bill. "A Virtue Ethics Approach to Aldo Leopold's Land Ethic" *Environmental Ethics* 19 (1997), pp. 53-67.

Sikora, R.I., & Barry, B. (eds.) Obligations to Future Generations (Philadelphia: Temple University Press, 1978)

Singer, Peter. (ed.) Companion to Ethics (Oxford: Blackwell, 1993)

Singer, Peter. Practical Ethics 2nd edition (Cambridge UK: Cambridge University Press, 1993)

Singer, Peter. One World: The Ethics of Globalisation (Yale University Press, 2002)

Smart, J.J.C, & Williams, B. Utilitarianism: For and Against (Cambridge UK: Cambridge University Press, 1973)

Smith, Adam. An Inquiry into the Nature and Causes of the Wealth of Nations (New York USA: PF Collier and Son, 1909)

Smolkin, Doran, "The Non-Identity Problem and the Appeal to Future People's Rights" *The Southern Journal of Philosophy*, Vol. 32, No. 3, (Fall 1994) pp. 194-208

Smolkin, Doran, "Towards a Rights-Based Solution to the Non-Identity Problem" *Journal of Social Philosophy*, Vol. 30 No. 1, (Spring 1999) pp. 194-208

Stearns, J.B., "Ecology and the Indefinite Unborn" *The Monist*, vol. 56 (1972) pp. 616-617

Swanton, Christine. "A Virtue Ethical Account of Right Action" *Ethics* 112 (October 2001) pp. 32-52

Tae-chang, Kim (ed.) Self and Future Generations (Cambridge UK: The White Horse press, 1998)

Taylor, Paul. Respect for Nature: A Theory of Environmental Ethics (New Jersey USA: Princeton University Press, 1986)

T'Hooft, Hendrick, Justice to Future Generations and the Environment (Dordrecht, Netherlands: Kluwer Academic Publishers, 1999)

Torrie, Bruce "Sea-Level Rise Alert" *CCPA Monitor* (Canadian Centre for Policy Alternatives, Ottawa, Canada) Vol. 6 No. 4 (September 1999), pg. 11.

United Nations Development Programme, Human Development Report 1992 (New York: Oxford University Press, 1992)

Urmson, J. O. Aristotle's Ethics (Oxford UK: Basil Blackwell, 1988)

Vellinga, P. & van Verseveld, W. J. Climate Change and Extreme Weather Events (Gland, Switzerland: World Wildlife Fund for Nature, 2000)

Wackernagel, M., and Rees, W. Our Ecological Footprint: Reducing Human Impact on the Earth (Victoria BC Canada: New Society Publishers, 1996)

Wallace, James. Virtues and Vices (Ithaca, New York, USA: Cornell University Press, 1978)

Wensveen, Louke. Dirty Virtues: The Emergence of Ecological Virtue Ethics (Amherst, New York, USA: Prometheus Books, 2000).

Woodward, James. "The Non-Identity Problem" *Ethics* 96 (1986) pp. 804-831

Woodward, James. "Reply to Parfit" *Ethics* 97 (1987) pp. 800-816

World Commission on Environment and Development, Our Common Future (Oxford University Press, Oxford UK, 1987)

Zimmerman, et. al., (eds.) Environmental Philosophy 3rd Edition (New Jersey USA: Prentice Hall, 2001)

Index

Hume, David, 113-114

Hursthouse, Rosalind, 2, 15, 26, 221, 272, 302, 305-307, 311, 375

Husserl, Edmund, 341

Hutchinson, D.S., 244

illegal dumping, 154-5

Johnson, Lawrence, 270

Johnson, Robert, 307-308

just savings principle, 101-102

justice (defined), 98

Kant, Immanuel, 1, 15, 29, 80, 95, 118, 139, 146-217, 226, 299, 303, 337, 341, 373, 376, 383

Kaplan, Richard, 208

Kawall, Jason, 267-268

Kipling, Rudyard, 8, 11

Kyoto Protocol, 107

land planning, 298-299, 355-357

last acts, 350-351

Leopold, Aldo, 7, 10-11, 16, 26, 146

Lévinas, Emmanuel, 341

Lewis, C.S., 8

lexicality, 65-71

litter, 154

Locke, John, 122

Louden, Robert, 300

Lovelock, James, 270

MacIntyre, Alasdair, 2, 15-16, 193, 238-239, 241, 246-247, 256, 260

May, J.A., 182, 185, 191

McMurtry, John, 140, 212, 367

mere addition paradox, 27, 62, 84, 92, 361

Mill, J.S., 37, 42, 65-66

Miller, David, 103

Millgram, Elijah, 378

Milne, A.A., 8

mobile phone radiation, 235-236

motorways, 259

Muir, John, 7, 11

Ricoeur, Paul, 341
rights, human (defined) 195
Risky Policy, 50, 52, 55, 64, 74, 76, 78, 199-203
Rolston III, Holmes, 11, 325
Rousseau, Jean Jacques, 7, 226
Salk, Jonas, 258
Sandler, Ronald, 237-238, 347
Sellafield nuclear fuel plant, 76
Sessions, George, 11
sewage treatment, 298-299
Shaw, Bill, 270
Shaw, William H, 37-38,
Shell Oil, 169
Singer, Peter, 10, 14, 40-47, 108-109, 241
Slote, Michael, 309
Smart, J.J.C., 36-37
Smith, Adam, 331, 367
Swanton, Christina, 306, 309
Sylvan, Richard, 9, 12
T'Hooft, Hendrick Visser, 14, 60, 72, 82, 115-116, 119-129-132, 137, 139, 339-340, 350, 373
Taylor, Paul, 11, 15, 170-177, 180, 241, 299
Thoreau, Henry David, 7, 11
Tolkien, J.R.R., 8, 11
Tuvalu, Republic of, 5, 25
Urmson, J.O., 250
utility (defined), 36-39
Van Wensveen, Louke, 15, 255, 265-266, 334, 385
veil of ignorance, see original position
virtual reciprocity, 119-128, 138-139, 160, 196, 201, 255, 382
virtue (defined), 218-219
Wallace, James, 15, 299
waste disposal, 3, 52, 154
wealth, world distribution of, 108
weather disasters, 63-4
western rail corridor (Ireland), 63

CPSIA information can be obtained
at www.ICGtesting.com
Printed in the USA
LVHW03s2356060918
589445LV00008B/309/P